STEPHEN

BREAKING LAW

The Inside Guide to Your Legal Rights & Winning in Court or Losing Well

Published July 2016

ISBN 978-0-9935836-0-5

Bath Publishing Limited

27 Charmouth Road

Bath

BA1 3LJ

Tel: 01225 577810

email: info@bathpublishing.co.uk

www.bathpublishing.co.uk

Bath Publishing is a company registered in England: 5209173

Registered Office: As above

For Pie

Contents

Part 7 RIGHTS AND WRONGS

Foreword

What would a judge say? Never a bad question to ask before you undertake any form of legal action. And that's the joy of this book - it reveals what someone, who until very recently wore a wig, thinks and how he'd approach an enormous compendium of problems.

Legal knowledge is one of the bedrocks of consumer empowerment. Often common sense sadly isn't enough - there is a system and you need to know the rules and how to play the game to get justice.

Those who know the system inside out have an unfair advantage. Senior lawyers, including Stephen (I've heard him myself) boast of times when they encountered life's challenges, they took action, and found their weight of knowledge speeded them to an easier resolution. This book exposes the truth, that some of life's real super-complainers may be squirrelled away among the judiciary themselves.

Thankfully though it also helps redress that balance allowing us, the mere reader, to don a gown too. It's not written as an academic text book but in an easy and accessible style which doesn't soft soap the technical expertise that underlies it.

And that's important. Be under no illusions - dealing with the law is a mix of research, knowledge and negotiation. The subject range covered here is huge, from help for tenants who may lose their claim, to divorce, or just tackling shoddy service. There's practical guidance and a number of template letters (something I know a little bit about myself).

Like me, as you pilot through this mammoth work, you may find it tough to decide whether it's a comedy romp through a legal life well lived or probably more importantly a text book for action. The first is well worth a read, but its longer term importance is as a place on your bookshelf as an emergency legal handbook.

Martin Lewis

Money Saving Expert

Introduction from the author

The legal aid scheme has been virtually decimated and lawyers' fees can go through the roof. The result? Litigants are increasingly turning up at court without any, or any proper, understanding of how they legally stand, without preparing their cases in a way which will do them justice and so help them and the judge and without a clue of what is going to happen when they get there.

If you have gone it alone with no lawyer, you won't qualify for special treatment by the judge who is meant to generally require you to comply with court orders and deal with case preparation in the same way as a party who is represented by the most eminent and expensive lawyers in the land. It's not good enough to say to the judge "But I'm only a litigant in person and I have never been to court before. I didn't know that by yesterday morning, I had to send in a statement under rule 1,689 (16) (A)(viii). I was making the kids' breakfasts then."

It doesn't have to be like this. I have written this book to help you survive without a lawyer when a dispute first rears its ugly head and later if there is a court case and to find one when that is what you need to do. And if you happen to be a lawyer then you should find the book of interest and use to you too. Whatever induced you to acquire the book, I hope it benefits you and you may even enjoy it!

The law in the book is that applying to England and Wales as at 25 July 2016 and I'll be updating it in my blog at breakinglaw.co.uk to which you are welcome. No extra charge - and no court fee!

Stephen Gold

Part 1

SOME FUNNY THINGS HAPPENED TO ME ON THE WAY TO COURT

Chapter 1

Look, No Maths

At 16, armed with a mediocre five GCE 'O' level passes and the tops of six Weetabix packets but limited small change, I rang the Law Society's careers department from a button A and button B kiosk round the corner which, being long distance, required the reinsertion of a coin every couple of seconds.

"I've got five..." Beep beep beep

"O's but I haven't got..." Beep beep beep

"maths. Sorry, can you..." Beep beep beep

"hear?"

It was all very unsatisfactory but they would send me a booklet. I managed to spout out my address and left it at that. We did have a land line at home but this was my own enterprise and I was wanting to keep it from my parents. I was suffering the sixth form at Portsmouth Grammar School at which I had been slippered on the backside by a prefect for talking at the notice board and wanted out. The booklet arrived. I found I could scrape into training as a solicitor and escape school. The training would involve entering into articles of clerkship for five years with a principal who was a qualified solicitor and passing the exams. Even if it meant joining a profession which would have an innumerate as a member, I was game. All I had to do was to find the solicitor.

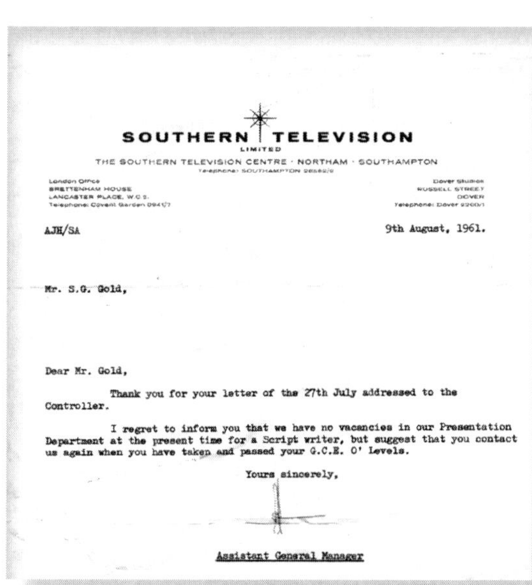

SOUTHERN TELEVISION
LIMITED
THE SOUTHERN TELEVISION CENTRE · NORTHAM · SOUTHAMPTON
Telephone: SOUTHAMPTON 28582/9

London Office
BRETTENHAM HOUSE
LANCASTER PLACE, W.C.2.
Telephone: Covent Garden 0941/7

Dover Studios
RUSSELL STREET
DOVER
Telephone: Dover 2200/1

AJH/SA

9th August, 1961.

Mr. S.G. Gold,

Dear Mr. Gold,

Thank you for your letter of the 27th July addressed to the Controller.

I regret to inform you that we have no vacancies in our Presentation Department at the present time for a Script writer, but suggest that you contact us again when you have taken and passed your G.C.E. O' Levels.

Yours sincerely,

Assistant General Manager

"Thank you but no thank you"

Taking knocks is part of growing up and I had been well rehearsed for what was to follow. Southern Television had rejected my pre-'O' level application for appointment as a scriptwriter in its presentation department. Around about the same time, Associated-Rediffusion which held the commercial television franchise for London had turned down my play, the BBC my "kind offer" to take part in *Juke Box Jury* and ABC Television my request for an audition for the 'Spin-a-Disc' panel of *Thank Your Lucky Stars*.

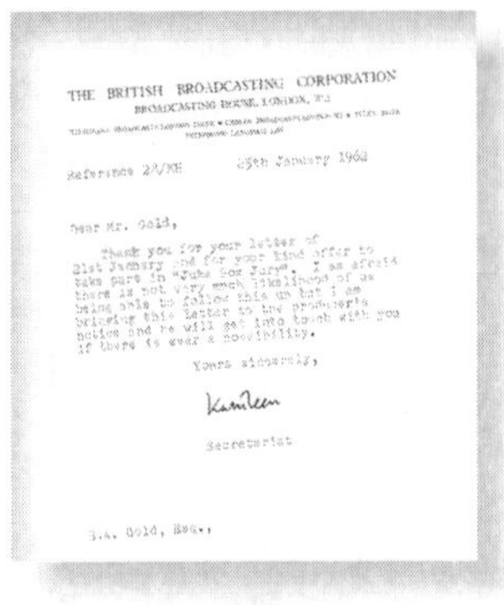

THE BRITISH BROADCASTING CORPORATION

Dear Mr. Gold,

Yours sincerely,

Secretariat

"A Miss!"

"My word, Gold. You are small." Having pushed out around 30 letters to every firm within bus travelling distance of my home, I had arrived at the top of the staircase of Churchers, solicitors of Gosport in Hampshire (so a walk, bus and a ferry) for my first interview. The firm's senior partner, Pip Churcher no less, had written to "grant" me an interview in view of the keenness displayed in my communication although he had not contemplated having another articled clerk. "He has one already." Here was Pip towering over me and telling me how small I was. 5' 6" actually which was short enough to give me a complex. I had prepared well and had a speech which I was to recite at every one of the dozen or so interviews which followed and which involved the interjection of such words as *contentious* and *non-contentious* and *litigation* and *conveyancing* which I had borrowed from the Law Society's booklet and I was off. Pip Churcher didn't want me.

PLEASE REPLY TO GOSPORT.

CHURCHER & CHURCHER,
SOLICITORS.
COMMISSIONERS FOR OATHS.
A.K. CHURCHER.
TELEPHONE GOSPORT 82288 (4 LINES)
COSHAM 76422 (2 LINES)
PLEASE QUOTE: RC/CRC

28 High Street,
Gosport.
AND AT 62, NORTHERN ROAD, COSHAM.

21st February, 1963.

Dear Mr. Gold,

We thank you for your letter of the 19th instant.

At the moment Mr. Churcher was not contemplating having another articled clerk - he has one already.

However, in view of the keeness displayed by your letter, Mr. Churcher personally would be pleased to grant you an interview.

Perhaps you will either telephone Mr. Churcher or write saying which times of the day are convenient to yourself.

Yours sincerely,

"First interview, First rejection"

The severe partner at Hubert Way, Malpas and Stanley of Portsmouth told me that if he accepted me into articles he would require a premium of £250 and I would not be paid. Even then he didn't want me, not even with a firm name which closely resembled that of a local shoe shop. No maths and my age were said in the rejection letter to have been against me.

A Chichester firm Arnold Cooper & Tompkins (walk, bus and train) preferred me to finish my 'A' levels than join them. Large & Gibson of Southsea referred me to the secretary of the Hampshire Law Society "who sometimes knows of solicitors in the county who are looking for a suitable man to be articled." And so it went on until I was back in Gosport and performing before Richard (Dick) Elliott who was one of two partners in a medium sized firm of family solicitors with a litigation bias. It was called Donnelly and Elliott. I didn't buy the firm but I did become the senior partner from which you will deduce that he took me on and things went relatively well.

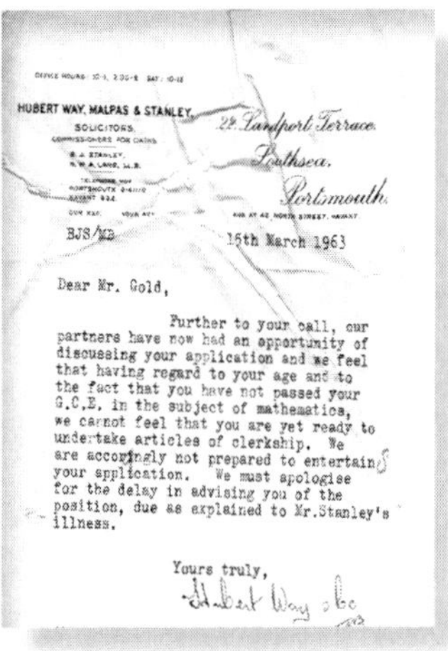

HUBERT WAY, MALPAS & STANLEY,
SOLICITORS.

24 Landport Terrace,
Southsea,
Portsmouth.

BJS/MB 15th March 1963

Dear Mr. Gold,

Further to your call, our partners have now had an opportunity of discussing your application and we feel that having regard to your age and to the fact that you have not passed your G.C.E. in the subject of mathematics, we cannot feel that you are yet ready to undertake articles of clerkship. We are accordingly not prepared to entertain your application. We must apologise for the delay in advising you of the position, due as explained to Mr.Stanley's illness.

Yours truly,

Hubert Way & Co

"Your application doesn't add up"

By deed of articles of clerkship I of my own free will, and with the consent of my father, bound myself to Dick (I called him *sir* then and later, with his permission, *Mr Elliott* and once I had passed my exams I was entreated to call him Dick) to "truly, honestly and diligently" serve him for five years as a faithful clerk ought to do.

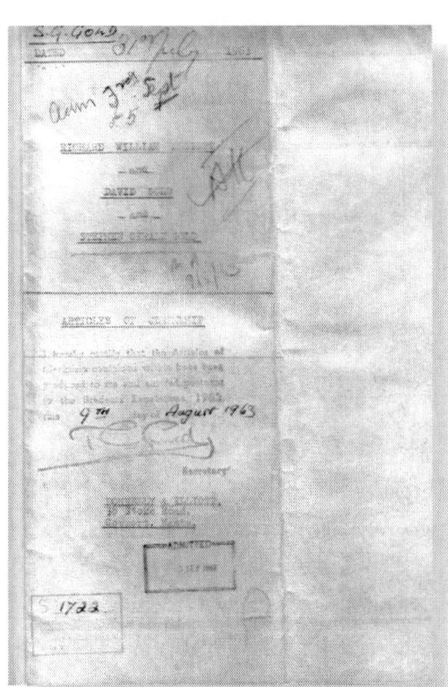

S.G. Gold

9th August 1963

Secretary

S 1722

"The deed is done"

By virtue of my tender years, there was not much enforceable covenanting I could do so it was my hapless father who had to promise I would not at any time during those five years "cancel obliterate spoil destroy waste embezzle spend or make away with any of the books papers writings money stamps or other property" of Dick or any of his clients and I would cheerfully obey and execute Dick's lawful commands. In those days, punctuation in legal documents was anathema lest it should change the sense - or nonsense - of what was being stated or enable any lay person to understand the document. I see that Dick stuck in a further promise by my father that for five years after I qualified as a solicitor (if ever) I would not practise in the law in the Borough of Gosport or down the road in the Urban District of Fareham. This was known then, and is still known now, as a covenant in restraint of trade and stops you walking off with the hard won clients of your employer for the benefit of yourself or your new employer. To be enforceable it has to be reasonable in radius and time. This covenant was neither. Dick is no longer with us but he would forgive me for saying it was very cheeky. He would also forgive me for telling you that I was not paid a penny for the first two years of my articles. This was overshadowed by the fact that in this instance no premium was required. It would have enhanced my self-worth if I had been allowed just sufficient to buy a couple of tubes of *Rolos* each week. When Dick announced after two years that I was to be paid a fiver a week, I

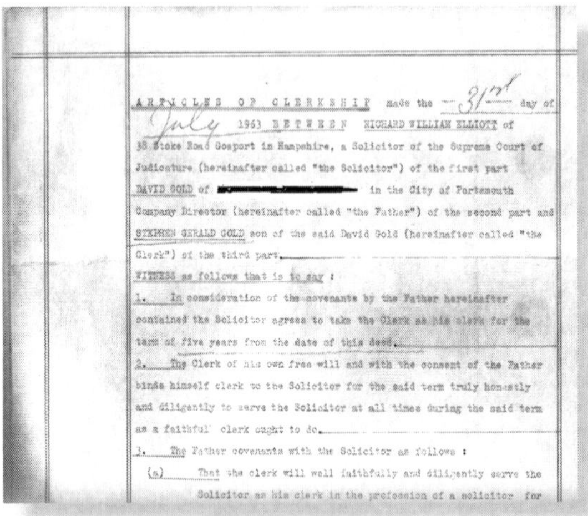

ARTICLES OF CLERKSHIP made the 31st day of July 1963 BETWEEN RICHARD WILLIAM ELLIOTT of 38 Stoke Road Gosport in Hampshire, a Solicitor of the Supreme Court of Judicature (hereinafter called "the Solicitor") of the first part DAVID GOLD of [redacted] in the City of Portsmouth Company Director (hereinafter called "the Father") of the second part and STEPHEN GERALD GOLD son of the said David Gold (hereinafter called "the Clerk") of the third part

WITNESS as follows that is to say :

1. In consideration of the covenants by the Father hereinafter contained the Solicitor agrees to take the Clerk as his clerk for the term of five years from the date of this deed.

2. The Clerk of his own free will and with the consent of the Father binds himself clerk to the Solicitor for the said term truly honestly and diligently to serve the Solicitor at all times during the said term as a faithful clerk ought to do.

3. The Father covenants with the Solicitor as follows :

(a) That the clerk will well faithfully and diligently serve the Solicitor as his clerk in the profession of a solicitor for

"Though shalt obey"

almost prostrated myself before him and thought I had won the pools. Not that any of this came to matter as I stayed on for another 27 years once I qualified.

I loved my training. Dick specialised in crime and litigation. Before admission as a solicitor he had assisted in the investigation of war crimes and in the preparation of cases for the Nuremburg trials He was one of the most eloquent and persuasive advocates in the south of England and attracted not only a mass of criminal defence work but prosecution work for the police (this was way before the creation of the Crown Prosecution Service) and for the NSPCC (he was honorary secretary of its local branch) and the RSPCA. Of the many celebrated cases in which he had been, or was to be, involved was the 1971 court martial following the sinking of the submarine HMS Artemis at which he advocated. His one weakness was an inability to bill his clients. And so it was that, seated in the corner of his room, following him around to court and prison like a lap dog and given my own workload very soon after I started, I learnt the trade. As I attended many criminal trials, I was able to study the styles of some of the finest jury advocates on the Western Circuit and observe the idiosyncrasies of some of the most eminent judges including the Chairman of Hampshire Quarter Sessions Sir Eustace Roskill QC (later to become a Law Lord) who had the unfortunate habit of picking his nose whilst up there on the bench. I borrowed not this habit but his name, occasionally signing in as him at the Pomme D'or club in Southsea but without the title.

It could have been so different if I had been articled to a conveyancing specialist with all their dry pieces and parcels of land and easements and quasi-easements. That would probably have driven me back to the sixth form. But I was not permitted to shun the conveyancing as I would be tested on the law of property in the exams which were to come my way and ultimately as a solicitor I would combine my contentious work with a large volume of conveyancing. I came to realise that for lies and deceit those involved in property sales and purchases strongly rival convicted criminals which makes litigation and conveyancing suitable bedfellows.

Barely out of short trousers and with the sexual experience of a monk, I was dazzled by the frequency with which sex manifested itself in one form or another in so many cases. Dick's secretary soon drew my attention to one file in the cabinets for which no bill had been rendered concerning a case which had gone to the Court of Appeal in which Dick had successfully represented the husband being sued by his wife for divorce on the ground (as it then was) of sodomy. It was there held that the wife's consent to the act was a good defence. And within weeks of starting my articles, Dick asked me if I knew what incest was. By coincidence my parents had recently and in complete advance ignorance of the subject matter taken me to the theatre to see a new play starring Robert Beatty and Diane Cilento. Beatty made a short curtain call speech at the end and told the audience to urge their friends to go and see the play. "Tell them," he said, "it is about incest - something the whole family can enjoy." I was able to give Dick a short definition and referred amongst others to a relationship between brother and sister. "And step-brother and step-sister," he corrected me for he was just about to call in a soldier charged with incest with his step-sister and who was soon to appear at the Hampshire Assizes. The couple had fallen deeply in love, completely unaware that their active sexual relationship was criminal. I attended the client's trial when having pleaded guilty and undertaken never to revive the relationship he was granted a conditional discharge.

I relished the opportunities to question clients about their sexual lives. Accident plaintiffs (as they used to be called) were asked whether their trauma had prevented them from engaging in intercourse and, if so, over what period, how frequently intercourse had occurred before the accident and whether abstinence had been a strain (for this was factor which could quite properly be reflected in an award of damages as my researches had established). It was in the field of matrimonial law, however, that I was able to excel. Divorce on the basis of two years' separation with consent or five years' separation without consent was not to arrive for another seven years and most divorce petitions were then founded on adultery or cruelty. In Gosport there was a large community of servicemen and a disproportionate number of them allegedly treated their wives with cruelty which ordinarily involved excessive sexual demands, foul and abusive language and intoxication. There was heavy concentration in the divorce petitions I drafted on the sexual demands. One particular lady had been required to submit to what seemed to me to be the most remarkable practices which she claimed she had abhorred. I spent most of that evening preparing a most comprehensive account of them in terms which would be suitable for a court of law and was bereft when the next day the lady telephoned me to say that she had decided on reconciliation. Such an outcome is something for which matrimonial practitioners now pray. As to the language and intoxication allegations, these rarely varied from one case to another and before long I was able to jog the client's memory by putting the list of the usual swearwords to her and invite her to confirm or deny what was in her spouse's vocabulary. The only variation in the allegation of intoxication related to where the spouse would urinate. It was almost invariably in the wardrobe of the matrimonial bedroom (and would often be accompanied by vomiting under the influence) and, in one case, out of the front window of the matrimonial bedroom down on to the footpath.

A very refined lady had made an appointment to see Dick on a matrimonial matter. Dick, alas, had gone missing and it was left to me to stand in for him. By now I was 17 and an expert on sexual practices so was well qualified for the task. The lady tentatively made her way up the staircase. I extended my arm to greet her whereupon she exclaimed with horror "I'm not seeing you am I?!" turned and ran down the stairs never to reappear at Donnelly and Elliott. This was the second Gosport top of the stairs rebuff for me and it took a little time for my confidence to be restored.

Sex or No sex was the issue in a defended divorce case, the conduct of which was entrusted to me in the first year of my articles because the firm's managing clerk Gerry Combes (he became a close friend with me regularly leaving the empty shells of a packet of monkey nuts to which I was addicted on his office at lunchtime) was terrified of the client respondent. It was alleged by her husband that she had committed adultery with the naval rating who was half her age and lodged with her. She admitted habitually sleeping with the man but denied that she had been penetrated and, hence, that intercourse and thereby adultery, had occurred. Her GP compiled a report which explained the physical conditions with which she was afflicted and which he confirmed would have prevented intercourse. The cards on the table approach to litigation did not then exist and so the killer report remained secreted in the file - until the morning of the hearing of the case in the High Court. Barristers change for court in their robing rooms. It is there that outcomes are negotiated, bluff is met with counter-bluff, each side ridicules their adversary's case and - in those days at least - crushing pieces of unexpected evidence were produced and flourished, as if by magic. In our case it was the medical report. The husband's barrister turned pale, conferred with the husband and then announced that the husband had decided he must abandon his petition. Today, all would not be lost for the divorce petitioner who is unable to prove that their spouse has gone as far as having sexual intercourse with another person. Instead of alleging adultery the petitioner could rely on the alternative ground of unreasonable behaviour. No court should strain to find that having an improper relationship with someone other than your spouse (whether it is confined to sexting or fumbling in the office broom cupboard) amounted to unreasonable behaviour.

During my articles Dick undertook the defence case for a man charged with the murder of an elderly woman. The man was a part time fireman and had allegedly killed the woman, set fire to her home and later gone out on one of the appliances which attended the scene to extinguish the fire. His trial was held at the assizes at Devizes where the difficult defence to be run for him was that he had not committed the murder but, if he had, he was suffering from diminished responsibility at the time. The prosecution were seeking to rely on evidence of a previous arson at which the accused had attended in the course of his part-time work with the fire brigade. This is known as *similar fact* evidence and the trial judge was to be asked by the defence to exclude the evidence on the ground that the facts of the two incidents were not sufficiently similar and that, in any event, the prejudice to the accused of allowing in the evidence would outweigh its probative value. There was a leading case on the subject which had been decided by an appeal court and represented a legal precedent. Norman Brodrick QC who Dick had instructed as the leading barrister for the accused should have come to court with an authoritative report of the case to which the trial judge could be referred.

This is how it is done - or should be done. He had forgotten it.

I had attended the trial with Dick. The trial was memorable for me for its drama and two other reasons. The first was that Muggins was sent out into Devizes in heavyish snow to locate and borrow an authoritative report of that leading case - on foot. I eventually found a local solicitors' firm with a decent library and a volume of law reports which included the case in question. I talked them into lending it to me. The trial judge decided - naturally, in the absence of the jury - that the prosecution could not rely on evidence of this previous incident and the law book was returned. The second ground of fascination was that Dick had instructed as junior barrister for the defence David Webster who was to become my BBC referee. So? Well, before going to the bar he had worked as an actor and appeared in *Dixon of Dock Green* on BBC television as the young police cadet Jamie. Having a celebrity in the defence team was a really big deal - for me.

The accused was convicted and sentenced to life imprisonment. Dick went down to the cells to see him afterwards and reported back that the accused had thanked him for all he had done. Dick did not speak on the journey back.

That duty of consulting with the client after a guilty verdict or custodial sentence has its inherent difficulties although the judge tends to be the target of the client's grievance. The client is entitled to advice on his rights and especially on the prospects of a successful appeal against conviction or sentence although a considered opinion a day or so after the event is probably the best time for its delivery. In the case of Robert Malcolm Weeks, this articled clerk copped out of an instant post-sentence encounter with his firm's client.

Mr Weeks at the age of 17 entered a pet shop in Gosport with a starting pistol loaded with blank cartridges, pointed it at the owner and told her to hand over the till. He stole 35p which was later found on the shop floor. Later that day, he telephoned the police to say that he would give himself up. He was apprehended locally by two police officers. He took the pistol from his pocket and it went off. In the ensuing struggle, two more blanks were fired, one of which caused a powder burn to the wrist of one of the police officers. It emerged that Mr Weeks had committed the robbery because he wanted to pay back £3 which he owed his mother who had told him that morning to find lodgings elsewhere.

Just 18 days after all this, Mr Weeks appeared before Hampshire Assizes. Dick had never expected the case to be listed so fast. We were told the day before that the case would be on. My frantic telephone calls to the prosecutor's office and the court to get the case put off were of no avail. A brief was hurriedly prepared by Dick and a barrister instructed to appear at the Assizes the next day. I was sent to represent the firm. Me and my sandwich box. Mr Weeks pleaded guilty to armed robbery, assaulting a police office and being in the unlawful possession of a firearm. The trial judge was the terrifying Mr Justice Thesiger. A prison medical officer testified that he could find no evidence that Mr Weeks was suffering from mental instability which would justify sending him to a mental institution. But a probation officer who was present characterised him in his report before the judge as being susceptible to fluctuation in mood and emotionally immature and as showing a morbid interest in the literature of violence and a fascination for guns. The officer had also written that he had taken to drinking heavily from time to time and had a high potential for aggression.

The judge passed sentence. I can hear him now. I can see his reddened face now.

> *"The facts of the offence and the evidence of the character and disposition of the accused ...satisfy me that...he is a very dangerous young man...I think that an indeterminate sentence is the right sentence for somebody of this age, of this character and disposition, who is attracted to this form of conduct. That leaves the matter with the Secretary of State who can release him if and when those who have been watching him and examining him believe that with the passage of years he has become responsible. It may not take long. Or the change may not occur for a long time - I do not know how it will work out...So far as the first count of the indictment is concerned [robbery], I think the right conclusion, terrible though it may seem, is that I pass the sentence that the law authorises me to pass for robbery and for assault with intent to rob with arms, that is life imprisonment. The Secretary of State can act if and when he thinks it is safe to act."*

Our barrister was stunned. The probation officer whose report had been instrumental in the judge's sentence was stunned. I was stunned. Perhaps everyone apart from the judge had been thinking about borstal or a fixed term of a few years. But life had not crossed minds.

It was getting late. The barrister left court without seeing Mr Weeks. I left court without seeing Mr Weeks. The next morning, back in the office, I reported to Dick. He was stunned. "What did Weeks say?" he enquired. I confessed he had not said anything to me as I had not seen him afterwards in the cells. Dick ordered me back to Winchester immediately (which was a bit rich as it was <u>his</u> case) and I duly saw the client there in prison. I explained the rationale of the sentence almost selling it to myself as I did so. He expressed gratitude that I had turned up because he had convinced himself that he would die in prison. Never again did I flinch away from the post conviction and post custodial sentence conference.

And what happened to Mr Weeks? He made his own attempt at getting his sentence reduced on appeal to the Court of Appeal but failed. Nine and a half years after the robbery he was released from prison on licence. Nine months later he turned up at my firm's offices asking to see me. I was then a qualified solicitor. He had broken into a beach hut and stolen a pullover. I represented him at Portsmouth Magistrates' Court where he pleaded guilty to a couple of charges and was conditionally discharged and fined. I never saw him again. After recalls to prison and further offences he was paroled and re-paroled but when some 20 years after the robbery he was required to return to prison he was at large having gone to France. Whilst in prison he had taken his case to the European Court of Human Rights which held, whilst he was still at large, that his human rights had not been violated by the recalls. A tragic story of a troubled young man who was charming and courteous in the dealings I had with him.

Before I leave this section of my life, I feel obliged to explain the maths. I had no trouble with my tables and could mentally aggregate the prices of a packet of gobstoppers and a sherbet fountain. I started to be thrown by the equations and things took a sharp turn for the worse when I stumbled upon a set of answer books at W H Smith & Son.

Chapter 2

Let Loose

At 22, I was deemed fit and competent to practise as a solicitor. Frightening, eh? I stayed on with Donnelly & Elliott in Gosport where I had trained. My qualification meant I was no longer commanded to run errands for my former principal Dick Elliott. The last completed fag had been executed after I had returned to the office from law school to await the results of my final exams and involved the purchase of a loaf of sliced white bread for his wife. There was no doubt that I would specialise in a wide spectrum of contentious work including crime with some conveyancing thrown in and a sprinkling of probate. And that's how it turned out with, in due course, a heavy concentration on media law. At Donnelly & Elliott I was to remain initially as assistant solicitor, then as partner and then as senior partner.

My first case was the defence of a young man charged with taking an E-type Jaguar without the owner's consent. It had been 'prepared' by Dick. The file consisted of the charge sheet and Dick's note to the effect that the car taken was red and, because of the poor street lighting when the client had driven off at night in the unlocked vehicle, he had thought it was the maroon coloured E-type that he did in fact have permission to drive. The owner of the maroon car was not to be produced by the defence. I was to meet the client for the first time at court. Mindful of Dick's mantra that it did not matter too much if you lost a case so long as you lost well, I proceeded to court with severe nervousness and the skeleton of a closing speech in my head during which I would suggest to the magistrates that driving an E-type through the streets of Portsmouth late at night was the equivalent of a naked Lady Godiva riding a horse through Coventry and was inconsistent with a guilty mind and not wanting to be noticed. As I paced the foyer of the court awaiting the client's arrival, another defendant approached me and asked: "What's up, mate? Is this your first case?" I used the Lady Godiva analogy to the magistrates. The client was convicted.

An early diversion from the staple diet of the litigation biased solicitor arrived in 1969, a few days after the end of the Isle of Wight Pop Festival which I did not attend. I was instructed to render post-festival advice to the organisers. This had been the second music festival on the Island but in terms of buzz and legend it was in a different class to the first or anything since. Brothers Ron and Ray Foulk had run the event through their company Fiery Creations Limited and associated companies and Rikki Farr, the exuberant son of boxer Tommy Farr, managed it. He was also a booker. My brother Clive knew him well and swears that his booking activities involved him running up a phone bill of £29,000. Clive was given a concession at the site to sell leatherwear and accessories. He talks of a massive volume of drug consumption (not you, dear reader), a disproportionate volume of arrests and a crude toilet system involving a pit with planks over and much falling into the pit as revellers attempted to position themselves on the planks whilst they went about their business. Around 150,000 people had attended over three days. The festival turned out to be a commercial failure for the organisers and they along with two associated companies also involved could not pay their debts. There I was just as soon afterwards standing in eerie silence on flat and unremarkable land, pondering what had been. Bob Dylan, The Who, Joe Cocker, the Moody Blues and others had performed on stage and (so they say) three of the Beatles, two of the Stones, Yoko Ono and Taylor and Burton had been among those to dip into and out of the long weekend. The organising companies had to go into voluntary liquidation. Creditors of two of the companies were summoned to meetings at which it was announced that there was no alternative to a winding up. Some of them were local businesses which would be hit badly by the losses the liquidations would bring and were enraged. There was shouting and there was waving of fists. The third company to publicly collapse was Solent Graphics Limited and it was my unenviable task to turn up to a meeting of the assembled thirteen creditors and a vocal solicitor at the Clarence Pier Pavilion in Southsea as sole representative of this company, walk unaccompanied along what seemed an eternal plank (with no pit thereunder) from the entrance

Mr. Ray Foulk (left), principal director of Fiery Creations, Ltd., addressing creditors, stands up to leave the Clarence Parade Pavilion, Southsea, with his brother Ron (right), just before the abrupt ending to the meeting.

"That's my forehead"

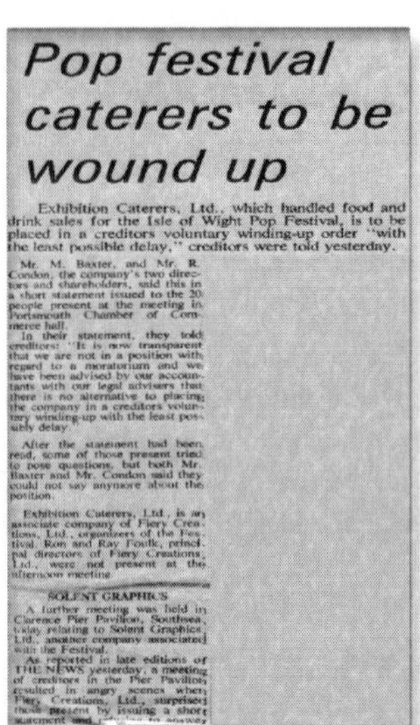

Pop festival caterers to be wound up

Exhibition Caterers, Ltd., which handled food and drink sales for the Isle of Wight Pop Festival, is to be placed in a creditors voluntary winding-up order "with the least possible delay," creditors were told yesterday.

Mr. M. Baxter, and Mr. R. Condon, the company's two directors and shareholders, said this in a short statement issued to the 20 people present at the meeting in Portsmouth Chamber of Commerce hall.

In their statement, they told creditors: "It is now transparent that we are not in a position with regard to a moratorium and we have been advised by our accountants with our legal advisers that there is no alternative to placing the company in a creditors voluntary winding-up with the least possibly delay."

After the statement had been read, some of those present tried to pose questions, but both Mr. Baxter and Mr. Condon said they could not say anymore about the position.

Exhibition Caterers, Ltd., is an associate company of Fiery Creations, Ltd., organizers of the Festival. Ron and Ray Foulk, principal directors of Fiery Creations, Ltd., were not present at the afternoon meeting.

SOLENT GRAPHICS

A further meeting was held in Clarence Pier Pavilion, Southsea, today relating to Solent Graphics, Ltd., another company associated with the Festival.

As reported in late editions of THE NEWS yesterday, a meeting of creditors in the Pier Pavilion resulted in angry scenes when Fiery Creations, Ltd., surprised those present by issuing a short statement and [illegible] questions.

Third 'pop' company liquidates

door to a platform and announce: " It is now apparent that the company is not in a position to put forward any proposals for a moratorium and it has been advised by its accountants and lawyers that there is no alternative to placing the company into liquidation with the least possible delay. The present situation results from circumstances beyond the control of the directors." And then, as reporters of the *News of the World* were accustomed to do in other situations, I made my excuses and left.

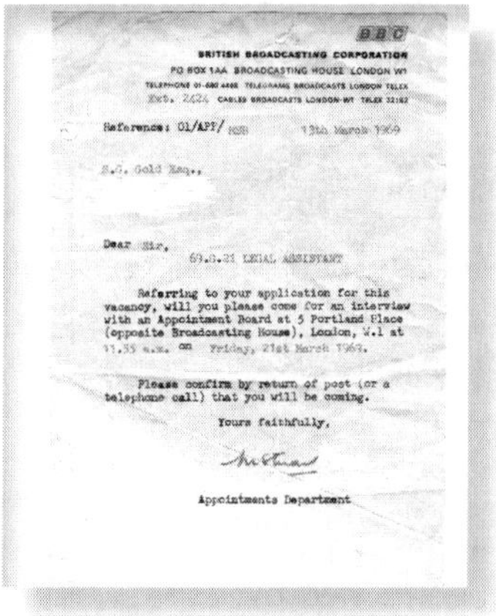
BBC
BRITISH BROADCASTING CORPORATION
PO BOX 1AA BROADCASTING HOUSE LONDON W1

Reference: 01/APT/ 13th March 1969

E.G. Gold Esq.,

Dear Sir,

LEGAL ASSISTANT

Referring to your application for this vacancy, will you please come for an interview with an Appointment Board at 5 Portland Place (opposite Broadcasting House), London, W.1 at 11.55 a.m. on Friday, 21st March 1969.

Please confirm by return of post (or a telephone call) that you will be coming.

Yours faithfully,

Appointments Department

"It's 11.55 and there's no Gold. Here is some music"

For a short period I knuckled down to the law as a qualified solicitor. The work was stimulating and satisfying but then I saw an ad for a legal assistant - at the BBC. Yes, the station of the nation, the BB Corporation, wanted a lawyer. I could tear round the studios shouting "Broadcast and be damned "and eventually become legal correspondent on air. Or maybe I would be stuck at a desk in a pokey office approving wayleave agreements between my employer and the water authority. I got in my references and sent off the application. I was given an interview for 21 March 1969 at 11.55 am before "an Appointment Board". This worried me. Who makes an appointment for 11.55 am? A little pedantic or were they seeing 63 people and allocating just five minutes to each of them? I consulted one of my referees, the barrister David Webster we have already met and who by now I was regularly briefing in criminal cases. He went on to become a QC and then a circuit judge so the boy did well. He talked me out of going to the interview. I would be far removed from "the action" he wisely predicted. What in the event the Board did at 11.55 am on that Friday, I have never discovered. Perhaps they saw the 12 noon candidate early?

Criminal work is serious stuff, for the reputation and livelihood, if not also the liberty, of the defendant are at stake, but it can also be the most exhilarating with its heavy demands and theatre. Over the years I mainly acted for the defence but also regularly prosecuted for the Crown Prosecution Service. As it had done throughout my training, the element of sex was to figure in so many cases. Frequent prosecutions were brought against men for alleged persistent importuning at public conveniences. There were many sad cases where the defendant was entrapped by plain clothed police officers effectively posing as homosexuals. One defendant I represented claimed that on the occasion charged he had positively not been importuning but since he had in fact importuned on many previous occasions and never been detected, he thought the unfounded allegation was a "fair cop" and he was insistent on pleading guilty to the charge. And another defendant was so embarrassed by the allegation against him that he could not bring himself to enter a solicitor's office. He turned up at Portsmouth Magistrates' Court as I was prosecuting a case and planted a note in my hand asking me to ring a given number so that I could arrange to represent him.

But the defence I had to run for one man charged with importuning was so incredible that I strained to keep a straight face. The reason he was seated on a promenade bench a few yards away from the gents, he claimed, was that it was a hot day (conceded by the prosecution) and on account of this, he was avoiding dehydration by drinking large quantities of water from bottles he was carrying. This in turn induced a need for urination and so it was that he entered the toilets several times over a relatively short period of time. On the last visit, he was standing by the urinal having urinated and bent down to tighten his shoelaces. These had become loose as the act of urination had caused the foot swelling from which he suffered (verified by medical evidence) to subside. He also suffered from vertigo (verified by medical evidence) and upon rising from a bending position, he lost his balance. This led him to stumble forwards. As he was doing so, the door of a cubicle opened and my client fell into it. This was his explanation for being found by two police officers inside the cubicle with another man whose trousers were down to his knees. My client was convicted.

The *Identical Twin* defence which I had to argue was successful. It won't be available to you unless you are one of identical twins or are prepared to undergo extensive plastic surgery to give you an identical appearance to your sibling. It is essential that you are both of the same gender. In my case, the twins were male and so identical that they had trouble from telling each other apart. Twin 1 committed a string of motoring offences, ended up at the police station and passed himself off as Twin 2 to the point of producing Twin 2's driving licence which just happened to be in his pocket. Twin 2 was accordingly charged with these offences. He protested that he was not the culprit: it was my brother wot done it! Twin 1 had signed various bits and pieces at the police station in the name of Twin 2. I had the relevant documents examined by a forensic expert who compared them with the handwriting of Twin 2 and had no hesitation in concluding that the writing was not that of Twin 2. It was unnecessary to call Twin 1 to give evidence. Anyway, he was probably some miles away at the Blackpool illuminations on the day of the trial. The magistrates could not be sure beyond reasonable doubt about the true identity of the offender and so all charges against Twin 2 were dismissed and the prosecutor's face was extremely sour.

I see that the *Identical Twin* defence was set to be run in a trial at Gloucester Crown Court in February 2016 when a man was charged with dangerous driving and possessing an offensive weapon. The prosecution offered no evidence. The court was told that inquiries to try and verify which of the twins had been arrested had drawn a blank. The charges were dismissed.

The deceiving twin could always be charged with perverting or attempting to pervert the course of justice but even that could have its difficulties. With the innocent twin unlikely to cooperate in such a prosecution the deceiving twin could always insist that it was his brother and not him who had been arrested.

One speech in mitigation to a bench of magistrates went down flat. My butcher client was prosecuted for a series of food hygiene offences by the local authority. The thrust of the case was that what sounded like a very large number of mice droppings had been found where meat was prepared and sold. The authority's solicitor who had a rodent appearance around the mouth area produced with enormous relish several packets of the droppings which had been scrupulously collected and carried away by council inspectors, no doubt before they had taken their luncheon break. "But your worships," I said. "One single mouse can be responsible for 80 droppings a day. All we are talking about here is one and a half mice on the premises."

But I did win cases too on some interesting little points (which you would call technicalities). I successfully submitted that there was no case to answer against the defendant who was summoned for breaching a local authority abatement notice which prohibited her from causing a nuisance through *barking* dogs when the evidence of the neighbours was that they had been disturbed by *howling* dogs. Another client had a charge dismissed for allegedly carrying an offensive weapon in a public place when he had spontaneously picked up a piece of wood and immediately used it offensively so that it could not be said he had *carried* it. A diner at a Gosport Chinese restaurant had a charge of stealing a salt pot dismissed on the ground that he had no case to answer and a charge of stealing a pepper pot on the same occasion dismissed after he had given evidence. I was able to submit that only a gastronomic pervert would act in the dishonest way alleged. My racing tipster client saw off 19 charges relating to the alleged dishonest reuse of postage stamps on the envelopes he sent out daily to his punters. My market trading client who sold foodstuffs close to or over the 'sell by' date and who had previously been convicted of attempting to bribe a health inspector with two tins of dried peas (really) was found not guilty of a series of public health offences and then proceeded to bung £50 in cash into my hand in court to show - to me and the magistrates - his gratitude. A woman client charged with aiding and abetting her husband to live on her immoral earnings as a prostitute was acquitted on the basis that she could not be guilty of aiding and abetting an offence which had been created for her own protection and the husband for whom I also acted was acquitted of living on her immoral earnings on the basis that she had spent all those earnings buying jewellery for herself and so he had not derived any benefit from them. A youth alleged to have attempted to steal sweets from a stall was found not guilty as I was able to submit that, whatever his dishonest intent, there was no evidence there had been any sweets present. This element of impossibility is no longer a defence to a charge of attempt. And two clients during my career as a solicitor were rightly acquitted of charges of manslaughter but this had nothing to do with technicalities.

There were frustrating instances. A rural bench of magistrates rejected my submission that there was no case to answer for my client summoned for speeding because the one police officer giving evidence for the prosecution had failed to identify him as the driver he had stopped. The clerk to the justices asserted that the officer had pointed to the client from the witness box when he mentioned his name but I would have been unable to see this from where I was standing! Another was the falling ill of one of the three members of an employment tribunal after the 14th day of my client's application for unfair dismissal compensation which we had been winning and the opting of the employer to require the hearing to restart before a fresh tribunal before whom we lost. More frustration at the decision of magistrates before whom I was prosecuting a defendant for theft of a hat to dismiss the charge. This was notwithstanding that although he said he had selected it for himself but forgotten to pay, the hat was patently no less than four sizes too big as demonstrated when I insisted he tried it on in court. On another prosecuting outing, I opened a fairly complex case to the magistrates and then asked for the first witness to be called only to discover that there were no witnesses at court. The police had messed up.

The frustrations were eclipsed by the humour which was often lurking. There was the insistence of a particular magistrate for production of a plan of the area in which the offence charged was alleged to have been committed, however straight the road or unremarkable the features. It would come fairly early on in the case. "Is there a plan?" When the enquiry was made one afternoon on the hearing of an indecency case in which I was defending, the prosecutor offered to go out and draw the plan of the relevant section of the High Street close to the court if the hearing could be adjourned and I enthusiastically agreed. We went for a cup of tea after which the prosecutor sketched out what amounted to little more than two parallel lines and this was gratefully accepted into evidence. During the course of my questioning a strange client in a domestic case about his penchant for adult pornography, my opponent lawyer passed me a note which was calculated to make me corpse and it succeeded immediately on reading. We had to adjourn.

And then there was the 1980 case of the LBC traffic reporter who successfully claimed for unfair dismissal. LBC was under different management in those days and it was to be some time before I began participating in legal phone ins on the station. So they never held it against me! The reporter's job was to broadcast live from Scotland Yard and the dismissal came after a series of incidents in which traffic control room staff wound her up. She alleged that whilst on air one officer had stood behind her and made a lewd remark. She also alleged that the staff put a dead mouse on her chair resulting in a bit of a scream just as the main studio went over to her, whistled whilst she was broadcasting, tampered with her broadcasting equipment and failed to give her adequate traffic information so that she could do her job properly. The onus was on LBC to justify the dismissal and so it was that they had to call their evidence before us. The first question to be put to their first witness was "Did you ever say to the applicant 'I am going to pull your knickers down and smack your bum?'" It was a bizarre opener and the single agency reporter present must have thought Christmas had come early. Within ten minutes, half of Fleet Street (they hadn't moved out yet) were in residence. The tribunal decided that LBC was 80% to blame and we subsequently agreed on compensation.

In 1989 my first book, the catchily entitled *Gold's Law or how to beat the system*, was published and in my drive to sell a couple of copies, I did radio and telly. One of the radio phone-ins was with Johnnie Walker on BBC Radio London who asked me to comment on a news story which broke during the programme that a Capital Radio technician had been arrested for alleged criminal damage for trying to drive his car away as it was being raised by a crane following impoundment for unlawful parking outside the Capital studios. Different. I declined for legal reasons which was just as well because the man was subsequently charged and engaged me to defend him. He was convicted.

I have made two visits to the House of Lords. The second was in connection with an attempt at a career change to which I shall come. The first was for a case in 1978. My client got himself into difficulties over some cannabis leaves and was charged with their unlawful possession.

But was it a criminal offence to possess cannabis leaves? It seemed to me that it was not. Cannabis was then defined by statute as meaning the flowering and fruiting tops of the cannabis plant and leaves didn't look like fruiting or flowering tops to me. I advised my client to plead not guilty and to elect to have his case tried at the crown court. This is what he did and I briefed barrister Randolph Boxall who, as it happens, was then on the select panel of barristers who prosecuted cases for HM Customs & Excise so he knew his drugs and, usefully, he had read chemistry at Cambridge. For the purposes of the trial, we needed to show the jury a cannabis plant. I was granted a special license to hold onto to one. A label distinctively marked **CANNABIS** was attached to it and I ensured it was seen by as many people as possible. The argument that leaves were not fruiting or flowering tops did not go down well with the Crown Court judge at round 1 and my client was convicted. He appealed against that conviction to the Court of Appeal on round 2 where he won but they gave permission for him to be returned to the Crown Court to be tried on an alternative charge of possession of a cannabinol derivative (which is hard to say even after just two modest glasses of white wine).

Back at the Crown Court then for round 3. The prosecution contended that the cannabinol derivative was present in cannabis leaves so that if you had the leaves, you had the derivatives they contained. This was akin to saying that if you were holding an orange you were in possession of sugar. The judge did not agree with the defence and my client was convicted of this alternative offence. He put in an appeal to the Court of Appeal.

Back to the Court of Appeal for round 4. The conviction was upheld. My client asked for permission to appeal. It was refused. My client applied to the highest court in the land the House of Lords (which has since morphed into the Supreme Court) for its permission to appeal to them. At round 5 permission was granted.

And so to the House of Lords for the substantive appeal at round 6 and my first visit there. Mr Boxall - who throughout had been assisted by another barrister Roderick Cordara who is now a QC - argued that at least ten drugs classified in the same way as the cannabinol derivative relied on by the prosecution were to be found in various plants, toadstools and toads. Three types of toad produced venom in their granular and mucus glands and that venom contained bufotenine which was a controlled drug. Was it intended that possession of a toad should be a criminal offence, he asked rhetorically? The House of Lords quashed the conviction. The law was changed. It is now an offence to possess cannabis leaves. And, quite outrageously. HM Customs & Excise never gave Mr Boxall another case to prosecute.

There are stars of the law as there are stars of every profession. I had a good grounding in idolatry. I started where we all start, as an autograph hunter. I was in my early teens. The stage door at The King's Theatre, Southsea became my habitat for a season. I gazed at Margaret Lockwood and Zachary Scott as they rushed through. I had no idea who they were but they looked glamorous. I arrested Mr Scott for a photograph and he said that he would send one if I left my details with his dresser. It arrived a month or so later. I was very impressed. Nigel Stock dropped a bogey on page three of the autograph book after it had been left with him. I was not impressed. On Sunday steamer trips with my parents in the Solent between South Parade Pier and Ryde one would often encounter a star due to perform at a concert on the Isle of Wight. Eric Robinson and Dickie Henderson Junior signed my book. So did the orange haired Wee Willie Harris but he found the task arduous and applied so much pressure with my biro that it made an impression on several pages underneath. I almost passed out as I encountered Bob Monkhouse on South Parade Pier. He seemed to be in an enormous hurry. I stopped him and asked for his autograph. He pleaded for time. "I'm dying for a wee." This indulgence I extended to him and when he emerged from the gents, he duly obliged.

As an articled clerk and later a solicitor, I was not averse to sitting in the awe inspiring Lord Chief Justice's Court in the Strand Law Courts, soaking up the atmosphere and fixated at the intellect of the appeal judges. For even the most experienced criminal barrister, an appearance before the Lord Chief Justice and his two judicial colleagues to each side was an occasion for trepidation. Only once did I encounter a joke cracked there. A barrister had turned up to argue that his client's conviction had been wrong but he had received late instruction to abandon the appeal. "My Lords, I came to curse but now I bless." Not ribcage fracturing stuff but it got a laugh. At the lower end of the scale, a visit to Marlborough Street magistrates' court to listen to a stipendiary in action was always good entertainment. A street vendor convicted of obstruction of the highway asked for time to pay his fine. "Get in a moneylender," he was instructed.

These judicial heroes do not have fan clubs or sign autograph books. I suppose at the request of a law student they might be persuaded to sign a legal tome written or edited by them and I see that even Lord Neuberger, the president of the Supreme Court, who once balked at the idea of television cameras in the Court of Appeal, is nowadays posing for selfies on conducted tours around his Westminster base when not being broadcast with his co-Justices. The proper way to worship a judge is read their judgments and listen to their reply to the toast to the guests at an occasional pain inducing legal dinner. In respect of the great Master of the Rolls Lord Denning, however, I did get a bit silly.

By 1982 I had notched up quite a few television and radio broadcasts as a legal talking head initially as a Law Society spokesman and then in my own right and then, quite extraordinarily, I was engaged to present a weekly current affairs programme *7 Days* on the now defunct Television South. There was some pre-series editorial disagreement about its ethos. Whilst this was going on I had the hare-brained idea of a slot in which Lord Denning who had by then retired and lived on the station's patch would arbitrate on disputes between parties who were willing to bring them to the programme. This was presumably before Judge Judy had learnt anything about the burden of proof. I couldn't see how such a slot would comfortably meet the criteria of a current affairs programme but no matter, this would get the punters watching. I wrote off to Lord Denning who was media friendly and got a charming refusal.

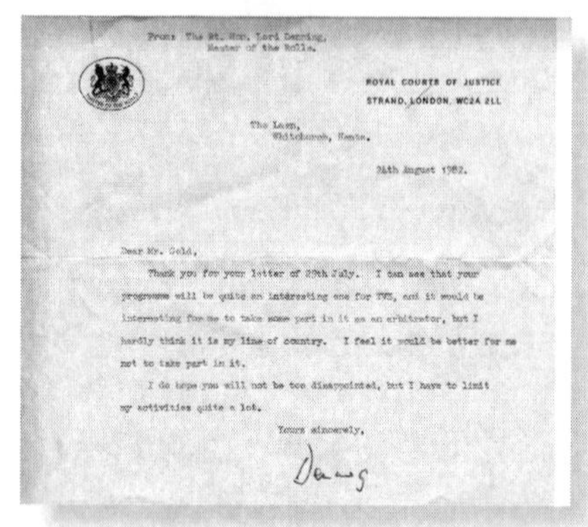

From: The Rt. Hon. Lord Denning,
Master of the Rolls.

ROYAL COURTS OF JUSTICE
STRAND, LONDON, WC2A 2LL

The Lawn,
Whitchurch, Hants.

24th August 1982.

Dear Mr. Gold,

Thank you for your letter of 29th July. I can see that your programme will be quite an interesting one for TVS, and it would be interesting for me to take some part in it as an arbitrator, but I hardly think it is my line of country. I feel it would be better for me not to take part in it.

I do hope you will not be too disappointed, but I have to limit my activities quite a lot.

Yours sincerely,

Denning

"Lord Denning regrets"

Then there were Ron and Reg with a smattering of Charlie.

Chapter 3

Ron And Reg

The place: Old Bailey, London EC4

The date: 5 March 1969

The occasion: Day 40 of the trial of Ronald Kray, Reginald Kray and others

Mr Justice Melford Stevenson sentences Ronald having been convicted of the murder of George Cornell and Reginald having been convicted of the murder of Jack McVitie.

> *"Ronald Kray, I am not going to waste words on you. The sentence upon you is that you will go to life imprisonment. In my view society has earned a rest from your activities and I recommend that you be detained for 30 years. Put him down."*

To Reginald Kray:

> *"Now, on the third count of this indictment, on which you have been convicted of murder, you will go to imprisonment for life. For reasons I have already indicated in the case of your brother, Ronald - I don't propose to repeat them - I recommend that you be detained for 30 years; and on the second count of this indictment, there will be a sentence of 10 years to run concurrently."*

They were then 34. 26 years on Ron Kray was dead from a heart attack having spent that time in prison and later as an inmate in Broadmoor, the maximum security psychiatric hospital in Crowthorne. 41 years on Reg Kray was dead from bladder cancer having spent the whole time in prison until eight weeks before his death when he was released to hospital on compassionate grounds.

I acted for both the Kray twins, not in connection with any criminal defences but on a myriad of civil matters over some six years until Ron's death and then for a little longer for Reg until I ceased to practise as a solicitor. Whatever their past misdeeds, they were entitled to legal advice and representation on their personal affairs and they got it from me. All my dealings with them were in person and by post and 'phone. So far as Ron was concerned, I would see him at Broadmoor where for the greater part of the period of our association he shared a ward with, amongst others, the *Yorkshire Ripper* Peter Sutcliffe (he told me he refused to have anything to do with him). Reg I would see at one of the various prisons in which he was incarcerated and at which he held considerable sway but mainly at Gartree Prison near Market Harborough in Leicestershire.

When Reg was subsequently transferred to Nottingham Prison I drove there at his request to discuss what I expected to be serious business to find him under the influence of alcohol and insistent that the interview be conducted in the presence of a young man who had become his cell-mate and was in the same condition. Reg explained they had both been drinking 'hooch' which was an alcopop. It was necessary to summarily terminate the interview.

The authorities would make a private room available for legal consultation at all the venues. Reg was accustomed to direct an adjournment when parched and ask me to get him a cuppa and possibly a biscuit from the prison canteen. Letters from each of them were regular and would end with a *God Bless* unless I had displeased so that one would check the sign-off first. The handwriting was sometimes hard to decipher, especially Ron's. They both seemed to have ready access to phones. I amused myself by pondering how the conveyancing and probate clients waiting in the reception of my Gosport office a few yards away from the trilly telephonist, reacted to hearing "Reg/Ron Kray for you, Mr Gold" as they raised their eyes from antique editions of *Horse & Hounds*. One Sunday afternoon I received a call from Ron at home instructing me to take out an injunction against Broadmoor for keeping him locked up in his room for unacceptable hours because of industrial action by staff. It was not an instruction to be relished and happily the problem was soon resolved. You may rest assured that I was not asked to do anything illegal or professionally improper but occasionally my instructions were unusual. Reg once asked me to take out the twin's brother Charlie for lunch - on him. I thought it would be an interesting experience. I met him at Graham's fish restaurant in London's Poland Street where two of the waitresses regaled him like a long lost friend. We occupied a table at the front window. During the meal, I half expected to see a limo pull up outside and a machine gun penetrate our dover soles.

The most serious mischief perpetrated by either of the twins over this period of which I was aware was on the part of Reg in reading my regular columns in the New Law Journal without having taken out a subscription though he had a good defence, namely that I had sent them to him and on the part of Ron in receiving visits in Broadmoor from members of the Mafia (or so he said).

In September 1989 BBC 1's, *South-East at Six* regional news programme broadcast an item about the Krays presented by Duncan Kennedy to which they took exception. They claimed that what was said on air by Mr Kennedy and an unidentified male witness amounted to allegations that the Krays were mass-murderers who had committed countless killings which had gone undetected and unpunished and that if released they intended to re-embark on their earlier careers as mass-murderers. Reg was particularly anxious about this publicity for his dream, periodically snatched away from him with parole application kick-backs, was to get out of prison.

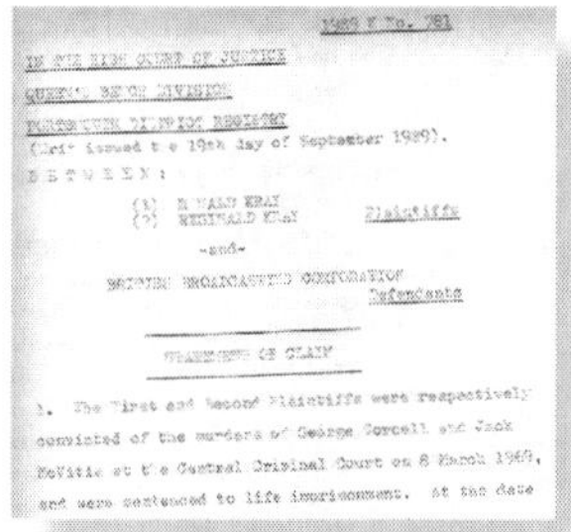
IN THE HIGH COURT OF JUSTICE
QUEEN'S BENCH DIVISION
(Writ issued the 19th day of September 1989).
BETWEEN:
(1) RONALD KRAY
(2) REGINALD KRAY — Plaintiffs
-and-
BRITISH BROADCASTING CORPORATION — Defendants

STATEMENT OF CLAIM

1. The First and Second Plaintiffs were respectively convicted of the murders of George Cornell and Jack McVitie at the Central Criminal Court on 8 March 1969, and were sentenced to life imprisonment. At the date

5. In their natural and ordinary and/or inferential meaning, the said words meant and were understood to mean:

(i) that the Plaintiffs were mass-murderers who had committed countless killings which had gone undetected and unpunished;

(ii) that if release, the Plaintiffs intended to re-embark on their earlier careers as mass-murderers;

(iii) that in March 1965, the Plaintiffs had managed to avoid conviction for a number of serious crimes of which they were plainly guilty.

6. In consequence of the said broadcast and publication, the Plaintiffs and each of them have suffered considerable distress and have been brought into public scandal, odium and contempt.

"The Krays in the High Court"

The twins instructed me to bring libel proceedings against the BBC, the very hand that fed me £2 or sometimes a little more for my own local radio broadcasts. Although libel is generally devoted to defamatory words which are written rather than spoken - slander is for the spoken stuff - what is defamatorily broadcast on television and radio is classified as libel. A claim for libel had no chance of getting off the ground unless as the law then required it could be proved that the words complained of had "lowered the reputation of the claimant in the minds of right-thinking members of society." Now, you might reckon it was a pretty tall order to prove that anything said to the detriment of the Krays would make right-thinking members of the public think any less of them than they already did. The Krays were under no illusions about the hurdles in their way but they wanted to have a bash at trying to extract some partial withdrawal or apology from the BBC. I had to get a defamation barrister on board to draft the court document to go with the High Court writ I was to issue. The barrister's name would appear on the document and without a name there, the BBC would have deduced that yours truly, a mere solicitor, had done the drafting and so the twins were not serious about taking the case the distance if it did not capitulate. I had a furious row with the first barrister I went to, a self-satisfied practitioner who was highly regarded by his peers and the judiciary. He refused to accept that it could be respectably argued that the Krays would be thought any less of if accused of a catalogue of murders instead of the single murder for which each of them had been convicted and clearly had no desire to dirty his hands with the likes of the Krays. The second barrister I went to readily accepted the job.

A writ was duly issued. Asked by the media for a statement on the Krays' behalf I said this: "They do not seek to make any complaint about legitimate discussion of their crimes for which they have been severely punished. But what they do object to is that having been incarcerated for so long, they should be subjected to unfounded and unsubstantiated allegations of misdeeds which have not previously been made."

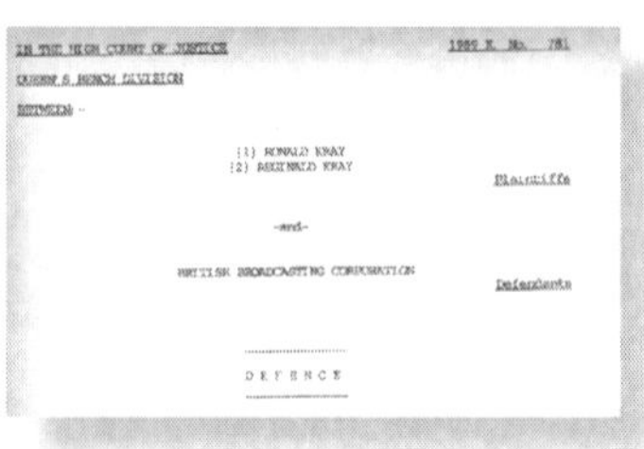

IN THE HIGH COURT OF JUSTICE 1989 K. No. 781

QUEEN'S BENCH DIVISION

BETWEEN:-

(1) RONALD KRAY
(2) REGINALD KRAY

Plaintiffs

-and-

BRITISH BROADCASTING CORPORATION

Defendants

DEFENCE

The BBC put in a spirited defence. They contended that the words complained of were true in substance and in fact and were a fair comment on a matter of public interest which was whether or not the Krays should be released from detention before their 30 years were up. The Krays, they argued, had terrorised people by proving their readiness to carry out killings and maimings and had committed countless serious crimes for which they had managed to avoid conviction and punishment. The defence pleaded that "people have good reason to be fearful at the prospect of the Plaintiffs' release from detention." The BBC also relied heavily on what the Krays had gone on record as saying in the book *Our Story* published by Sidgwick & Jackson which with Fred Dinenage they had written in 1988. In the BBC's assessment the twins had in that book exposed themselves as cruel and ruthless men whose sole regrets lay in the mistake they had made in themselves carrying out the murders of which they had been convicted instead of

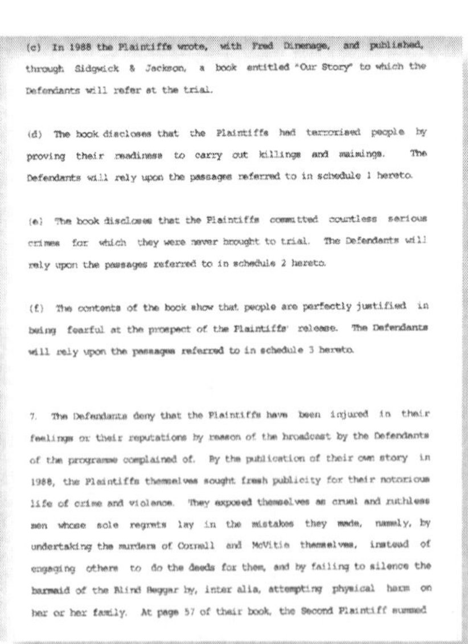

(c) In 1988 the Plaintiffs wrote, with Fred Dinenage, and published, through Sidgwick & Jackson, a book entitled "Our Story" to which the Defendants will refer at the trial.

(d) The book discloses that the Plaintiffs had terrorised people by proving their readiness to carry out killings and maimings. The Defendants will rely upon the passages referred to in schedule 1 hereto.

(e) The book discloses that the Plaintiffs committed countless serious crimes for which they were never brought to trial. The Defendants will rely upon the passages referred to in schedule 2 hereto.

(f) The contents of the book show that people are perfectly justified in being fearful at the prospect of the Plaintiffs' release. The Defendants will rely upon the passages referred to in schedule 3 hereto.

7. The Defendants deny that the Plaintiffs have been injured in their feelings or their reputations by reason of the broadcast by the Defendants of the programme complained of. By the publication of their own story in 1988, the Plaintiffs themselves sought fresh publicity for their notorious life of crime and violence. They exposed themselves as cruel and ruthless men whose sole regrets lay in the mistakes they made, namely, by undertaking the murders of Cornell and McVitie themselves, instead of engaging others to do the deeds for them, and by failing to silence the barmaid of the Blind Beggar by, inter alia, attempting physical harm on her or her family. At page 57 of their book, the Second Plaintiff summed

"The BBC defends"

engaging others to carry out the deeds for them and by failing to silence the barmaid of the Blind Beggar who had given evidence for the prosecution at the Old Bailey trial by threatening physical violence against her or her family.

The defence did the trick for the BBC. The twins decided to extricate themselves from the proceedings as fast as possible. I spoke to the BBC's lawyer who was handling the case. I tried to persuade him to drop any claim for costs if the Krays withdrew. He wasn't having it. He joked that the BBC didn't usually win civil cases and wanted to make the most of this victory. The BBC was insistent on the Krays paying the costs they had incurred. In June 1990 the High Court ordered with the consent of both sides that the action should be dismissed and that the Krays should pay the BBC's costs. The prospects of those costs ever being extracted by the BBC were as great as me making it to Lord Chief Justice. Wisely, they did nothing about enforcing the costs order which meant, dear licence fee payer, they were borne by you (and me) or your forefathers. And three years after that dismissal the Home Office was giving feedback to Reg to the effect that he was unlikely to be released before his 30 years were up. A probation officer in her parole report was saying that clear messages needed to be given about expectations he needed to meet before he would be fully considered for release and he would have to work on those areas. Otherwise, release would not happen. As for Ron, he never expected to get out of Broadmoor. But did he want out?

In 1989 Ron instructed me to bring divorce proceedings against a woman who had befriended him during his time in Broadmoor and whom

Kray away day

GANGLAND killer Ronnie Kray this week divorced his wife for desertion.

Kray (55), who is serving a 30-year sentence at Broadmoor Psychiatric Hospital, was refused Home Office permission to attend the hearing at Portsmouth County Court on Monday, after concern about the effects the trip and the 40-minute hearing would have on him.

Kray, represented by lawyer Stephen Gold, brought the action on the grounds of desertion — and it was not contested by his wife, 32-year-old Elaine Mildener.

The one-time gangland chief, who with his brother Reggie was once ring-leader of the London underworld, claimed she had not visited him at Broadmoor.

"Divorce court report"

he had married. He was inside: she was outside. That made living together very problematic. He claimed that for more than two years she had ceased to visit him or to have anything to do with him. There was no suggestion that she would consent to a divorce and so the only basis on which it was likely Ron could secure his liberty from the marriage at that point was to allege that his wife had deserted him for the minimum period required of two years. And that is precisely what we did. Proceedings were started in Portsmouth county court. His wife did not take any steps to defend them. However, a district judge had declined to grant a divorce on the papers because of the relative novelty of the desertion argument we were putting forward and a hearing was ordered at which the court would need to have Ron's live evidence. Arrangements were made for him to be taken to the Portsmouth hearing from Crowthorne and the police were anticipating the possibility of a large public turn out. In the event, the day before the hearing I was notified that Ron did not wish to be there: either that or the Home Office had refused to let him out. I was to attempt to persuade the judge to pronounce a decree of divorce without the client. Fortunately, I had a sworn written statement from him setting out all the alleged facts and would have to do my best with this.

The case came before His Honour Judge Michael Brodrick. "Your Honour. I appear for the petitioner in this case. My client had the misfortune to appear before the Central Criminal Court on 5 March 1969 when he was convicted....." The judge stopped me. With a rueful smile, he said "We all know who Ronald Kray is" so I was able to cut short my introduction. Apart from a limited number of things like the date and that there are one hundred pence in the pound, a fact has to be proved by evidence and an advocate is not entitled to assume that a judge will take anything unproved for granted. That is why I had to proceed on the premise that Judge Brodrick lived in different world to everyone else. Ron's case was that although he and his wife had never lived together, she was in law capable of deserting him if she had ceased over at least two years to have anything more to do with him in the ways which had been available to her. We were looking at desertion from a state of affairs rather than a place and, given that she could have visited him in Broadmoor as formerly she had done and he had wished these visits to continue, she had deserted him at Broadmoor. The judge agreed and pronounced a divorce decree. Ron later married Kate Kray who subsequently divorced him.

In 1990 *The People* revealed that the twins were to profit substantially from *The Krays*, the film of their lives which was then about to be premiered in which they were being portrayed by Martin and Gary Kemp. The Inland Revenue had a couple of inspectors who spent their time or much of it trawling through newspapers to pick up on stories of money received but tax not paid. They read the story and made contact with Reg requiring a full disclosure of income. Serving prisoners like prostitutes are as chargeable to tax as judges and vicars. I was instructed to negotiate with the Revenue and came to an agreement subject to an interview by inspectors with Reg in prison which I set up. I attended and two Revenue men were there. Little or nothing was asked about relevant transactions. Reg treated the men to a daytime cabaret and they lapped it up. They were totally mesmerised by the man and his notoriety. Thereafter, Reg instructed me not to proceed with the agreement. I have no reason to believe that the Revenue ever collected a penny from him. In Ron, no doubt by virtue of his mental condition, they had no interest. What did happen is that a senior Revenue investigator was subsequently convicted of corruption in the course of his duties and ended up in prison. Whether or not he ever served time under the same prison roof as Reg, I know not.

I heard of Ron's death on the radio as I was driving back from London on the M3. I was an executor of his will and being relatively close to Broadmoor decided it would be prudent to divert there and take charge of his personal property or at least check what was there before the memorabilia hunters burst into action. My accelerator foot got carried away with the moment and I was stopped by a traffic police officer on a motorbike for speeding, albeit modest. It was not unknown for the motorist's words of excuse on being cautioned for an offence to make their way on to the offence information with the summons and to be passed on to the magistrates. Say "Sorry, officer. I had just heard that my client Ron Kray has died and I needed to get to Broadmoor fast?" Hardly. I accepted with grace that I had offended and without excuse and in due course collected the summons, the fine and the endorsement with no Kray mitigation put forward.

ST. MATTHEW'S CHURCH
BETHNAL GREEN

In Loving Memory
of
RONALD KRAY
BORN 24th OCTOBER 1933
DIED 17th MARCH 1995

OFFICIATING PRIEST
FR. CHRISTOPHER BEDFORD

WEDNESDAY 29th MARCH 1995
at 12 NOON

"Ron Kray's order of service signed by Reg Kray"

Reg was suspicious of the circumstances in which Ron had died and wanted me to investigate. I contacted the coroner and ascertained that he had held an inquest at his place of residence in the absence of any member of the public. There is no suggestion that he had been seeking to cover up evidence but he did offer to reconvene the inquest at which I could have appeared. I also arranged to instruct a private pathologist to carry out a post-mortem on behalf of Reg. Both the fresh inquest and the post-mortem were aborted after Reg telephoned me to say that he had that day seen his twin's body at the undertakers. Because he had looked so peaceful he did not wish to see the body subjected to a second post-mortem and he would accept the cause of death as certified - a heart attack - without a fresh inquest or post-mortem. What he did not know and what I could not bring myself to disclose to him was that Ron's brain had been removed for examination on what may have been the request of the Home Office. This information had been passed on to me by the private pathologist and the likelihood, it seems to me, is that the brain was sought for research purposes there being special interest in it having come from a twin. In the event, Reg later discovered what had happened and was none too pleased.

It is not uncommon for the brain to be removed at post-mortem where this is required for the purpose of determining the cause of death. Removal for legitimate research purposes should not take place without consultation with the relatives and their consent. I have spent the last year seeking an authoritative explanation of how the brain came to be removed without apparent consultation with and consent from any family member and what has become of it. The Home Office says that it does not hold any of the information I have requested. I am satisfied that West London Mental Health NHS Trust which is responsible for Broadmoor acted with propriety. Having drawn a blank with other health trusts who might have been able to shed light on the mystery, I have come to rest with Oxford University Hospitals NHS Trust which has responsibility for the neuro-psychology unit in Oxford to which I believe the brain was taken. I made my Freedom of Information Act request of the Trust on the night of 31 December 2015. I was not going out. Having asked for the current location of the brain, the result of any research carried out on it and by what authority it had been removed, I was informed two months plus later that, after careful consideration, it had been decided that the information requested would not be disclosed. "It is the Trust's responsibility to maintain the confidentiality of a patient's healthcare information, even after the death of a patient, and this duty of confidentiality will apply to all information requests."

I asked for a review of the refusal arguing that the grounds for withholding the information were misconceived. "None of the information requested is for data from the deceased's health records. By definition such records must relate to an individual's health. What happens to the person's organs following death cannot pertain to their health. Further and in any event, none of the information requested would or should be contained within health records of the deceased in question but elsewhere. Since health records are not involved the question of confidentiality is not engaged."

Reviewing the situation was taking an unreasonable period of time and so I referred the matter to the Information Commissioner. On 20 June 2016 I heard from the Oxford Trust. Here are my main questions and their answers.

> **Q1** Where is the deceased's brain presently located?
>
> **A1** Brain samples including blocks and histological slides, but not the whole organ, were kept as part of medical pathology records at the John Radcliffe Hospital.
>
> **Q2** If the brain is no longer in your possession when was it last in your possession?
>
> **A2** We can confirm that the Trust did not receive the deceased's brain at any point, only the samples as referred to in question 1.
>
> **Q3** On whose authority and with whose consent was the brain removed?
>
> **A3** We do not hold this information, as we did not remove the brain. We were commissioned to conduct certain tests but had no other involvement in the matter.
>
> **Q4** In what way was the Home Office/Broadmoor Hospital involved?
>
> **A4** The Trust was instructed to conduct the neuropathology tests for this patient by Wexham Park Hospital.
>
> **Q5** What tests have been conducted on the brain and with what results?
>
> **A5** The Trust holds this information, but considers that details of medical examinations and any results fall outside the proper scope of the Freedom of Information Act, by virtue of an obligation of confidence to the patient and/or the body commissioning our services in respect of such tests.
>
> **Q6** Has it been accepted that the brain should not have been removed?
>
> **A6** The Trust does not hold this information.

So Wexham Park Hospital asked for the tests? I had already put a similar series of questions to the responsible Frimley Health NHS Foundation

Trust. Their reply? "The information you have requested is personal information of the deceased. The Trust can confirm that this information is not held. As per the Department of Health's Records Management Code of Practice, the Trust is required to keep medical records for 8 years after the date of last treatment or 8 years after the death of the patient."

And what did West London Mental Health NHS Trust responsible for Broadmoor Hospital have to say to me? They do not hold the brain and do not know where it is. It did not hold any information relating to research carried out after death and was not a party to the decision to remove the brain.

I have more questions to put and shall keep you updated on my blog. In the meantime, Reg's widow Roberta tells me that Reg had related to her that he had instructed solicitors to procure the release of his twin's brain once he knew of its removal and that it had been released and placed in a casket in Ron's coffin subsequent to interment.

Incidentally, I still have the pocket watch gifted to me by the twins which is inscribed "Mr Gold From the Kray Brothers". When it needs attention, I prevail on someone else to deliver it to and collect it from the repairers lest they should think I am on day release from Parkhurst. And, no, it's not for sale on eBay.

Chapter 4

Legal Print

I've put my pen to a fair bit of use. For a couple of years in the 1980's I contributed to the law page in *The Independent*. And in the 1990s I wrote a legal question and answer column for *House Beautiful*. The occasional letter seeking advice did come in from a reader but largely I made up the questions in addition to composing the answers. This is not an uncommon practice and I regard it as unobjectionable because questions and answers tend to be a lively way of disseminating diverse and sometimes technical information but so long as the published question is not succeeded by naming or indicating a fictitious reader. "My husband will not speak to me unless I wear a tight rubber skirt which I find most uncomfortable especially when shopping. Should I leave him? Mrs R. K. Macclesfield." During the lifetime of the *House Beautiful* column I was asked to sit on a panel of a couple of the magazine's experts at the Ideal Home Exhibition to answer questions from an uninvited audience and unwisely agreed. Around a paltry 30 people plonked themselves down in a lecture hall which would have accommodated several hundred to give themselves a respite from traipsing around laden with goodie bags. No audience questions emerged and so there was nothing for it but to pose a succession of questions - "I expect you want to know whether you can cut the branches of your neighbour's tree if they overhang into your garden don't you? etc etc - and proceed to answer. Very hard going but not as bad as opening the summer fete for the 7th Gosport Group Council on 3 July 1976 where I had to deliver a short opening speech and then tour the stalls in company with the chairman and make a complete fool of myself whilst failing to hit any of the usual targets. I had agreed to subject myself to this humiliation following the entreaty of a secretary in my office. I fancy that of those present, only she had a clue who I was.

For a couple of years in more recent times, I penned an anonymous spoof agony aunt column with a strong legal bias for the *New Law Journal*. 'Ask Auntie' was the inevitable title and Auntie unashamedly made it known that she would be delighted to hear from readers but could not guarantee to reply or, if she did, to be of any real help at all. In the event, Auntie never heard from anyone except the editor Jan Miller for whom I have deep respect. She thought I had gone over the top with one of my spoof questions and we sort of mutually agreed that Auntie should put her pen away. That question? It was supposedly from a judge who sought advice on how to dispose of wax if it dropped out of his ear during the course of a hearing and landed on a notebook which could be seen by the advocates and parties who were seated opposite. The irony was that a wax incident had actually happened to me. I shall spare you the solution.

One of my odder questions was from a supposed retired High Court judge on the subject of the legal principles of equity. Judges in search of a means of doing what is fair in a case may pluck one of these discretionary principles out of the sky and rely on it. If a party expects an equitable principle to be employed in their favour then it is important that they have not been up to any monkey business themselves. And so it is said *He who comes into equity must come with clean hands.* My invented retired judge wrote: "As a practical joke, I weaved a spoof maxim into one of my judgments a decade ago - Equity does to a cream trifle what cheddar cheese never did to clean hands. It has since been cited with approval in a number of judgments on appeal and appears in several works on the law of equity. I have discussed the situation at dinner parties with a number of friends including the editor of *The Lancet* and received conflicting advice about what I should do. Do you advise me to own up and if so should I see the Lord Chief (Justice) or Max Clifford?" Obviously, the retired judge was unaware that Mr Clifford's hands were stained.

Auntie advised: "Don't be daft. Equity is a load of nebulous you-know-what and much the better for a couple of good recipes. Incidentally add a drop of cherry brandy and ensure the sponge cakes are fresh."

In October 1994 I received a telephone call from *TV Quick*, as one does. The marriage of Prince Charles and Princess Diana had broken down, ITV was about to broadcast "Diana: Portrait of a Princess" and the magazine wanted a phantom High Court judgment on issues relating to finance and the children of the family - for the next day. I'll be frank. The money offered was so good (and as I am not before the House of Commons Public Accounts Committee, I'll not tell you how much but give you my assurance that I paid tax on it) that I agreed despite it meaning a late night. I wasn't being identified as the writer thank you very much and so it was that the judgment of Mr Justice Piranha was duly published. I did my best with the limited information publicly available on the parties' capital and income and taking account of the law as it then was in big money cases. I awarded the Princess a lump sum of £10m on a 'clean break' basis. I ruled that the Princes' relationship with Mrs Parker-Bowles and the Princess's relationship with Major James Hewitt did not amount to conduct which was so gross and obvious that it ought to have any bearing on what the Princess should receive. In the event, rumour has it that the ultimate settlement several years later provided for a lump sum of around £17m. In relation to Princes William and Harry, I made a residence order in favour of the Princess with reasonable contact to Prince Charles which I envisaged would be liberal but limited the Princess taking the children to America for more than one month at a time without the permission of the Prince or the court. Mr Justice Piranha has not been seen or heard of since.

Which brings me back to the *New Law Journal*. Poor Auntie apart, for 33 years I have written a regular column for this respected publication. The column has for the most part appeared fortnightly and designed to inform lawyers of legal developments and entertain them at the same time so that the overarching theme has been one of irreverence. I am not immune to the (hopefully, very) occasional error and so a lack of reader response to what I have written has always been a relief for a response generally spells trouble. I have been acidly corrected on one occasion by a former senior law lecturer and another reader's justified stricture resulted in a *mea culpa* but my warning that if he detected two further errors in the following six months, he would be required to take the column over. A practising law lecturer wrongly complained that I had misquoted him and Boy George's then solicitor that I had libelled his client. No damages have ever been paid.

My best story was exposing the conveyancing ineptitude of former Grimsby MP Austin Mitchell. In December 1983 he moved the second reading of his private member's House Buyer's Bill which was to lead to the abolition of the solicitors' conveyancing monopoly. He told the Commons that no particular skills were required for drawing up conveyancing documents other than perhaps the ability to put right and put names on a standard form. Two months later I discovered that Mr Mitchell had just bought and sold homes on behalf of himself and his wife with some help from a *Which* guide and also a public spirited solicitor acting for their purchaser who told me that Mr Mitchell has started off better than the average DIY conveyancer and got worse. He had made a considerable mess of things as he disarmingly admitted to me when I tracked him down at his Grimsby surgery at the 200th attempt one Friday evening soon after he had got back from buying some fish and chips. He told me he would get a professional to do the conveyancing work on his next transaction and that if the fee was reasonable, he would prefer to instruct a solicitor than a licensed conveyancer. Alas, all a bit late for conveyancing solicitors. How things might have been so different had the Mitchells bought and sold a bit earlier.

And then there was the case of Christmas Bigamy in 1987 which arose out of an error in the drafting of legislation which gave county courts jurisdiction to deal with defended divorce cases. The error was the inadvertent exclusion from county court jurisdiction of cases which had previously been transferred from the county court to the High Court when they became defended and then sent back to the county court. The error was not picked up for around 20 months during which time several thousand divorces were pronounced by county courts which they had no business to pronounce. It was an error which was highlighted in a case which came before the High Court and from which I concluded that those several thousand divorce decrees were null and void and that if any of the parties to them had remarried their remarriages were null and void: worse still, any children born following the remarriages would be illegitimate. The government was forced to introduce emergency legislation which was duly passed and resulted in retrospectively validating the invalid divorce decrees and any subsequent remarriages on the strength of them. I made BBC 1 6 o'clock news on that one.

In my *New Law Journal* column I closely followed the performance of the then controversial changes in the drink-drive laws which came into force in 1983. The Home Office had approved two machines for measuring the quantity of alcohol in a suspect motorist's body through samples of their breath. Things looked a bit dodgy for the new laws when one of the machines, the Intoximeter 3000, was demonstrated to magistrates in Cannock. Despite much huffing and puffing, at least three of them found it impossible to provide the breath specimens required and could have been facing 12 months' disqualification if it had been the real thing. Every technical defence which could be conceived was run by creative lawyers on which I regularly reported. Some failed and some succeeded. In *Gold's Law* I summarised 14 of the defences which had succeeded. These included *The Archbishop Defence*, a form of which did lead to the dismissal of a drink-drive charge against one motorist. This is how it goes. Motorist dines with archbishop before driving. His liquid intake during the meal is restricted to two glasses of mineral water and a bowl of non-alcoholic consommé. He appears quite sober to the archbishop and to other persons with whom he is in contact before he has the misfortune to be arrested. He calls these people as witnesses in his defence. Oddly, the breath machine shows him to be over the legal limit. In the course of the driver's attempts to impugn the breath machine's accuracy, the court may hear evidence of the lack or quantity of alcohol which the motorist had consumed prior to occupying the driving seat. So evidence from persons of high moral standing, like the archbishop, could make the court sit up and wonder whether the machine might have had a bad day. But the evidence will need to be very powerful indeed and, ideally, linked with some evidence suggesting former strange breath machine behaviour if the court is to be expected to contemplate that the machine suffered an aberration when our motorist patronised it. Records of how the machine had been doing previously could be crucial.

Writing profusely about drink-driving will eventually persuade the media that you are an expert on the subject. So it was with me. I see that *The Sun* described me in 1987 as a leading breath-test lawyer. If you are going to write about a subject then you have got to be prepared to 'do it'. I did. Firstly, I 'did it' as an alleged suspect. After a hard day's work as a solicitor I repaired to a wine bar a couple of doors away from the office where I consumed two small glasses of house white whilst reading that week's edition of the *New Law Journal.* On my way back to the office to collect my car I passed two police officers who were unknown to me. I duly collected my car and drove off whereupon I was stopped by the officers. The lead officer asked me whether I had been drinking and I admitted to consumption of the wine. He then initiated the drink-drive procedure by requiring me to give a roadside screening sample of my breath and outside my law office. Fail that and you get arrested and have to give the substantive breath test at the police station. He was out of luck because the officers did not have the breath kit with them. This was delivered after 10 minutes by a sergeant whom I knew well. During the wait, the officer refused to allow me to take the screening test out of public view and in answer to my enquiry as to why he thought I might be over the limit, all he would say was "policeman's nose" and "gut feeling". The screening test was, of course, negative which meant I was free to go off and write up the episode for.....the *New Law Journal.* The officers were aware of my displeasure at this indignity and the failure to answer my enquiry in a more satisfactory way. "That's it," said the lead officer. "I told you your nose would get you into trouble. Do you want to apologise?" "No." I later established that the lead officer was new to the locality and had filed a report claiming that I had been unsteady in the gutter as they passed me by. And so it was that I did write up the episode in the *New Law Journal* under the strapline "Sober In Charge of NLJ."

Second, I 'did it' as an advocate, winning and losing. I was irked by one particular failure because I thought I - and more particularly the client-deserved a success for initiative. The point I took was highly technical. You may yourself be irked by highly technical defences but they are legitimate and it is the advocate's duty to take a point which is reasonably arguable even though it has 'technical' pouring out of its ears. The client, a film cameraman, was charged with driving with excess alcohol in his body and I was appearing for him at Thames Magistrates' Court. I took the precaution of examining the breath machine print-out showing the result of the police station test when it was produced in evidence by the police officer who had conducted the test. My client had signed the print out as required but where the police officer should also have signed there was a blank. I unsuccessfully submitted that my client had no case to answer on the basis that the printout did not satisfy statutory requirements and so was not admissible in evidence. Without the print-out there was no evidence that he had been over the limit, as alleged. My client appealed against the conviction to the High Court which dismissed the appeal on the basis that the print-out was admissible under common law rules of evidence whether or not it complied with the statutory requirements.

Chapter 5

Let Right Be Done

In July 1988 it arrived. The letter. It came from the office of the Lord Chancellor at the House of Lords and invited me to apply for appointment as a deputy district judge (then known by the inferior title of registrar). The idea of going over to the establishment on a part-time basis was intriguing. I flattered myself by wondering whether somebody, somewhere, wanted to shut me up. I applied. Just in case you've had enough of working in the chippie and fancy a judicial role, starting with appointment as a deputy district judge, you may find, as did one solicitor aspiring to such an appointment, that traffic convictions could disqualify you on the ground that you are of "bad character." He had two live endorsements for speeding and breaking traffic lights which had earned him seven penalty points. He challenged the decision to rule him out for appointment on the strength of that record and failed in the High Court in 2014.

Naturally, I disclosed that I had collected some speeding convictions. I must come clean with you about these. On 6 November 1970 I was about 10 miles per hour over a 40 limit on my way to Lewes Prison in a hire car on a dual carriageway, perplexed why other drivers were travelling slower than me. I, idiot, never saw the police car. I shot off a letter to the police to try and persuade them not to prosecute. The summons arrived.

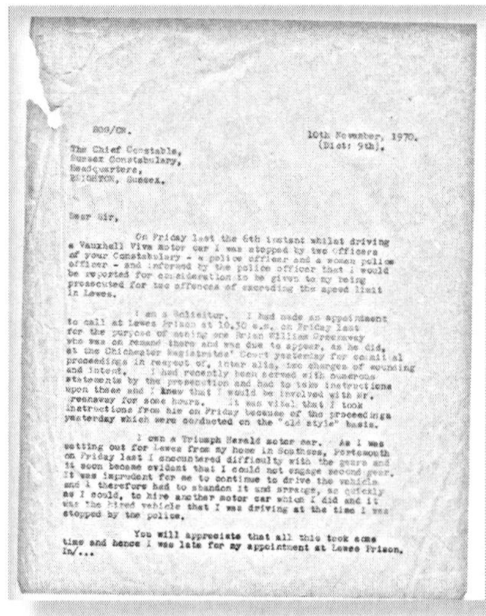

RDG/CR.

10th November, 1970.
(Dict: 9th).

The Chief Constable,
Sussex Constabulary,
Headquarters,
BRIGHTON, Sussex.

Dear Sir,

On Friday last the 6th instant whilst driving a Vauxhall Viva motor car I was stopped by two officers of your Constabulary - a police officer and a woman police officer - and informed by the police officer that I would be reported for consideration to be given to my being prosecuted for two offences of exceeding the speed limit in Lewes.

I am a Solicitor. I had made an appointment to call at Lewes Prison at 10.30 a.m. on Friday last for the purpose of seeing one Brian William Greenway who was on remand there and was due to appear, as he did, at the Chichester Magistrates' Court yesterday for committal proceedings in respect of, inter alia, two charges of wounding and intent. I had recently been served with numerous statements by the prosecution and had to take instructions upon these and I knew that I would be involved with Mr. Greenway for some hours. It was vital that I took instructions from him on Friday because of the proceedings yesterday which were conducted on the "old style" basis.

I own a Triumph Herald motor car. As I was setting out for Lewes from my home in Southsea, Portsmouth on Friday last I encountered difficulty with the gears and it soon became evident that I could not engage second gear. It was imprudent for me to continue to drive the vehicle and I therefore had to abandon it and arrange, as quickly as I could, to hire another motor car which I did and it was the hired vehicle that I was driving at the time I was stopped by the police.

You will appreciate that all this took some time and hence I was late for my appointment at Lewes Prison. In/...

"Late for prison"

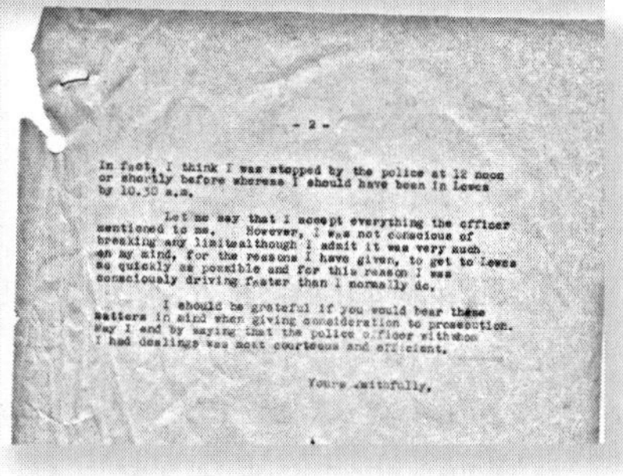

- 2 -

In fact, I think I was stopped by the police at 12 noon or shortly before whereas I should have been in Lewes by 10.30 a.m.

Let me say that I accept everything the officer mentioned to me. However, I was not conscious of breaking any limit although I admit it was very much on my mind, for the reasons I have given, to get to Lewes as quickly as possible and for this reason I was consciously driving faster than I normally do.

I should be grateful if you would bear these matters in mind when giving consideration to prosecution. May I end by saying that the police officer with whom I had dealings was most courteous and efficient.

Yours faithfully,

The inevitable followed. Then on 25 December 1971 I was clocked at 70/72 miles per hour on a 30 mph section of a dual carriageway going out of Southampton (oh, you have been done there

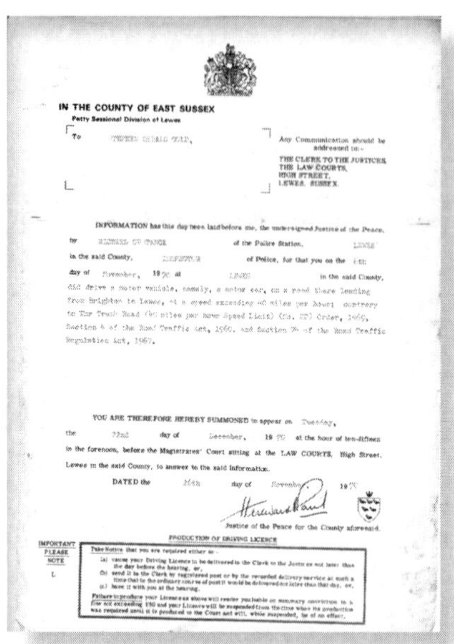

IN THE COUNTY OF EAST SUSSEX
Petty Sessional Division of Lewes

To [illegible] GOLD,

Any Communication should be addressed to:-
THE CLERK TO THE JUSTICES,
THE LAW COURTS,
HIGH STREET,
LEWES, SUSSEX.

INFORMATION has this day been laid before me, the undersigned Justice of the Peace, by [illegible] of the Police Station, Lewes in the said County, Inspector of Police, for that you on the [illegible] day of November, 1970 at Lewes in the said County, did drive a motor vehicle, namely, a motor car, on a road there leading from Brighton to Lewes, at a speed exceeding 40 miles per hour; contrary to The Trunk Road (40 miles per hour Speed Limit) (No. [illegible]) Order, 1969, Section 4 of the Road Traffic Act, 1960, and Section 78 of the Road Traffic Regulation Act, 1967.

YOU ARE THEREFORE HEREBY SUMMONED to appear on Tuesday, the 22nd day of December, 1970 at the hour of ten-fifteen in the forenoon, before the Magistrates' Court sitting at the LAW COURTS, High Street, Lewes in the said County, to answer to the said information.

DATED the 26th day of November 1970

Justice of the Peace for the County aforesaid.

IMPORTANT PLEASE NOTE

PRODUCTION OF DRIVING LICENCE

Take Notice that you are required either to -
(a) cause your Driving Licence to be delivered to the Clerk to the Justices not later than the day before the hearing, or,
(b) send it to the Clerk by registered post or by the recorded delivery service at such a time that in the ordinary course of post it would be delivered not later than that day, or,
(c) have it with you at the hearing.
Failure to produce your Licence as above will render you liable on summary conviction to a fine not exceeding £50 and your Licence will be suspended from the time when its production was required until it is produced to the Court and will, while suspended, be of no effect.

"But be early for court"

too). There was no other traffic on the road apart from a police car and I had overlooked that I was in the slower section. No defence but I thought it worthwhile sending off a letter to the police to - you know the rest. The summons duly arrived and the inevitable followed. You may wonder if prosecutors can ever be persuaded not to prosecute when an offence has been committed. I once extricated a BBC television presenter from a prosecution for failing to hold a current television license, through representations to the prosecuting authority. They may have seen the force in my argument that the media publicity which a conviction was likely to generate would be self-defeating for some of the public might conclude that if it was good enough for a BBC presenter then it was good enough for them. My success rate on no prosecution persuasion was never high but put it this way: whilst there's life, there's hope.

By the end of 1989, I had been appointed a deputy district judge. Those stale convictions did not turn out to be any hindrance. I got myself a few more white shirts (tab collars, mind you), cleaned my shoes and for the next four years and a bit and at the rate of about once a week, I was highly respectable and sat as a deputy judge doing much the same

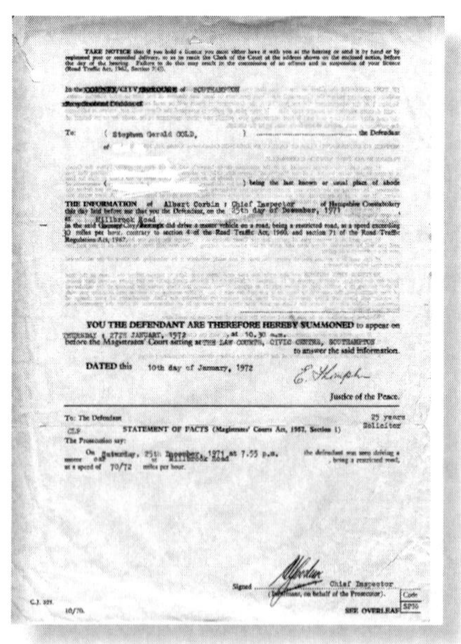

TAKE NOTICE that if you hold a licence you must either have it with you at the hearing or send it by hand or by registered post or recorded delivery, so as to reach the Clerk of the Court at the address shown on the enclosed notice, before the day of the hearing. Failure to do this may result in the commission of an offence and in suspension of your licence (Road Traffic Act, 1962, Section 7(4)).

In the COUNTY/CITY/BOROUGH of SOUTHAMPTON
Petty Sessional Division of

To: (Stephen Gerald GOLD,) the Defendant
of
( ) being the last known or usual place of abode

THE INFORMATION of Albert Corbin : Chief Inspector of Hampshire Constabulary this day laid before me that you the Defendant, on the 25th day of December, 1971 at Millbrook Road in the said County/City/Borough did drive a motor vehicle on a road, being a restricted road, at a speed exceeding 30 miles per hour, contrary to section 4 of the Road Traffic Act, 1960, and section 71 of the Road Traffic Regulation Act, 1967.

YOU THE DEFENDANT ARE THEREFORE HEREBY SUMMONED to appear on THURSDAY, 27TH JANUARY, 1972, at 10.30 a.m. before the Magistrates' Court sitting at THE LAW COURTS, CIVIC CENTRE, SOUTHAMPTON to answer the said information.

DATED this 10th day of January, 1972

Justice of the Peace.

To: The Defendant
25 years
Solicitor
STATEMENT OF FACTS (Magistrates' Courts Act, 1957, Section 1)
The Prosecution say:
On Saturday, 25th December, 1971 at 7.55 p.m. the defendant was seen driving a motor car at Millbrook Road, being a restricted road, at a speed of 70/72 miles per hour.

Signed Chief Inspector
(Informant, on behalf of the Prosecutor).
C.J. 371.
10/70.
SEE OVERLEAF
Code SP30

"Merry Christmas!"

work as a permanent judge would do and at a number of courts in southern England. It was fascinating to be looking at those legal situations with which I had been dealing for years in my practice as a solicitor but from a different standpoint. And it was enormously satisfying to be able, wherever possible, to apply the law so that a fair result was achieved. What I was not prepared to do was eat lunch in the judges' mess. This was asking too much and I disregarded the advice given to me by one permanent judge to the effect that I could never hope to secure a full-time judicial post if I did not socialise at lunch. Though I judged, life otherwise proceeded much as usual and I certainly carried on writing and broadcasting on the law. When I was doing phone-ins for London's LBC I relaxed a little in the belief that nobody connected with the administration down south would be listening and permitted callers to address me as *Stevie Boy*.

I did not always feel completely comfortable as a deputy judge. At Newport, Isle of Wight the county court sat once every fortnight or so at the Guildhall for cases that had to be heard in public. What seemed like hundreds congregated in an enormous council chamber. The route from the retiring room outside and through the chamber to a bench at its head - robed! - was for this newcomer to the part-time judiciary a walk too far (a little like the one after the Isle of Wight pop festival). But not as embarrassing as the ceremony for the swearing in of the new Lord Lieutenant of Hampshire in court number 1 at the Winchester Crown Court. As I was sitting there as a deputy judge for the day, I was roped in to attend this session of excruciating pomp. I was in my civvies and, happily, they couldn't find me a wig to fit my bonce which meant I could

"For painful looking judge, go to back row, second from right"

remain unrobed. I was directed to enter the courtroom and take a seat on the bench but to go in first. Since I was to be followed by a line of the most worthy including Mr Justice Ian Kennedy, I assumed in my naivety that this was an irrational honour. I soon discovered the truth. First in, last out. At least I didn't have to clear up after the others. One other unfortunate experience at the Winchester Crown Court was on the steps outside. It had snowed and nothing had been done to clear any of it away. I slipped on what was by then an icy step and twisted my ankle. A & E and a stick and the rest succeeded. Claims for damages arising out of snow trips are not the easiest to succeed in though in the particular circumstances I reckoned I had a good case. Put it this way. I would have awarded myself damages had I heard the case. I concluded that my prospects of a full-time position would not be enhanced by litigation and so on this rare occasion I held off. It's too late now (see chapter 10).

In due course, I applied for a permanent post as a district judge. I was

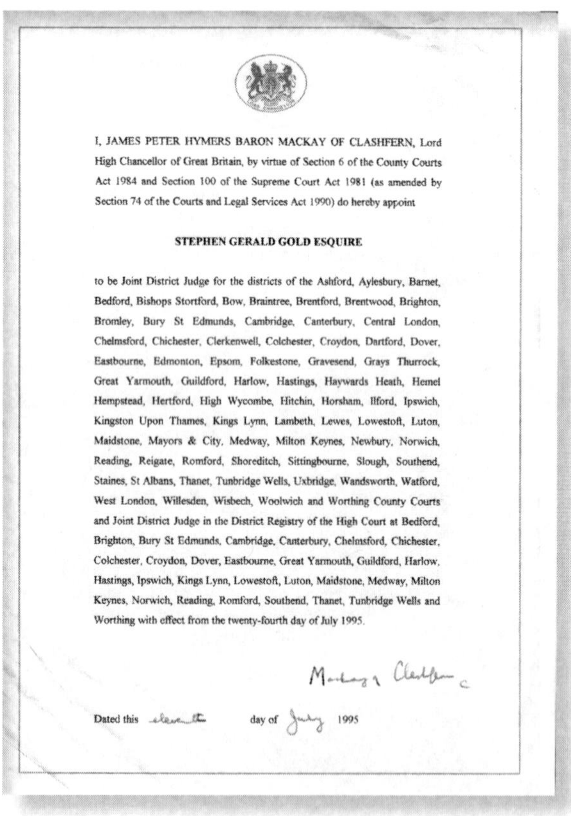

I, JAMES PETER HYMERS BARON MACKAY OF CLASHFERN, Lord High Chancellor of Great Britain, by virtue of Section 6 of the County Courts Act 1984 and Section 100 of the Supreme Court Act 1981 (as amended by Section 74 of the Courts and Legal Services Act 1990) do hereby appoint

STEPHEN GERALD GOLD ESQUIRE

to be Joint District Judge for the districts of the Ashford, Aylesbury, Barnet, Bedford, Bishops Stortford, Bow, Braintree, Brentford, Brentwood, Brighton, Bromley, Bury St Edmunds, Cambridge, Canterbury, Central London, Chelmsford, Chichester, Clerkenwell, Colchester, Croydon, Dartford, Dover, Eastbourne, Edmonton, Epsom, Folkestone, Gravesend, Grays Thurrock, Great Yarmouth, Guildford, Harlow, Hastings, Haywards Heath, Hemel Hempstead, Hertford, High Wycombe, Hitchin, Horsham, Ilford, Ipswich, Kingston Upon Thames, Kings Lynn, Lambeth, Lewes, Lowestoft, Luton, Maidstone, Mayors & City, Medway, Milton Keynes, Newbury, Norwich, Reading, Reigate, Romford, Shoreditch, Sittingbourne, Slough, Southend, Staines, St Albans, Thanet, Tunbridge Wells, Uxbridge, Wandsworth, Watford, West London, Willesden, Wisbech, Woolwich and Worthing County Courts and Joint District Judge in the District Registry of the High Court at Bedford, Brighton, Bury St Edmunds, Cambridge, Canterbury, Chelmsford, Chichester, Colchester, Croydon, Dover, Eastbourne, Great Yarmouth, Guildford, Harlow, Hastings, Ipswich, Kings Lynn, Lowestoft, Luton, Maidstone, Medway, Milton Keynes, Norwich, Reading, Romford, Southend, Thanet, Tunbridge Wells and Worthing with effect from the twenty-fourth day of July 1995.

Mackay of Clashfern C

Dated this eleventh day of July 1995

"Licence to Judge - from Ashford to Worthing"

selected for interview at the House of Lords. This was to be my second visit there. The first was for my cannabis leaves appeal case. I was to be grilled by an informal board: a judge to fire legal conundrums at me and two senior members of the Lord Chancellor's Department. I realised I didn't like boards. I was terrible. I was not selected but persisted. By the time of my next but differently constituted board, the administrators had moved from the House of Lords to common offices in a London street and one of the civil servants had been replaced by a lay person. I was a little disturbed as I sat in the waiting room by the appearance from the interview room of another deputy district judge whom I knew well and was also up for a post. I say disturbed because my application had been a secret from the outside world. Indeed, when the lay board member asked me what my firm's partners thought of me seeking a judicial appointment, I chose to tell them in all honesty that I hadn't breathed a word to them of what I was up to as I wanted to limit the damage if I was turned down. It seemed to amuse and I got the job. I was sworn in on 24 July 1995 at Kingston-upon-Thames county court by the resident circuit judge who wondered in his short speech why on earth I had wanted to become a district judge.

After five years as a district judge I was invited to become the public relations officer of our trade union - the Association of Her Majesty's District Judges as it is now known. I remained in post for 15 years. It brought me into contact with print and radio and television legal journalists. I organised the setting up of regular columns penned by district judges in three rival legal periodicals and arranged for district judges to contribute articles to a variety of legal and non-legal publications including some which were syndicated to local newspapers. A couple of national television packages featuring a district judge were run and my colleagues began editing or writing for some of the major legal works. I arranged for a group of the better looking district judges to be media trained. The annual inauguration of the Association's president led to full coverage in the broadsheets. One president who I rang at around 10pm one night to seek to persuade him to be interviewed on a commercial station before midnight complained that I had interrupted him in a long delayed sexual act with his wife and chose to decline the invitation. The profile of district judges was gradually enhanced. We were really punching above our weight. When I bowed out, the district judges were directed from above to cease publicising themselves by way of presidential interviews and media statements without prior authority.

May I briefly digress? One of those national television packages involved a mock matrimonial dispute resolution hearing which was being filmed by Channel 5 (as it then called itself) in Harrogate. Although I, in typical self-effacing style, was not appearing, I needed to poke my nose into the filming and so made my way up to Harrogate with thoughts of afternoon tea at *Betty's* which tragically never materialised. I was booked into a hotel in the town for the night before. That experience was pretty tragic too. They had central heating problems and my room was freezing. A temporary heater never materialised. It was October. The lighting in the room was dim. There was said to be a shortage of restaurant staff and so I had to eat dinner in the room. My hotel bill was due to be reimbursed by my Association but, in all conscience, I could not countenance them having to pay out for such agony. I did not have the stomach for a reception confrontation the next morning. I paid what was asked of me and endorsed the credit card voucher "up" intending to be short for "under protest". This was evidentially important for it obviated any later suggestion by the hotel that I had accepted the accommodation and service had been satisfactory by tendering payment. Back home and thawed out, I asked the hotel for my money back. I got it without a quibble.

Then in 2007 (with a little pressure from the Lords Select Committee on Constitution) the former Lord Chief Justice Lord Phillips set up a panel of media spokespersons to represent the judiciary, when appropriate, to which I was appointed. The panel members, now pared down to five circuit judges, were given special training. It was similar to the training I had received years earlier when working as a solicitor before being appointed as a Law Society spokesman. Mock interviews were recorded on video and then played back for verbal lashings delivered by the professional trainer and, this time, fellow panellists but always in the best possible taste. The training is occasionally refreshed. I've appeared on *Panorama* (BBC1) talking about mortgage repossessions and there is an extended version of the interview to be found on the internet. And I have participated in a *One Show* (BBC1) package dedicated to the small claims scheme and, for some of it, attired in the modern Betty Jackson designed robe for district judges (which I rarely wore in court and that positively does not mean that I sat naked). On national radio I have been interviewed on several programmes including *Live Drive* (5 Live) on bankruptcy from my court car park in a radio car which was a new experience for me. And I was permitted to assist the moneysaver.com website on its small claims guide. Not much. The panel is reactive and only to a very limited degree and not proactive. No member will be allowed to rear their head unless the senior judiciary on advice from the judiciary's communications unit is satisfied that it is in the interests of the judiciary that they should do so. Quite rightly, the panel will never comment on another judge's decision. My personal view is that the panel is underused. I have advocated an extension of its remit to inform the public on their legal rights and obligations and to regularly seek to influence public opinion and decision makers. Not a view which has found favour in the right places although I accept that there are respectable arguments against. Incidentally, when Lord Phillips gave an early report to the Select Committee on Constitution about how the panel was doing in 2008 he said: "I certainly have not received any expressions of dissatisfaction about these interviews." That included mine. The higher judiciary does not go in for rave reviews.

District judges deal with the vast majority of cases in the County Court and a substantial proportion of cases in the now separate Family Court although both courts are more often than not run out of the same building. All judges from the bottom to the top rung of the judicial ladder do their utmost to give every party before them a fair hearing and to reach the right decision. They would go bonkers if they became emotionally involved in the cases they hear. At the same time, they would be inhuman if they did not sometimes agonise over the right thing to do and did not find to be very heavy the burden of deciding the more substantial cases and the cases in which their judgment is to be everlastingly impacting on the parties. Decide the facts and apply the relevant law to those facts is what has to be done. Sometimes there is discretion to be exercised. It has to be exercised in a just way.

The judicial workload is intense. For district judges, at least five hours a day will usually be spent deciding cases in open court or in their private room which is sometimes called their chambers. Familiarisation with the papers before a case is called will usually be desirable. The papers will have to be read on the morning or when hearings have finished on the previous afternoon or evening. Frequently papers will be taken home. If a hearing has taken longer than predicted or the judge needs time to consider their judgment, that judgment will have to be put off - reserved - to another day and it is common in that situation for the judge to prepare their judgment in writing and for it to be circulated to the parties before being formally handed down on another court day. Preparing reserved judgments will frequently have to be squeezed in between other duties or tackled at home. But there's the so-called boxwork to be attacked as well. Lots of decisions will be made on paper involving case management, enforcement of judgments, queries from parties, complaints by parties, applications for adjournments et al. 85 out of every 100 pieces of paper which come into the court will land on a district judge's desk for attention. On top of all this the district judge will be working closely with court management on administration and doing extras in training, monitoring and appraising deputy district judges and liaising with the community and various agencies on diversity matters and making life easier for litigants in person. And there are would be judges who wish to sit in with - shadow - a proper judge and there's tea to be made and departing staff to be thanked and law reports and new legislation to be read. Life is much the same for judges in the upper echelons.

Yeh, the judiciary is marvellous. But it isn't loved and it is in desperate need of some tender care. Governments have been keen to blame all manner of wrongs onto the judges when all they have been doing is interpreting the legislation using the words Parliament has given them and applying that law. The pension arrangements on which judges relied when they took their jobs have been cut down without their agreement. The dismantling of the legal aid system and the advent of lawyers' charging rates beyond the reach of most of the population have left judges with soaring numbers of litigants in person. The result? Chaotic paperwork frequently from which it is often impossible for the judge to work out what the case is about; the litigants' failure to comply with procedural directions; litigants engaging before the judge in shouting matches with their opponent; an understandable difficulty for the litigants to appreciate what is relevant to the case and what is irrelevant; the judge having to effectively undertake the questioning and the cross-questioning of the litigants and their witnesses which should not be their function; and an inability by so many litigants to look objectively at the strengths and weaknesses of their case and so compromise where compromise is the obvious course. What ensues are lengthier hearings, an increased burden on the judge and a nightmare for the litigants themselves.

Against this background, most of the judiciary lacks the support which is essential for their job to be done efficiently and without having to pull out what little hair they have left on their heads. The root cause of the problem is that there are insufficient members of court staff and, whilst the staff in post are totally dedicated and overworked, some lack the capability to do what is required of them - they are faced with a wide, complicated and forever changing raft of procedures - and have insufficient training. Sometimes, the untrained are training the untrained. Clerical positions are habitually filled on a temporary basis by casual workers who cannot reasonably be expected to know how to do what they are told to do after five minutes in their chairs. In most courts, a single usher can be found serving four or more judges leaving it to the judge to swear in witnesses and wait for the parties and any legal representatives in an individual case to be brought into court so that the case can commence. Many district judges at least feel that they are not trusted by the administrators as they should be. In April 2011 - after 16 years of service with just a couple of days off sick - I absented myself from work for a single day due to illness. My court sent off notice of this very serious absence to someone regaling in the title of District Bench Judicial Business and Deployment Officer, Judicial Secretariat for London and the South East Region who was doing her thing on the third floor of a London office. But my court had not specified from what sickness I was suffering. The officer, Helen, courteously notified me that the Presiding Judges requested to know what had been wrong with me. I assure you that the Presiding Judges - they are High Court judges who in association with HM Courts & Tribunal Service watch over judges, pull them back if they look like straying, counsel them if they appear to be twitching too often and do a host of other good things but normally follow what HM Courts & Tribunal Service would wish them to do in the context of suspected skiving - were only constructively interested in what this little judge had been up to. I asked Helen for confirmation that the Presiding Judges wanted to know from precisely which malady I had been suffering and the symptoms. She replied that the malady was wanted. So I gave it to 'em in these terms:

"Virus causing chronic fatigue, nausea and migraine and approximately six other symptoms. Will that do? I returned to work after one day but if it recurs I shall take a proper period of time off and send in samples."

The deficiencies of the present system are now coming to be recognised and plans are afoot for a technological revolution which will see the internet as being the default position for all steps in proceedings apart from nose blowing and final hearings and the system for small claims will be transformed. But that's around another three years plus away so don't ask for your money back on this book - yet. And, anyway, the law as this book presents it will remain relatively intact for some time.

PART 2

HELP!!!

Chapter 6

Lawyer Or Litigant In Person?

You would probably prefer to use a lawyer to advise you on a legal dispute and represent you in court if that is where the case has to end up. That's their job and not yours. For a start, you can sue a lawyer should their advice be negligent and you suffer loss as a result. But while you may self-mutilate for getting it wrong, suing yourself is not an option though, having said that, you might be able to achieve it with *Money Claim Online*. Still, what a terrible waste of a court fee.

The internet is overloaded with information about how you can find a lawyer and how you can manage without one. A good deal of it is misleading and many of the plugs are from organisations and people whose hidden agenda is to empty your pockets of what money may be left inside them. But much of it is also well meaning and often from charities committed to helping those of you caught up in a legal dispute and not having a clue where to turn. This goes some way towards filling the chasm created by the brutal axe taken to the legal aid scheme in April 2013. What is lacking is a central organisation which can coordinate the activities of all the good guys: an organisation to which you can go to advise on the best advice which may be available to you wherever you may be and to get you to it as soon as possible. There is an organisation which goes some of the distance to achieving this goal. It's called Law for Life (lawforlife.org.uk) which runs a great website (advicenow.org.uk) full of stuff for litigants in person - do go to it when you have had enough of me - and they work in partnership with a handful of other charities. I am going to give you my take on what's about and how you can get it - if you want it!

Legal aid fade

That beautiful legal aid scheme we had for bringing and defending civil cases through a solicitor plus a barrister, if necessary, is no more. Generally, legal aid is not now available for consumer and breach of contract cases and for negligence and other accident claims for compensation. It is also out for family law cases (like divorce and disputes over children) except where strict criteria are met regarding child abuse or domestic violence and cases over child protection brought by local authorities so a temptation there is often succumbed to for parents to make allegations against the other which previously would never have seen the light of day and so bring themselves within the scope of legal aid. There's a useful list of what you might still get legal aid for at lawsociety.org.uk.

The only way of securing legal aid in one of the myriad of excluded cases is to go for *exceptional funding* on the basis that a denial of legal aid would be a breach of your human rights. It is only intended that this exceptional funding should be available on rare occasions. For the 12 months to September 2015, of the applications for this funding made to the Legal Aid Agency, 394 were granted (for the whole of England and Wales!) and 519 were refused. Up until July 2015 applications were being refused for full legal aid if the applicant was not thought to have at least a 50% chance of success in the relevant proceedings but, following a successful High Court challenge, the law was changed and full legal aid can be granted where the prospects of success are borderline or poor (but not very poor). This should lead to more emergency funding. There is a fly in the ointment. The High Court decision was overturned by the Court of Appeal in May 2016 though I reckon there is an evens chance at least that the case will go to the Supreme Court. For the time being the new criteria for exceptional funding continue in force. You can make an exceptional funding application yourself but it would be prudent to have some professional guidance. The Public Law Project is a charity which, if it can, will help you to apply or reapply if you have been turned down. The problem is that the charity is a small one with limited capacity and they may find it impossible to give help to everyone who needs it.

See publiclawproject.org.uk and contact exceptionalfunding@publiclawproject.org.uk.

Using a lawyer without legal aid

No win, no fee agreements

These were formerly known as conditional fee agreements and, in theory, are available for all civil cases except family cases such as divorces, financial disputes within matrimonial proceedings and children disputes. They often figure in commercial, insolvency, debt collection and defamation cases and in claims for accident compensation (as well as employment tribunal cases which are mainly outside the ambit of this book). Effectively, you and the solicitor share the risk of you losing. The best deal you are likely to reach with the solicitor where you are bringing (instead of defending) a claim is that (a) you pay them no fees if you lose, (b) if you win, the solicitor accepts for the work they have done the amount they can collect from the loser but (c) the solicitor charges you a success fee which can be anything up to 100% of what they are entitled to collect from the loser for their work and this success fee comes out of the money you have been awarded. In claims for personal injuries (other than for diffuse mesothelioma) the success fee is capped at 25% of your compensation other than for future loss (such as for future care).

The capping does not apply to an appeal against a defeat in court where the success fee can be up to 100%. The solicitor may want you to take out an insurance policy for their basic bill so that they are protected if you lose. You will pay the premium but the solicitor may agree to foot it until the case is concluded. If a barrister is brought in, you can hopefully come to a similar arrangement with them. Where use is being made of an expert who won't wait around for payment you may have to advance their charges. It is usual to insure against the winner's legal costs being ordered against you should you lose; that's an after-the-event policy and the premium on that would also be down to you though, again, the solicitor may be prepared to pay it up front and get it back from you later.

But will a solicitor - and maybe a barrister too - take you on? They are unlikely to touch you unless they reckon you have at least a 60% chance of winning and you may have to yourself advance not only experts' fees but court fees and other expenses which are incurred by the solicitor as the case progresses. The solicitor may also wish to have the right to charge you for the work they have done at a rate which is higher than your loser would have to contribute. This is all up for negotiation with the solicitor. Particularly in accident claims brought by an adult on behalf of a child, I have frequently encountered scandalous conditional fee agreements providing for a 100% success fee where the risk of failure is close to non-existent, typically whiplash claims where the child has been a passenger in a stationary car which has been hit in the rear by the defendant's vehicle and the defendant's insurers have already admitted that the defendant was to blame.

You may need to haggle over the success fee sought. The solicitor will assess the risk they would be taking on in accepting the case. The bigger they assess the risk to be, the higher the success fee which will be sought. An assessment of a 60% chance of you winning may well justify a success fee of around 67% as against around 11% for a 90% chance of winning. The solicitor might be prepared to accept a staged success fee arrangement: if the case settles within say three months you pay them a success fee of x%, if it settles within say nine months you pay them a greater success fee of y% and if it settles or you win any later you pay them a success fee of a dreaded 100%. If you manage to negotiate the ultimate of not a penny from you if you lose and a success fee if you win, the level of that success fee is going to reflect the fact that no risk is being assumed by you. Where you are convinced that you have a strong case, you may wish to shop around. Sizing up the case and drafting a proposed conditional fee agreement will absorb any solicitor's time. Check beforehand whether they would charge for that and, if so, how much.

So the key info you want from the solicitor about a conditional fee arrangement is:

- Will you charge me for looking into the possibility of it and then setting it up and, if so, how much?
- If I lose, do I have to pay anything towards the cost of your work and disbursements you incur and, if so, how much do you estimate that will be and when will I have to pay?
- If I win, do I have to pay anything towards the cost of your work and disbursements you incur and, if so, how much do you estimate that will be. And what will be the rate of your success fee and will it be reduced if the case settles before trial and, if so, by how much and, if not, why not?

OK, I know you were desperate to ask. You've been charged with driving whilst disqualified and with excess alcohol in your body, you've got this cracking defence, you need an ace lawyer to argue it in court, you haven't got a black and white tv to your name and can you hire that lawyer under a conditional fee agreement? No. These agreements cannot apply to criminal proceedings except magistrates' court cases under section 82 of the Environmental Protection Act 1990 by any person aggrieved by a statutory nuisance at premises (smoke, dust, insects, badly kept animals and Uncle Tom Cobley).

Damages based agreements

Here is another deal you may reach with your solicitor which only became legal in April 2013 - the damages based agreement. The solicitor agrees to act for you in return for a cut of your compensation. If you lose, they get nothing. But if you win, they may do very nicely or very badly. Depends. There is a cap on their cut depending on the type of case. In personal injury cases, it is 25% of the compensation but the solicitor cannot share in any part of compensation for future loss. In other civil cases the maximum cut is 50%. In employment tribunal cases it is 35%. Any expenses which the solicitor has had to pay out such as court fees and fees for medical reports which for whatever reason the loser escapes having to reimburse will be reimbursable by you. Should you lose, you would have to reimburse disbursements except for any barristers' fees. These caps do not apply to appeals where you and the solicitor are free to negotiate the percentage cut. A damages based agreement will have the solicitor in hindsight laughing if they settle the case in five minutes but they could be weeping if it goes to trial five years later. A lousy idea is for you to agree to a damages based agreement where your case is oozing with strength and the opposition is weak or non-existent or liability has already been conceded.

Lawyer charges but you don't pay or you borrow

Third party litigation funders, they are called. Companies who will pay your legal fees in return for a cut of the damages you recover. The Judge Ltd (www.thejudge.co.uk) is a leading broker which arranges this kind of funding. But what funders really love is multi-million commercial litigation. Could little you (or little me) ever hope to secure third party funding? The broker's associate director Robert Warner says that there is a handful of funders who will consider "smaller" value claims but they would normally need to be worth at least £100,000 and are most likely to be negligence claims against professional advisers such as lawyers (oh no!), accountants and surveyors, contested will and intestacy claims, financial mis-selling claims (not PPI) and breach of contract and employment claims.

The funder would usually be looking for the claim value to be at least four times that of the costs which will be involved. They will usually require you to take out an insurance policy to cover any costs which may be awarded against you if you lose and the insurer would want to be satisfied that you had a minimum of a 60% chance of winning. In the current climate, it is unlikely the funder would take you on without full legal representation. Acting in person or with a direct access barrister (see below) would be a non-runner. Robert Warner is coy on the amount of the funder' s cut: "It is too difficult to say as each funder operates a different "success fee" model and these largely depend on the amount of capital committed, the actual fees drawn and the length of time that the money is committed. To give you a fixed answer would not be representative of the market." Matrimonial financial remedy and clinical negligence claims are usually avoided although some specialist lenders may back a financial remedy claim with a loan where there is a property that can be offered as security but expect to pay high interest within the range of 1.5 to 2.5% per month (that's 18 to 30% per annum).

Novitas (novitasloans.co.uk) is a leading player in the market for lending for legal fees in matrimonial financial remedy cases between opposite and same sex couples without taking a share of the spoils (and they will also similarly lend for claims for clinical negligence and 'you left me out of your will' - see chapter 40). The finance can cover proceedings under the Children Act 1989 which are running in tandem with a financial remedy application but not under schedule 1 to the 1989 Act (see chapter 32). They will lend to either side of a case and often lend to both sides of the same case. You can draw down tranches of the loan as and when you need the money but only be liable for interest on what you take from the date you take it. The interest rate works out at 18% per annum. However, there is a set up fee in family cases of the greater of £500 or 1% of the loan agreed which along with the interest is rolled up into the loan. The period of the loan is a formal 12 months but 30 days' notice can be given calling it in after 11 months have run. Novitas' managing director Jason Reeve stresses that his company seeks to be flexible about the length of the required loan period in practice and they have some loans which have been allowed to be out for three years.

There is no prescribed maximum loan at Novitas but it will want to be satisfied that the money will be available at the end of the case to repay what has been lent along with the interest. Secondary considerations include credit and reconciliation history (after all, you could be reuniting after a few months which would bring the proceedings to a close). They will arrange to have first call on the settlement proceeds to the extent necessary to get their money back and take a charge on your interest in the family home as security where that is available. If there is no security available then Novitas may wish to insure the risk of going unpaid and you would be responsible for the 10% premium; so if you were after £10,000, you would have to draw down £11,000 of which £1,000 would be passed to the insurer. About 20% of their loans are insured in this way. Novitas will insist on you taking legal advice on the proposed arrangement with them and for that advice you will have to pay.

Back to a sharing of the spoils. Augusta Ventures (www.augustaventures.com) describes itself as the leading provider of litigation finance in the UK which has shelled out over £15m to date in backing suitable claims. Its no go areas primarily include matrimonial applications and claims for personal injury, defamation, breach of privacy, housing disrepair and professional negligence which has allegedly led to an insufficient financial recovery (for example, against a solicitor who has acted in your litigation) although other negligence claims against solicitors will be looked at.

Augusta have financed claims worth between £20,000 (so lower than the norm) up to £40m and as a general rule of thumb look for a budget to damages ratio of 1 to 3 (that's the client seeking at least £300,000 for every £100,000 to be spent on legal costs). The legal work will be done by a firm out of their approved panel of solicitors or, if you already have a solicitor, they will work with them provided they satisfy their due diligence process. What they will not do is fund you as a litigant in person. The assessment process - it looks rigorous though they say it is no worse than applying to a bank for a loan - will include obtaining a barrister's opinion on the merits of the claim unless the matter is "small and simple". They will extend early action finance covering initial costs and a barrister's fee on merits where required and if the claim is then fully financed by them and you win this expense will come out of the spoils plus a 25% mark up. If they refuse finance or they finance and you lose, there is no charge for the assessment.

What's in it for Augusta if they fully finance? Nothing if you lose. If you win then out of the compensation (and in this order) they are reimbursed for their outlay plus 14% per annum on the capital they have advanced, your lawyers who would have acted under a conditional fee agreement are paid (but not their success fee - yet) and you are reimbursed any funds you have contributed. Out of the balance, Augusta collect an average fee - wait for it and they aren't shy about giving us the figure - of 20%, the lawyers are paid their success fee. And the rest is yours.

Augusta's director of strategic engagement Jeunesse Edwards tells me they will not finance litigation unless the claimant will end up with no less than 50% of the compensation awarded after the deductions I have mentioned have been made. Oh and Augusta will want an after the event insurance policy taken out to protect you against an adverse costs order. If you have made any cash contribution to the claim costs then the policy can extend to 90% of the contribution which means that, should you lose, you will only be down for 10% of any cash contribution made and will not be in debt for costs to Augusta or the winner. The policy will involve a 15% premium. Augusta will include the premium in their finance.

Selecting a solicitor or barrister

or

"That Ponsonby-Smythe is red hot"

Like judges and weather forecasters, there are brilliant lawyers and lousy lawyers. Choose one who specialises in the type of case for which you want to *instruct* them. Yes, you don't take on a lawyer or buy their services. You *instruct* them though with most lawyers I have encountered, it is they who do the instructing. If you are embroiled in a boundary dispute with your neighbour, steer clear of a lawyer who spends most of their days on criminal trials. A friend may recommend a "good lawyer". You might even be able to extract an off the record recommendation from someone in the know, perhaps from the CAB or other advice agency. Or if your case is about making a claim against the domestic help you dismissed who went off to a tabloid newspaper with lurid details of your private life, research on *Google* which lawyers have been involved in cases on breach of confidence and who may still be alive - and won! If you want a powerful advocate to destroy your lying opponent in the witness box and can't get a recommendation from a reliable source, pop along to your local civil court, ask the usher if there are any good advocates in action that day and listen and watch but make sure you have a note of their name and address before you hop it. Advocacy can make the difference between success and failure. Any judge who swears that they will never be swayed by a persuasive advocate should be taking a lie detector test.

Should the lawyer's name play any part in the selection process? A really grand name like Ponsonby-Smythe could impress the opposition but distract the judge like a twitch, very greasy hair or an old-world charming barrister who sometimes appeared before and insisted on referring to his female clients as "my lady". The most intimidating name for a firm of solicitors that I have ever come across is Wright Hassall who are based not in the East End of London but tranquil Leamington Spa and who count debt collection as one of their specialities. Their marketing director Vikki Whittemore fears that some people are likely to question the firm's credibility because of the name. Is it a joke or is the firm some sort of commoditised legal practice rather than a full service law firm with a 170 year heritage?

Solicitor, barrister or both: the choice is yours

You now have a choice of lawyer in that you can go for a solicitor or a barrister - or both. Traditionally, a litigant's first stop was a solicitor's office. The solicitor may have had someone else in the firm with legal experience (often a legal executive who can also sometimes advocate in court) who would advise and prepare the case for battle and the solicitor, especially in a complex case, would bring in a barrister to advise and also to appear in court as the advocate. If the case was proceeding in the High Court, Court of Appeal or Supreme Court the solicitor would be compelled to use a barrister for advocacy unless they had acquired authority to advocate there themselves. The majority of solicitors do not have this authority although numbers have recently been increasing. But now the solicitor can be dispensed with and you can directly engage a barrister not only to appear in court as your advocate but to advise on the law, prepare paperwork and do other things along the way. We will look at how you can source such a barrister shortly. Some barristers will only accept work via a solicitor; some will be prepared to have the litigant directly instruct them, without a solicitor, to appear in court as the advocate (and, with that axe taken to legal aid work, an increasing number are so prepared); and some will agree to do the whole case - advice, preparation and advocacy - directly instructed and without solicitor involvement.

Dilemma

What the hell do you do? Using a solicitor plus a barrister is going to be more expensive than using just one of them as there will inevitably be some duplication of work for which you will pay. For example, if a meeting with the barrister is needed - it's called a *conference* but you are unlikely to get a lousy lunch thrown in as you do with most conferences I go to - the solicitor will charge you for telling the barrister in writing all about the case and the barrister will charge you for reading what the solicitor has written. The solicitor will charge you for attending the meeting with the barrister and the barrister will charge you for advising at the meeting.

That doesn't make the decision open and shut. Some cases are so complex that they demand the application of two legal brains. Less complex cases may still justify both solicitor and barrister because the preparation will be quite extensive and there may need to be quite concentrated contact between you and whoever is in charge of preparation. And you could also want to call on your lawyer in an attempt to settle the case, be it before proceedings have been started or hand in hand with the proceedings. Generally, solicitors and others in the firm who are on the case are better at preparatory work and they are better placed to be available to you when you want them and to keep up the momentum of settlement negotiations with the opposition. That's because they are unlikely to be occupied advocating in court with the same intensity as a barrister and they will have the office back up which will not normally be available with a barrister. "My Lord, whilst my learned friend was cross-examining, I took the liberty of checking my messages and I see that another client for whom I am in court next week urgently wants to speak to me about a settlement offer and is desperate for help on compelling some witnesses to come to court if the case does not settle. My Lord, would you be prepared to indulge me and stop this case for a few minutes so that I can deal with these matters and I apologise to your Lordship and my learned friend but, you see, I operate on direct access." It couldn't happen except in a nightmare or occasionally when only a barrister is handling the case.

Beauty parade

If you are going to instruct a solicitor with or without a barrister, you find the solicitor first. They will almost certainly have a barrister in mind who they think is suitable for the case although you may have decided on someone else. You call the tune. Some solicitors have pet barristers and fall into the trap of using them on all their cases when sometimes a particular case may not really be in their comfort zone. In the absence of a recommendation for a solicitor or a Ponsonby-Smythe, you can use a pin in a directory - and remember that a flashy advert on a full page with a teaser on the preceding page could spell danger - or you can use the *Find a Solicitor* facility run by the Law Society (lawsociety.org.uk or telephone 020 7320 5650) or check out the websites of local law societies which are mainly established on a county basis. If I woke up one morning with every legal principle erased from my mind and needed to instruct a solicitor then unless the case revolved around a remote area of law in which the only firm having any expertise operated out of London's West End charging £2,000 an hour plus VAT, I would pick a local medium sized firm with a member who knows their stuff, would prepare, negotiate and advocate at all stages from start to finish and would not charge me an arm and a leg.

You ought to be able to locate a solicitor who will see you free of charge for at least half an hour so that you can size them up and they can size you up and, with a bit of luck, extract a bit of legal advice at the same time. You don't want a wimp and they don't want a lunatic. Ensure it is agreed when you make an appointment that there is no charge for this initial session. You will decide when you see them whether you would be able to get on with them - pompous, prat or personable - whether they appear confident and whether you would have confidence in them. And here are the questions you want answered:

- What is your experience in this sort of case?
- From what you have heard, do you think I have a good chance of success?
- Who would be dealing with my case - you personally from beginning to end? If not, what other members of your firm would be involved and what would their tasks be?
- Will you advocate for me in court or take in a barrister?
- Why would you take in a barrister?
- Can you and will you take my case on a no win, no fee basis (and, if so, see above for the questions to ask about a no win, no fee agreement)?

If no win, no fee is out of the question:

- What will be the amount per hour you will charge me for your time and the time of anyone in the office to whom you will delegate and what do you estimate your charges will amount to for the whole case?
- How much would I have to pay you up front? How often would you send me interim bills?

Where a no win, no fee is not to be the arrangement, you could ask whether the solicitor would be prepared to take the case on a fixed fee basis so that the actual fee is fixed in advance and neither you nor the solicitor would be justified in departing from it no matter how straightforward or problematic the case turned out to be. In the world of litigation, it is unlikely that the solicitor would agree to this should you be looking at them dealing with the case in its entirety because the course of litigation is so difficult to predict. An unbundling situation is another matter (see below under **Dipping in and out with a lawyer**).

If you are going to instruct a barrister without a solicitor and are not following up a recommendation, you can go to barcouncil.org.uk which will not help you a lot except it will tell you about the Direct Access Portal. This is the website for barristers who are prepared to be instructed directly without a solicitor - directaccessportal.co.uk. For the privilege of being included on the portal, the barristers pay £100 a year. Barristers who don't want to be instructed by you directly or to pay £100 a year, won't be on the portal. Of the 6,000 barristers who will take on direct access work, around one-half of them are on the portal. The minority of portal barristers who will conduct the whole case and not just advocate for you say so on the portal. A similar website is run by www.mybarrister.co.uk which has 500 barristers on board but claims far more hits than the relatively new portal. Its barristers pay an annual subscription to be included on the site of between £480 and £1,440 depending on how long they have been practising.

clerksroom.direct.com works on a different basis and has over 1,000 barristers on its books who are available for advocacy work and drafting documents. You can select the barrister you want or ask them to find you a suitable barrister who they are satisfied is right for the job and will take it at a fee you have named or within a budget agreed in advance of the case. They will deal with all the administration involved including getting the fee agreed in advance of the case. For their service they charge you anything up to 20% of what is to go to the barrister. You'll be aware of the split between the barrister and clerksroom before you accept or reject. Most of their barristers will be prepared to spend up to half an hour by phone with you to understand precisely what service you are after and whether you are suited to direct access.

What makes Cotswold Barristers distinct is that they are a set of chambers targeting direct access work for their smallish band of barristers - you can see who they are, their specialist areas and what they look like on cotswoldbarristers.co.uk - and so leaving solicitors out of the reckoning. 90% of their work comes through direct access with solicitor involvement in the remainder. They have a Cheltenham base but their barristers will advocate anywhere in England and Wales - and Gibraltar - and litigation services are also available. Barristers will assess a case - and you - on a free 15 minute telephone conference for which it is suggested you fully prepare. Their head barrister Mark Smith represented around 250 buy-to-let tracker mortgage borrowers who took on West Bromwich Mortgage Company for increasing their interest rate by 1.99% without any change in the Bank of England base interest rate. They won their case on appeal to the Court of Appeal in June 2016. Mr Smith dealt with the litigation work and acted as junior barrister to the QC taken in from other chambers.

What sort of fees are charged by the Cheltenham barristers? "This information is not made public" says chief executive Carla Morris-Papps - even to me! But she maintains that prospective clients are encouraged to compare fees and level of service before committing. Client meetings can take place in Cheltenham, at your premises or by video link from their dedicated suite. Fees are payable in advance and are fixed.

Some barristers personally advertise their availability for direct access work. Take a look at the classified ads in *Private Eye* and go onto the web and you will find plenty of barristers chambers - groups of barristers operate out of an office which they call chambers (see old videos of *Rumpole of the Bailey*) where they are terrorised by their clerk and it is probably the clerk you will speak to if you contact a set of chambers to talk about direct access - with websites imploring you to engage a barrister directly.

The minority of barristers who will conduct the entirety of the litigation for you will be no keener than a solicitor to undertake a fixed fee arrangement - if anything, even less keen. In fact barristers won't generally even go in for advertising a fixed fee tariff for dealing with advocacy alone. One London set of chambers, however, did brandish a rather inviting list of fixed fees on their website. Alas, this took the head barrister by surprise when I questioned him about it and he said they didn't go in for fixed fees and they had been planning to alter the website the next week!

The majority of barristers operate out of clusters in London but there are plenty of sets of barristers' chambers in large cities and towns, sometimes linked to the main chambers in London. The idea that provincial barristers are second-rate is a cruel myth. The closer the base of the barrister you choose to the court at which you want them to advocate, the lower will be their fee - hopefully. I've got a flavour of the going-rates from two higher flight London sets of chambers which both hold themselves out to be eager for direct access work.

Over at 1 Gray's Inn Square (http://www.1gis.co.uk) they cover family work on direct access. The more senior the barrister, the more you pay.

To advocate in a financial remedies case at one of the preliminary hearings (see chapter 48) a barrister who has been mouthing it for five years would be looking for the first appointment to charge up to £850, for the financial dispute resolution appointment up to £1,250 and for the final hearing up to £2,000. A more senior barrister who has been going for 14 years would be after up to £850, up to £1,750 and up to £2,500 respectively. And for someone from the most senior echelons, "fees to be agreed on review of the papers" so a little shy there. For Children Act cases not brought by a local authority, the fees will generally be lower and pitched for a junior barrister for a preliminary hearing at up to £600 or if the case is to take three hours up to £1,000 and for a final hearing up to £2,000. For a barrister of middle ranking seniority these figures rise to up to £850, up to £1,250 and up to £2,500 respectively. Going to the even more senior boys and girls, "fees to be agreed on review of the papers." Where have we heard that before? All the figures given are exclusive of VAT.

At 4 King's Bench Walk (http://www.4kbw.co.uk) a highly competent barrister with 13 years' experience under his wig will usually charge £750 for a first appointment, £2,000 for a financial dispute resolution appointment and for a final hearing, £3,500 and if the case goes over one day £2,000 for each successive day. For non-family litigation, his advocacy will cost £500 for up to one hour, £1,250 for up to three hours and £2,000 for the day. For advisory work he charges out at around £250 per hour. Again, VAT is on top. These fees will reflect an extra 10% to 20% over the fee which would be charged if he was instructed by a solicitor instead of by direct access because of the additional work that is involved with no solicitor. If any barrister makes that point to you then you might say that the fee should be 10% less because they are going to be paid in advance. Seldom will you get credit on a direct access instruction.

A barrister can act on a direct access basis under a conditional fee or damages based agreement (see above under **Using a lawyer without legal aid**). I would be surprised if the barrister queue to do so is very long. If you see a queue of posh lawyers, it will probably be outside a *Costa* outlet.

In the battle of solicitor v barrister, my efforts to get some representatives from each profession to come to blows at a hearing centre near me didn't come off and the bosses of *mybarrister.co.uk* wouldn't be drawn. "We would prefer not to comment." In desperation, I invited the Bar Council and the Law Society to slag off the other. A Bar Council spokesman argued that it *can* be more advantageous to instruct a barrister instead of a solicitor (though this isn't always the case) and relied on the lower overheads of barristers meaning that their rates were "often very affordable" and their expertise in disputes and, in turn, their understanding of how to avoid disputes reaching the court room. And he threw in that complaints against barristers are low in number. Statistics from the Legal Ombudsman showed that in 2014/15 just 4.6% of all complaints against lawyers related to barristers. He did point out that a barrister might actually refer a case to a solicitor if they felt they were not best suited to take it on.

Alright, we get the drift. Over to the Law Society for a knock out. Their spokeswoman said: "Solicitors provide vital support to clients in contentious matters. While clients can still instruct barristers directly and have been able to do so for some time, solicitors provide a wider range of services, which is why many clients choose to instruct a solicitor first."

If you bought tickets for the fight, you might want your money back.

Dipping in and out with a lawyer

Barristers traditionally dip in and out of a case. So it is that a barrister will take on the advocacy at a final hearing though they have never met you or the case before and, as we have seen, so many of them now will take it on without the involvement of a solicitor. The fee will be agreed with you in advance and if you don't have to pay it before the barrister steps into court, I'll eat another one of my hats. A solicitor may possibly be more flexible than a barrister about reaching an instalment plan for their fees which has you plunging into your pocket even after the final hearing. Be it barrister or solicitor, they need to guard against the possibility of you losing and having to pay the winner's legal costs. Who will get to you first - lawyer or successful opponent- and is there enough for both? A mortgage on your home in favour of the lawyer might well be sufficient protection for them should you be desperate for their representation but lacking ready cash and unable to negotiate a loan.

If you intend to hire a barrister for the final hearing only, you should give them an opportunity as long as practically possible ahead of that hearing to see the papers and you so that they can advise on whether they have everything they require to do the best for your case.

Will a solicitor with their office backup be prepared to dip in and out of a case rather than act from start to finish should that better suit your pocket? Could you ask them just to advise whether your case is legally strong or a stinker? Just to draw up the court papers so that you can start the proceedings yourself? Just to advise you whether or not you need a particular witness or what questions to ask in cross-examination? Just to deal with the advocacy at the final hearing instead of a barrister? Just to act as *McKenzie Friend* (see more below) at a final hearing and not an advocate which perhaps a more junior and less expensive member of the firm could more than adequately do? To look over a document setting out proposed terms of settlement of the case to ensure you are not being ripped off or that it is watertight? They would be performing what they call an *unbundling* service dealing with a discrete aspect of the case and for most solicitors it's a novel concept. Until recently, the vast majority of solicitors were nervous about it for fear that they would be highly vulnerable to a complaint by the client - or worse still, a client claim for damages - because something went wrong after they had overlooked some feature of the case they could not have known about as they were so limited in the case information available to them and the time a modest fee would allow them to spend on it.

Then along came a decision of the Court of Appeal in November 2015 which should have put their minds at rest. There a lady had reached a financial remedies agreement with her husband dealing with property and finance in the course of divorce proceedings. She consulted a solicitor to deal with the redrafting of the order which set out exactly what was to happen between the couple after the unsatisfactory paperwork which had so far been prepared was rejected by a judge. She wanted the solicitor to amend the order so that it was in a form which would meet with the judge's approval. This the solicitor duly did. Subsequently, the lady came to regret the order. She sued the solicitor for damages claiming that the solicitor should have advised or warned her against going ahead with the order as she could have done better and that the solicitor had failed to do so. When the claim was thrown out the lady appealed. The Court of Appeal upheld the throw out. They ruled that the solicitor had not been under a duty to give the broader advice or warnings for which the lady argued. There would be very serious consequences for both the courts and litigants in person if solicitors felt unable to act on a discrete part of a cased for fear of being sued in this way. This sort of solicitor service was invaluable. It was vital though that where a solicitor was consulted for an unbundling service the limitations of what they would be doing were carefully set out in writing.

So I asked the Law Society what they had done about compiling and publishing a register of solicitors who are prepared to do unbundling work. Nothing. So I asked the Law Society what were their plans to compile and publish such a register. None. So I put the same questions to the local law societies and generally the response was no more encouraging. However, Nottingham Law Society did rise to the challenge and they have compiled a list of unbundlers in their town and county. Go to www.nottslassoc.org. If a visit to Nottinghamshire to discuss the particulars of claim against your dentist after your dentures fell out and cracked into tiny pieces would involve more than six hours travel, you will need to ring round some local firms and ask whether they will unbundle. The receptionist may query with a "Do what?" so ask if you can speak to a solicitor about the possibility of instructing them on a discrete litigation matter and hopefully the line won't go dead. The level of enthusiasm for unbundling will vary. Probably better to try a smaller or medium sized firm and steer away from West End firms who may be concerned that you will spoil their waiting room carpet with your muddy boots. Some firms may prefer to reserve their unbundling services for established clients. What I am confident about is that unless the profession as a whole does show more enthusiasm and gets its unbundling act together it will find it has lost its litigation business to barristers doing direct access work and showing much more enterprise.

Free legal help

Citizens Advice

The good old CAB. They are brilliant and operate out of 3,500 locations. You can search for your nearest location on citizensadvice.org.uk or call 03444 111 444 for pointing in the right direction in England and 03444 77 20 20 in Wales.

RCJ Advice Bureau

This is affiliated to the CAB and dispenses legal advice for unrepresented litigants from two venues: The Royal Court of Justice in London's Strand for those involved in a court case proceeding in the county court, High Court or Court of Appeal other than contested probate and Court of Protection cases (telephone for an appointment to 020 3475 8996 on weekdays between 10am and 1pm for an appointment) and from the Principal Registry of the High Court's Family Division in London's Holborn (telephone for an appointment to 020 3137 6935 Monday to Thursday) for those after legal advice on any area of family law including divorce financial remedies and appeals. Appointments are at the appropriate venue although it is possible to obtain advice by telephone and, where feasible, by email. It matters not where the case is being heard: Wigan will do. Except for emergencies such as evictions, you are likely to be seen within one and seven days of booking. The bureau may be able to help get you free representation by a barrister in court through the Bar Pro Bono Unit (see below). The bureau's advice is designed for those who cannot afford to pay for it. You won't be subjected to a formal means test but the bureau will want to know that the resources are not there for you to pay a lawyer. Five leaflets have been produced ("Are there alternatives"; "Before you start"; "First steps"; "Starting your claim and the pre-trial process"; and "Hearings, the trial and appeals") which can be downloaded on www.courtnav.org.uk/going-to-court.php). The bureau is also concerned in the running of Islington CAB (020 3475 5080). See www.rcjadvice.org.uk.

Law works

They provide free initial advice for those who are ineligible for legal aid and cannot afford to pay for a lawyer. They cover various areas of law, in particular employment, housing, consumer, debt and finance. You can expect a 14 to 45 minute session to explain and be advised and some clinics may draft a letter for you where that is appropriate. Search for a clinic at lawworks.org.uk

Law centres

They offer free face to face advice and some run a telephone advice line for those who cannot afford a lawyer. You can search for your nearest centre on lawcentres.org.uk. You will find a mapped list of them on this website. Some may have closed down since you opened this book because of loss of funding but the website is kept up to date. Eleven centres have closed since the scope of legal aid shrivelled to a microdot. Each existing centre focuses on core areas of work which are normally firmly within social welfare law and targeting their help at the most disadvantaged. Put it this way: you are more likely to get help if you are an employee or tenant rather than an employer or landlord.

Surrey Law Centre (http://surreylawcentre.org/contact/) is one of the liveliest about and a good example of what can be on offer from solicitors and some barristers, particularly from chambers in Guildford in Surrey's case who volunteer their services. For domestic abuse cases, they run regular clinics at Guildford, Reigate, Godalming and Epsom and for the rest there are regular evening clinics at Dorking, Epsom, Walton-on-Thames, Oxted, Reigate, Godalming, Woking, Camberley, Sutton and Crawley. Do they have any qualifying financial criteria? Mark Gough who runs the centre says they let anyone come to their clinic for initial help and will see what they can do to get them more help via legal aid or from a pro bono lawyer where that is appropriate.

Some law centres have set up subsidiaries which charge for representing those who are on low incomes but outside the legal aid scheme to deal primarily with employment and immigration cases. They are run under different names from different addresses. Rochdale Legal Enterprise and Islington's Green Roots are examples. Charges look to be on the modest side and the lawyers doing the legal work are likely to be highly specialised in the cases they deal with so you would be doing well to get them to take you on.

Law centres also provide free help at a number of county court centres - civil hearing centres we must call them now, remember - for those caught up in housing possession cases whether as tenants or mortgage borrowers. Where the law centres do not operate there are other initiatives so that the current position is that free expert advice will be available on the day at every civil hearing centre for housing possession cases.

Civil legal advice

This is provided by the Legal Aid Agency (www.gov.uk/civil-legal-advice telephone 0345 345 4345). "Could you repeat that, please?" Yes, certainly. The Legal Aid Agency. It's nothing like the legal aid that used to be around. It's just legal advice and often by telephone, post or email for those who pass a means test and is limited to a mere five areas of law: debt, housing, education, discrimination and family. You can have a go at working out if you would qualify financially by going to www.gov.uk/check-legal-aid and, if you succeed, they may offer you a job in their accounts department. If you are telephoning to find out if you are financially eligible you should have available recent payslips, bank statements, details of any savings and investments, details of any benefits, and mortgage statements and a current valuation of any property you own. You will be relieved to hear that you can ask them to call you back. Once it is established that you are likely to be financially eligible, you will be put through to an adviser immediately. Alternatively, you can have a face to face meeting with a legal adviser from a firm of solicitors or law centre who are contracted by the Legal Aid Agency to provide it in one of those five areas of law. Where do you get hold of one of these advisers? You can make a search on find-legal-advice.justice.gov.uk which I have just tested. It works. Or phone the number above.

Bar Pro Bono Unit

We have briefly met the unit under ***RCJ Advice Bureau*** above. The unit can provide a barrister to represent you free of charge for a specific part of your case which could be the main hearing. Where your needs would involve more than three days of the barrister's time (including the hearing) the unit will have to decline help. In deciding whether a barrister can take you on, consideration will be given to the legal merit of your case, your financial circumstances and the time the barrister would be occupied on the case. Find out more at www.barprobono.org.uk. You will make yourself very unpopular if you apply to the unit direct. It will only allow a litigant to be referred by an advice agency such as RCJ Advice Bureau, a solicitor or your member of parliament.

Insurance

Perhaps you have a legal expenses policy. Then you are laughing provided you didn't take it out after the dispute for which you want help actually arose. It could be that some other policy you hold, like one for household contents, includes cover for legal advice and representation. Go through your drawers. You may be pleasantly surprised.

Other advice centres

There may be other sources of legal help in your area which you can *Google* or one of the sources I have mentioned can point you in the best direction where they cannot themselves assist you. Law schools throughout England and Wales offer free legal advice from students training to become solicitors or barristers in specified areas of the law. This is part of that training. I accept that you might be terrified about acting on their advice but worry not because they will be closely supervised by a qualified lawyer. Indirectly, it will be that qualified lawyer who will be telling you or endorsing or revising what the trainee has told you about how you legally stand. If you *Google* "legal advice from law school students" you will be able to access details of the law schools who offer this service. Among them are University of Law (telephone 0800 289997), London's City Law School (telephone 0207 4045787 ext 353/391) and Nottingham Law School (telephone 0115 8484262). Toynbee Hall (info@toynbeehall.org.uk) will give you free advice if you live, work or study in the City of London with an emphasis on debt, benefits, landlord, housing and dealing with the financial aspect of cancer. For those who live and work in London, the Mary Ward Centre (www.marywardlegal.org.uk) will help with free of charge advice on the main areas of debt, benefits and housing and, through their pro bono clinics, on employment disputes as well as with services targeted at those on low incomes. You will find a myriad of other sources of free legal help at www.advicenow.org.uk/guides/help-directory in various areas including domestic violence (and there's a separate source for victims who are men and children), education, disability rights and mental health.

Mckenzie Friends and other friends

"This is my friend, McKenzie"

If you don't have the benefit of a lawyer in court, you will almost always be allowed by the judge to have help from a *McKenzie Friend*. You may be forgiven for thinking that this is what they are called so that litigants in person won't have a clue what they are. Actually, it's just the law being daft with titles. *Litigant's Assistant* (even *Litigant's Mate*) would be better - or *Court Supporter* as a consultation paper from the judiciary suggested in February 2016. *McKenzie* was the surname of a divorce petitioner in a 1970 case who had been denied proper help from a friend in court. The denial was successfully challenged and the Court of Appeal ruled that help to a litigant in person from somebody they take along to court should in the ordinary course of events always be available. So now we are stuck with the unfortunate title.

Holding your pencil

Certainly the *McKenzie Friend* can do this: even a biro or a quill pen, if you have ink at the ready. They can sit by your side in court and provide you with moral support, take notes, help with case papers (find exhibit 1278b when all your documents have crashed to the floor) and quietly give you advice on any aspect of the conduct of the case by a discreet whisper into the lughole. What they cannot do is to speak to the judge on your behalf, suggest how you answer questions when you are giving evidence or cross-examine witnesses which means, in short, that they cannot perform the role of a lawyer. That's the theory and that's more often than not the practice. However, with lawyer help being so hard for so many to come by, many judges will now allow the *McKenzie Friend* to do more. If they appear to have a better grasp of the case and the procedure than you - especially, if they have some legal or semi-legal or other professional knowledge or background - the judge may well allow them to speak on your behalf though never, never, never, ever give evidence on your behalf. After all, what's the point in insisting they whisper into your lughole so that you can then repeat to the judge exactly what you think you have heard although it is a complete corruption of what was actually said.

> *McKenzie Friend whispering into litigant's left ear: "Tell the judge that in your submission the evidence of the witness was a tissue of untruths."*
>
> *Litigant whispering into McKenzie Friend's right ear: "Don't fudge what?"*
>
> *McKenzie Friend whispering a little louder into litigant's left ear: "Tell the bloody judge that in your submission the witness told a pack of porkie pies."*
>
> *Litigant to Judge: "Your Honour, my mission was to do up my flies."*

Friendzie to McKenzie

Your *McKenzie Friend* can be anyone you trust to give you the support and assistance you may need. You can take a family member, friend or that baker or candlestick maker so long as they are willing to accompany you. Be discriminating about who you choose. If they get up the noses of people who know them they will probably get up the nose of the judge. And be careful about using someone from a pressure group who may well have their own agenda and fail to help you in the objective way that is good for you. Research by the Legal Services Consumer Panel shows that a large proportion of *McKenzie Friends* got into the job following negative experience of courts during divorce and child contact cases.

Or you can hire a *McKenzie Friend*. There are loads and loads of paid *McKenzie Friends* out there and on the internet you will find plenty of plugs by them or agencies they work through. Some are brilliant and some are dreadful. Steer clear of former solicitors and barristers who have been thrown out by their professional body for some misdeed, not because they won't be up to the job but because the judge may well be disapproving of them. Steer clear too of those who have no background in the area covered by the case. If you are involved in a dispute about the welfare of a child, for example, an ex-senior Cafcass or social services welfare officer would be handy but not an ex-electrician. Don't engage someone simply because they sound very sympathetic to your case - if they are wildly sympathetic it could be for the reason that they are desperate for your cash. Ask for a copy of their CV.

What do the paid *McKenzie Friends* charge? You can expect to pay anything within the range of £35 to £60 an hour or £100 to £400 for a full day with travelling expenses being added on. If you win, the court cannot order the loser to reimburse these charges to you. However, you might get the charges back from the loser if the court has taken the ultimate step of allowing the *McKenzie Friend* to advocate for you in court as if they were a qualified lawyer.

But for how much longer will *McKenzie Friends* be able to charge for their services? That consultation paper in February 2016 nudged towards putting a stop to it by banning them from helping in court where they are directly or indirectly being paid. My prediction is that charging will not be outlawed and, if it is, I think I'll eat my wig this time. Anyway, for the time being, McKenzie Friends can certainly carry on charging.

Pros and cons

An unpaid, sane, respectful and grudgeless *McKenzie Friend*? Go for it every time if you can't get a lawyer. An unpaid, sane, respectful and grudge bearing *McKenzie Friend*? May be better than nothing. A paid *McKenzie Friend*? They are more likely to be allowed by the judge to do more for you in court than an unpaid one. But they are not answerable to a regulatory body like a qualified lawyer and they may not be covered by insurance for any claim you wanted to make against them for negligent advice. Generally, you are better off in court with a qualified lawyer than a *McKenzie Friend*. Compare what you are quoted by a solicitor or barrister for representation in court with what a *McKenzie Friend* would cost you. Sometimes, there may be little or nothing in it. Alternatively, you may be able to obtain free help in court from a support agency (see below).

Permission to use

You will need to ask the court for permission to use a *McKenzie Friend*. You should do this as soon as possible. Preferably, write to the court before the case and ask for the permission with details of the person's name and connection with you, although judges will normally allow permission to be sought on the day at the beginning of the case. Permission would almost certainly be refused if the judge thought that the *McKenzie Friend* was using you as a puppet or was giving assistance for some improper purpose.

No McKenzie Friend

It may not be legal advice you want or it may be you want it but cannot get hold of it when you need it. In this situation, support from someone who knows the system could be your salvation. That someone might well be legally qualified or experienced. Over then to the Personal Support Unit (www.the.psu.org.uk, rcj@thepsu.org.uk, telephone 020 7947 7701)) which operates out of the Royal Courts of Justice in London's Strand, London's Central Family Court, the County Court and Family Court hearing centres at Wandsworth and Nottingham, Birmingham Civil Justice Centre, Newcastle upon Tyne Combined Court Centre, Preston Combined Court and Sheffield Combined Court Centre. The Combined Courts referred to there house the Crown Court and the county and family courts' hearing centres. A South Coast unit is due to open soon and four others probably in the East, South-East, Midlands and Wales in the near future. Volunteers provide practical and emotional support to those involved in civil and family cases. They do not offer legal advice and will not speak for you at the hearing but can be present there with you and, if a hearing is adjourned, support next time can be made available. Where more is required they will signpost or actually refer you to other organisations. They will also help you fill in court forms and, as they put it, help you to organise your papers and thoughts and think about your next step.

Part 3

IS THE REST OF THIS BOOK WORTH READING?

Chapter 7

Preserving My Premium Bonds

It's far too early to sell this book on eBay. Anyway, there could be a glut of them on offer for a while. Read on and discover a myriad of legal rights - many will surprise you - which are there for your use and protection. Allow me to show you how to achieve a good result in civil and family court cases and that may sometimes mean losing well. And better still, see how you can avoid having to sue or being sued in the first place.

It's unlikely that any of us will get through life without some involvement in a legal dispute. I've had my own fair share. Hopefully, you will feel well equipped to cope with any that come your way by the time you invite any eBay bids. What I ask of you is this. Don't sue me because you reckon you followed one of my tips and lost out as a result. That's because I can't afford to pay you out and would have to argue that, in law and just like the radio racing tipster who gets it wrong, I don't owe you a duty of care and so am not liable for any mistake that has caused you loss. But most important of all, legal rules and principles can easily be dislodged by some peculiarity in an individual situation. For that reason, I implore you where you possibly can to check out with an expert (see chapter 18) whether there is a peculiarity in your situation before embarking on a legal course of action that could go wrong and cause you both anguish and expense. That's the end of my disclaimer.

Court proceedings should be the last resort. There are other ways of settling a dispute apart from thumping the opposition or going to court and they should be explored. Constructive negotiation is the most obvious. Try it and occasionally it will succeed. For the alternatives to actual court proceedings see alternative-dispute-resolution/settling.ou which I cannot improve on (and, no - they don't pay me commission).

There are two points to be alive to with out of court arbitration, where an arbitrator decides who is in the right and who is in the wrong and how much the winner gets. Most consumer arbitration schemes provide for a decision based on paperwork so you don't get to tear the other side to pieces in the witness box. They also bind you to the arbitrator's decision even if you think it stinks so you can't follow up the dispute with proceedings unless the arbitrator has had a seriously bad day. The Ombudsman schemes are different in that you can have a second bite of the cherry with court proceedings when the decision goes against you and you will sometimes achieve compensation which a strict legal interpretation of the facts by a judge in court would have to deny you.

I gave the Financial Ombudsman Service a go a couple of years back. My complaint was that Santander UK plc failed to notify me that a bond I held with them was about to mature. If I had had any sense, I would have jotted down the maturity date and asked for withdrawal before it arrived but I was too busy judging the negligence of others. They proceeded to reinvest the money in another bond for 12 months paying puerile interest which their terms and conditions entitled them to do when they had not received instructions to the contrary. Had I been alerted to the maturity, I would have withdrawn and reinvested elsewhere at a superior rate. The Ombudsman recommended that Santander should compensate me for my loss. Santander refused to accept the recommendation, claiming that I had been given advance notice of maturity. The Ombudsman had to make a ruling. She decided in my favour. She was not persuaded that there was sufficient evidence Santander had given me notice of maturity. Whatever the terms and conditions said, that notice should have been given. I was awarded my loss of interest and £100 for distress and inconvenience. Santander proceeded to reinvest my money for a second 12 months just 13 days after the ruling and without prior notice to me. Then they failed to pay the full award on time and I secured an additional award - around £25 - to take account of the delay. In a court of law, the result on the basis of the terms and conditions could well have been quite different. The interesting postscript is that I later received a letter from Santander about someone else's account and that someone else just happened to be called Stephen Gold. I wonder at night whether they had sent him my notice of maturity.

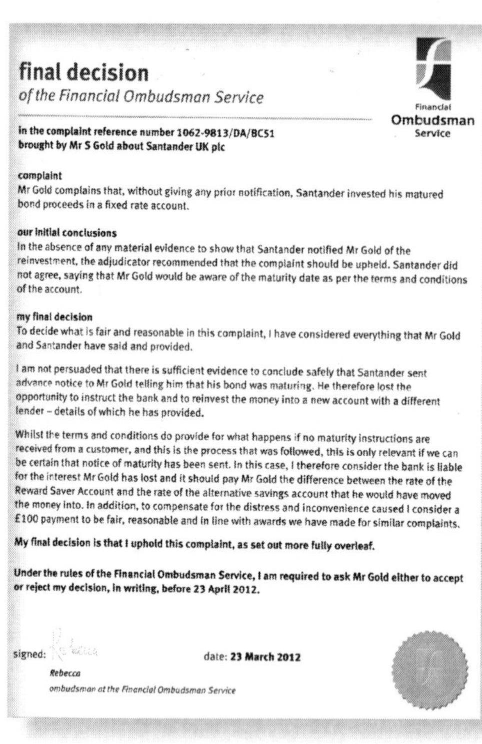

final decision

of the Financial Ombudsman Service

Financial Ombudsman Service

in the complaint reference number 1062-9813/DA/BC51
brought by Mr S Gold about Santander UK plc

complaint

Mr Gold complains that, without giving any prior notification, Santander invested his matured bond proceeds in a fixed rate account.

our initial conclusions

In the absence of any material evidence to show that Santander notified Mr Gold of the reinvestment, the adjudicator recommended that the complaint should be upheld. Santander did not agree, saying that Mr Gold would be aware of the maturity date as per the terms and conditions of the account.

my final decision

To decide what is fair and reasonable in this complaint, I have considered everything that Mr Gold and Santander have said and provided.

I am not persuaded that there is sufficient evidence to conclude safely that Santander sent advance notice to Mr Gold telling him that his bond was maturing. He therefore lost the opportunity to instruct the bank and to reinvest the money into a new account with a different lender – details of which he has provided.

Whilst the terms and conditions do provide for what happens if no maturity instructions are received from a customer, and this is the process that was followed, this is only relevant if we can be certain that notice of maturity has been sent. In this case, I therefore consider the bank is liable for the interest Mr Gold has lost and it should pay Mr Gold the difference between the rate of the Reward Saver Account and the rate of the alternative savings account that he would have moved the money into. In addition, to compensate for the distress and inconvenience caused I consider a £100 payment to be fair, reasonable and in line with awards we have made for similar complaints.

My final decision is that I uphold this complaint, as set out more fully overleaf.

Under the rules of the Financial Ombudsman Service, I am required to ask Mr Gold either to accept or reject my decision, in writing, before 23 April 2012.

signed: date: **23 March 2012**

Rebecca

ombudsman at the Financial Ombudsman Service

"The Financial Ombudsman be praised"

For an arbitration scheme which caters for financial claims in matrimonial proceedings where it is close to certain that the court will endorse the outcome, see chapter 49.

I'll be in trouble if I don't specifically mention mediation. That's the process by which an independent person who has been trained in getting parties at war to settle their differences will apply their skills to you and your opponent. The mediator could see you separately and then together. If the animosity between you is intense they may prefer to avoid damage to the furniture by keeping you apart under the same roof running messages from one room to another. They could try and rubbish the case of each of you so as to extract a bit of compromise here and a bit of compromise there and with the moon about to appear in a few hours and a coffee and smoked salmon sandwich consumed by each side, there's a deal. They'll have their individual styles.

Mediation could take place before court proceedings have even started or hand in hand with the proceedings. Sometimes, parties alarmed at how protracted proceedings have become and how destructive the legal costs will be for them if they lose will ask the court to halt the proceedings for a month or two so that a settlement outside the proceedings might be reached through mediation. I wouldn't expect the court to refuse because judges love mediation. Even the civil division of the Court of Appeal will ask the parties to an appeal to consider mediation where this seems appropriate. None of this mediation is compulsory but the court can take into account the unreasonable refusal of a party to participate or consider participating in it when the court ultimately comes to deal with who pays the costs of a case or an appeal.

Here's the rub. Generally, mediators are in the game to earn a living so they will charge a fee and the parties will share it. The Civil Mediation Council has a list of professional mediators who can be used (see civilmediation.justice.gov.uk/) and will bang your heads together - sorry, I mean who will mediate - at a fixed fee but it is important that you tell them you have located their details through the online directory of mediators. That fixed fee will be based on how much is in dispute and how long the mediation session is to last. For a claim of up to £5,000, each party pays £50 for one hour and £100 for two hours; between £5,000 and £15,000 in issue and it's £300 per party for a three hour session; and between £15,000 and £50,000 you are looking at £425 per party for four hours. Once you top £50,000 in issue you will have to negotiate the fee. VAT is on top. There could be an extra charge for the use of the mediation venue. If the mediation is unsuccessful then that money has gone down the drain but the coffee and smoked salmon sandwich were nice.

Where a consumer has a dispute over goods or services bought online, resolution without proceedings has been facilitated with the setting up in February 2016 of a European Online Dispute Resolution Platform (the ODR platform - and it's multilingual!). Feast on http://ec.europa.eu/odr. It catches deals entered into here and across the EC. And if the time limit for bringing court proceedings is close to running out (see chapter 10) and you and the online trader want to attempt resolution of the dispute through the route of the ODR platform that time limit will generally be extended by eight weeks from the end of the resolution procedure. If you get into an argument about this with a bouncer outside a ballroom, refer them to the Consumer Disputes (Amendment) Regulations 2015.

In the county court there is a more simplified form of mediation for the majority of small claims - no more than £10,000 being claimed - which is free (see chapter 18), but this facility is not available unless proceedings have already been started and are being defended. And in the family court, you will be prevented from starting an application relating to financial proceedings or the care of a child unless you have found out about mediation by attending a mediation information and assessment meeting - they call it a MIAM - but there are a number of exceptions to this requirement. If you are hard up, you may qualify for legal aid to cover the cost of the MIAM. If one party qualifies then the legal aid people will foot the bill for the other party to have a MIAM even though they would be financially ineligible. And since May 2016, if the financially ineligible party pays for a MIAM out of their own pocket and attends it and then the other party attends a separate MIAM through legal aid, the first party can ask the legal aid people to refund the fee they bore.

Part 4

STARTING A CASE AND BEFORE

Chapter 8

Before Starting A Case

Pre-match muscle flexing

How you handle a dispute before court proceedings are started may be just as important to the outcome as your conduct during proceedings - or more so. Using the right tactics may actually avoid proceedings and bring you a good result. What those tactics should be is dependent on the legal strengths or weaknesses of your position.

Supposing you owe money but less than is being demanded from you. Then it is desirable to set out your complaints, strongly and concisely, and make an offer which takes them into account. Your letter to the other side should be calculated to give them something to seriously think about. And I advisedly urge conciseness. Too much verbiage is a sign of weakness. As a solicitor, I took great joy in answering six pages of nonsense with: "*We thank you for your letter of the 12th instant, the contents of which we have noted. Yours faithfully.*" The best put down ever.

One ingredient to be avoided in correspondence is aggression. Its use may be cathartic for you but, that apart, it achieves nothing. If the dispute ever reaches a court trial, the judge will be singularly unimpressed by it and, if you lose, the aggression could even earn you a more severe order for costs against you than you might otherwise have been condemned to pay. Try and achieve a balance: a sort of cross between a Russell Brand interview and a chat with the Queen.

Lawyers occasionally try and impress their clients with aggression directed to the opponent, especially where the opponent is a litigant in person. Solicitors, barristers and legal executives should keep to guidelines set by their governing bodies in June 2015. These lawyers must adopt a professional, co-operative and courteous approach at all times when communicating with a litigant in person. An initial letter from them should briefly address the issues and avoid protracted, clearly one-sided and unnecessary arguments and assertions. In both that initial contact and at other suitable stages in any dispute, they should recommend that you seek independent legal advice or point you to other advice or support agencies. They should avoid technical language and legal jargon or explain jargon where it cannot be avoided. And they should take extra care to avoid using inflammatory words or phrases that suggest or cause a dispute where there is none or inflame a dispute that already exists. Expressing any personal opinions of the behaviour of a litigant in person is also taboo. On the other hand, the lawyer need not tolerate unacceptable behaviour from you and you have no right to expect an **immediate** response to a call or other communication.

If the lawyer on the other side has overstepped the mark with you, a carefully crafted letter to them may turn out to your advantage where they shake at the prospect of it being seen by the trial judge should the claim not settle.

"You may be pleased with your aggression and your client may be more than impressed but it does you no credit. May I respectfully draw attention to Excalibur Ventures LLC v Texas Keystone Inc and others [2014] EWHC 3436 (Comm) in which Mr Justice Clarke warned that parties who engage in aggressive correspondence run the risk of an order for indemnity costs against them. Further, you would do well to read - I fancy, for the first time - the guidelines jointly agreed by the legal professional bodies in June 2015 for communication with a litigant in person such as myself. A professional, co-operative and courteous approach is demanded without the use of inflammatory and technical language and unexplained legal jargon. I reserve my right to bring this correspondence to the attention of the trial judge should my dispute with your client not be resolved to my satisfaction."

Without prejudice

But you may be concerned about putting into writing an offer which could damage your defence to a later claim if it were to come to the attention of the trial judge. Fear not. You can genuinely attempt to negotiate a settlement by marking your correspondence "*without prejudice*" (or if you are talking about settlement with the other side, by telling them at the start that you are talking on a "*without prejudice*" basis.) Then, nothing written (or said) can be used in evidence if no agreement is reached.

However, the magic words "*without prejudice*" won't give you a guaranteed licence to write or say absolutely anything and get away with it if they were a cloak for perjury, blackmail or what has been described as "unambiguous impropriety". This won't work when I say to you at the start of our discussion: "We're talking *without prejudice* now. You understand that. We'll try and settle but if we don't, lips must be sealed in court about what we say. And what I say to you sunshine and no hard feelings and that but if you don't agree to what I am going to put to you to get rid of this ruddy litigation then I will tell a pack of lies in court and I will be believed as I've got the gift of the gab and I will probably get my heavy mob friends to pop round to yours as well. Can't be fairer than that." But this would work.

149 Magnolia Crescent

Twickenham

KT89 4XZ

14 July 2016

Dear Credit Controller

WITHOUT PREJUDICE

Re Invoice A10/88675

I have your invoice for advertising in two consecutive editions of The Middlesex Pet Fanciers' Recorder in the sum of £2,750.69. My principal - but not exhaustive - complaints about your services are that:

(a) in the photograph you took and published of my shop frontage, the depiction of a double tripe sandwich in the bottom left hand corner of the window was obscured.

(b) I have evidence that over 300 copies of both relevant editions had been abandoned by your distributors in a receptacle outside St Margaret's Railway Station.

(c) My takings since the advertisements have appeared have plunged, leading me to the conclusion that your publication does not enjoy the volume of readership your salesman represented to me when he induced me to take advertising space and/or that few of the copies of the relevant editions were actually delivered.

I have been legally advised that you are in breach of contract and that I have no liability to make any payment to you at all. Notwithstanding this advice and solely with a view to avoiding the distraction of litigation, I am prepared to make a payment to you of £750 in full and final settlement of the invoices. If I receive a written acceptance of this offer from you within 14 days of the date of this letter, I will remit the £750 to you immediately. If I do not receive such acceptance within that period, this offer will stand withdrawn and I will defend any proceedings you choose to bring against me and counterclaim for damages for loss of business.

Best wishes

Clive Troublesore

The fact that a letter has not been endorsed with, or a meeting has not been preceded by, the use of the words "*without prejudice*" is not fatal if it is clear from the surrounding circumstances that in that letter or at that meeting you were seeking to compromise the litigation. As a general rule, evidence of the content of the negotiations cannot be used at a later trial should those negotiations come to nothing. But both sides should realise that the communication or meeting is about compromise. Say you write to your opponent a letter which is littered with uncomfortable admissions but do not head it "*without prejudice*". Although you send it in an effort to strike a deal in the case, it can still later be used against you in court unless your opponent knew or should have known that you were writing because you were seeking to compromise.

The Court of Appeal recognised in a case it decided in January 2016 (a case, incidentally, in which I have a special interest as I dealt with a good deal of preliminary hearings before it got to trial) that where litigants in person are involved in discussions, it may be more difficult to establish whether they were for negotiations genuinely aimed at a settlement. In this case, one of two tenants of a restaurant had at her own initiative gone to the offices of the landlord's solicitor to discuss the landlord's proceedings against her and the other tenant. She allegedly said things at the meeting which were used in evidence against the tenants at the ultimate trial. "*Without prejudice*" had never been mentioned. The Court of Appeal ruled that the only sensible purpose for such a meeting must have been to seek some kind of solution to the litigation for the tenant who attended and that meant that the meeting could not be relied on in later evidence. There was no justification for salami slicing an interview into bits that could be used in evidence and bits that could not be used in evidence. And the consequence? The trial that had taken place would have to be rerun - without the "*without prejudice*" evidence.

Boot switch

When the boot is on the other foot and it is you who have been poisoned, whiplashed, libelled, mis-sold or falsely imprisoned (or, on a *dreadful* day, poisoned, whiplashed, libelled, poisoned, mis-sold *and* falsely imprisoned), the approach should be different. Do you start court proceedings the moment you swallow the snail in the bottle of ginger beer or are bashed in the rear? No. Thou shalt follow a protocol which is a set of rules about claiming nicely and although there is no bar against you starting proceedings as though the protocol never existed, this could lead to the proceedings being halted for a period to give the other side an opportunity to carry out investigations which would have been available under the protocol. Non-compliance might also go against you when the court comes to deal with the costs of the proceedings. Each protocol kicks off with you sending the other side what is called a letter of claim with full details of what you are alleging and wanting.

In one situation you will not be criticised for starting proceedings without following the protocol. That's where the time limit for doing so is about to expire. There are specific time limits for bringing different types of claim (which sometimes, and not easily, the court may be prepared to extend): three years for a claim for personal injury compensation, six years for breach of contract and one year for libel or slander (see chapter 10). But, again, there may be a halt of the proceedings for a couple of months to enable the other side to catch up with their enquiries.

There are separate protocols for different types of case - for personal injury claims with a value of up to £25,000 which is designed for road traffic, pavement type tripping and slipping and accident at work cases; clinical negligence (surgeon falling asleep during the op); construction; defamation (libel and slander); professional negligence (cock ups by lawyers, accountants, surveyors and the rest); disease and illness; housing and repair; and judicial review. You will find the protocols with the Civil Procedure Rules 1998. They are composed in digestible language. The time for the other side to respond to your letter of claim ranges from a fortnight to three months. Some of the protocols were revamped in April 2015 so if you are relying on a third hand law book you bought in a car boot sale in 2000, check out the up to date protocols on http://www.justice.gov.uk.courts.

A debt protocol for claims by a business against an individual (including a sole trader) is on the cards before Jools Holland welcomes in 2017. It is expected to require that the debt information provided in the letter of claim includes details of whether interest is continuing; how the debt can be paid (under Margate Pier at eleven minutes past midnight to a monacled debt collector carrying a copy of *How to Stab a Debtor Without Really Trying* under his left armpit); why a court claim is being considered if you are paying or offering to pay instalments; and what you should do if you want to discuss payment options. If you fail to respond, you should not be sued until 30 days are up. You should be allowed a reasonable period to obtain advice if you indicate you are seeking it and at least 30 days from sending back an information form about your circumstances or, if later, being given copies of any relevant documents you have asked to see. That's what the protocol when it arrives is very likely to say and it will also want the creditor to inform you that free independent advice and assistance can be obtained from organisations including National Debtline, Consumer Credit Counselling Service and Community Legal Advice. But it has to be emphasised that default by the business in complying with the protocol will not provide you with a valid defence to the claim. What it should do is allow you some more time to win the National Lottery and it may give you grounds for resisting a claim by the business for their costs of bringing proceedings on the grounds that, had they complied, proceedings would not have been necessary.

And now for everything else

Many cases will fall outside the scope of all these protocols. Fear not. There's a general protocol to catch all other cases so that might include a claim for an unsecured debt before the debt protocol is introduced and compensation for substandard goods. Again, it's to be found in the Civil Procedure Rules in the swingingly called *Practice Direction - Pre-Action Conduct and Protocols*. Here, the other side should respond to the letter of claim within a reasonable period of time. Eh? Some guidelines are given on how you might quantify this. A fortnight where the matter is straightforward; no more than 30 days in a very complex case.

The Part 36 offer

This is a reference to Part 36 of the Civil Procedure Rules 1998. We've seen how to use the "*without prejudice*" communication when you wish to try and reach a settlement because you owe something to the other side. And we have seen how to follow a protocol when you are the one wanting to push a claim forward. But there's something else you can do in addition to protocol compliance and it will usually be bonkers not to do it. This is because it will concentrate the mind of the opposition more potently than a high voltage electric shock and, if it doesn't lead to a fast settlement, it could earn you mega bucks down the line. Take your partners for the Part 36 frightener offer.

Part 36

Lawyers talk about Part 36 all the time and not simply because non-lawyers haven't got a clue what they are talking about. "Had a fantastic day, Rodney. Made a Part 36 for £3m. Gave the b.......s 21 days to stump up. They came back with a counter Part 36 at £750,000. Said 'See you in court" and just settled at £1m and the client wasn't expecting more than 500 quid. Another double, Rodney?"

You can read Part 36 if you must - it was substantially amended in April 2015 so, again, don't rely on old law books - but I would recommend a damp cloth and a bottle of aspirin to go with it. Note it does not apply to small claims (see chapter 18). Although we talk of an offer, you won't be paying any money. You will be offering to the other side to accept a stated sum of money in settlement of the claim. You can make an offer like this not only after you have started proceedings but beforehand.

The consequences for the other side could be dire if the offer is not accepted and the trial judge ultimately awards you at least the amount you offered to settle for or more. Then the likelihood is that you will collect an extra 10% of the sum you are awarded. If it's a mega-award of over half a million, it will be 10% up to half a million and only 5% on the rest. There's a limit on this bonus which is £75,000. Shame. And hold on, there are further bonuses of getting your legal costs with interest of up to 10% above base rate from the losing side along with interest on what you are awarded of up to 10% over base rate usually running from three weeks after you made your offer. If that is not enough, there are other advantages in relation to the costs you can collect. These bonuses will come your way unless the court reckons it is unjust to condemn the losing party to pay them. It will consider whether the offer was a genuine attempt to settle the case and won't lightly let the loser off the hook for the whole package of the extras.

The other side of the coin is that if the opposition made a Part 36 offer to you which you did not accept and you failed to better the offer with the judge's award, you will be condemned to pay their legal costs with interest, usually from three weeks after the offer unless - altogether now - the court reckons this would be unjust.

Pitching an offer at the right level is an art and it could pay you dividends to obtain legal advice just on this aspect of the case. Bearing in mind the consequences for the other side should they fare no better at a court trial then they would have done if they had accepted your offer, they will start sweating the moment your offer whizzes through their letterbox. It is also conceivable that they will have convinced themselves that the value of your claim is higher than the actual value. You might consider offering to settle high and see how they respond and subsequently go lower.

There's a form you can use - not essential but I recommend it - to make a Part 36 offer which you can adapt if it is made prior to proceedings. It's form N242A (the 2015 version is what you want). Good luck.

It is open to you to withdraw a Part 36 offer which has not been accepted within the period you have set. You should do this in writing.

You can also specify when you make it that the offer will lapse if not accepted after a stated period which must generally be not earlier than 21 days.

"Hands up. I was going too fast"

You can make a Part 36 offer which is limited to the issue of liability - not how much you want but whether you are prepared to concede that your compensation should be reduced to reflect your own conduct. It can take two to tango and to bring about an accident. If say you were one-half to blame the court will reduce your compensation by one-half. You know it makes sense. All the time, judges are having to decide whether the claimant was partly to blame and, if so, by what percentage and how much dosh they should receive. Perhaps you aren't yet ready to put a value on your claim but you want to get any argument about blame out of the way. Perhaps your prime witness on liability is about to take off for Abyssinia and is not planning to return until Aldershot Town have won the Premier League. Making a Part 36 offer to the other side to concede 25%, 50% or whatever negligence on your part would be open to you. It could entitle you to your legal costs from when the time for acceptance is up if the case goes the distance and the judge decides you were blameless or no more to blame than you had offered to concede.

An alternative approach

In some situations, it can be tactically wise to hold off making any formal claim against the other side but instead to write explaining what you are complaining about and inviting their observations. This tends to work better when dealing with service industries and the bigger businesses. Why do this? The response is more likely to come from management or customer services rather than in-house or outside lawyers and so couched in less defensive terms and to contain an apology at the least (which could be of high evidential value to you if a claim is made later). There may even be an *ex gratia* payment which will not usually reduce your compensation on any later claim. Be careful, though, not to accept any payment in full and final settlement of any claim you were intending to make - unless it's fat enough (see chapter 12).

In my 2013 complaint to Salcombe Harbour Hotel & Spa's general manager, I outlined in a three page letter what had gone wrong with a one week's stay by me and my companion. The hotel had reopened following substantial renovation but, unbeknown to me when I booked, works were behind and this resulted in our effectively occupying a building site instead of a prestigious hotel for the period of the stay. I acknowledged that the location was idyllic and that, when fully operational, the hotel would clearly be quite excellent and a success. In this particular instance, I went further than simply asking for comment but fell short of threatening proceedings. I put it like this:

> *"In the light of the above, I have to ask you to put forward some realistic proposals to compensate us. I would ask you to return to me with the proposals within the next seven days..."*

I declined an offer of a 25% bill refund plus two complimentary nights at the hotel, followed by offers of a £1,000 refund and then a £1,500 refund and finally settled at £1,800 which meant I paid for our food and got back the accommodation charges. This was fair to both sides. It was almost a pleasure negotiating with the hotel and I still get generic emails inviting me back. Perhaps one day - with a false beard and moustache.

Out of court

Negotiation and court proceedings are not the only ways of achieving a settlement. There are ombudsman schemes run by trade associations and others, mediation and arbitration (see chapter 7). We also have early neutral evaluation. This involves a judge reading the papers and hearing the parties or their legal representatives before proceedings go too far and then giving their opinion on the strengths and weaknesses of each side's case. The parties can heed what the judge has said or ignore it. What they get is a pretty good idea of who will win and who will lose and how well or how badly if the case continues to the bitter end. If it does continue, that judge will play no further part in the proceedings. Either of the parties or both of them can request an evaluation or the judge may float the idea. An evaluation is more likely to be ordered if the parties consent to it but their consent is not essential. It is also more likely in the High Court than in the county court.

Chapter 9

Where To Start

"This was a court. Do you want mushy peas with your fish and chips?"

You might just happen to live round the corner from a building at which civil or family cases - or both - are heard but most of the population does not. There have been dramatic changes in the court system and plenty more are in store. We no longer have a county court here, there and everywhere. Instead we have a single county court with hearings and offices at civil hearing centres and they just happen to be at the very same buildings which used to house the local county courts. Loads of these buildings have been closed down and loads more are to follow. The county court buildings at Hammersmith and Bow will be locked up before you reach the end of this book and, among others, those at Lambeth, Lowestoft, Tunbridge Wells, Chichester, Colchester, Kettering, Halifax, Bolton, Bury and Oldham will be gone by the end of 2017 or, as it is euphemistically put, "cease to provide a public-facing service." This is all to finance massive investment to belatedly bring the justice system administratively up to date and hopefully make it efficient - 'cos it creaks badly. The closed buildings will be sold off where possible. If you have the money you might want to put in a bid for one of the dilapidated buildings which would make a quirky restaurant complete with bench for the maitre d' and witness box for the waiter or could be turned into a block of luxury flats to be known as *County Court Towers*.

In the family arena where parties are ending their marriages and civil partnerships and battling over property and maintenance and the welfare of their children and the rest, we have a single family court. It does its thing out of family hearing centres. Sometimes they will be in the same building as the county court civil hearing centres: other times they will be on their own. The family sections of magistrates' courts have been killed off although magistrates now often hear family cases at the new family hearing centres.

High Court or County Court for civil claims?

If you are going to bring civil proceedings - or someone brings them against you - that will most probably be in the county court. The High Court generally deals with very substantial and complex cases and those in which the outcome is important not just to the claimant but to the public in general. Trying to impress and frighten your opponent by suing them in the High Court for a case which is neither substantial nor complex won't work. The High Court will transfer to the county court where the case should have been started. In fact, you cannot bring a claim in the High Court for personal injury compensation under the value of £50,000 unless it is for clinical negligence, or for any other claim involving money unless it has a value of more than £100,000.

Civil claims online

Using the online procedure is not compulsory. You can claim online for the defendant to pay you money (in the early hours and with some suitable background music) provided:

- You have access to a computer (ha ha).
- The claim is for less than £100,000 and for this purpose you disregard any interest and costs you are after but if the amount is say £100,002 you can be a devil and abandon £2.01 of it so that you qualify.
- The claim is for a fixed amount so you cannot claim say for a sum to be assessed by the court up to a specified ceiling. But you could - though few people do - quantify a claim for damages at a specific sum. That specific sum would need to be a reasonable and properly considered one. Otherwise, the defendant would be in a strong position to subsequently have the judgment set aside.
- You are over 18.
- You are claiming against a single defendant or just two defendants but for the same amount.
- Generally, your base and the defendant's base are in the UK.

Advantages. Speedy. No risk of the court losing the paperwork. Cheaper court fee (see chapter 13). Disadvantages. Fee remission unavailable. The capacity for the content of the particulars of claim which must be completed online is limited with the result that neither the judge nor the defendant may have a clue as to what the claim is about and the particulars might have to be amended with you possibly being ordered to pay some costs to the defendant. The limit is 1,080 characters and that includes spaces and the situation can be made more serious if the claimant's typing skills aren't up to much. You might get tommyrot that goes something like this - "*Ct compute not staingand smahed with hammershop rude said me fort and me mumsays claim 4 losuy hlidays.*" It is possible in many uncomplicated cases to include everything that needs to be stated within 1,080 characters and you will find that we have succeeded with this on some occasions in later pages with our template particulars. Otherwise, there is a way round the potential problem for a case that cannot be adequately particularised within the available limit. In the section of the online claim form headed "Particulars of Claim" give just a brief summary of claim and say detailed particulars will follow.

PARTICULARS OF CLAIM

The claimant claims specified damages for breach of contract arising out of his purchase of a computer at the defendant's Twickenham store on 14 July 2016. Detailed particulars of claim will follow.

At the end of the detailed particulars when they do follow add this:

I am the claimant. I believe that the facts stated in these detailed particular of claim are true.

(signed) C Troublesore

Dated 14 July 2016

The detailed particulars of claim must then be sent to the defendant within 14 days of the defendant having been treated as receiving the claim form from the court. Within 14 days of the defendant getting the detailed particulars, you have to send the County Court Business Centre a certificate to the effect that the detailed particulars of claim were sent out (in form N215). You won't be able to obtain a judgment against the defendant for failing to respond to the proceedings until time has run out for them to do so after they have had the detailed particulars.

I have tried out the online system as a claimant. I had been handling the winding up of the estate of my late uncle who held an account with Nationwide. It paid out the money due to the estate but drew its cheque in his favour which was of no use at all. When it neglected to issue a fresh cheque in favour of the personal representatives including me or to respond to correspondence, I claimed - online. Nationwide failed to put in a defence and so I obtained judgment - online. I then put in the bailiff - online. This did the trick. Nationwide threw itself into action and settled the claim including interest and costs. I then made a claim for inconvenience under their internal complaints procedure and they paid up £200.

Other civil claims

A claim which is for money only and is not started online should be sent to the County Court Money Claims Centre, PO Box 527, Salford M5 0BY or, if you are in Wales, to the County Court Money Claims Centre (Wales), PO Box 552, Salford M5 0EG. This assumes you are using claim form N1 under the so called part 7 procedure which will usually be the case. A claim for money plus something else (say damages and an injunction) or a claim which is not for money at all (say only for an injunction or a declaration) - whether you are using form NI or form N208 for the so called part 8 procedure - may be sent to any county court civil hearing centre but it will probably avoid delay if it goes to your local centre although these days that may be some miles away. The same applies to certain applications to the court before a claim - for example, for your prospective defendant to hand over documents (see chapter 11) - which are made under part 23 of the Civil Procedure Rules 1998. Go to courttribunalfinder.service.gov.uk and search for your local court hearing centre and for a really digestible summary of starting your claim and the pre-trial process go to www.courtnav.org.uk/going-to-court.php. There is also a worthy 'Handbook for Litigants in Person' written by six circuit judges on behalf of the Council of Circuit Judges which you can access on judiciary.gov.uk. It runs through the litigation process and I would commend it to you if you haven't got a clue what I have been on about. 160 pages but no jokes. It's up to date as at 1 April 2013. On the same site you can also devour 'Interim Applications in the Chancery Division: A Guide for Litigants in Person' and 'The Interim Applications Court of the Queen's Bench Division of the High Court: A Guide for Litigants in Person' though, as is evident from their titles, these guides are for the heavy stuff and not your perishing hot water bottle claim in the county court. If you want to see a human being at your local hearing centre instead of posting papers there or using a drop-box there - perhaps you are after an emergency injunction or need to make an emergency application to stop the bailiff evicting you - then you should telephone or call at the centre and ask to be seen.

Matrimonial and family cases

For where to kick off a matrimonial, child or other family case, use courttribunal.service.gov.uk. Divorce, nullity, judicial separation and civil partnership dissolution cases now have to be started out of one of four regional centres. The head family law judge threatened in a speech in February 2016 that before long there would be an online start for these cases. So much for the sanctity of marriage and civil partnership. Click in haste and repent at leisure.

Chapter 10

Time Limits For Starting Court Proceedings

Disaster or windfall

Success in your claim may be a dead cert but if you fail to start court proceedings within the stipulated time limit for that type of claim, the general rule is that you have had it. Too late for justice. Nobody will stop you from starting the proceedings because the fact that you are late is a defence which is for your defendant, and not the judge or the court staff, to raise. If it is not raised because your defendant is too idle to take steps to defend the case or is simply unaware of the time limit law and of the cracking defence that is available to them, then you could conceivably end up with a judgment in what is a stale claim. I have seen the "too late" (lawyers call it the "statute barred") defence successfully raised many times and it has usually brought the proceedings to an end at a very early stage. This had been especially so in credit card and other loan claims where the borrower has defaulted, the lender has lost track of them and then, some years later, sold on the debt for next to nothing to aggressive debt recovery businesses which have traced and sued. It has transpired that there has been no activity on the account for more than six years before proceedings were started. Six years is the period a lender has to sue for this sort of debt.

The law in this area is complicated and you will find chapter and verse, if you must, in the Limitation Act 1980. Generally, the time limits you are up against, counting from when your right to claim arose, are these:

- six years for a breach of contract (for example, a duff purchase or an unpaid loan) or 12 years if the contract was made by deed which will be readily apparent from the document as it will start with the words *THIS DEED*, look all fancy, have signatures witnessed by the vicar and make you tremble when you look at it;
- three years for a claim for compensation for a personal injury, whether the claim relates to a breach of contract (for example, you bought a used car, the brakes failed and you ran into a brick wall) or negligence (pedestrian knocked down by car) but claims for personal injuries or anxiety compensation under the Protection from Harassment Act 1997 can be brought within six years;
- six years for a nuisance (for example, habitually kept up by next door neighbour playing Delilah on Hammond organ);
- six years for a negligence claim relating to damage to property

rather than body;

- one year for claims for defamation (libel or slander) or malicious falsehood (see chapter 42);
- six years for unpaid rent running from when it became due; and
- within six months of probate or letters of administration for claims for provision out of a deceased person's estate although the court does have the power to allow more time (see chapter 40).

Try by the various routes available to get your claim settled without court proceedings but the moral is that if you want redress and none of those other routes bring it, pull your finger out and start proceedings. The law does not allow you to wait for ever and the longer you leave it to bring actual court proceedings, the greater the risk witnesses may disappear and that memories will fade - yours and those of your witnesses - making it difficult to prove your case. *"It's nine years since the accident, Mr Troublesore. You waited five years and 364 days before suing and the case has taken some time to get to court. I put it to you that you cannot possibly now be as sure as you make out that the driver of the other car was wearing a red polka dot dress with beige shoes and had rings in her nose and left ear lobe."*

On your marks

When does your right to bring a claim arise (or as the law and lawyers poshly put it, your cause of action accrue) which sets the clock ticking? Generally, in a breach of contract claim this will usually be when the contract is broken (the date on which duff goods are purchased or a payment is missed on a loan agreement). In other claims such as negligence, the right arises when you suffer some loss - even though you are not conscious of it at the time! (see though **Messing with the clock** below). In claims for defamation and malicious falsehood, you have one year from the date on which the words complained of were published in writing or out of the defendant's mouth.

Exploding washing machines

The clock may tick for longer before you have to start proceedings for compensation claims relating to defective products which are brought under the Consumer Protection Act 1987. Here, the manufacturer and importer of unsafe items can be rendered liable to you even though you didn't have a contract with either and without you having to prove they were negligent. You are given three years to start proceedings running from when you had knowledge about certain factors such as the effect of the defect and the identity of the defendant with a long stop of ten years.

There is a similar - but not identical - set up for negligence claims which do not involve personal injuries, such as claims for defects in property (usually buildings but not necessarily so) against builders, architects, surveyors and the rest, but here you need to claim within six years or, if later, three years of acquiring the necessary knowledge with a long stop of 15 years.

Messing with the clock

The clock won't tick while you are under 18 or of unsound mind. So, for example, if you are injured in an accident because of someone's negligence when aged four, you have until 21 (18 plus the normal three years) to start proceedings although an adult can still sue on your behalf - the adult is called your *litigation friend* - before you reach 18.

Where the claim is for compensation for personal injuries (whether on the basis of a breach of contract or negligence) your three years to start proceedings can run from when you have gained sufficient knowledge about things to be able to make a claim if later than when you actually suffered some loss. The knowledge the law says you need is that your injury was significant, that it was down to some legal wrong and the identity of the person responsible.

And even more time than this could be available. Although three years from the date on which your right to claim arose and you knew about it have expired, the court may still be prepared to allow a later claim which is for personal injuries compensation if it would be "equitable" to do so. The court will take into account a host of factors: the length and reason for the delay; how stale the evidence may be for both sides; and how promptly and reasonably you acted once you knew you had a case. These are some of the factors.

The judge's discretion to allow late claims is now of special significance in civil cases arising out of sexual abuse. We are on *Jimmy Savile* type territory here. The law was effectively reversed by the judicial arm of the House of Lords (before it morphed into the Supreme Court) when it decided that the court would have to look at whether there would be a reasonable prospect of a fair trial if more time were given. And this would depend as usual on a number of matters, not least when the complaint of abuse was first made and with what effect. If a complaint had been made and recorded and, in particular, if the defendant had been convicted of the abuse, that would be one thing. On the other hand, if a complaint came out of the blue with no apparent support for it (other perhaps than that the defendant had been accused or convicted of similar abuse in the past) that would be quite another matter. By no means everyone who brings a late claim in a sexual abuse case, however genuine their complaint might be, can reasonably expect the court to allow it to continue. This is how the House of Lords set out the law which now applies.

Very tricky Troublesores

Say you have a claim based on the defendant's fraud or the defendant has deliberately concealed from you some fact which is relevant to your right to make a claim against them. Or say you have made a mistake: perhaps you have continued to pay Clive Troublesore for eight years after you sacked him for gross misconduct. And say you haven't started a claim within the usual time limit which applies to it on account of that fraud, concealment or mistake. In these instances, the clock may not begin ticking until you have discovered the fraud, concealment or mistake.

Acknowledgment and part payment traps

A sum of money is owed under a contract and within the six years you have to start proceedings the debtor acknowledges the debt or makes a part payment towards its settlement. Then the six years restarts from the date of the acknowledgment or part payment. In fact, the six years could repeatedly restart with each acknowledgment or part payment which is made and you, your children and your children's children might still have a right to sue although they could have to go to the debtor's graveyard to serve the court papers. But before an acknowledgment will be effective to start the six years running, it must be in writing and signed by the debtor.

Dear Whitewash Credit Controller

I acknowledge that I still owe your company £15,000 for goods sold and delivered. I will pay as soon as I can.

Yours faithfully

Clive Troublesore

14 July 2016

PS I'll be in on Saturday for some paint and grouting. Just add it on to the £15K.

That would be more than sufficient. As the creditor, it could be worthwhile you procuring a written acknowledgment where you are close to the six year expiry date for starting proceedings PLUS you are pretty sure that at long last your debtor is to show you the colour of their money PLUS you prefer not to invest time and money into beginning a claim simply to preserve your legal right to do so. A belated acknowledgment after the six years are up, however, is no good. Once a right to claim is time-barred, that right cannot be revived by a later written acknowledgment or even a part payment. A crafty debtor might try and trick you into postponing the commencement of proceedings beyond the six year limit by a *verbal* acknowledgment.

> *"Hello, Whitewash man, Troublesore here. You said you were about to sue me before it was too late. Don't trouble. My life assurance is maturing next month and I'll clear what I owe with 20% interest. You can write and confirm our conversation."*

Useless to you. Not in writing and any writing must emanate from the debtor and not you.

There aren't any formalities that need to be observed to make a part payment effective for the purpose of restarting the six years. But it would be wise for you to send your debtor written acknowledgment of its receipt, especially if payment has been made in cash. A payment made on behalf of the debtor and at their direction will be as effective as a payment by the debtor themselves.

24 hours to go

Your time limit runs out tomorrow? Get the ruddy claim form issued SOMEWHERE. If it's a claim for money and you can't get to the County Court Money Claims Centre at Salford then you should insist on your nearest county court civil hearing centre accepting it and passing it on to Salford. If it's for a remedy other than the payment of money or a mixture of money and something else, get it to any county court civil hearing centre. And should a hearing centre refuse to let you in, insert the claim form into their drop box. And don't forget to accompany the claim form with the correct fee. No fee or an insufficient fee will make the claim form a non-event. You will be treated as having started the proceedings when the claim form in triplicate and the correct fee with it were received at the court destination and not when they were subsequently formally issued.

For defendants' eyes only

If you want to defend a claim on the ground that it has been made too late, your defence should run something like this:

> *1. The limitation period for the claimant's claim as alleged under the Limitation Act 1980 expired before the commencement of the claim and the claim should accordingly be struck out.*
>
> *2. The defendant makes no admissions as to the allegations of*

fact contained in the particulars of claim.

or

2. Further and alternatively, the defendant denies the allegations of fact made in paragraphs 1 to 13 of the particulars of claim. [go on to set out your defence to the claim to be considered by the court in the event that it rules against you on the time point or the claim is one in which the court has power to extend the claimant's time for making a claim and the claimant successfully applies for it to do so].

Now say for whatever reason the claim against you is not too old but you have a valid claim which arises out of the same events which is too old for you to bring your own proceedings. Perhaps you haven't paid money due up front five years ago for building works and have been sued by the builders for what they say is owed, but you maintain that the works which were completed more than six years ago were messed up by them and that they were in breach of contract. In that situation, you could defend the case relying on the old breach of contract so as to knock out the claim entirely or reduce it. What you could not do is to also counterclaim in the proceedings and in addition to knocking out the claim, recover some damages from the builders.

Usual time limits for starting court case*	
Type of case	***Time limit***
Breach of contract including debt	6 years
Breach of contract made by deed including debt	12 years
Claim for personal injury	3 years
Claim for negligence not including personal injury	6 years
Libel, slander or malicious falsehood	1 year
Money claim under Protection from Harassment Act 1977	6 years
Claim for provision out of deceased's estate	6 months (from probate or letters of administration)
*But see above for how a longer period may sometimes be gained	

Chapter 11

Getting Your Opponent's Documents

The sooner the better

Whether you begin court proceedings or how you frame your case in any proceedings you do bring may be dependent on what will be revealed by certain documents held by your opponent - but not you. If these are documents which the court would compel your opponent to reveal to you as part of the process of what is called *disclosure of documents* in the course of proceedings which were brought then you may well be able to get hold of them earlier rather than later. If the documents would sink you, good to see them before you launch a claim with all the preparatory work and expense that could involve. If the documents would sink your opponent and you can demonstrate that you know it (and your opponent knows it) that may force them to capitulate and settle without proceedings. If the documents would reinforce your case and your opponent is denying any liability to you, good to see them to help you assess the risks of litigation. And if the documents would discourage you from making certain allegations in the particulars of claim but encourage you to make others, good to get them in and avoid having to amend the particulars of claim later on which might slow down the case and incur unnecessary expense.

Philip Kanal of Chichester - fresh from his 1994 success in obtaining a £300 settlement from British Airways after starting county court proceedings for allowing passenger smoking in a non-smoking row close to that occupied by himself and his family travelling from Heathrow to Toronto and because of crew neglect obliging him to attend to an adjacent passenger who was vomiting - was recently back on the litigation trail. On a dark night in March 2015 on the B2178 his car struck a pothole and split a tyre and buckled the wheel. The highway authority West Sussex County Council rejected his claim for £629.16 but thanked him for reporting the incident. He insisted on being provided with documents relating to the authority's inspection and maintenance of the road. These documents destroyed their argument that they operated a reasonable system of maintenance and repair. When further documents were requested they offered to settle at £314.58. When told that a court claim was ready, they coughed up the full amount.

Where a pre-action protocol letter has been sent (see chapter 8) and has been met with a denial of liability, it may be that the documents you are after should have been provided by your opponent but were not. It may be that you have not reached the stage of a pre-action protocol letter.

Either way, the documents you want could well come to you by courtesy of a court order on an application by you under part 31 of the Civil Procedure Rules 1998 for a *pre-action disclosure order*. The application is made on form N244 and should be backed by a written statement explaining what you want and why you want it.

Before you make your application, write to your opponent. The court will expect you to have done so. Who knows, your opponent may actually agree to comply with the request.

"Pursuant to rule 31.16 of the Civil Procedure Rules 1998, I hereby request you to supply me with copies of the documents specified in the schedule to this letter within 14 days of the date of receipt of this letter. It is my intention to bring proceedings against you in relation to the claim about which we have already been in correspondence if you will not settle with me; the documents would be disclosable by you in such proceedings as part of standard disclosure; and disclosure before proceedings is desirable in order to dispose fairly of the proceedings or, by actually assisting us to resolve the dispute without proceedings and, in any event, would save costs.

I have to require you to take this letter as formal notice that if my above request is not complied with, I shall issue an application in the county court for an order compelling you to disclose the documents to me and I shall ask the court to order you to pay the costs of such application. I am a litigant in person and will ask for such costs to be assessed on that basis.

I confirm that I undertake to pay your reasonable photocopying charges for providing me with the documents in question.

Schedule of Documents

(specify the documents you want)

And when you are met with a refusal or silence, you can issue your application and send it to a civil hearing centre. There will need to be a hearing of the application (unless your opponent capitulates in the meantime) and so choose the most geographically convenient hearing centre. If you and your opponent are miles apart, you may well choose the centre which is closest to you. When describing the order you want on the form N244 you can adopt the wording you have utilised in the letter you sent to your opponent (unless it was unmitigated nonsense). With the application, include a draft of the order you are inviting the court to make. Not only is this good practice, but it will put you in the judge's good books.

Case no: BY4999786

IN THE COUNTY COURT

SITTING AT PEARDROP

BETWEEN

CLIVE TROUBLESORE Applicant

- and -

WHITEWASH LIMITED Respondent

Before District Judge Wisdom-Solomon on (date to be inserted in due course)

Upon hearing the applicant in person and legal representative for the respondent

IT IS ORDERED that-

1. Subject to paragraph 2 of this order, the respondent must disclose to the applicant copies of the documents specified in the schedule to this order within 28 days of the date of this order.

2. In the event that the respondent asserts that any of the documents referred to are no longer in its control, the respondent must serve on the applicant within 28 days of the date of this order a written statement (verified by a statement of truth) specifying which of such documents this applies to and what has happened to such documents and shall further specify such documents (if any) in respect of which it claims a right or duty to withhold inspection.

3. The respondent do pay the applicant's costs of this application summarily assessed on the litigant in person basis at £(amount to be inserted in due course) within 14 days of the date of this order.

Schedule referred to above

(specify the documents you want)

In your written statement in support of the application, describe what your claim is about and how your opponent comes to be involved; produce with the statement copies of the relevant correspondence you have exchanged with your opponent about the documents in question; and explain why you say that you should have the documents at this early stage. Do not go over the top with your document requests. If you have done so in your original letter of request, there is no shame in cutting down what you ask for in your later form N244. If it is important for you to see the originals of certain documents instead of just photocopies (because, for example, you have some doubt about their authenticity) then you should adapt the paperwork to require production of those particular documents at a set time and place.

If your opponent can persuade the court that your claim is dotty and does not stand a hope in hell of success then your application will fail. That's why your statement should cover the merits of your claim.

Costs are a little unusual in these cases. If you succeed, the likelihood is that the judge will make no order for costs in favour of either side and only if your opponent has behaved particularly unreasonably, an order that they pay your costs. If you lose, you will probably be ordered to pay your opponent's costs. You should send the court and your opponent a statement of your costs before the hearing (see chapter 26).

Your opponent cannot be compelled to come up with documents they do not have in their possession and do not control - before or after proceedings have been brought. Should they say following the start of proceedings that Joe Bloggs down the road has this crucial document and they are not entitled to extract it from him themselves then you could make an application to the court against Joe Bloggs. The procedure follows a similar pattern to the application before proceedings against your opponent. You will find more about it in rule 31.17 of the Civil Procedure Rules 1998.

Chapter 12

In Full And Final Settlement

Take it or leave it

Plump and sweet fresh strawberries dipped in the finest milk chocolate, served with a glass of chilled vintage champagne on a warm summer's evening in the gardens of your employer's estate. You reckon that's tempting? In the Temptation Stakes, it doesn't come within a mile of this (even if you could get another two glasses out of it). A cheque for £5,000 from someone who has owed you £7,000 under an invoice you sent out seven months ago and who you have been chasing for settlement ever since and who has written to say that they have tendered the cheque in full and final settlement of the invoice. That's what you call temptation, eh? Gift in the hand and all that so do you present it and write off the balance or return it and say that you are owed £7,000, it's nothing less than £7,000 that you want and it's £7,000 that you are going to get, you indescribable piece of dirt and son of unmarried parents?

Take it and DON'T leave it

But how about turning the temptation into a dilemma and consider paying in the cheque and suing your debtor for the balance? Can you successfully do this? It depends! What it depends on will usually be whether or not the debt is disputed. If it is not disputed then it should be safe for you to expeditiously bank and claim the balance, provided, that is, you do not delay in letting your debtor know that you do not accept the lesser amount in full and final settlement for otherwise the delay may be treated as evidence that you have accepted in full and final settlement. Of course, you will want the cheque to be paid out on before you break the bad news to your debtor for otherwise the likelihood is that they will cancel it. And immediately you know that the cheque has cleared, you get off a communication to your debtor.

> *"Dear Mr Tryon*
>
> *I acknowledge receipt of your letter dated 14 July 2016 enclosing cheque for £5,000 which you have tendered "in full and final settlement" of my invoice. I have presented the cheque for payment but I positively do not accept it in full and final settlement and I have never given you any reason to suppose that I would accept anything less than the full amount due to me. The invoice has never been disputed and, as you well know, there are no grounds for dispute and you have no legitimate reason for withholding a single*

penny of what you owe me.

I give you notice now that unless the balance due to me is paid within seven days of the date on which you receive this letter, I shall institute proceedings against you for the recovery of the £2,000 balance together with interest and costs.

Yours faithfully

Clive Troublesore"

Disputed debt

The tender of a lesser amount for a disputed debt is another matter. Then your debtor may be treated as providing some legal consideration for tendering the payment - that is, providing a benefit to you by paying an amount they contend is not due - so that, if you bank the cheque, you are likely to lose out in respect of the shortfall. I suggest that the dispute must be a genuine one. It would not be enough, for example, for your debtor to invent some fanciful reason for short changing you. So a serious dilemma does kick in when Mr Tryon, with justification, takes issue over the invoice, and writes to you - and all the Tryons in England and Wales might adopt wording along these lines in a genuinely disputed situation - like this:

"Dear Mr Troublesore

Without Prejudice*

You have invoiced me for £7,000. I do not owe you £7,000. You are in breach of our agreement in a number of respects. In particular, you were two months late in completing the works and various of the materials you supplied were not of satisfactory quality as I have already informed you. These breaches have caused me considerable loss which I am advised I can set off against the invoice.

I prefer to settle this matter without suffering the expense and inconvenience of court proceedings although, rest assured that if it does not settle as now offered by me, any proceedings you choose to bring will be defended with vigour.

I enclose my cheque in your favour for £5,000 which I tender in full and final settlement of your invoice and with a denial that you are entitled to this sum. My calculations point to the value of the set off for my own losses to which I am entitled equating to a sum in excess of £3,000 and I am advised that I would be entitled to set off the entirety of those losses against your invoice. However, I am prepared in the spirit of compromise to forgo obtaining compensation for all those losses by way of set off.

Your presentation of the enclosed cheque for payment will constitute acceptance of the £5,000 on the basis on which it is tendered and, subject to such presentation, it will not be open to you to make any further claim against me in respect of the invoice or the works and materials supplied to which the invoice relates.

Yours faithfully

Bernard Tryon"

*The words "*without prejudice*" are important (see chapter 8). If Mr Troublesore banks the cheque but sues Mr Tryon for the balance, Mr Tryon has a choice. He can ask the court to throw out the case on the basis that he and Mr Troublesore concluded a compromise agreement which binds Mr Troublesore and rely on the letter as evidence of the agreement. The inclusion of the words "without prejudice" will not prevent this. Alternatively, he can decide that he does not want to be bound by the agreement and claim that he owes nothing to Mr Troublesore because of his contract breaches. In that event, the judge will not be able to see the letter before they decide the case in view of the inclusion of the words "without prejudice" and so Mr Tryon will not be prejudiced or embarrassed by the offer.

Undisputed debt but payment by third party

For your debtor, there is one possible way round the rule that you are not barred in the case of an undisputed debt from chasing the balance when you accept a cheque for a lesser sum which is tendered "in full and final settlement". It is to procure payment by a third party.

"Dear Mr Troublesore

My nephew Bernard Tryon has referred me to your outstanding invoice against him for £5,000. I am assisting him in connection with it. I am prepared to pay you on his behalf a lesser payment but on the strict condition that the lesser sum is accepted in full and final settlement of the debt.

Therefore, I now enclose my own cheque in your favour for £3,000 which I tender in full and final settlement of the invoice and the works and materials supplied to which it relates. If you present the cheque for payment then this will be an acceptance of the terms on which it is tendered and it will not be open to you to make any claim against my nephew for the £2,000 balance or any part of it or for the works and materials which are the subject of the invoice.

Yours faithfully

A Vuncular Tryon"

There the payment by the uncle being someone who has no legal responsibility to Mr Troublesore constitutes the legal consideration which is likely to bind Mr Troublesore if he banks the cheque.

Undisputed debt: lump sum payment

Your debtor can put forward a settlement proposal for payment themselves on a debt which they do not dispute which, if accepted, will bind you. Suppose they owe you £5,000 which they are paying off at the rate of £5 per month when out of the blue comes this.

"Dear Mr Troublesore

Without Prejudice

Remember me? You agreed to accept instalments from me at the rate of £5 per month when I was in dire straits and that was, let me see, more than 20 years ago. If at all possible, I would now like to get the noose of this debt removed from my neck. I could:

borrow £1,000 from my uncle;

or

now I am 55, take £1,000 out of a small pension fund that I own;

or

sell some household items for around £1,000 which are protected from being seized by a bailiff or enforcement officer,

which I would then be prepared to pay to you provided you accepted that sum in full and final settlement of the debt so that I was then fully discharged from any further liability to you.

Please let me know whether you are prepared to settle with me on this basis."

Yours faithfully

Bernard Tryon"

If you accept and you are paid out the lesser sum in one go as agreed, you could not legally chase the rest of the money. Mr Tryon would be doing more than discharging part of his legal obligation to you. He would be doing something he was not legally obligated to do: that's the legal consideration for the deal.

Chapter 13

Court Fees

Save £s £s £s

Civil and family cases would be so much more enjoyable if it wasn't for the court fees. When you start a case and when you subsequently take some formal step during the case at court, you will almost always be asked to pay a fee for the privilege unless, as does sometimes happen, the court forgets to ask. The money is used to run the courts. If you win the case, the loser will probably have to pay those fees back to you. There are ways of making savings on the fees. You might even be able to escape paying them entirely by getting them waived under the fee remission system.

Fee saving tip 1

I was in the back of a taxi - as one is - and the driver was talking - as they do - and having covered Margaret Thatcher, Brexit and the state of the prisons, he moved on to small claims. He had brought a succession of them in his local county court which he had meticulously timed to coincide with the regular summer break he took when he signed on. By doing so, he managed to get the court fees waived by courtesy of the fee remission system. At the end of the journey I told him I was a judge. He made off just as my feet touched the pavement and before I had had the chance to tip him. A gratuity remission situation, in fact. This was a few years back. The system is still with us but because it was costing the state a cool £28m a year, it was tightened up in 2013. Here's how it works now.

To get a fee remitted, you must pass a financial test. The merits of the case you want to start or application you want to make don't come into it. It may be a bag of tripe. Not too much capital and not too much income. On capital, the higher the fee, the more capital you are allowed. Take a fee of up to £1,000. It would require capital of £3,000 or more to disqualify you from remission (or £6,000 or more if you or your partner are 61 or over). Your home will be disregarded.

If you aren't knocked out on capital, you then have to pass the gross income test which applies a series of thresholds to single persons or couples with an allowance for children. Below a certain threshold, you will be granted full remission. Otherwise you will be required to make a contribution towards the fee of £5 for every £10 of your monthly income which is over the relevant threshold. There is automatic remission for the main state benefits.

Where your partner has a contrary interest to you - for example, you may be litigating against your partner - their capital and income will not be taken into account: otherwise, they will.

Should you have struggled to pay a court fee and only later discovered that you could have successfully applied for remission, you are able to make a retrospective application and obtain a refund. But don't hang about as you have just three months from the date on which you paid the fee to apply for its return.

And should your day be ruined by a court notification that your application for remission has been refused, you might want to put up a fight and ask the hearing centre's so-called delivery manager to reconsider it on the grounds of *exceptional circumstances*. There is discretion to still allow remission even though you have too much capital or income but you would have to satisfy the manager that there were extenuating reasons to remit. If, for example, your claim would be stifled by not receiving remission and though you enjoyed a relatively high income on paper you had no disposable means, you could be in with a chance but don't hold your breath.

> *"Dear Delivery Manager*
>
> *I ask you to consider/reconsider my application for fee remission under the schedule to the applicable fees order at paragraph 16. I submit that there are exceptional circumstances which justify remission and without remission I will be unable to raise the money I need to pay the fee. This would be contrary to justice because it would prevent me from pursuing a meritorious claim and to obtain the relief to which I am entitled to make the application in these proceedings which is essential if justice is to be done. The exceptional circumstances on which I rely are [specify the circumstances].*
>
> *Yours faithfully*
>
> *Clive Troublesore"*

It is not possible to claim remission for the fee on starting a claim when you are doing so through Money Claim Online.

Fee saving tip 2

You can pay a court fee by debit or credit card and, with the latter, earn cashback or points on it.

Fee saving tip 3

Use the Money Claim Online system (only available if the claim is less than £100,000 - see chapter 9) where you are not seeking fee remission because the fee for starting the claim is cheaper than claiming offline. On a claim for up to £300 the fee would be £25 instead of £35. At the other end of the scale, a claim for over £10,000 attracts a court fee based on a percentage of the amount you are going for. That percentage is 4.5% for an online claim as against 5% for an offline claim. On a claim for say £90,000 there would be an online saving of £450 which you could spend on two West End theatre tickets and a hamburger beforehand.

Fee saving tip 4

In a defended civil case a number of procedural steps have to be taken - for example, relevant documents and witness statements exchanged. If your opponent has failed to do as ordered, the court has the power to strike out their claim or defence. Or the claim or defence may be complete nonsense and the court could strike it out at an early stage of the case (see chapter 15). In this sort of situation and in a multiplicity of others, you can apply to the court to exercise one of its appropriate powers. Trouble is a formal application is usually expected (in form N244) and that will cost you serious money (recently made even more serious) unless the fee is remitted (see Fee Saving Tip 1 above). By serious money I mean £255 - pick the readers of this book off the floor, usher, they have just passed out - or if you are contemplating that a judge will decide the application 'on paper' without a hearing at court, the fee is a trifling £100. What you do, therefore, is try and save paying a fee by refraining from the use of a formal application form and sending a letter to the court which says:

> *"I am the claimant. The defendant has failed to comply with paragraph 8 of the order made on 14 July 2016. The defendant has previously been in breach of four orders in these proceedings. I respectfully invite the court to exercise its case management powers and to order of its own initiative that the defence be struck out and judgment be entered in my favour for the sums claimed and costs to be assessed in detail in default of agreement on the litigant in person basis.*
>
> *Yours faithfully*
>
> *Clive Troublesore"*

The judge could treat that as a formal application and direct that you pay a prescribed fee. Or the judge may let it go.

Fee saving tip 5

If you do make a formal application in the course of civil proceedings (see Fee Saving Tip 4 above) the form N244 will invite you to say whether you want it dealt with at a hearing or without a hearing. By opting for no hearing you can tender the lower fee of £100 instead of £255. Now the court may direct a hearing even when you have not asked for one but it may well not trouble to collect the fee balance of £155.

Fee saving tip 6

Do not over exaggerate your civil claim. It looks naff to the judge. The financial reason for not doing it is that it may waste you money. The more you claims, the more you pays. Take an online claim which is worth say £250. You could allow a bit of manoeuvre for negotiation by claiming £300 which would cost you a court fee of £25. But by going the next band up and claiming over £300 and up to £500 you will incur a fee of £35. If the case is defended and in due course you win and are awarded no more than £300, the probability is that the judge will order the loser to pay you back £25 and not £35. The value you have placed on your claim will also affect the hearing fee you will later have to pay where the claim is being defended (see ***Fee saving tip 8*** below). You could be limited in what you get back from the loser towards the hearing fee in the same way by having gone after too much money.

Fee saving tip 7

When a civil claim is going forward as defended, there will be a full hearing: let's call it a trial. You as the claimant will be charged a hearing fee. We are looking at big money. For a small claim the hearing fee depends on how much you have claimed and ranges from £25 on a claim for up to £300 to £335 on a claim for over £3,000. On a fast track claim it is £545 and on a multi-track claim (are you seated?) it is £1,090. If, having paid the hearing fee, the case settles you may be entitled to have it refunded. For a small claim, you get a full refund - it's all or nothing - when at least seven clear days before the hearing you are able to tell the court in writing that there has been a settlement (or that, for whatever reason, you are discontinuing the claim). For other claims (on the fast track or the multi-track) you will enjoy some refund provided that you can give this written information to the court at least one week before the hearing. The earlier you can do it, the more you save. So you get the full hearing fee back when you have done the necessary at least four weeks before the hearing; 75% back when you have done it between 15 days and four weeks before the hearing; and a return of 50% when you have done it between one week and a fortnight before the hearing. Don't fall into a trap that's waiting for you. On a strict interpretation of the relevant legislation, the hearing must have been fixed when the settlement is notified. You will often have paid the hearing fee beforehand. If reasonably possible, do not notify the settlement until after you have been given hearing date. You could always hasten the court for that date. Naughty. But nice.

The potential saving in the hearing fee can be used as a negotiating tool like this:

> *"Dear Whitewash Limited*
>
> *I am writing to remind you that you have not responded to my offer to you for the settlement of my claim.*
>
> *The hearing fee is £x. I must pay it to the court by 14 July 2016. I do not have to pay it if the claim settles before then.*
>
> *Or*
>
> *The hearing fee is £x which I have already paid to the court and the trial is listed for 14 July 2016. If I can notify the court of settlement of my claim by 5 July 2016 at the latest then some of the fee will be refunded to me.*
>
> *The hearing fee will be part of my costs and so, in the absence of a settlement, you will be obliged to pay back that fee to me should you be required to meet those costs, as I expect to be the position. Settling with me timeously will save you money. I hope you realise this.*
>
> *Yours faithfully*
>
> *Clive Troublesore"*

Fee saving tip 8

The hearing fee (see ***Fee saving tip 7***) for a fast track claim is cheaper than for a multi-track claim and the hearing fee on a small claim is the cheapest of all. Although the small claim limit is usually £10,000 and the fast track limit is usually £25,000, the court may be persuaded to "track down" - try a claim for over £10,000 as a small claim or a claim for over £25,000 on the fast track provided in either case it won't take longer than one day to hear. There may be considerations other than the hearing fee but by securing a "tracking down" the hearing fee will be substantially reduced.

Fee saving tip 9

Don't ask the court to photocopy a document for you. Unless you are a female with a Leicester City Football Club season ticket and the request is directed to a lecherous looking male usher, the charge will be £10 for ten pages or less plus 50p for each subsequent page. And fee remission (see ***Fee saving tip 1***) does not apply to copying charges.

Some of the other fees

The prescribed court fees can be found at court form EX50 www.hmcts-formfinder.justice.gov.uk. In addition to recent fee increases reflected above, the fee for starting a possession of land claim has risen to £355 (or £325 online) and for applying for divorce, nullity, judicial separation or civil partnership dissolution to £550.

Part 5

CRIKEY, PROCEEDINGS HAVE STARTED

Chapter 14

Witnesses And Their Statements

Sock it to 'em in writing

There was a time when neither the court nor the other side had a clue what a witness was going to say until they got into the witness box and opened their mouths. Now we have a 'cards on the table' approach to evidence. Each side will almost always (though occasionally not so in the very simplest of small claims) be required by court order to disclose their evidence in writing in the form of a witness statement to the court and the opposition before the hearing - that's the evidence of the parties as well as the others they intend to drag along to court to back up their truths, lies or mistakes.

The court will set a deadline for this to be done. If the court has ordered documents to be disclosed, this deadline will be afterwards and if it has given permission for an expert's report to be used which has not yet been prepared, it will probably be before it has been prepared so that the expert can see the statements prior to doing their job (see chapter 18).

Failing to adhere to the deadline is dicing with death. You will be prevented from calling a witness whose statement has not been handed over in time without the court's permission and such permission may be hard to come by unless you were slightly late and had good reason for it. The burning down of your house and the sustaining of a double fracture to the leg the day before could be sufficient provided it was not a case of your own arson and your dirty tackle on the referee that were responsible.

The order will usually say that the statements are to be exchanged. This simply means they are swapped round so neither side has an advantage over the other by seeing the opposition statements before they release their own. Otherwise, they might be tempted to revise their statements because of what they read from the opposition camp. Occasionally, exchange of statements will be inappropriate. In a family case, for example, where one party is alleging that the other has used domestic violence towards them, the court would order that the party making the allegations should come up with their statements first so that the other party knows what they have to answer and that the other party follows on later.

Exchange without pain

How the exchange takes place is left to you. Meet up on platform 1 at St

Pancras at 4.30pm on Thursday and do it or both undertake to pop the statements into a letterbox or email them at the same time and do it. Where the process gets intriguing is with a case involving twenty parties and not just two, some of whom have lawyers and some of whom are doing it themselves. Incidentally, if one party cheats by holding on to their statements until they have peeked at those of their opponent and this can be proved, their evidence will be treated by the judge with enormous scepticism.

"He's mine. Stay away"

No party can be forced by another party to rely on the evidence of a particular witness but say you are desperate for that witness to be heard by the court. Well, try and get them to make a statement for you. They work for the other party and so you can't approach them? Actually, you can approach them. It is a well established principle of law that there is 'no property in a witness'. In other words, you cannot be prevented from making an approach to anyone you believe may be able to assist your case whatever their allegiance may be to the opposition. Obviously, you must not make a nuisance of yourself but you do not need opposition permission before making the approach. If the opposition is their employer, the chances of them helping you would be somewhat reduced by an approach at work. Sometimes in this situation, a statement is refused but some useful information is gathered. "Sorry, mate, the gaffer is due back in minute. I know you were stitched up and, yeh, I did hear him tell you the old banger had never been involved in a crash though you're not getting me to court. Cheerio."

"She 'aint talking"

The next step where a witness will not cooperate? You can ask the court for permission to rely on a witness summary instead of a statement. The procedure is under rule 32.9 of the Civil Procedure Rules 1998 but does not apply to small claims (see chapter 18). The summary should set out the evidence the witness would have given in the statement if they had made one or, if this is not known, the matters about which you propose to question the witness and the name and address (care of address, if that is the best you can do) of the witness. You should explain to the court why you have not obtained a written statement and what steps you have taken to secure one. The permission application should be made and the summary sent to the other side before the deadline for exchanging witness statements.

Now, it's one thing to produce a witness summary. It's another to get the body of the witness to court. You do this by applying to the court for the issue of a witness summons which compels their attendance and which must be handed to them at least seven days before the date on which they are wanted at court and at the same time the witness must be offered their travelling expenses in getting to and from court and compensation for their loss of time. The amounts should be equivalent to what they would be entitled to if attending to give evidence at a Crown Court criminal trial and the figures which are updated from time to time can be discovered on http://cps.gov.uk.

And here comes the warning. Seeking to rely on a witness from the enemy camp without their written statement in advance is a risky business. They might just sink your case on the day. What might be less risky if not downright delicious is to procure permission to rely on a witness summary without necessarily following it up with a witness summons and scare the pants off the opposition before any hearing so that they settle your claim or drop the claim against you. This might happen if they have not relied on the witness themselves or they have produced a statement from the witness which is at odds with what you have put in the witness summary.

We're dealing here with witness statements and not *War and Peace* so, if you can restrain yourself, don't produce books. Your statement and the statement of each of your witnesses should contain a chronological account of the relevant evidence which each of you can give as if recounting it from the witness box and be in the first person. The statement may refer to documents which are copied with it. It is a statement of fact and should not contain comment or argument about the case or the relevant law. "I consider the defendant to be a liar and, in my opinion, his witness must have Mafia connections as my wife commented on our way back from the car showroom that he was wearing a double-breasted suit that was miles too big for him and had a slight Sicilian accent." No thank you. You omit relevant facts at your peril. The judge could well preclude evidence being given in the witness box which has not been incorporated into the statement although the opposition can cross-examine on any relevant events or conversations about which there has been no or only limited mention in the witness's statement.

How to lose in one easy lesson

Now for a tip on how to lose your case. Draft the witness statements of all your witnesses in your own language. Ensure that you and each and every one of your five witnesses all refer in exactly the same words to the used car salesman mentioning that the vehicle had only clocked up 25,032 miles with a single previous owner who was a glass-eyed Peruvian belly dancer and that the salesman's boss would put in a new Doublesock multi killer blow sound system before delivery. Nobody sees the same action or hears the same words in identical manner. It would be obvious to a judicial moron in a hurry that the words of your five witnesses were your words and that the witnesses could not all possibly recall what the salesman had said word for word in precisely the same way. Claim dismissed. So let the witnesses use their own words and, if possible, write or type their own statements. And unless a written statement is agreed by the opposition, ensure that the maker of the statement attends court and is called by you to support their written statement and is available to be cross-examined by the other side and questioned by the judge.

Naughty statements

If a statement contains irrelevant or disproportionate material or something improper then an application can be made to the court for an order that the passages objected to be excised and the statement re-served without them. That's not the sort of application that should be rushed into. Objection could always be taken at the trial instead of beforehand. "Judge, I did not want to burden the pressed court previously but I must object today to paragraphs 146 to 279 of the defendant's statement on the grounds that they are unduly prolix, irrelevant and contain extracts from 'without prejudice' correspondence I sent to the defendant before proceedings began. I ask that those paragraphs be removed from the copy of the statement in the bundle of documents."

"Without prejudice"

Of course, if any of the opposition's witness statements contain something that could actually damage your case, you would not want it to be seen by the trial judge and in that situation an application before the trial day for it to be removed may be essential. Say you have claimed damages of £10,000 but before you brought your claim you wrote to the other side to say you would be prepared to accept £50.42 rather than have the hassle of litigation. It would be better if the judge did not know about the communication for they might just possibly think your claim was a try-on. The law encourages parties to a dispute to try and settle it and details of written or verbal communications (or both) which they exchange in a genuine effort to settle should not be referred to before the judge in advance of them giving their decision on who has won and who has lost or in any documents prepared for the judge. The way to ensure that such communications with their offers and counter-offers are protected from disclosure to the court is to write at the top of the written communication the magic words "without prejudice" or say at the start of the conversation that you are speaking on a "without prejudice" basis (see chapter 8).

Second bite

Only in an exceptional case will you be granted permission to rely on a further witness statement which is designed to reply to what the opposition have said in one or more of their statements. Permission might be granted if this further evidence is really important and you could not reasonably have contemplated the points in question would be covered by the other side when your own statement was prepared.

I say, hearsay

"Max informed me that the defendant had told him he had stitched me up proper." "Max informed me that Ron had told him that the defendant had mentioned to Ron that he had stitched me up proper."

That's hearsay. These days, hearsay evidence can be used so either of those pieces of hearsay could go into your witness statement. But hearsay evidence - it could be third hand and, in theory, twenty hand hearsay by which time you would want to turn it into a song - has limited and in many cases no value whatsoever unless Max and Ron are both dead or have disappeared into oblivion and your best efforts to trace them by placing a full page ad in *The Sun* have been to no avail. If possible, you want Max in the first instance or Ron in the second instance.

Formalities

There are certain formalities which generally need to be observed in the format of a witness statement. This is not so with small claims unless the formalities are directed by the court. Nevertheless, even in small claims the observance of the formalities is no bad thing. It may well impress the judge so long as the substance of the statements does not amount to tommyrot of the highest degree.

With all the formalities - you will find them at Civil Procedure Rules 1998 Practice Direction 32 - a compliant witness statement may look like this:

Case no 97P0000678

Claimant

F Smyth-Jones

7 July 2016

FS-JD1-2

IN THE COUNTY COURT

AT PEARDROP

BETWEEN

WHITEWASH LTD Claimant

- and -

CLIVE TROUBLESORE Defendant

I FEDORA SMYTH-JONES state as follows:-

1. I live at 6b Millstone Parke, Twickenham KT46 1LA.

2. I am employed by the claimant Whitewash Ltd at its retail outlet at 149a Lower High Road, Twickenham, Middlesex KT46 1LA as a salesperson specialising in miniatures of footballers playing in the English Premier League.

3. The facts referred to at paragraph 4 of this statement are of my own knowledge and the facts referred to at paragraph 5 of this statement are based on information I have received from Ms Alethia Mcmorrow in my employer's accounts department and which I believe to be true.

4. On the 2 April 2016 at approximately 2.30pm a man I now know to be the defendant Clive Troublesore attended at the Twickenham outlet. He was accompanied by a woman who was carrying an empty beer bottle and a rattle and they were both wearing red scarves. They were unsteady on their feet and their speech was slurred. The defendant asked if we stocked Wayne Rooney miniatures and old Aldershot Town Football Club programmes. I informed him that we had no memorabilia or other products relating to Aldershot but that we had had a delivery of some very fine Wayne Rooney miniatures which were in the stockroom but unpacked. He asked me to show him every one of the miniatures which were available for purchase. I proceeded to the stock room, unpacked the miniatures and returned with them on a tray. The claimant's companion was by then lying prostrate on the floor by a full-sized cardboard cut out of David Beckham in underpants. I showed the miniatures to the defendant who said he would have them all, regardless of price. I informed him that the entire 64 could be purchased at a discounted price of £5,000. He replied that he thought this more than reasonable. He said he could give me £500 in cash with the balance to be paid within one week. He had sold some land in Spain and was awaiting a transfer to his bank account for the sale proceeds of over £1m within a matter of days. He was a "big shot at Old Trafford" and had once been a lay preacher. His word was his bond and he would not let me down. He showed me his passport and I satisfied myself about his identity. I re-wrapped the miniatures, accepted £500 in cash for which I wrote out a receipt a copy of which I produce marked "FS-J1" and handed it to the defendant. I also handed over to the defendant the 64 miniatures and woke up the companion who was still on the floor. The defendant and the woman left with the miniatures. On 4 April 2016 my employer's accounts department issued and posted to the defendant an invoice for the £4,500 balance due. I produce a copy of the invoice marked "FS-J2".

5. The invoice was not settled within seven days and remains unsettled at the date of this statement notwithstanding twelve telephone calls I have made to the number provided to me by the defendant and none of which he has answered.

I believe that the facts stated in this witness statement are true.

Signed ....F Smyth-Jones

Dated 7 July 2016

Chapter 15

Daft Cases And Daft Responses

The early kill

The claim or application may be bonkers or the defence or other response not stand a hope in hell of success. But because the case is defended it has to go through the usual procedures and end up with a contested hearing at which the inevitable occurs. Or are there alternatives? You bet there are.

The more bonkers the case, the more likely that the person who has started it is subject to an order of the court that, because of their track record in the civil courts, they are prevented from making a claim or application without the permission of a judge. That order could be one declaring them to be a vexatious litigant or otherwise a civil restraint order that is limited, (and we are getting more severe) extended or (and this is for the most extreme litigants) general. The likelihood is that they have not obtained permission to do what they are now doing and they could well have slipped through the net without this being picked up by the court. So check 'em out! Go to www.gov.uk/guidance/general-civil-restraint-orders-in-force for the list of general restraint orders in force and this will take you to the lists of the other types of order made against a number of our over-persistent lovers of the court system.

Otherwise, the case might be stopped in its tracks before time, labour and money have been wasted. You will usually have to make an application to the court. If what the other side have come up with is patently unadulterated rubbish, it could be worthwhile writing to the court and asking that a judge kill off (don't use that phrase whatever happens) the opposition's case of the court's own volition so that you don't have to issue an application or you can make that request when you come to complete a form called a directions questionnaire which you will be asked to do if and when a defence has been produced.

Some words

The application in a civil case should be on form N244 - it will cost you £255 unless the fee is remitted (see chapter 13) - and state that what you are applying for is:

- For claimant - "*an order that the defence [and counterclaim] be struck out and judgment be given for the claimant with costs because the defence [and counterclaim] discloses [disclose] no reasonable grounds for defending the claim [and counterclaiming]* *in accordance with CPR rule 3.4(2) and/or for summary judgment because the defendant has no real prospect of successfully defending the claim [and counterclaiming] in accordance with CPR rule 24.2.*" * **

- For defendant - "*an order that the particulars of claim be struck out and the claim be dismissed with costs because the particulars of claim disclose no reasonable grounds for claiming (in accordance with CPR rules 3.4(2)) and/or for summary judgment because the claimant has no real prospect of successfully claiming.*" **

*If there is no counterclaim or you are not after killing it off, delete the words in square brackets.

**You can rely on rule 3.4(2) or rule 24.2 or both. Frequently, both are put in. Delete as necessary. Should you at least be relying on rule 24.2, ensure that you add these words to the N244 application form (or there may be tears):

"*If the respondent to this application for summary judgment wishes to rely on written evidence at the hearing, they must file the written evidence and serve copies on each other party to the application at least 7 days before the summary judgment hearing.*"

In so far as the early kill application is based on the particulars of claim not disclosing reasonable grounds for claiming, the defence not disclosing reasonable grounds for defending or the counterclaim not disclosing reasonable grounds for counterclaiming, there is probably nothing you need to say in the written evidence you put in or with the application - the particulars of claim, the defence and the counterclaim and their weaknesses will speak for themselves.

But in so far as the application is based on your opponent not having a real prospect of success, there will need to be supporting evidence in the hope of proving that your opponent has no hope. Where you have documents which back up what you are saying then refer to them in your written statement and include copies. If you are the claimant suing for the price of goods sold and the defendant has put in a defence alleging that the goods are substandard then you will be assisted by that wad of correspondence from them promising to pay when they have won the football pools or inherited under the estate of their 40 year old wealthy father who is in excellent health and in which they make no complaint about the goods which they have continued to use. And if you are the defendant to a claim for the balance outstanding for the supply and installation of double glazing and the claimant has written to you apologising for the fact that due to their surveyor's defective eyesight the windows don't fit properly and they will be round to fix the problem and you haven't heard from them since and you have had the windows replaced and are out of pocket and you have an expert's report to verify your case - then shove all that in.

Beware

Don't go for the early kill unless you are pretty confident of success or you could suffer failure and an order for costs against you. If you are pretty confident go for it early and with a small claim (for up to £10,000 usually - see chapter 18) go for it before the claim is formally allocated to the small claims track (which will usually be *after* completed direction questionnaires have been sent in to the court). That's because, before allocation, the other side will lack the protection of the limited costs regime for small claims so that, if the case is killed off, you can expect them to be ordered to pay your costs which will be especially handy where you have taken in a lawyer. Bear in mind that a claimant can apply for summary judgment under rule 24.2 (see above) even before the defendant has put in a defence. This would happen where the defendant has notified their intention to defend in the form of an acknowledgement of service and the claimant reckons they are playing for time and that the claim is undefendable. Why wait for the defence to come in? Should this ever so early pounce be made by the claimant, the defendant need not put in a defence before the application for summary judgment is heard.

Family cases

You are not allowed to apply for an early kill in family proceedings relating to a child. However, you may do so in other family proceedings such as divorce and matrimonial finance although such applications are rare. This time the application should be made in form D11 and the court fee will be £255 unless it is remitted (see chapter 13). Any application needs to rely on rule 4.4(1) of the Family Procedure Rules 2010. It empowers the court to kill off where there are no reasonable grounds for bringing or defending (for example, it is impossible to fathom out what the document starting or defending the case is about; what has been said is incoherent and makes no sense; or in an answer to a divorce, nullity, judicial separation or civil partnership dissolution petition, all the respondent does is to deny every allegation made against them without advancing a positive defence) or where the document starting or defending the case is frivolous, scurrilous or obviously ill-founded. It would be extraordinarily hard to convince a judge that they should kill off a matrimonial finance application. Perhaps if you divorced 30 years ago, are on benefits, are worth a £3,000 ISA and your former wife is asking for money and property for the first time, you might just have a chance.

Chapter 16

Outside The Court Room For A Civil Case

Waiting around

"Would the parties in the case of Troublesore versus Whitewash Ltd report to the usher's desk immediately."

That's it. The judge is ready to start the case. No point now in lamenting the day you got into this. Too late to change your script. Possibly too late to expel bodily waste though if you ask them nicely and display sufficient facial tension, the usher may permit you a quick visit to the loo. After all, you could be inside the hearing room for up to a continuous three hours and the judge will have made themselves comfortable before calling for the case to come on. Judicial training urges a full wee before a full court session. Judges though do have little tricks at their disposal to secure a break if unexpected lavatorial demands are made of them. When once caught short in my previous incarnation as a solicitor, I pretended to the bench of beaks I had just remembered that I had an urgent phone call to make. They sympathetically allowed me to rush out of court at 280 urisweats per second. Later, as a judicial beginner, I relied once or twice on a need to research a point of law in the court library but as confidence has grown I have followed the more common practice of announcing a 'comfort break' which, more often than not, will be welcomed by all present. This is unlikely to last longer than five minutes so you need to get on with things.

It's vital to concentrate on the case rather than your bladder or anus or both so if nature makes its call whilst the case progresses and there is no sign of the judge being in trouble, simply ask them for a loo break. It won't lose you the case.

"Please tell the judge I'm ready - if they are"

The problem in sensibly timing the last pre-hearing court loo visit, collection of the kids from school after the case or popping out to Primark or for a smoke while the court is in session with other cases is that you can never be absolutely sure when your case will be called on. Of course, you will have been sent a *notice of hearing* telling you at what time the case will start and probably how long it has been estimated to last. Here's the catch. The case may be taken dead on time or some while after it was due. Certain categories of case are bulk listed. That means, for example, that 12 claims by mortgage lenders for repossession could all be listed to begin at 10am. You won't see the 40 people involved in them invading court at the same time. Each case will be heard separately and, if you are unlucky, your turn may not come until close on to 11am.

It could be even worse. The judge may not begin the 10am batch of cases until 10.45am because of urgent business that was not expected when those 12 repossession cases were arranged. Maybe a tenant is due to be evicted from their home by a court bailiff during the day because of rent arrears and is making a last minute desperate attempt to be allowed to stay put. Or a battered wife is asking for an injunction to forbid their violent husband from molesting them after a serious assault the night before.

If for whatever reason you are not around when the case is ready, it is likely to be dealt with in your absence. This might result in it being *struck out* if you brought it and an order that you pay expenses to the other side or say an order that you give possession to your building society of the home in which you had intended to die. Then you would have to make an application for the case to be reheard. If you had genuine and reasonable grounds for your absence, a rehearing is more probable than not but coupled with an order that you compensate the blameless opposition for the loss your absence caused them.

The runner

It has been known for litigators to try and drag out proceedings by 'doing a (surreptitious) runner'. This involves clocking in with the usher so that they get marked down as present and then departing. The case is called. It is dealt with in their absence with an adverse order against them. Later they return and ask the usher why they are having to wait so long.

> *"Your case was called one hour ago and the judge has dealt with it."*
>
> *"No it wasn't. I have been sitting here all the time and I never heard my name."*
>
> *"Well I called it loud and clear."*
>
> *"I want to see the judge immediately."*
>
> *"He won't see you now. He's busy and the other side has left."*
>
> *"This is terrible. What can I do?!"*
>
> *"You'll have to apply for another hearing. Go to the court office and they will give you an application form."*

Judges are adept at sussing out the 'runner' when several weeks later they attend and remain for the hearing of their application for the previous order to be set aside.

Hug an usher

That usher I mentioned. His or her job is to know who has turned up, ferry litigants and witnesses between the waiting areas and the courtrooms, act as a link between the judge and the outside world, occasionally pour out a cup of tea for the judge and do a million other things. They've drastically cut down on the number of ushers and the poor things are rushed off their feet. They - the ushers and their feet - come in all shapes and sizes. Sometimes they wear a black robe on their back. If no robe then they can usually be identified by a booming voice and a bad temper on account of poor pay, pressure of work and insulting litigants and members of the public.

Sneer at or underestimate the usher at your peril. The first usher I encountered as an advocate at Portsmouth Magistrates' Court was my former Latin master. Having failed on so many occasions to accurately translate "Greeks build walls" into the arcane language, I was thoroughly embarrassed when he held open the court door for me and called me 'Sir'.

You never know. Your usher might report back to the judge on waiting room activities involving....you! If the judge is going to have to decide whether you are a placid wallflower or a violent maniac, you won't want the usher telling them that you shouted 'slut' at your ex-wife when she sat down opposite you and have been making menacing faces ever since. So remember you could be on trial from the moment you step into the court building. Behave and strike the right balance in your dealings with the usher. A little flattery coupled with a sympathy inducing element. You might enquire whilst shaking nervously how they keep so calm with such a heavy workload or ask whether they once worked as a brain surgeon because they look so like the person who operated on you. Keeping in with the usher will do you no harm.

Dress code

Oh I do hope you have dressed appropriately. You wouldn't go to a place of worship or a school prize giving ceremony ready for an outdoor barbecue. Showing you have some respect for the judge and the occasion in how you are attired is recommended. I accept that the claimant masquerading inside a pin-stripe job with a silk handkerchief flowing from the breast pocket may turn out to be the mastermind behind the latest Ponsi scheme. However, if it looks like you don't give a damn for where you are, the judge may just feel that you don't give a damn about anything - your behaviour towards your opponent or keeping to court orders or whatever. The best dressed people in the past have been debtors who came to court asking the judge to make them bankrupt. Not too smart and expensive if you intend pleading poverty and not as if you have just risen from bed. Preferably, not completely naked either. A gentleman who insisted on walking without a stitch on from Land's End to John O'Groats in the course of which he was subject to arrest, prosecutions, convictions and imprisonment lost his complaint to the European Court of Human Rights in 2014. And men: definitely not in a tank top and a pair of shorts with your belly bulging out. And women, keep it discreet. A male judge may have a good time if ample cleavage is deliberately exposed - and I've seen many a female try it on with a bust heave or two - but the exposer will not gain any advantage in the case.

Watching lawyers go by

There's no entertainment laid on for you whilst you are waiting for your case. Watching the other litigants and, better still, their lawyers can be quite absorbing. It's not so easy these days to identify the lawyers by appearance: easier by behaviour. The solicitors are likely to rush in late with sweat running down their faces and papers spewing out of an obese file under the arm. I've had two male solicitors recently appear before me unjacketed. This is as serious as hitting an old lady over the head with a mallet. When I enquired of one of them whether he normally came to court unjacketed, he apologised without offering any explanation. His client who was immaculately attired put him to shame. As to the other, I asked him whether he was going to the beach. He apologised profusely and stated that he had been late setting off for court from his office and had simply forgotten to put his jacket on. The inspiration for the enquiry was an experience many years ago on entering Portsmouth Guildhall auditorium with a friend and very casually dressed for a Julie Felix concert - late. She publicly enquired of us: "Going to the beach?" My instant retort which, like the best of them, stayed in my head and did not leave my mouth, was: "No, the zoo, zoo, zoo. How about you?"

Barristers dealing with civil cases tend to be better attired than their solicitor counterparts (though the younger ones specialising in criminal legal aid cases for which the pay is appalling sometimes have frayed shirt cuffs) and the VPC - that's Very Posh Counsel, as they are known - can be spotted by dress and demeanour. Pinstripes for the men and fine silk tops for the women, they glide rather than walk, with the hint of an aroma under the nostrils.

Water and biro

There might be a refreshments machine or, if you are very lucky, a public canteen should you be in the mood for food or drink. Safer to carry a bottle of water with you though anything larger than a half litre may look over indulgent and if you feel constrained to have a swig after your case has started, ask the judge for permission. And you may want to arm yourself with a biro (those *Barclays* freebies are to be recommended) and paper because you will not find a stock of stationery available in the hearing centre for your use. There are two reasons for biro. First, in the longer cases you are well advised to make notes of the evidence being given by your opponent and witnesses and this will act as a memory jog when you come to cross-question them. And, secondly, the judge may be impressed by the care you are applying by writing down what you can. It could mean you will be writing down their judgment and are in appeal mode (after all, you're *Mr Troublesore*, aren't you).

Leave the tape recorder at home. If you record any part of the hearing without the judge's permission, which would be refused, you would be in contempt of court and that's serious because it can lead to imprisonment, a fine or confiscation of your assets. The hearing will be tape recorded by the court and you can obtain a transcript of it or just part of it afterwards provided you pay the transcriber's charges for which you can ask for a quote.

Music while you wait

Unlike most public buildings, there's no background music in court buildings which is a bit of a shame. Carefully selected, it could act as a relaxant to all involved. After all, soothing music is played to womb occupants who tell me it calms them down nicely. Here's a name drop. One my nephews is Murray Gold who composes the *Doctor Who* music and also wrote the music for the David Attenborough *Life Stories* series. I asked him what he might write for a county court waiting room. He wasn't too keen. He has obviously had bad experiences. He says music designed to calm him in public places actually puts him more on edge and he is worried about how it would affect conversation. "If people are talking over it, everything becomes louder," he says. "Conversation is at a specific range of the frequency spectrum. Musically it is pitched in a range that is only a small part of the piano keyboard. But the more the music is in the same frequency range as human voices, the more difficult it is to hear people while it is playing because it competes. In terms of music style, the human heart tends to imitate pulses so that when there is a fast base drum that resembles a heartbeat, our hearts speed up and we get excited, agitated or nervous."

Cancel the Abbey Road Studios booking and the harpist.

> *"This is the second call. Would the parties in the case of Troublesore versus Whitewash Ltd report to the usher's desk immediately".*

Who's that woman over there? Is she holding a notebook? Has she come to report my case? Blimey, the neighbours might turn up too. Should I get out of here fast? Generally, the media's obsession with criminal court cases is not matched in civil cases. Unless you've just indulged in sexual intercourse on a television reality programme, it is highly unlikely that your case will be reported on. There's one exception. If your opponent has tipped off the media and the case is offbeat or otherwise highly newsworthy, either nationally or, more probably, locally then some coverage there might well be. A tactic adopted by one persistent litigant is to alert his local newspaper cronies to an upcoming hearing and have them make contact with his opponent before the hearing for a comment. This is calculated to induce the opponent to settle the case before the hearing out of fear of adverse publicity. It has worked.

Public or private

Whether or not the reporter can get into the hearing depends on the type of case. For civil cases, the general rule is that the hearing is open to the public and so a reporter can sit in and report what happened. This includes the hearing of a small claim but here the judge may decide to keep out the public and media if the litigants agree or one of certain grounds exist (for example, the hearing involves confidential information including information relating to personal financial matters and publicity would damage that confidentiality or a private hearing in necessary in the interests of justice). Certain hearings will almost invariably be in private. Principally, these are for cases where repossession of a property is being claimed by a mortgage lender against their borrower or a landlord against their tenant. So if there is someone at the back of the court you would prefer to see suspended from a very, very tall crane stationed in a dumping ground for putrid rat flesh, ask the judge to hear the case in private and boot them out, explaining why.

Sorry, I digressed. The usher will take you into court unless you are at one of the rare court buildings in which they operate a doctor's surgery type system of moving you from waiting room to courtroom by electronic board message or tardis. You enter. It may be a grand courtroom just like off the telly or it may be a shoebox. The longer and more substantial cases are likely to be in the grand courtroom. The shorter cases and small claims are likely to be in a shoebox or a room akin to an office with the judge sitting at a desk and seats for litigants and others opposite the judge. The judge or usher will tell you where to sit. You can keep your mouth shut until the judge asks you to open it. The cocky, feeling resentful that they are in court and wishing to convey an air of indifference, will come out with an "Alright, mate?" class of greeting. Never attempt to shake hands with the judge or kiss them. To do so would be construed as an attempt to curry favour which would be quite improper and could backfire. Should you take the judge by surprise and succeed in either, they might feel constrained to demonstrate that they are not partisan by shaking hands with your opponent or, worse still, kissing your opponent! I'm not serious.

Addressing the judge

"Blimey, what do I call the judge?" I have had *My Lord*, *Your Highness*, *Your Honour* (all of which are wrong but none of which I have corrected because I enjoyed them too much) and *Sir* (which is right). District judges who deal with the vast majority of county court hearings should be addressed as *Sir* or *Madam*, depending on their gender and, if you aren't sure of that, remain silent until you get some clues. Circuit judges who are senior to district judges deal with the remainder. They should be addressed as *Your Honour*. The list of cases on display in the public areas of the building will show which judge is taking which cases so you will know before whom you will be appearing. Establishing the judge's gender if not obvious from the list of cases or disclosed by the usher, will not be hindered by the judge wearing a wig. These days, wigs are passé except for ceremonial occasions. More often than not, the judge will be robed if sitting in open court.

In the absence of a robe, what can you expect? Neither nudity nor gardening clothes.

In guidance given eight years ago by Lord Justice Leveson (who as a barrister unsuccessfully prosecuted Ken Dodd for allegedly fiddling (no, not tickling) the tax man but has put that all behind him with a distinguished judicial career - and an enquiry) it was stated that the civilian clothing should be "a dark coloured business suit or similar" so if your judge is clad in pale blue or something off the shoulder, you might turn wardrobes and suggest that they refresh their memories on that guidance. Or you might not. Perhaps just save that in case there is a judicial attempt at rebuke for your own appearance.

"Where's the jury?"

The judge will decide your case on their own. You only get a jury in a criminal case at the Old Bailey or in a Crown Court and sometimes at an inquest into a person's death. Once in a blue moon there may be a jury in a civil case which involves a claim for damages for defamation (libel or slander), malicious prosecution or false imprisonment. And you only get magistrates at - you guessed it - magistrates' courts and for some less complicated family court cases. You will have more than one judge for your money on most appeals to higher courts.

Enough of this. Let's get into court.

Chapter 17

In Court For Your Civil Case

"What am I doing here?"

Getting rid of the judge

Thinks. "I've seen that judge before. It's that b......d Gold." You can't cherry pick your judge but you are entitled to a fair hearing and so in certain situations you are entitled to ask the judge to stand down - to 'recuse' themselves as we say - and hand over to another judge. The judge should stand down if they are actually biased against you. That's notoriously difficult to prove and few attempt to do so. It's more common for objection to be taken on the ground of the judge's apparent bias. You have to show that a fair-minded and informed observer would reckon there was a real danger or possibility of bias - it stinks a bit. I'll give you an example. In a big money divorce case in 2007 a High Court judge had made a number of remarks about the Egyptian husband's ethnicity during preliminary hearings (see chapter 48). When the husband attempted to get rid of the judge for the final hearing, he refused to stand down. The Court of Appeal overruled him. Yes, he talked too much but he was a good judge. However, his remarks had been regrettable and unacceptable and it could be thought that the scorn and contempt that his words conveyed might be carried into his decision.

But say you are confronted by a judge you have met before in another case which you lost after the judge had decided you were the most odious, contemptible, immoral piece of excrement he had had the misfortune to encounter and had failed to utter a truthful word in evidence apart from your name and there was even some doubt about that. You would stand a good chance of persuading the judge to stand down. It is a question of the extent to which the judge had previously taken against you. The mere fact that the judge had ruled against you before or had been critical of you will usually be insufficient to warrant a recusal.

No judge should be a judge in their own cause so if they have a vested interest in the outcome of a case, they should hand over to another judge. And guidelines to judges about their conduct make it clear that a judge must not decide a case in which a member of their family legally represents a litigant or is in any way associated with the case.

The recusal request should be made at the start of the case unless you know in advance that the particular judge is due to preside, in which event you should write to the court and state your objection to the judge. If the judge refuses to stand down then you may be given permission to appeal that decision.

A warning. If your request to the judge to stand down is unsuccessful then with that judge you are stuck. Judicial continuity is often the aim. Therefore, in cases where there may be a series of preliminary hearings before the final trial, you are likely to have the same judge presiding on each occasion. In fact, that same judge may even preside over the final trial. If you have attacked them for alleged bias just be ready to be embarrassed as they continue to handle the case. Wear that false beard and nose in future in the hope that the judge does not remember you? Don't bother. The judge will remember but arguably they will bend over backwards to be fair lest it should be suggested they put the boot in out of revenge.

Order in court

The judge is there to control the hearing. You should submit to this control. It is self defeating to shout, be rude or offensive or interrupt the judge or, indeed, in the presence of the judge, to act in such a way towards your opponent (whose guts you may detest) or their lawyer (whose face you may like to thump with the force of a tornado). You will be given an opportunity to reply to whatever is being said against you. Wait until your time comes to crush the other side's allegations. Two caveats: if your blood is boiling at a temperature in excess of 35 degrees Celsius or the other side has got it so wrong that this may send the judge off on the wrong track and an instant correction is the only reasonable course, then attempt an interruption.

> *"Madam, I am sorry to interrupt but I must correct what you have been told. It is said I have made no payments under my mortgage since the 20th July 2013. I paid £7,500 off the mortgage arrears last Monday and have the lender's receipt here. The lender's representative has clearly not been fully instructed by his client."*

Game, set and possibly match to you and achieved with such courtesy.

It is just conceivable that you have made a cock up by failing to follow pre-hearing directions or to comply with an order made at a previous hearing: or perhaps you did your best but through no fault of your own you were unable to do what was expected of you. It will go down much better with the judge if you cough your default at the start.

> *"Madam, I now realise I should have sent to the court and the claimant copies of the invoices for fresh fish purchased by me over the last six months and I have not done so. I sincerely apologise. I did not read the court's order as carefully as I should have done. There is no satisfactory excuse I can offer but if the case can proceed without*

the invoices, I would be extremely grateful."

Another warning. That cock up could have triggered some sanction against you such as an ability to rely on certain evidence. This could be fatal to your case. You should apply before the hearing to be excused for your default: it's called an application for relief from sanctions. Where you haven't done so, you can try your luck with the grovelling apology as suggested but don't hold your breath.

Shorter hearings

A myriad of reasons could have got you to court. The nature of the hearing will determine the procedure. Shorter hearings take place for such cases as claims for repossession because of mortgage or rent arrears, return of cars and other goods on the ground of arrears under credit agreements, petitions by creditors for bankruptcy and enforcement of judgments by way of charging order or attachment of earnings and so on. And there may also be a short hearing in what will be a long case. Take a substantial claim for damages for a serious injury sustained in a road accident which is being defended. Quite early on in the case the court will probably fix what is called a case management conference at which it will give directions to the parties about how they must prepare for the ultimate trial. Then there are those longer hearings like the full trial of that road accident claim and other defended cases where the judge has to hear evidence from the litigants and their witnesses, consider possible legal points and decide who wins and who loses. Generally, the shorter hearings will be decided by the judge on the basis of written evidence and representations on the day from each side without anyone going into the witness box. Whichever side is making the claim or application will normally go first and have its say and the judge will then turn to the other side to hear whether they oppose what the court is being asked to do, and, if so, why.

Whether or not prior to a shorter hearing you have sent to the court and your opponent any written representations about what order you are inviting the court to make, be ready to verbally repeat your main points to the judge. If the judge has had an opportunity to read and digest what you have written, they will ask you in felicitously couched judicial language to belt up. In fact, the greater impact may well be made by what you say, concisely, on the day rather than what you have written in the tiniest green biro scrawl. And that reminds me. If you have the ability to type any document for the court, type it instead of putting the judge through the torture of trying to decipher your handwriting.

You may have been required in advance of the hearing to send to the court and probably the other side details of your evidence or argument.

If that was so, please, please, please make copies of what you have written and any documents that have accompanied it and also write covering letters with what you are sending and keep copies. There is a real possibility that your paperwork is not on the court file for your case which is in front of the judge (because it has been lost, misfiled, gone to sleep under a court staff member's in-tray or is in a queue for attention). Alternatively or in addition, your opponent may deny ever having received what you sent them, the reason being that they are a bare-faced liar. Where you are lodging a document with the court in person and there is a human being there to take it, ask for a receipt. Where, as is the more likely, you are inserting a letter into a court 'drop box', take a selfie of you putting it in with a newspaper front page for that day visible in the pic but don't drop your lunch box in the process. I have actually seen the selfie being done!

Longer hearings

The longer hearings are different (and for the rather different procedure on small claims hearings, see chapter 18 exclusively devoted to them). Usually, the litigant bringing the case - the claimant or applicant - will kick off because it's their job to prove what they are alleging. The position will be reversed where the other side - the defendant or respondent - has the task of proving the central allegation. Perhaps a manufacturer is claiming for the price of goods it has sold to a retailer and the retailer is admitting the transaction but defending on the grounds that the goods fell to pieces the moment they came out of their boxes and the retailer immediately returned them. The onus is on the retailer to prove that the goods were substandard and so the retailer would go first and give their evidence before the manufacturer. In the more complex cases, any lawyer representing the claimant will seek to make an opening statement drawing the judge's attention to the main factual issues and points of law they will have to decide. However, the trend is for the lawyers to have put in a written summary of those matters before the hearing in what is called a skeleton argument or position statement - only in exceptional cases would that be required from a litigant in person - and for the judge to discourage any oral opening statement from them. An unrepresented litigant will get a copy of the written summary but it may only be thrust into their hands outside court by the lawyer who has prepared it and very close to the time for going into court. If that unsettles you as a litigant in person then you should explain to the judge what has happened (to generate a few fluid ounces of sympathy) and, if it is genuinely desired, ask for a little more time outside to study the document. So, generally speaking, straight into the evidence. The claimant or applicant will almost invariably be the first witness and the evidence they give before they are cross-examined is called their 'evidence in chief'. Having declared their name, address and occupation, they proceed to confirm the truth of the contents of their written statement. If legally represented, their lawyer may try and squeeze in some additional oral evidence under the guise of wanting to clarify some matters.

> *"Ma'am, if I may seek your indulgence to just put one or two supplementary questions to the witness for the assistance of the court."*

Very often, the real reason is that some essential matter has been left out of the statement which could damage if not be fatal to the success of their case if not dealt with. This might be due to the incompetence of a lawyer or someone in their employ who has drafted the statement for the witness. Be quick to stop that.

> *"Objection, Ma'am. We should be told precisely what questions Mr Harbottle-Fraser-de-Monfort wishes to put to this witness and may I respectfully draw the court's attention to the fact that the witness statement should have contained all the witness's evidence in chief and I should not be ambushed with fresh evidence at this juncture. It is unfair."*

If it transpires that all the lawyer wants to do is get the witness to indicate on some photographs of the accident scene which have been produced whether they had been travelling from the bottom of the photographs to the top or vice versa, the objection to this innocuous supplemental evidence can be withdrawn. Perhaps even with the mildest whiff of humour.

> *"Ma'am I had been wondering whether the witness had actually been present at the accident and so this clarification is to be welcomed."*

Keep an eye on where the witnesses for your opponent are looking when they are testifying. If they are asked a question they appear to be finding awkward they may look towards your opponent for a nod or some other sign before they answer. This would almost certainly be picked up by the judge if they can spot it but the courtroom geography may make this difficult so be quick to score a point.

> *"Ma'am, the witness needs to be true to his oath and not my opposing party. Would the witness stop looking towards him."*

When the witness has completed their evidence in chief, you get the opportunity to cross-examine them. This does not mean being angry with the witness. After that, they may be asked questions by their lawyer in what is called 're-examination' but this should be restricted to dealing with matters which have been raised in cross-examination and not with fresh matters. Then the judge may ask the witness some questions of their own which are frequently the questions that the litigants or their lawyers forgot to ask, were afraid to ask or were not entitled by the rules of evidence to ask. The remaining witnesses for the claimant or applicant are then questioned in the same sequence. Thereafter, the other side and their witnesses go into bat and we have more of the same.

Each side has the right to make a closing speech to sum up at the end. Generally, the defendant or respondent sums up first and the claimant or applicant goes second. The defendant or respondent may be given the opportunity to reply purely on a point of law or to correct any inaccurate statement made by the claimant or applicant in their summing up. Phew! Summing up is not compulsory but the right to do so should be seized with both hands if it can be done well. A judge could be swayed at this late stage of the case. But if all you are going to do is to repeat your evidence then keep your trap shut and certainly don't open it to try and squeeze in some new evidence or you will be jumped on. The idea is to show why the judge should make findings of fact which are favourable to your case by linking together the salient points of evidence which the judge has heard and drawing attention to any relevant support for your account and inconsistencies in the other side's evidence. It will help you to jot down on a piece of paper the bits of evidence you may wish to refer to in your summing up as the evidence is given. And if there is a difference between you and your opponent about the relevant legal principles, this is your opportunity to argue for your interpretation of the law and to draw the judge's attention to any legal precedents that assist you. You are also meant to draw the judge's attention to any legal precedents that don't assist you! When a precedent is relied on a copy of a recognised law report of the case should be shown to the judge and your opponent. You should be able to source these reports through the internet - take a look at BAILII, British and Irish Legal Information Institute, at www.bailii.org.

Cross-examination

Back to cross-examination. There's probably not a lawyer in the world who doesn't give some thought before he gets into court to what they are going to say to the judge. A prominent London QC professes to spend one hour in preparation for every minute of his court speak. If it's good enough for them, it's good enough for you. It shouldn't be hard to predict which areas the other side will wish to concentrate on when cross-examining you - the weak areas of your case. If you have asserted that it was definitely the other side who was at the wheel of the Mercedes when it drove into the back of your Skoda and that you recognise them in court, be ready to be questioned about your fishbowl-lensed specs and when you last had your eyes tested, what the driver was wearing and precisely what it is about his appearance in court that you recall from those two seconds of observation three years earlier.

Get a loved one to be cruel and put you through your paces with some really tough cross-examination involving a hypothetical situation such as whether it was you or the babysitter who stole half a cream meringue out of the fridge. Don't over rehearse or your evidence may sound false. When in that former incarnation I cross-examined a store detective giving evidence against my client who was charged with shoplifting, I put it to her that she was plainly wrong. She insisted that her evidence was correct and she knew it was correct because she had gone over it at home when practising for court many times. I had little difficulty in securing the dismissal of the charge on the basis that this key witness had not been testifying about the facts as she recalled them but had been delivering a learnt speech.

Conversely, think about any questions you may wish to put to the other side and their witnesses in your own cross-examination. The object of this cross-examination should be to flush out points that haven't been mentioned and will help your case - though one of the cardinal rules of cross-examination is never ask a question if you do not know the answer it will get or you could risk opening up a can of worms - and to put your own version of events to them so that they can comment on it. Make notes beforehand about the questions you want to put. Try to start and end the cross-examination with a strong point. If you possibly can - and this requires a mixture of concentration and luck - start your cross-examination with a question which bounces straight off the last statement the witness has made. It might go something like:

> *Opponent answering his own lawyer: "Because of the way the claimant behaved towards me, I had to take a fortnight off work and stay in bed the whole time."*
>
> *You with your first question in cross-examination: "Apart from the Saturday when I saw you at the Spurs match, that is?"*

Be circumspect about alleging that the other side or any of their witnesses have told untruths. The judge may be more susceptible to persuasion that they are mistaken than that they have deliberately lied. But if the only reasonable conclusion to be drawn from their evidence is that they have lied and it is important to your case then you will need to put that allegation to them in cross-examination. Do it with a flourish. "You were a liar then and you are a liar now." Or if you want something wordier: "I put it to you that your evidence is a farrago of lies. Lie upon lie to cover up the truth."

Giving your evidence

When you give evidence yourself, turn towards the judge and look them in the face - but not in a threatening way! While answering questions which may be coming from your own lawyer or your opponent, the temptation may be to turn towards and look at them but it is better to focus on the judge. After all, it is for the judge's benefit that you are answering questions so that they can reach a decision. In a difficult case I once tried relating to the welfare of a child, the father who was a psychiatrist of some years standing and his wife gave a master class in the technique, actually moving the witness chair so that they had a direct line to my face and stuck rigidly to that line from the beginning to the end of their testimonies. Yes, the father won but on the merits of his case.

When giving evidence, will you have to take an oath to tell the truth (the whole truth and nothing but the truth)? Something along those lines except on a small claims hearing. Under the Oaths Act 1878 - still going strong despite intermittent attempts to kill it off - a witness must take a religious oath to tell the truth or may affirm, in non-religious terms, that their evidence will be true. This is arguably a pointless exercise because a sizable proportion of witnesses then proceed to lie their heads off though there are instances of witnesses pulling back from the utterance of a porkie by virtue of the fact that they have sworn to tell the truth. Some defendants at their criminal trial are prone to declaring that they must be 'not guilty' because whenever they have been 'guilty' in the past, they have admitted the offence. That rarely works before a jury. And it never works before a civil judge to suggest they should accept your evidence is true because you have sworn on a holy book to tell the truth and you went to church only the day before. I once dismissed a claim for personal injury following a road accident by a claimant who testified to his God fearing nature and produced statements by a series of acquaintances from his religious order as to his excellent character. He had been involved in around seven previous accidents over the preceding few years and I had to decide on the evidence that his latest accident was just one whiplash too many.

One of the possible consequences of a witness telling lies at a civil trial after they have taken an oath or affirmed is that they can be charged with perjury and brought before a criminal court. If convicted, the likely sentence is one of imprisonment. If every witness who the civil judge decided had lied were charged with perjury, the queue to the Old Bailey dock would stretch to Bognor Regis promenade. And so it is that only in the more flagrant and consistent cases of porkie pieing will the civil judge refer the matter to the Director of Public Prosecutions.

It's cold outside

You will stay in court for the entire hearing but what of your witnesses? The practice in civil cases is the dead opposite to criminal cases in that the witnesses being called by each litigant come into court at the start and so hear the evidence being given before their turn arrives. Bonkers? It does give them what is sometimes perceived as the advantage of being able to change what they were going to say on account of what they have heard from the witness box. If they did so, though, they would have to explain why their written statement copies of which the judge and opposition had before them differed from the verbal evidence they were now giving. The evidential u-turn would probably reduce the value of their evidence to the price of a used pilchard. The judge always has a discretion to direct that the usual practice be dis-applied and that witnesses only come into court when they are to be called into the witness box. This might follow a request by one of the litigants or their lawyer who believe that their witnesses are going to be strong and impressive and that even greater weight will be attached to their evidence if they all stand up to cross-examination and give substantially the same evidence on a crucial matter as each other without having been present when the others testified.

Witness familiarisation

Of course, if you are flush with money, you will have undergone a professional witness familiarisation session. Eh? You'll recall the bitter High Court case in 2012 between the late Boris Berezovsky and Chelsea Football Club boss Roman Abramovitch. The trial judge found Abramovitch who won to be a truthful and on the whole reliable witness. She said: "Where he had relevant knowledge, he was able to give full and detailed answers; he took care to distinguish between his own knowledge, reconstructed assumptions and speculation." The fact he had given the entirety of his evidence in Russian through the use of a translator didn't operate to his detriment, then. Abramovitch, you see, had been through witness familiarisation with Bond Solon, the UK's leading firm specialising in the area. Firms like this won't coach anyone by guiding them through the evidence they should give in their own particular case because that's taboo. But they may subject you to a mock cross-examination similar in ferocity to the wife when investigating over the half cream meringue which has gone missing from the kitchen and will tutor on such things as the theory, practice and procedure of giving evidence. Perhaps on the lines of some of this book, only more expensive.

For a one-to-one three hour session, Bond Solon charge a fee of £850 and boss Mark Solon assures me that Abramovitch paid that amount. I didn't ask if he collected a free Chelsea season ticket for his trouble. The fee and time increase with the number of participants but they would not take you on with more than five of your witnesses in a single session.

If you won the case after undergoing witness familiarisation and were awarded your costs, you could include the fee paid for your session in your bill. If you were allowed the fee, I would eat another of my hats.

Pass the tissues, please

Worth crying at the hearing? If you are genuinely so distressed by the possibility of an adverse outcome of the case for you, at what is being said against you or what you are describing in your evidence that you lose control and shed a tear then, so be it. The judge may feel that your reaction is relevant to your credibility. Anything from wailing to snivelling which is falsely induced so as to invoke sympathy along with manufactured panic attacks can only assist your opponent. I usually kept a box of paper tissues to produce at vapour time. It would obviously give the game away to readily produce your own box. I have come across a couple of lawyers who were moved to tears in their closing addresses to me which I found puerile. Highly emotive representations to a professional judge are a no-go area. Possibly, they would be productive before a bench of lay magistrates. One experienced defence magistrates' court solicitor I knew would plead with the bench in these terms: "God never gave this man a chance. Will you?" But he never cried in court.

Putting a sock in it

It is a mistake to go on too long in cross-examining a witness or addressing the judge. This could irritate the judge. Use the judge's face as a barometer. If it goes bright red, their eyebrows rise to the ceiling, their cheeks expand and they exhale hot air or words are emitted from their mouths along the lines of "How much more of this are we going to have, Mr Troublesore?" or "I've got the point" or "You've asked that question five times already" then you should think very carefully about shutting up. It is important not to misread what is in the judge's mind. A lay magistrate - he was a professor who was chairman of the bench - before whom I regularly appeared when advocating criminal cases had what I can only assume was an affliction in that he would smile broadly throughout proceedings no matter what he may have been thinking. I had not been tipped off about this when I first encountered him in court and made the mistake of believing I was doing very well and could be economical in the mitigation I had to offer on behalf of my convicted client. In the event, a severe sentence was passed. The mistake was never repeated.

Occasionally it may be necessary to fall out with the judge albeit you must surrender to his control of the proceedings and accept that he is entitled to impose a time limit on cross-examination and other stages of the case. If the judge's impatience is obvious but you have not got round to your killer question or point then you must stand up for yourself and attempt to press on. You will be forgiven some mild impertinence once you have demonstrated that you had good reason to keep going.

> *Judge: "Mr Troublesore, surely we don't need any more of this?"*
>
> *"Sir, I regret just a little more."*

The judgment

Where the judge has to decide the result of a case because the litigants have not agreed it, one of them will be disappointed and possibly enraged. Unruly behaviour in court when the judge gives their decision is most unwise. It's worth remembering that, quite apart from the fact that it could well lead to you being locked up for contempt, after the judge has announced his decision they will go on to deal with the costs of the case - who picks up the winner's expenses which may include their lawyer's fees if they have been legally represented at the hearing and may include a lawyer's fee for advising or otherwise helping with the case before the hearing even though they have not been legally represented at the hearing. So something like this would be unfortunate:

> *Judge: "Accordingly, Mr Troublesore, your claim is dismissed."*
>
> *Mr Troublesore: "You idiotic cow. About time you learnt some law."*
>
> *Representative for Whitewash Ltd: "Most Gracious Madam, I apply for an order for costs against Mr Troublesore. I have sent him and the court a statement of my company's costs which I ask you to assess now on the litigant in person basis. You will see the amount asked for is £15,689. 23 and on top of that........."*

And then there's the question of when you have to pay those costs. Oh dear.

Chapter 18

Small Claims

Small but beautiful

Anyone who hasn't heard of the Small Claims Court must have been away on Planet Mars. As it happens, that's not quite right. The Small Claims Court does not actually exist except in the imagination of many or possibly at Uranus Town Hall. What does exist is a regime in the normal county court which is dedicated to small claims - generally, those for up to £10,000 - and is the pride and joy of the courts service which breaks its neck to get those of them which are defended, heard within 30 weeks of being started. The regime is notable for protecting a litigant who loses against a thumping great big costs order in favour of the winner and for the relative informality of the hearing. These claims are said to be on the *small claims track* where we see real life at its rawest. Contests between buyer and seller, landlord and tenant, motorist and motorist, holiday-maker and package travel company, neighbour and neighbour and that Uncle Thomas Cobley and all again. Before they get onto this track, they are started in much the same way as a massive claim and things can go horribly wrong if they are nutty. But more of that later.

County court arbitration was the forerunner of the modern small claims track and started in the 1970s for county court cases involving a bag of sweets or a grain of sand. Lawyer involvement was considerably rare in those days. It mainly occurred when the wife of the senior partner in a solicitor's office bought a pound of cheese that was off or a solicitor owed a client a favour. As a solicitor myself, I often advised on whether the law was on the side of a client or their opponent and on the tactics to be adopted but my experience as an advocate on a county court arbitration was limited to two cases. The first was a road accident claim where for no fee I represented a female friend I was trying to impress. Whilst she had been standing in the road by the partially opened offside door of her kerb-parked vehicle, an elderly driver out for the afternoon with his wife decided to make contact with the door and remove it from its hinges. Fortunately, the client's body was left intact. The arbitrator - he was a county court judge who was then called a registrar - decided that the client was 20% to blame for having opened the door whilst parked near a slight bend in the road and the elderly motorist was 80% to blame. The result was that the client had to bear 20% of her repair charges. A peculiar decision which was probably intended as a consolation to the likeable elderly driver.

In my second arbitration outing as an advocate I was representing a

Pompey fan against Oxford Football Club in the days of Robert Maxwell. The teams were playing in the Milk Cup quarter final. My client had bought stand tickets at £10 a time for himself and his three children. The tickets stated that they were sold subject to conditions displayed at the ticket office but it transpired that at the time there were no conditions displayed there. It was a disastrous evening for the family. They had a poor view of the match due to barriers and pitch perimeter fencing in front of the stand and Pompey lost. My client sued Oxford United for damages. He lost too but on the facts of the case and not the relevant law. The judge decided that the family had been able to see the flow of the game, how it evolved and how the goals were scored. As poor as their view was, it was not so poor that Oxford were in breach of contract in selling the seats. Had the seats not been reasonably fit for purpose, my client would have scored. Some years later, I used this area of the law to obtain a refund for the price of two tickets for an Abba tribute band concert at Richmond Theatre which had been ruined by most of the audience ahead spending the whole concert on their feet. I tend to prefer sitting down at concerts except when purchasing the ices.

The modern small claims scheme got going in 1999 and looks like being given a monumental facelift but not for another four years so plenty of time to enjoy what we have got. The same law of England and Wales that applies to an oligarch's case before the Supreme Court applies to your small claim in the county court and that will continue to be the case under the new regime. If the law is against you, the judge will be - must be - against you. That's why I had to throw out one person's claim against another for damages on the ground that the other had stared at them in a supermarket. If you have any doubt about the legal validity of your claim, check it out with a lawyer or advice agency first.

I need to make a confession. I have brought small claims during my judicial career (and before). Judges bleed when they are pricked and think about suing when they are wronged. Only occasionally, having thought about it, will they actually launch a claim. It's not the done thing. All a bit embarrassing. Difficult to find a judge who doesn't know you and just think of the humiliation if you lost. That makes me something of an exception. I have always claimed using Money Claim Online (see chapter 9) and without disclosing that I am a judge. Every time it has been my intention that, should the defendant be misguided enough to defend the case, I would either abandon it or, more probably, ask that a judge or deputy judge who didn't know me from Adam should hear the case in my absence. Happily, I have never lost and either obtained a judgment in default (see below) or negotiated a settlement after a defence has gone in.

Alas, there is a further confession about which I cringe and contort every sinew of my body in shame. I, me, Judge Clever Dick, was conned. In 2008 a builder induced me to pay him £3,500 on account of his charges and those of a structural engineer he said he was to engage in connection with the preparation of plans and an application for planning permission for a loft conversion at my home. He did little or nothing but pay the money I handed over towards the debts he had incurred. In mitigation, I plead that I agreed to do this by telephone over dinner and after a hard day's work and the builder had been highly recommended by a friend (whose assassination I have arranged) and I had seen some impressive work the builder had done for someone else. This is scant mitigation, I know, and is not deserving of a discount of more than 10% on the number of lashings I should receive for my stupidity. And if I had taken the elementary step of making a search at the Register of Judgments, Orders and Fines (see chapter 20), I would have discovered that my plausible builder had a string of unsatisfied county court judgments registered against him. So I sued him and then came the not uncommon scenario. He didn't put in a defence and I obtained a default judgment. He applied to set the judgment aside and failed to turn up for the hearing of the application in Oxford County Court where I had instructed a local solicitor to represent me. His application was dismissed with costs in my favour. I then put in the bailiff. The builder was never at home when the bailiff called and nobody who was at home would open the door. All the bailiff could find outside the house that he could seize was a water feature - not even a bird seed container - but the advice was that it would cost more to remove than it would sell for. Next I obtained a charging order against his interest in his home (see chapter 22). That was one of the better moves I had made since meeting my builder.

Then he was made bankrupt by someone else. The bankruptcy did not lose me the value of my judgment because of the charging order for this generally takes priority over other creditors who have not obtained such an order. The builder's trustee in bankruptcy had the builder's property sold and, once his mortgage was paid off along with the bankruptcy costs, the surplus was available to pay me my £3,500 and costs due to me and other charges were also paid off with the balance available for unsecured creditors to share. By the way, do you know any good loft converters who do cheap plans and don't telephone during dinner?

A chocolaty story

It's as important to know when not to make a small claim as when to make a small claim. In 2012 my brother Clive gifted me a Marks & Spencer bottle of champagne with chocolates which he ordered online. On a peckish night around three months later, I ripped open the box of chocolates to find they were past their scoff by date. They had been given a life of just two and a half months from the date of delivery. I wrote Marks and Spencer a 'letter before action' - yes, I know I was not a party to the contract for the purchase of the gift but the Contracts (Rights of Third Parties) Act 1999 gave me the standing to make a complaint and claim in my own right without involving my brother and, anyway, I could hardly have troubled him - contending that it had been implied on purchase that the scoff by date would be reasonable and that two and a half months was unreasonably short. I argued that the chocolates were not an accompaniment to a short life product but to champagne. If they had accompanied some other perishable product then I conceded that a different situation would have prevailed. Not a bad argument, eh?

MARKS & SPENCER

Mr S Gold

Our Ref: 1-421236117
12 November 2012

Dear Mr Gold

The quality of our food is extremely important to us. We want you to enjoy our food at its very best and we carry out extensive tests to establish the natural life of each of our products.

We also want you to enjoy food that is as natural as possible and free from any unnecessary additives or preservatives.

As a result, some of our foods may have a shorter life than our competitors' products. We believe the benefits of our approach outweigh the negatives of a shorter shelf life, and help us achieve the higher quality our customers have come to expect.

Having said this, we are always pleased to hear from our customers on any issues that are important to them, and I have passed your comments on to our buyers. They will take them into account when we come to review the recipe and guidelines for this product.

We must also advise, that is a customers responsibility to check the best before date on items they receive, in case of any errors that may have occurred during the picking.

Concerning the chocolate in question, we do feel that 2.5 months from the date of delivery to the best before date is more than reasonable. And in this instance we would not offer anything further.

I am sorry you were disappointed with this product. I hope my letter has been helpful in explaining how and why we date our food as we do, and that you will continue to shop at M&S with confidence.

Yours sincerely

Customer Adviser
Retail Customer Services
We're keen to know what you thought of our service. If you'd like to share any feedback, please let us know by completing our short automated telephone or online survey. You can give us a call on 0333 20 20 500 or use the web link www.mandssurvey.co.uk/500.

"The life expectation of a chocolate"

As I pictured no less than the chief choc buyer from M&S's head office turning up with the biggest hamper known to man and sufficient *Mountain Bars* to keep me stuffed for twenty years, customer services were instead composing a letter rejecting my claim. They wanted me to enjoy food that was as natural as possible and free from any unnecessary additives and preservatives, they said, and, as a result, some of their foods might have a shorter life than some of their competitors' products. They were sorry I had been disappointed and hoped I would continue to shop at M&S with confidence etc etc. I shook the envelope after removal of the letter but nothing dropped out: not even a chocolate peanut.

I gave judgment against myself. A softer centred judge might well have awarded me the retail price of the chocs but a hard centred judge such as the one I saw in my mirror was not persuaded that two and half months was unreasonable.

What's the big deal?

This is all about the cost of a case on the small claims track. If you are making or defending the claim and you lose, there is a ceiling on what you will have to pay to the winner for their expenses. For a start, where the winner used a lawyer (whether for advice and help in preparing for court or just for appearing at the hearing or both) you won't have to make any contribution towards that lawyer's fees. Those fees have to be borne by the winner out of their own pocket. Apart from one ruddy great big exception (see below), there are two modest exceptions to this. If the winner made a claim for an injunction (no drum practise in the flat above after 10.30pm) or for specific performance (my landlord to be compelled to eradicate dry rot in the main bedroom) he can recover from the loser up to £260 for the cost of obtaining legal advice and assistance on the case. And if the winner made the claim and had a lawyer issue the claim form for them, then there is a standard allowance which the loser will almost invariably have to pay which takes some account of what the lawyer would have charged. This allowance depends on the amount claimed and is usually between £50 and £100 (show me a lawyer who will charge no more than £100 and I'll show you a happy corpse). Should you lose but for less than the amount which had been claimed, it would be reasonable to ask the judge to keep this allowance down to the amount applicable to the award rather than the higher figure claimed. Then the loser can seek payment of other expenses though, mostly with maximum sums:

- Any court fees paid by the winner (for a winning claimant who has not enjoyed remission from fees, these would be the commencement fee when you kicked off the claim and a hearing fee: the so-called allocation fee has now been abolished) - see chapter 13 for details of these fees and the system for remitting (excusing) litigants from having to pay court fees.

- Travelling expenses and expenses in "staying away from home" so as to enable court attendance for the winner and any witnesses who have attended court with them (noisy overnight box room and a sandwich at *The Wig and Duck* might get through with a double bedroom at *The Dorchester* and a Full English being more problematic). No maximum but the expenses must have been reasonably incurred. Don't get too panicky here as expenses tend in the majority of cases to stay under £100. Nevertheless, there is potential in some cases for the bill to be quite substantial. The court will direct the hearing to take place at the most convenient venue and the number of witnesses to be called by each side and where they live or carry on business will be highly relevant. If you live on the Isle of Wight and the other side have three witnesses all of whom come from Cumbria it might be worth agreeing to a hearing in Carlisle unless you are as sure as eggs that you are going to win so won't be saddled with having to pay one new pence by way of travelling or accommodation expenses. It may be productive to challenge such expenses claimed on the grounds that they are unreasonable and/or that one or more of the witnesses were unnecessary and/or that you were not alerted by the other side before the hearing that a particular witness was to be relied on. Further, it is always prudent when having sight of copies of the other side's witness statements in advance of the hearing to consider agreeing one or more of those statements and letting the other side know that you do agree so that the agreed witnesses are not dragged along to court. You won't want to agree the statement of a witness where you dispute the truth or accuracy of something in their statement which is material to the issues in the case. You will want the witness at court so that you can cross-examine them and the judge can question them too.

- Loss of earnings for attending at court or "staying away from home" so as to enable a court attendance for the winner and any witnesses who have attended court with them at the rate of £95 each per day (increased from £90 in April 2015). If time off in lieu of holiday has been taken so that there is no financial loss but loss of holiday, the same allowance applies. Take home pay only will be reckoned and the employed and self-employed can qualify because they both (hopefully) "earn". The comments above on challenges to travelling and accommodation expenses and how to try and avoid exposure to liability for them equally apply.
- Experts' fees with a maximum of £750 per expert. The majority of small claims do not involve an expert's report. Sometimes, though, the court will give permission for an expert's report to be obtained (see below).

The ruddy great big exception

Here it comes. It's the major exception to the rule that the loser is protected by the limits on what they have to pay in respect of the winner's expenses. Where the judge decides that the loser has behaved unreasonably then the judge can order the loser to pay the winner expenses which fall into the categories summarised above but uncapped PLUS any other reasonable expenses on the case that the winner has incurred (for example, on postage, telephone calls and stationery used for the case) PLUS an allowance to a litigant who has conducted the whole or any part of the case without a lawyer at the rate of £19 per hour (up from £18 since April 2015) for the time they have been personally occupied on the case or an hourly sum to compensate for the actual earnings they have lost if more than £19 per hour (see chapter 26). And it's getting potentially worse. If the winner has been represented by a lawyer then the unreasonable loser could have to compensate the winner for the lawyer's fees or part of them. Big Businesses may well be represented by a lawyer and defend the case not because it is financially viable to do so but because they do not wish to be regarded by the social media community as a soft touch and thereby vulnerable to those claimants who are out to make a fast buck.

What's unreasonable behaviour?

Very good question, There's no definition of it. Like that elephant, it's hard to describe but you know it when you see it - and so does the judge. It could be doing everything required to defend the case and then failing to turn up for the final hearing. Telling lots of small whoppers or a couple of sizeable ones could amount to unreasonable behaviour. The judge will be used to a bit of lying by one of the litigants (sometimes both!) in a high proportion of cases so it would probably take some serious stuff before they were prepared to remove costs protection on the basis of unreasonableness. Behaviour both before and after a claim has been started can be reckoned. Take a claimant who alleges he was sold substandard goods but makes no contact with the seller and simply launches a court claim without any warning. Then when the seller puts in a defence saying they need an opportunity to examine the goods so that they can decide on their stance, the claimant denies them that opportunity. Finally, the judge concludes that the goods were up to standard when sold but were damaged when the claimant threw them at his wife the next night. In my book, that's unreasonable behaviour.

Staying small

There's nothing to stop you gaining the benefits of the small claims track by limiting a claim to £10,000 even though it is actually worth more. This would involve giving up the chance of recovering the excess over £10,000 in return for lower court fees, an earlier hearing, the more informal procedure and the normal shield against a swingeing bill for the other side's costs if you lose. A calculated decision has to be made.

In assessing whether the claim goes over £10,000, you disregard any interest sought, any costs you intend to seek including the court fee for starting the case - and any undisputed amount. So, for example, if the claim is for repayment of a loan made of £25,000 and in their defence the other side admits they owe you £17,000 but deny the rest, the claim should go onto the small claims track because the amount in dispute is only £8,000.

You won't normally be allowed onto the small claims track where the hearing is likely to take longer than one day - that generally means five hours of hearing time - or one side is alleging dishonesty against the other side and the allegation is disputed. Other types of claim which are excluded from the small claims track are those for personal injuries over £1,000 (that's compensation for pain and suffering and loss of amenity and other compensation for say vehicle repairs, damaged clothing and loss of earnings can be asked for on top - the chances are that this will be increased to £5,000 in the foreseeable future as part of the war against whiplash victims) and sometimes for housing repairs involving over £1,000.

Now to what could be your saving grace. The court has a discretion to allocate a claim involving more than £10,000 to the small claims track whether or not the parties consent. It is not something which is often done and the power to do it is not always in the forefront of judges' minds but the power is there. You might be able to persuade a judge to exercise the power where, for example, both sides are litigants in person, the case is uncomplicated, the hearing will take less than one day and the judge is in a good mood.

You will get an opportunity to make written representations about whether a case should be allocated to the small claims track when you complete a form called a *directions questionnaire*. This will be sent out for completion (to litigants in person but lawyers for the parties have to download their copies) if and when a defence is put in. It solicits information to enable the court to ensure the case is allocated to the appropriate track and that it is not listed for hearing on your silver wedding anniversary when you are due to be baking on a Mediterranean beach.

The wobbles

You've made or defended a claim and notice of the hearing arrives. The hearing is 500 miles away or you have a panic attack - or both. Is there an alternative to throwing in the towel to avoid the hassle of a long return journey or palpitations? Yes. You can approach the other side and ask whether they would agree to dispense with an oral hearing and, if they do, write to the court with a copy of their letter of agreement and a request that a judge decides the case on the papers in the absence of the parties. The other side would be daft to agree because they should realise you might capitulate if they disagree and the court might well refuse the request. But you can always try.

And without the permission of anyone you can request the court in writing to decide the case in your absence but it must receive the request at least seven days before the hearing date. Also, you must have told the other side that you will be absent and sent them copies of your statements and any other documents at least seven days before the hearing date.

"Pursuant to rule 27.9 of the Civil Procedure Rules 1998, I hereby give notice that I will not attend the hearing of this case. I request that the Judge please decide it in my absence taking into account the statements of evidence and other documents I have already lodged with the court. I confirm that I have given the other party notice of my intended absence and sent them copies of my statements and other documents so that they will have received them at least seven days before the hearing date".

Absence is by no means the best way of dealing with the case and may put you at a disadvantage. You will not be present to answer what your opponent in attendance and their witnesses have to say and personal representations and evidence have the potential to be a million times more powerful than the written word. However, if a personal attendance is not economically viable - and commercial organisations sometimes take this view - or is just too much trouble or panic has set in, this may be the answer for you.

Experts

An expert is someone who tells you what you already knew but in words you cannot understand. That tends to be the general view held by judges. The trend is to keep an expert out of a case if at all possible but sometimes you just can't do without one. The judge knows the law but they may not be too hot on whether the reconditioned engine caused the car to conk out on the M25 1,000 miles after it had been fitted or whether the windows fell out because of subsidence or the stupidity of the builder. In that sort of situation the judge might be assisted by the opinion of someone who is qualified in the discipline concerned like a vehicular mechanical engineer or a building surveyor. The expert does not decide the case and the judge is quite entitled to form the view that the expert is wrong if factual evidence in the case strongly points in an opposite direction. An expert can be relied on in small claims just as in the bigger cases but the court's permission to take advantage of an expert's report must be obtained. The time to ask for that permission is usually in the directions questionnaire we have already met which you will be asked to complete once a defence has been sent to the court. It is rare for an expert to give live evidence in a small claim. What the expert has to say will be said in a written report. The court frequently directs that an expert be allowed but that a single expert be used who is jointly instructed by both sides. That almost invariably means that both sides will have an input in what the expert is told about the case - one side should take the lead in drafting a letter of instructions to the expert which should be accompanied by copies of all documents including the claim form and particulars of claim and the defence (sometimes witness statements as well) and then send it to the other side to approve and if there is any dispute about what should go into or with the letter then the court would have to be asked to resolve it - and will usually be required to shell out for the expert's fees and expenses up front on a 50-50 basis. The court will probably order the losing party to reimburse the winning party for the share they have borne.

Experts can be expensive and, if at all possible, the fee paid to them should not exceed the £750 which the loser can be ordered to pay to the winner for an expert's report (see above) or the parties to the case or one of them will find themselves having to meet the excess. The court does have the power to impose a limit on the amount of the expert's fee and often does so when giving the necessary permission for the expert to be used. Anecdotal evidence suggests that experts' fees range from £32 to £500 an hour with an average of £177. You may have to haggle over the fee. Don't be afraid to do that. The volume of work for experts has dropped significantly in the last couple of years. You can always remind them of the fee they would be paid if they were producing a report in a legal aid case: £85 for a housing repair surveyor (£115 if London based), £64 for an accountant and £72 for a cell telephone site analyst or telecoms expert. This might lead to a reduction in what they were asking or an invitation for you to take a one-way standing room only trip to Hell.

It's risky to pay out for an expert's report before the court has given permission for an expert to be relied on. The reason is that the court might well order that a single expert jointly instructed by the parties be used even though you had already obtained your own report. Then the cost of your early report would be money down the drain.

> *"But I got this builder bloke in and he told me that Whitewash had really cocked up the job and he said he'd give me a report I could take to court and he also said that he would come in and do the job for half the price Whitewash had ripped me off for."*

That sort of report would be as good as a chocolate teapot. An expert's report must be independent and the expert's overriding duty is to the court and not to the person who is paying their charges. If the expert has a vested interest in the outcome of the case - for example, they will get a job from you if the case goes your way - then the expert lacks independence and relying on them could severely prejudice your case.

The formalities that have to be observed in relation to the contents of the expert's report and certain other matters which apply to the bigger cases do not apply to small claims. Nevertheless, you don't want the report typed out on the back of a bus ticket and it's useful even in a small claim for the expert to confirm that they understand their duty to the court and that they have complied with that duty and also to give details of their qualifications.

Because an expert will not normally attend the actual small claims hearing, it is crucial that if they have failed to deal with a particular point they were asked to address, there is some ambiguity in the report or a question screams out to be answered, that you put written questions to the expert and ask that they answer them by a particular date: say by 14 days from receipt. You should send a copy of the questions to the other side where the report is from an expert they have alone instructed or the expert has been jointly instructed. Beware. This may generate a fee for replying so be selective in what you ask.

Preparing for the hearing

Before the hearing the court will probably have required each side to send to the court and each other statements of the evidence of themselves and their other witnesses and copies of any documents they will be relying on. Ensure that is done by the deadline set. In the bigger cases, statements are exchanged: swapped. That way neither side gains an advantage over the other by seeing their statements before they have parted with their own. In small claims, exchange is unusual so there may not be any merit in getting your statements in before those of the opposition. You could legitimately hang fire in the hope that you get to see the opposition statements first so long as you beat the deadline but it's not a good idea to blatantly comment on their statements in your own. Incidentally, as a party to the case, you are your own witness so don't answer the questions in the directions questionnaire about how many witnesses you have with 'none' unless you intend to be mute at the hearing. In chapter 14 we look at how a witness statement should read.

The claim will be decided on the evidence and the evidence comes from you and your witnesses. In so far as there is a dispute between you and the other side about what was or was not said and what did or did not happen, anyone who can back up your account or can deal with some relevant event at which you were not present, is a potential witness and you should consider relying on them. Obviously you don't want a busload of witnesses or the hearing might never end. You need to be selective about this too. The directions questionnaire will ask you to state how many witnesses you will be relying on. Whenever I saw an answer in a small claims questionnaire that more than say four witnesses were to be used, I had a pretty good idea that the party was "having a laugh". Not only will each witness in addition to you need to make a written statement but they will need to come to court if any real weight is to be placed on what they say unless the other side is prepared to agree their statement in advance. That's so they can be questioned by the other side and the judge. Should you drag a witness to court who had nothing of relevance to say and win, the judge will probably refuse to order the other side to pay that witness's expenses. Ouch.

If you follow the tips at chapter 17, your chances of winning should be enhanced. Be ready though for the judge to seize the case by the scruff of the neck, suspend the court niceties and weigh in at an early stage. Each judge has their own way of conducting a small claim hearing but the majority will be interventionist and will get to the root of the dispute pretty quickly so that you will be in no doubt what they think may be the strengths and weaknesses of each side's case. Concentrate on any indication the judge gives to you about any aspects of your case which concern them and attempt to persuade.

Mediation

You can take advantage of the court's own mediation scheme for most small claims which you will be told about if and when a case becomes defended. You cannot be forced into it but the number of cases which are settled through the scheme is enormously high. Trained mediators will speak to each side separately and usually by telephone to sound them out about a compromise. What is said in the course of mediation will not reach the ears of the judge and a willingness to use the scheme will not be construed as any sort of acceptance that you are legally liable to your opponent. The service is free.

Small intellect

Copyright claims ("I took those snaps of you naked on Brighton Beach and own the copyright in them and you've put them up on the internet without my permission"), trade mark claims ("My trade mark is registered here and the EEC and you have been illegally using it") and passing off claims ("I've been running *The Clive Troublesore Café* and you've stolen half my business by opening up *The Clive Troublesoretothesky Cafe* and the public reckon it's my joint") are specialised intellectual property claims. There's a court dedicated to them in which the judges have expertise in this area of the law. It's the Intellectual Property Enterprise Court at The Rolls Building, 7 Rolls Building, Fetter Lane, London EC4A 1NL. The good news is that it has its own small claims track which operates in a similar way to the general small claims regime in the county court for claims of up to £10,000. The same costs protection applies as does the free court service mediation scheme. A claim intended to be dealt with in the Enterprise Court should be started at The Rolls Building from which a guidance booklet is available. The small claims though are actually heard at The Strand's Royal Courts of Justice where the judges are treated as sitting in the Croydon District Registry of the High Court. Now should you think that sounds bonkers, you would be right. It is bonkers and it has happened to get over a legislative drafting cock up but that's another story.

Chapter 19

The Tomlin Order

Kissing and making up after proceedings started

The *Tomlin Order* is a very fine order indeed. Where litigants have reached a compromise agreement after a court case has been started, they can jointly ask the court to make this order which records the terms of the agreement and halts the case so that the agreement can be implemented. At the same time it gives the litigants permission to return to court to enforce any of those terms should one of them fail to do what they agreed to do. Those terms sometimes go beyond what the court would have the jurisdiction to direct if it was deciding the case although the terms should not be remote from the subject matter of the case as there could then be difficulty in getting the court to enforce them should default occur.

So what's the big appeal of it? It doesn't constitute a judgment and so is not registrable in the Register of Judgments, Orders and Fines (see chapter 20) but it commits the litigants to keep to the agreement and formally sets out all its details. Not a black mark against the debtor's credit record and protection for the creditor as he can obtain a judgment based on the broken agreement should the debtor default. The *Tomlin Order* can be used to replace a judgment which has already been entered (if the judge who considers it is prepared to allow it to go through) or, and this is more common, before any judgment has been obtained.

Pick and Mix the paragraphs which might be suitable for your very own *Tomlin Order*. Here goes.

Case No 97P0000678

IN THE COUNTY COURT

SITTING AT PEARDROP

BETWEEN

WHITEWASH LTD Claimant

- and -

CLIVE TROUBLESORE Defendant

UPON the parties having reached terms of compromise

IT IS ORDERED BY CONSENT that-

1. Judgment for the claimant entered on 14th May 2016 be set aside.

2. The claim be stayed on the terms set out in the schedule to this order save and except that there be permission to the parties to apply for the purpose of enforcing any of such terms.

The schedule

1. The defendant will pay to the claimant the sum of £4,500 to the credit of the claimant's account numbered 1098667 with Comic Bank plc sort code 14-09-06 by 4 pm on 14th July 2016.

or

1. The defendant will pay to the claimant the sum of £4,500 by instalments of £500 per calendar month payable calendar monthly on the first day of each month with the first instalment being made on 1 July 2016 (time being of the essence) to the credit of the claimant's account numbered 1098667 with Comic Bank plc sort code 14-09-06 and in the event of default in the payment of any one instalment on the due date then the full outstanding balance shall become immediately due to the claimant who shall be entitled to the entry of judgment against the defendant for such outstanding balance together with interest thereon from the date of the default until the date of judgment at the rate of 8% per annum.

2. The defendant will deliver to the claimant at its head office 65 Wayne Rooney miniatures (being part of the goods the subject of the claim) during normal business hours in the same condition as when sold and delivered to the defendant by 4 pm on 14th July 2016.

3. The claimant will send the defendant a VAT credit note for the sum of £750 plus VAT within 7 days of the date of the discharge by the defendant of his liability under paragraph 1 above.

4. The defendant will carry out the works of repair to the claimant's head office without payment in accordance with the specifications contained in the letter from the claimant to the defendant dated 11th June 2016 to a satisfactory standard and using good materials by 14th September 2016.

5. The claimant will accept the sum of £4,500 and the carrying out of the works referred to in paragraph 4 above in full and final settlement of its claim and costs.

6. The defendant withdraws any claims he has or may have against the claimant arising out of the sale of the goods the subject of these proceedings.

7. The claimant and defendant agree that the terms of this agreement shall be confidential and that they will not publish or otherwise disclose them to any other persons and through any medium whatsoever and, for the avoidance of any doubt, including radio, television, internet and social network sites save and except as may be required by law and to professional advisers in connection with satisfying legal requirements.

We hereby consent to this order

(signed) Arthur B Clematis (signed) C Troublesore

On behalf of the Claimant Defendant Dated 7 July 2016

Part 6

JUDGMENT HAS BEEN GIVEN

Chapter 20

The Register Of Judgments

The ugly face of proceedings

How do you avoid being sued? Stay at home, do not hang out of the window, feed the dog, eschew broadcasts and music, speak to nobody and never use the internet. If sued, how do you avoid a judgment being recorded against you in the Register of Judgments, Orders and Fines? That's more difficult.

The Register is run by Registry Trust Ltd and onto it go details of the majority of judgments that are given in the civil courts for the payment of money. Note, only money - so if the court has ordered you to take down an extension because it is partially encroaching on your neighbour's land, that won't be recorded. The register is checked out by would be creditors who are contemplating lending you money or extending you credit, and by wise would be claimants who have a good case against you but no wish to join a queue of creditors who have already obtained a civil court judgment against you but 'aint been paid. Inevitably, details of registered judgments are collected by the credit reference agencies. The longer term consequences of having a judgment recorded there can be more catastrophic than the judgment itself. For example, a business may find itself unable to obtain credit from suppliers and thereby strangled and an individual may be refused a mortgage loan all because there is a solitary judgment of which details are stained against their name on the register.

The job of sending details to Registry Trust of each judgment eligible for registration falls to staff at the court which gave the particular judgment. Human error leads to ineligible judgments being registered and eligible judgments not being registered. When the former occurs, the offending court should be told to cancel the registration immediately.

Registration Escapees

Let's have a look at some of the judgments which should not be registered.

- A judgment in family proceedings such as an order that you pay maintenance to your former spouse or partner or make a lump sum payment to them.
- A judgment where the hearing was contested. This is the Big One. If you put in a defence to the claim which led to the judgment, you escape its registration. It matters not that the defence was

spurious, farcical or the biggest load of nonsense ever to be committed to a piece of paper, or all three. It matters not that you failed to turn up at court when the case was heard. If a defence had gone in, then for these purposes the hearing was contested. In fact, it is not unknown for a defendant to put in a defence with no intention whatsoever of appearing at any hearing but simply to escape the registration of the judgment which they know will follow. But hold on to the champers. The court is required to register the judgment, though it was not previously registrable because of the contest, should your creditor apply for an order that the judgment be paid by instalments and such an order be made; you apply yourself for an instalment order; or your creditor takes certain steps to enforce the judgment.

- A judgment for you to pay money in a claim involving arrears of mortgage payments or rent - you may well have been ordered to give up possession at the same hearing - unless and until your mortgage lender or landlord takes a step to enforce the judgment.

Cancellation or satisfaction

If the judgment has been rightly recorded in the register then it stays put for six years from the date of the judgment (but not six years from the date of the registration which could be some time later). However, the registration will be cancelled should the judgment be set aside. Strictly speaking, judgments should only be set aside in limited situations (see chapter 16). Nevertheless, it is common for a debtor with a judgment against them to enter into an agreement with their creditor which provides for the judgment to be set aside so that hopefully its registration can be cancelled. The dialogue goes something like this.

Debtor: "You reptile. You are killing my business. May you rot in hell."

Creditor: " I'm not being spoken to like that. You've had the goods and sold them on and not paid me a penny. You are a despicable rogue."

Debtor: "Come on, angel face. Be reasonable. Tell you what, if my business goes down the pan, you'll get nothing. The judgment's for six grand. I'll sell the mother-in-law and borrow a few quid. I can come up with three grand in a fortnight. Accept that. I'll pay the money to my solicitor and he'll undertake to pay it over to you the moment the court makes an order setting aside the judgment and staying the claim on terms that I'll pay you the three grand and you'll accept it in full and final settlement of the claim and costs. I think they call it a Tommy Order or something.Have we got a deal. And if you happen to be my way over the weekend, pop in for a beer. It would be good to catch up."

So the creditor collects £3,000 and the debtor gets rid of the judgment and its registration. Everyone is happy - well almost. Some judges will go along with that sort of arrangement because there is some commercial sense to it in that it has the blessing of the creditor and it leads to the creditor collecting a substantial part of what they were owned when there was a real risk they might have had to whistle for the lot. Some judges may refuse to set the judgment aside even though the creditor will not enforce payment of what is unpaid because the strict criteria for setting aside a judgment have not been met.

Now there is a way of guaranteeing the cancellation of the registration. That's to pay the judgment in full. Novel, eh?! Time is of the essence. No guarantee here unless you pay within one month of the date of the judgment. Once the court has evidence of settlement in time, it will have the registration cancelled. However, this is not the same as the judgment being set aside. Setting aside means the judgment never existed. Cancellation where it has been paid off within one month means it existed but the world may never find out about it though if you were to truthfully answer certain questions put to you by a lie detector operator on the subject of your financial history you might find yourself having to cough it!

For debtors who settle a judgment after one month, there is a consolation prize. On the register, it will be noted by the entry relating to the judgment that it has been satisfied. At least anyone then searching the register will know that you are only 50% unreliable. You will need to apply to the court for a 'certificate of satisfaction' and, if you can, accompany the application with evidence that you have settled. Where you have no satisfactory evidence that you can produce in your possession, you should ask the creditor to confirm settlement. If the creditor returns your request torn into 1,006 pieces and then stapled, the court will write to the creditor and ask them to confirm within one month that you have settled and, when that meets with silence, the court will treat the judgment as having been satisfied.

"I've seen that face before"

It has occurred to some debtors who dwell within the register that a change of name could be their salvation. That does not overcome the problem that their address will still be blacklisted with credit reference agencies. Their greater problem is that even if they change their name and move, any dishonest information given to a prospective credit provider would probably earn them a charge of obtaining or attempting to obtain by deception. Mr Troublesore may now call himself Lord Lucan but he is still the subject of a county court judgment entered against him in Macclesfield County Court in 2013 for goods sold and delivered.

Tommy Order

Our rather dodgy debtor who we just met negotiating a deal to pay off his creditor £3,000 instead of £6,000 referred to a Tommy Order. There's no such thing though he was close. It's called a *Tomlin Order*. It's a gem (see chapter 19).

Credit repair services

Don't waste money on paying a firm to repair your credit by procuring the setting aside of a registered judgment. What they can do, you can do. They don't have a direct line to the judge. Applications to set aside judgments which have been prepared by a credit repair company can often be spotted in the dark. Some I have seen rely as grounds for setting aside that the defendant never received the claim form or, if he did, he was on holiday at the time and the dog ate it so that it was not available when he returned and that in any event he was too distressed to read any official documents that might have been delivered because his wife had just left him and that he may have just moved to another address and that he does not owe the claimant any money and he has never heard of the claimant and if he has heard of the claimant he demands a copy of any agreement he allegedly signed and that he reserves the right to contend that the claimant's charges are unfair and should be reduced. I exaggerate but only a bit.

Chapter 21

Challenging The Judge's Decision

After court

It is fashionable to complain about the judge after the hearing to the Judicial Conduct Investigations Office. No, I won't give you their address. You have three months from the date on which the judge allegedly transgressed to make the complaint although this time limit can be extended in exceptional circumstances. If you are saying that the judge has got it wrong then that's not a situation for complaint but for appeal to a more senior judge. The complaint route is often seen by the losing litigant as a means of reeking revenge or a cathartic experience after the shock of the case going against them. It is sometimes even threatened during the actual hearing in an attempt to put pressure on the judge to avoid trouble by finding in favour of the would-be complainant. Court staff are required to plaster waiting room walls with posters about how to make a complaint against the judge. One of my former colleagues was fond of ripping them down.

OK, so you think I've had a catalogue of complaints about me.

Complaints, I've had a few

But then again, too few to mention

I said what I had to say and saw it through without exemption

I judged each legal case, each stage along the byway

And more, much more than this, I did it my way

My first experience of a seriously unhappy litigant was at Guildford county court in the 1990s after I decided that a young motorist had negligently caused damage to the claimant's car in a road accident and so had to compensate him. He was the last to leave the court- always an ominous sign when the loser holds back and in due course I began to insist that everyone left together - and, as he departed, he called me a "four-eyed c..t" which deserved one month inside for contempt but with no usher or other member of court staff about - and, yes, I was and am bespectacled but, no, to the other thing - I had to let him go on his way.

At around the same time at Kingston-upon-Thames county court I heard a small claim in favour of the claimant dating agency. It had sued their female client for the cost of a dinner they had promoted and she had attended in the hope that it would lead to her betrothal. Her case was that the concert hall conductor she had expected to be at her side for the first course turned out to be an electric organist and the childless male (she had insisted on no offspring) substituted for consumption of the main course turned out to be the father of two children. She left the dessert unfinished and made her escape. Thereafter, she refused to pay on the ground of breach of contract and misrepresentation. My judgment in favour of the dating agency reduced her to a weeping state and so I exited the courtroom when she showed no sign of voluntarily removing herself. I took sanctity in a neighbouring courtroom of a free colleague along the corridor. As I was relating to him the unusual facts of the case I had just tried, the losing lady burst in and went to claw me with her very long talons. My colleague gallantly intervened and the lady was taken away with his assistance and that of some court staff who were hastily summoned. I survived intact.

In 2007 a litigant appeared before me claiming against the Courts Service certain losses he alleged he had suffered arising out of the misaddressing of communications relating to the hearing of an appeal he had launched against his conviction for a parking offence. You may have to read that again! The Courts Service was applying for the claim to be struck out. The claim was hopeless and the claimant sensed that the hearing was going against him. As I embarked on my judgment, explaining why the claim would have to be struck out, the claimant took to repeatedly banging on the desk at which he was seated. I warned him that I would be obliged to expel him from the hearing if he did not desist. He carried on. I expelled him. Subsequently, he complained about my conduct to the Office for Judicial Complaints (the forerunner of the Judicial Conduct Investigations Office). The complaint was thrown out. The claimant's response was to open a website partially dedicated to me. In the ordinary course of events I would have been flattered but not so in this instance because the site carried a photograph of a noose and promised that further photographs would follow. This suggested to me that he might have plans to secure my decapitation.

I was advised by the Judicial Office which looks after judges' welfare that if closure of the website was procured, this could backfire and fuel the claimant to go onto bigger and better things. Instead, a police officer was despatched to visit the claimant and warn him off. He was belligerent to the officer and promptly posted an update on the site to the effect that I had taken fright and involved the police. In due course and with my head still in position and my car tyres intact, the site disappeared. The man's conduct was seriously contemptuous and, on reflection, I believe it was a mistake to let him off the hook.

Later that year, a defendant who lost his case took his grievance towards me to the Office for Judicial Complaints. He suggested, among other things, that I had "stared down at his desk as if trying to conceal his impatience"; "had the characteristic of flicking his right hand as if flicking away an irritant"; and treated the claimants more favourably than him as exemplified by leaning encouragingly towards them and thereby increasing his sense of isolation. All these complaints were rejected though I now think twice before blinking lest this be construed as a wink at one of the parties and on no account will I scratch my ear for this could be taken as a secret sign to someone at the bus stop opposite the court that I am bored stiff and could do with a coffee.

At the start of 2011 a new complainant told the Office for Judicial Complaints that his mouth had dried up when appearing before me and when he asked for some water I refused point blank to give him some despite having a carafe (of the finest Thames non-drinking water) on my desk. There was some alleged rudeness thrown in. The complaints were rejected. As to the water deprivation, it was concluded that the complaint was without substance (!) or, even if substantiated, would not require any disciplinary action to be taken. In fact, I have never denied a request for water if there were water and a free glass available. In this instance, there was just my own glass and when there was a break in the hearing almost immediately after the water request, I asked my usher to fetch some water for the dry throated litigant.

Later in 2011 the Office of Judicial Complaints opened a letter from a claimant who was a former solicitors' managing clerk and whose case I had struck out at an early stage of its life on the ground that it had no real prospect of success. "Ethel, it's another one against Gold." "What's he done this time, Ron? Stared out of the window?" Not quite. This time I had allegedly told the complainant to sit down and keep quiet or I would otherwise have him removed from the court. He had also, he maintained, made five applications to the court to be heard and been refused by other judges and so "I can only assume that as colleagues of Judge Gold they are also on the square so they cannot contradict him no matter how wrong they know him to be." I have never been "on the square" - not even Albert's. This particular complainant had also taken to writing to me at court in abusive terms wondering how I could look at myself in the mirror. I agree this can be an uncomfortable experience. In the event, the complaint about my behaviour had no merit: the man had been represented by a barrister at the hearing before me who spoke on his behalf and the occasion did not call for any oral evidence or representations from the complainant. Because the complaint had come 18 months after the hearing in question, it was too late. In relation to the suggestion that I had wrongly struck out the claim, the man's application for permission to appeal was ultimately refused by a circuit judge.

Well, those are the complaints I can remember. That's probably a below-average number for a career spanning over 20 years. All judges including myself strive to give a fair hearing to every litigant and to treat them with courtesy and respect but pressure of court business does mean there may be a limit imposed on how long they can be given to state their case. And it does mean that very often they have to be curtailed and to this they do not always take kindly. The most innocuous gesture or judicial attempt to lighten the mood can be taken the wrong way and become a festering wound when a decision goes against the party to whom it was directed. Enter the Judicial Conduct Investigations Office.

Appealing

So what about an appeal then? That's certainly a more constructive approach to attempting to right what you see as a wrong. However, if for whatever reason you were absent from the hearing at which the decision about which you are aggrieved was made then the appropriate course is almost invariably to apply for the decision to be set aside and for a rehearing. This application would go to the same level of judge who made the decision.

The appeal route is for when you or your legal representative or both of you were present at the original hearing and either you reckon the judge made an error or some new evidence has come your way since the hearing which ought to result in a different outcome. The appeal would go to a superior judge.

It should be appreciated that you cannot appeal merely because you are cheesed off at the judge's decision. You will need to establish that they made a mistake of law: in deciding on the facts (what actually happened) or in exercising their discretion, they took into account something they should have disregarded, failed to take into account something they should have regarded or that they were plainly wrong (a decision only a crackpot would have made); the decision was clearly unjust because of a serious procedural or other irregularity; or because of fresh evidence you have obtained since the original decision, it would be unjust to allow it to stand (although it's unlikely you would succeed on this last ground unless you could not have reasonably obtained this evidence earlier, it is apparently credible and it would probably change the result).

Now that may all sound a bit complicated but it boils down to this. A mistake of law by the original judge is your best bet. When it comes to trying to show that the judge was wrong on their decision on the facts (what actually happened), you will have a more difficult task. The judge would have seen and heard the parties and their witnesses and so was in a better position than the appeal judge to assess their credibility. Decisions made by a judge when exercising their discretion such as who should pay the costs of a case and how much they should pay are notoriously difficult to successfully appeal as are case management decisions made as a case is being prepared for a contested trial.

You want to know how many times I have been successfully appealed? Mind your own business!

Permission to appeal

In three instances you don't need anyone's permission to appeal. Two of them are so remote, I won't bore you with them. The third I will bore you with. That's when a civil judge has sent you to prison (say for contempt of court). Otherwise, there can't be an appeal without permission so we aren't into parking ticket adjudicator type territory here. And from whom do you obtain permission? From the judge who made the decision you hate! Really. You wind them up when they have completed announcing their decision and say "I ask for permission to appeal" and go on to explain why (and be in no doubt, a losing advocate or party can assuage some of the anger they feel at defeat by attempting to needle the judge by criticism of their performance). The high chance is that the judge will refuse permission on the ground that an appeal would have no real prospect of success. The sort of exceptional situation in which the judge might grant permission is where the case has involved a novel or difficult point of law and they believe an appeal court might well reach a contrary decision. Where you are refused permission, the judge must tell you to which superior judge you can renew your permission request and give you certain other information which may appear in their written order you will receive after the hearing.

It is conceivable you want time to reflect on whether to try to appeal or to take legal advice about it. Should that be the position, you can ask the judge to adjourn the hearing so you can do so and then apply for permission to appeal next time. Not a brilliant idea to follow this course because it could increase your liability for the winning litigant's costs on a further outing. The better course is usually to write off the prospect of getting permission from the judge you wish to appeal and seek permission subsequently from an appeal judge. In the county court you would usually appeal from a district judge to a circuit judge (possibly in the same court building) unless you were involved in an insolvency case when the appeal would be to a High Court judge. An appeal from a circuit judge in the county court would also usually go to a High Court judge. Appeals from decisions on final hearings from circuit and district judges sometimes go straight to the Court of Appeal.

For the application for permission to the appeal judge, you have to put in a notice of appeal and generally do so within three weeks of the decision you hate. If you are late, you can ask for an extension of time for applying for permission. Should the original judge have failed to give you the required information when refusing you permission to appeal that might be a good reason for a late permission application to the appeal judge. The permission application is incorporated within the notice of appeal. The appeal judge will often decide whether or not to grant permission on the papers and so without a hearing. If you are refused permission on the papers you can insist on an oral hearing at which your application for permission is reconsidered except in some situations where the application is considered to be totally without merit (a complete waste of time).

Judgment transcript, please

It is almost certain that a transcript of the judgment you are attacking - the judge's summary of the case and the reasons they gave for their decision - will be required by the higher court when considering whether to grant you permission to appeal or when considering the appeal after giving permission. Sometimes, the judge will have supplied a copy of the judgment. That will suffice. Otherwise, the judge's words when giving the judgment which will have been recorded in court will need to be transcribed and that costs money. You would have to request the transcript through the office of the hearing centre where the decision under challenge was made. This will lead to a quote. You can't afford to pay? The court can order that the transcript of the judgment - and any part of the evidence given before the judgment - should be paid for out of public funds provided you qualify for fee remission or you are in such poor financial circumstances that the cost would be an excessive burden to you, plus that it is satisfied it is necessary in the interests of justice for the transcript to be obtained. If you are having an emotional discussion with a court official about whether this power really does exist, say "Civil Procedure Rules 1998 rule 52.5A, mate." If you have already put in your notice of appeal when you realise that the transcript is wanted then complete form EX105 which may be required of you anyway.

Anecdotal evidence suggests that permission to appeal within the county court is granted in around one case in every four and that around one half of appeals are then upheld. Appeals to the Court of Appeal succeed in around one-half of those cases in which permission has been granted.

Grounds of appeal

The notice of appeal will have to set out the grounds of appeal.

1. The Learned Judge wrongly refused my request for him to recuse himself from trying the claim which I had made on the ground that he was biased or gave the appearance of bias in that the claim was against a hotel at which, over the years, he and his wife had holidayed.

2. The Learned Judge closed his eyes and emitted a snoring noise during material parts of my evidence leading me to conclude that he was asleep or not paying any or sufficient attention to the evidence.

3. The Learned Judge wrongly refused to adjourn the trial so that I could take steps to compel the attendance of a material and necessary witness whose evidence was challenged by the defendant and who had failed to attend voluntarily notwithstanding his promise to me to be present.

Anything to lose by appealing? There's a court fee to be paid when you put in the notice of appeal (whether or not it incorporates an application for permission to appeal): in the county court that's £120 in a small claims case and £140 in any other, and in the High Court the fee is £240. An unsuccessful appeal is likely to increase the bill you have to face. Apart from what you shell out on appealing, you will probably have to pay the other litigant's expenses on resisting the appeal (which could be substantial if they took in a lawyer) and even an unsuccessful application for permission to appeal could add to your bill where it has led to an oral hearing. Any exception to this rule? Of course! The restriction on an order for costs against the loser of a small claim (see chapter 18) is replicated on an appeal (and application for permission to appeal). This means that unless the court finds that the loser has behaved unreasonably (and there has to be something more than just losing again) the appeal bill will effectively be limited to the other litigant's travelling expenses to and from court plus loss of earnings capped at £95 per day.

Some use the appeal route as a device to put off the evil day - the day they have to stump up what they have been ordered to pay to the winner - though they realise they have no prospect of an appeal succeeding, let alone procuring permission to appeal. If they have cash flow problems then the extra time may be invaluable though it carries the burden of an increase in their costs liability along with having to pay interest to the other litigant on the amount of the judgment, if that is at least £5,000, from the date of judgment until settlement. The device doesn't work unless enforcement of the judgment is stayed (paralysed) pending a decision on the application for permission to appeal (or the appeal itself where permission is actually granted). An application for the stay can be made at the same time as the application to the original judge for permission to appeal (where there is a reasonable chance it will be granted assuming permission to appeal is granted and, where permission is refused, the original judge can be invited to stay enforcement provided that a notice of appeal is issued within the 21 days available). The application can be repeated before the appeal judge. Where permission to appeal is obtained, it would be unusual for a stay not to be granted until the appeal is decided.

Chapter 22

Getting Your Money Under A Judgment

Can't pay, won't pay

"Two glasses of the finest champers - nicely chilled. And we'll both start with the fois gras. Is the lobster fresh?"

"Of course, Mr Troublesore. Are you by chance celebrating this evening?"

"Why yes. I have had a bit of a victory at the Peardrop civil hearing centre."

STOP!!!!! You've got the judgment. You haven't got the money. Hopefully, you checked up before you ever made a claim that the defendant was probably good for the amount you wanted out of them (see chapter 20). It doesn't follow that they are going to pay up without a bit of delay and a bit of evasion. The battle of wits may only just have started. It will be a consolation that so long as the county court judgment was for at least £5,000, interest on what is due will be attracted at the fixed rate of 8% from the date of the judgment until full payment (see chapter 24). It won't be a consolation to the defendant that the judgment will be recorded against them at the Register of Judgments, Orders and Fines in a case which was undefended if not settled within one month and, in a case which was defended, if and when the claimant takes enforcement action (see chapter 20).

There are a variety of lawful means by which you can extract from the defendant the amount they should be paying you. None of them involves a cut throat razor or any degree of intimidation (see chapter 30). Around one-third of judgments are settled in full and one-third are settled in part. No prizes for guessing what happens to the rest. Nothing is paid at all. The present system for judgment enforcement is highly unsatisfactory for the creditor. The court will not automatically do what is required to induce the defendant to settle. It will follow through whatever request or application you make for a particular means of enforcement but there is no point in kidding you. The process has sometimes reduced fully grown steroid ingesting body builders to a state of weeping. It could be much better. There is a brilliant system devised by section 95 of the Tribunals, Courts and Enforcement Act 2007 as an effective aid to enforcement for the court to get information about the true circumstances of the debtor from a government department and elsewhere. There's a problem. Nine years on the system has still not been brought into operation.

Let's see how we can use the lousy system we have got to some advantage. The methods to be looked at are available for the enforcement of maintenance orders as well as county court and High Court civil judgments although the process of an application for the court to consider the appropriate method of enforcement (see below) is peculiar to the enforcement of maintenance orders. For maintenance orders which used to be enforced by family proceedings courts (sometimes called magistrates' courts) the job of enforcement has now been taken over by the family court which is just as well 'cos the family proceedings courts were killed off in April 2014.

On your marks

You cannot enforce a judgment until the defendant has defaulted. If you have requested the court to enter judgment against them because they have admitted the claim or failed to put in a defence, you will be asked whether you want settlement forthwith - immediately - or within a fixed period or by instalments and, unless the defendant has asked for time to pay which does not coincide with your request, you will get what you wanted. On the other hand, if you have obtained the judgment at a hearing, the judge will usually direct that it be settled within 14 days of the hearing date although you can always ask the judge to make it sooner. Should you be pretty sure that you will have to take enforcement action, ask for payment to be made forthwith which would enable you to start the enforcement action immediately. The judge could well be sympathetic to payment forthwith where the defendant has put in a defence but then stayed away from the hearing as this indicates they were playing for time.

***a few words to our debtor friends:** If the court has ordered you to pay up sooner than you can afford then, whether you were present or absent when the order was made, you can do something about it. Where you admitted the claim once you received the claim form and made a proposal as to how you should pay which was opposed by the claimant, a decision - called a *determination* - on this will almost certainly have been made by a member of the court staff on paper. You have a right to ask for a *redetermination* which will result in a judge reconsidering how you are to pay at a hearing you would be well advised to attend. There's no fee for asking for the *redetermination* which you must do within 14 days of receiving details of what the staff member has decided. Where you put forward no proposals and an order was made without a hearing or there was a hearing at which the judge set a time for payment without an enquiry into your means, you can issue an application for the order to be varied to allow you to pay by instalments (form N245 costing a court fee of £50 but you could qualify for remission which would mean no fee - see chapter 13). You would be well advised to turn up at any hearing of that application if one is fixed. What is important is that you issue the application before the time for payment has arrived for once it has arrived and you have not come up with the cash, your creditor can start enforcement action. Where enforcement action has already started you can request the court to *stay* the enforcement action pending a decision being made on your application to vary. Should there be a change in your circumstances for the worse after a date for payment or a rate of instalments has been fixed on paper or at a hearing, you can ask the court to reconsider how you pay by making an application for variation (as above). Make at least two applications which are totally without merit and you can expect the court to put a stop to any more in the absence of a judge's prior permission and remember that each time you make an unsuccessful application which leads to a hearing, the chances are that you will add to the bill against you by being ordered to pay any legal costs and other expenses the claimant has incurred as a result.

***and a few more words to our debtor friends 'cos we can't stop:** A High Court judgment along with a county court judgment which is for at least £5,000 will attract interest at the rate of 8% as from the date of the judgment until you have settled in full. This is in addition to any interest ordered in favour of the claimant from when the money was due up to the date of the judgment. 8% is a swingeing rate but is automatic. Under the County Courts (Interest on Judgment Debts) Order 1991, the interest stops for a county court judgment, however, if the claimant takes enforcement action against you unless that enforcement action fails to produce a single new pence for the claimant in which event interest will continue to clock up as if the enforcement action had not been taken. Interest will not run while an attachment of earnings order or administration order are in force. An application for a charging order or for an order to obtain information from you will not rank as enforcement. It might be said that the kindest thing your creditor for a £5,000 plus judgment can do is to send in the bailiff who seizes your copy of this book (nominal value) and so stops the interest clock.

***and just a few more:** You can always attempt to do a deal with the claimant along the lines that "*Without Prejudice I owe you £6,000. I am unemployed with no prospects of a job. We live on benefits. My tenanted home has only basic contents. If you want to bankrupt me then so be it but I would just about prefer to stay afloat. How about you accept £750 in full and final settlement of the judgment which I could borrow from a third party?*"

Time limits and judgments on judgments

You need permission of the court to put in a bailiff or enforcement agent (see below) once the judgment is six years old. Otherwise there is generally no time limit on taking any enforcement action although you won't be entitled to interest on a judgment for any period beyond those six years. In certain circumstances it might be useful for you to sue the defendant for non-payment of the original judgment: a judgment on a judgment. Really. You would be obtaining a second judgment based on default under the first judgment and you could include in what you claim second time around any interest which had accrued since the first judgment to which you are entitled for up to six years from the first judgment.

What would be the purpose of this apparent madness? You would have six years to enforce the second judgment and would not have to apply for permission to put in a bailiff or enforcement agent to enforce the first judgment once it was six years old. You would also overcome the problem that any permission granted to enforce the first judgment after six years would have a life of only one year so that multiple applications to extend the one year could be necessary. The defendant might have gone missing with it likely to take a while to find him or the defendant might be down and out though with a good prospect of eventually becoming a multi-millionaire with an invention to prevent hard boiled eggs from stinking or perhaps you still lack sufficient information to decide on the most effective enforcement route to take. Words of warning. Going after the second judgment could lead to the defendant applying to the court for the claim to be struck out as an abuse of the court's process. So long as what you were doing was regarded as rational and reasonable in the circumstances, such an application by the defendant should fail.

Enforcement menu

Imprisonment

Calm down. Hardly ever. As a general rule, these days a debtor cannot be sent to prison for non-payment of a debt. Except in relation to certain taxes (and, in practice the tax collectors go for the loot and not the stir), prison is out unless the debt is for spousal or child maintenance payable under a court order and even then the court will not impose a sentence unless satisfied beyond reasonable doubt (no less) not only that the debtor has refused or neglected to pay but has had the means to do so: a high threshold. If a sentence is imposed in one of these excepted situations, it would probably be suspended so long as the debtor paid off the debt by a specified date or by specified instalments. There are a couple of indirect ways the debtor could end up being entertained by Her Majesty:

failing to produce a statement of means on an attachment of earnings application, for example (see below) but only then as a last resort.

Attachment of earnings

Generally available provided at least £5 is owed and the defendant is employed (and not self-employed or unemployed). The employer docks the defendant's pay each week or month for a sum fixed by the court and it is transferred to you through the court. Pretty useless unless you can identify their employer. The court can compel the debtor to disclose the employer's identity during the course of the attachment of earnings application or you can ascertain it by having the defendant forced to attend at court for questioning which is a step independent of any specific means of enforcement (see below). Should it transpire that the defendant is unemployed, ask the court to "adjourn the application generally with permission to restore it." This would enable you to reactivate the application if and when the defendant did get another job without having to make a fresh application and so pay a second court fee. The employed defendant would be well advised to ask for a *suspended* attachment of earnings order and state why and will be asked on the form they must complete about their financial circumstances, whether they seek suspension. With suspension, their employer would not come to know about the unsatisfied judgment unless any of the weekly or monthly payments required by the suspended order were missed and then you could ask for the employer to go into action and make the deductions. The managers of a pension scheme can be ordered to make regular payments from any private pension the defendant draws in the same way as an employer would deduct under the scope of an attachment of earnings order. For this purpose, the pension entitlements are treated as earnings. If you have the benefit of a High Court judgment, you will have to request the transfer of the case to the county court as only the county court has the power to make an attachment of earnings order.

As from April 2016 all applications for an attachment of earnings order (other than to the family court in connection with the enforcement of a maintenance order and some applications for a consolidated attachment of earnings - that's two or more attachment of earnings orders being lumped together) have to be issued in the County Court Money Claims Centre which will manage them until the making of an order. But should the debtor fail to complete a statement of their financial circumstances, the application will be sent to the hearing centre which covers the debtor's home or business address who will take it over.

a few words to our debtor friends: Note what I have just said about your ability to ask for any attachment of earnings order that is made to be suspended.

Third party debt order

Money which a bank or building society is holding in an account to the credit of the debtor is diverted to you up to the limit needed to settle the judgment. The same device can be used to divert money owed to the debtor by a customer or trader (for example, where the defendant has done some decorating work for Joseph Bloggs who has not yet settled the invoice the defendant has rendered to them). The court would initially make an *interim third party debt order* which effectively freezes the money and a hearing follows a month or two later at which the court decides whether or not to confirm the order and have the frozen sum thawed out and paid over to you. The magic is that the debtor does not find out about the *interim* order until after it has been made and so is robbed of the opportunity to withdraw money or ensure it is paid over to them before you engage your snatching tactic. Should the debtor who is an individual (not say a company) be suffering hardship in meeting ordinary living expenses because of the freezing of money in their bank or building society account, they can make an emergency application for a hardship payment to be made to them from the account. Where your application falls flat on its face as the defendant no longer has an account as you had believed or it is overdrawn, don't forget to ask the court to order the defendant to pay you the fee you have wasted on the application, to be added to what they already owe.

"I am the claimant. I refer to my application for a final third party debt order. In view of the information supplied to the court and myself by the third party, I am obliged to ask you to dismiss the application for the final order but I would respectfully request that the court should order the defendant to pay to me the court fee I have incurred on making the application, such amount to be added to the judgment debt and I would also ask to be excused attendance at the hearing in view of my work commitments."

That an account is in debit today does not mean that it will not be in credit next week. You can make a second or subsequent application in respect of the same account - I have seen it work - but eventually the debtor will cotton on.

Warrant of control

This used to be called a warrant of execution and meant then and means now that a county court bailiff will attempt to seize sufficient of the debtor's goods to sell and pay off the debt and fees. Sadly, using the bailiff can be a frustrating experience. The time and the resources are not there to prevent the wily debtor from playing the system and giving the bailiff a right run-around. For a judgment of at least £600 you can have the case transferred to the High Court for enforcement (completing form N293A) where the warrant of control becomes a writ of control: for a judgment of over £5,000 it is mandatory for you to do so (unless the judgment arises out of an agreement regulated by the Consumer Credit Act 1974 which can only be enforced in the county court). There are two advantages in a transfer. The enforcement will be carried out not by a court bailiff but possibly by a more savvy enforcement agent who is not in the court's employ but has been appointed by the Lord Chancellor to go about seizing goods and a county court judgment for less than £5,000 which would not otherwise attract interest will do so at the rate of 8% once transferred as from the transfer date. Enforcement agents are much more expensive than the county court bailiff which is worth considering in this respect - where the debtor has limited assets there may be less over for you once the agent's charges have been satisfied and you could end up paying all or some of those charges where little or nothing is available for seizure. Various items are exempt from seizure such as those which are essential in the household like clothing and bedding and, subject to a cap of £1,350, items or equipment for use in the debtor's employment or business. If property, including a motor vehicle, is owned not by the debtor but a finance company then it will not be taken.

a few words to our debtor friends: You can apply to the court to suspend the warrant (form N245 - £50 fee unless you are granted remission) which would have the effect of paralysing the bailiff or enforcement agent so long as you paid up by a specified extended date or by specified instalments. Fail to do so, and seizure of your goods could proceed without any further court hearing. The bailiff or enforcement agent should give you at least seven days' warning that they are coming in though the court is empowered to cut down on this time if it reckons you may otherwise make off with your goods and so frustrate seizure. They may come on any day of the week but generally only between 6am and 9pm unless the court has directed some other time. If you are trading from the premises at which the bailiff or enforcement agent seek to seize your goods outside of those hours then they can enter and do their business then. They may enter by any door or by "any usual means by which entry is gained" which rules out the chimney (unless we are talking about a grotto) and probably through the window. To use force to get in the court must give prior permission and even then the force will need to be no more than is reasonable. If the bailiff or enforcement agent has gone further than the law permits, you may be entitled to claim compensation (see chapter 23).

Charging order

This is mainly made in relation to freehold or leasehold property which the debtor owns, whether solely or jointly with others, but it can also be made in relation to the debtor's stocks and shares.

Let's concentrate on freehold or leasehold property. The order puts you in a similar position to a mortgage lender. In practice, the order is aimed at preventing the debtor from selling or mortgaging or remortgaging their interest in the property without paying you off. It is conceivable they would be disinclined to do any such thing for the next 75 years? Well, the court does have the power to follow up a charging order with an order for the property to be sold and the debt repaid out of the sale proceeds. That would involve an application by you for an order for sale and an application could well fail where the debtor was making headway with settling by instalments. Such an application is precluded where the judgment arises out of a regulated consumer credit agreement and the amount owed is less than £1,000. An order for sale is harder to obtain than a charging order.

The procedure for obtaining a charging order changed in April 2016. As with applications for attachment of earnings, charging order applications to the county court have been centralised and must now be made to the County Court Money Claims Centre. They are dealt with in two stages. The first stage involves a consideration of the application on paper without a hearing and without notification to the debtor. If the application is granted then an interim charging order is made and it is notified to the debtor and certain others including any co-owner, other creditors and, if they are known to you, the debtor's spouse or civil partner (which I can foresee leading to more than a few relationship breakdowns). The co-owner is interested because they could be losing their home if an order for sale was made subsequently. Where the co-owner is a spouse or partner and there are already proceedings for divorce etc, the court can be asked to link up the application for a final charging order to be considered alongside any financial remedy application in those other proceedings. The other creditors who are unsecured will be interested because a charging order in your favour will give you security which ranks in priority to them: should the property be sold (even after a bankruptcy) your judgment would be paid off before what they are owed.

The second stage has been streamlined. If nobody objects - and they have 28 days from being notified of the interim charging order to do so - then a final charging order will now generally follow on paper without a hearing. If there is any objection then the application will be taken over by the hearing centre covering the debtor's home or place of business.

There is no minimum debt required for a charging order to be made though some judges will be reluctant to make one for less than the £200 mark. Once upon a time, an application for a charging order could not be made where the judgment was to be paid by instalments and the debtor had kept them up. This is no longer the case if the judgment was applied for or the order was made after 30 September 2012. The charging order can be applied for immediately the time for payment of the judgment has passed: a nanosecond later. However, the absence of default will be taken into account by the court in deciding whether to make the order.

But if having obtained a charging order, you fail to register it against the property at the Land Registry, the whole exercise may turn out to have been a complete waste of time and you will be left feeling as sick as a cage of parrots whose sherry cream trifle has been stolen by an eagle. Where the debtor is the sole owner of the property you should register what is known as a *notice* and that ought to scupper a sale, mortgage or remortgage. You cannot do this, though, where the debtor is not the sole owner. Then, you need to register a *restriction*. There is a standard restriction and a non-standard restriction. With a *standard* restriction - which, unfortunately, is the norm - notice of a transaction has to be given to you but only after it has been effected. You're right. Potentially, rubbish. More often than not, once the prospective buyer or lender gets wind of the registered standard restriction which will happen when they make a Land Registry search before completing the transaction, they will require the charging order to be paid off but there is no guarantee this will happen. So, my prudent creditor, what you do is to instead request a *non-standard restriction* using land registry form L which will ensure you are given notice of the proposed sale, mortgage or remortgage before it takes place and can engineer getting paid out from the sale, mortgage or remortgage proceeds. You should ask the court when you make your application and again when, at the second stage, you request the final charging order to add this verbiage to the order:

> *"IT IS ORDERED pursuant to section 46 of the Land Registration Act 2002 that HM Land Registrar shall enter a non-standard restriction in respect of the title referred to in this order in these terms, namely:*
>
> *No disposition of the registered estate is to be registered without a certificate signed by the applicant for registration or their conveyancer that written notice of the disposition was given to Whitewash Limited of 231 Queen Alexandra Crescent, Richmond-upon-Thames, Surrey TW11 7FL being the person with the benefit of an interim/ final charging order on the beneficial interest of Clive*

Troublesore made on 14 July 2016 in the County Court in proceedings under claim number BLK161679 no later than 14 days prior to the disposition or without an order of the County Court which ordered this restriction."

Some creditors register both the interim and final charging orders: others just rest on the interim order. If you secured the extra wording on the final but not the interim order, you should be registering both.

***a few words to our debtor friends:** The charging order will not evict you from your home. Only a later order for sale would do that and different considerations apply when a court is deciding whether to order sale than when deciding whether to make a final charging order. The court might not make a final charging order if the property is in negative equity or close to it and/or the debt is small and/or you have already started to reduce the debt. Sometimes the creditor will say: "Just give me the protection of a charging order though I have no intention of trying to get the property sold so long as Mr Troublesore pays me regular instalments." If the judge says they are going to make an order, you pipe up with this: "I respectfully ask you to order that the claimant be debarred from applying for an order for sale so long as I pay instalments on account of the judgment debt at the rate of £x per month or at such other rate as the court may from time to time determine." But a charging order is an insidious form of enforcement because it gives your creditor security over your property and if you subsequently found that there was just no way you could settle the debt, you just might eventually be thrown out of your home where the order was against that property with the debt then being settled out of the sale price. Better off then without a charging order. You can object to an interim charging order being followed up with a final charging order and, if you were successful, the interim order would be cancelled. Persuading the judge to throw out the application may be an uphill task but you never know. You have 28 days from being notified of the interim order to send in your objection to the court and your creditor and, if you do so, there will be a hearing at the hearing centre covering your home or place of business. This document should contain a statement of truth.

"Pursuant to CPR rule 73.10(2), the grounds of my objection to a final charging order are that:

1. I was ordered to pay the judgment by instalments and I have religiously kept up those instalments.

OR

1. I have paid whatever my financial circumstances have permitted since the judgment was entered. Particulars of the dates and amounts of the instalments I have paid are set out on the attached schedule (complete and staple a schedule to the statement).

OR

1. I put forward written proposals to the claimant on 14 July 2016 to pay the judgment by instalments of £25 per month and to set up a standing order for this amount but despite hastening letters the claimant has completely ignored me (or refused to accept any instalments at all).

OR

1. On 1 June 2016 the claimant obtained a suspended attachment of earnings order against me under which I am required to pay £25 per month. I have already made the first payment and intend to comply with the order to the letter. In these circumstances, the making of a final charging order would be too severe and disproportionate.

OR

1. I believe that the claimant has purchased the benefit of the judgment debt from my original creditor for a tiny fraction of the amount involved since when it has pursued me with aggression and unreasonableness and refuses or neglects to engage with me in my attempts to reach an agreement with it.

2. The amount of the judgment debt is relatively modest and the making of a final charging order would be disproportionate and would involve me in costs which it would be inequitable for me to have to bear.

OR

2. The property against which the final order is sought is in negative equity. I attach copies of a market appraisal of the property from Flogarama plc and statements from my first and second mortgagees as to balances on my mortgage accounts (staple copies to the statement). There is no reasonable expectation that the property would go into positive equity within the next 20 years, if ever, and so to make the order final would be of no value to the claimant and involve me in costs which should never have been incurred and would not have been incurred had the claimant heeded these figures which I provided to them before this misconceived application was made.

OR

2. There is ample equity in the property against which the final order is sought. I attach copies of a market appraisal of the property from Flogarama plc and statements from my first and second mortgagees as to balances on my mortgage accounts (staple copies to the statement). I have no other debts and so the claimant does not have to compete with other creditors to gain priority over them in obtaining a charging order. There is no evidence that I would sell the property or remortgage it without paying off the claimant. I am paying the claimant by instalments. In all the circumstances, the claimant's application is disproportionate.

Statement of truth

I believe that the facts stated in this statement of my grounds of objection are true.

(signed) C Troublesore

Dated 14 July 2016

Appointing a receiver

This one is a bit of a secret and an application - the full blown title is an application for the appointment of a receiver by way of equitable execution - is fairly rare though, if granted, should be effective. Best for the larger judgment. What you would be asking the court to do is appoint someone to receive money which will fall due to your debtor and account to you for it after their inevitable bill has been met. You could ask for say your accountant to be appointed. The most likely straightforward situation in which an appointment might be appropriate is where your debtor is a landlord who is entitled to monthly rent for the premises they have let. The receiver could catch rent already due but unpaid as well as future rent as and when it becomes due and until the judgment debt has been satisfied. You would not be able to catch future rent with a third party debt order (see above). The procedure for applying is in Part 69 of the Civil Procedure Rules 1998.

Choosing the right course

Where your debtor is employed and you are willing to suffer payment by instalments, it's probably worth going for an attachment of earnings order. No good if you want your money quickly unless the debtor is a City trader. Swooping on a bank or building society account by way of a third party debt order makes a lot of sense if you reckon there is a reasonable chance it is in credit. And provided your debtor appears to have a reasonable lifestyle, trying the bailiff or an enforcement agent (concurrently with a third party debt order application, if you wish) could be a good bet, especially when they have a Morgan parked in the garage and it's not on HP. You can back up other action with a charging order application should your debtor own their home (even jointly with their spouse or partner). And, if you have patience, go for a charging order alone. The time could well come when your debtor wants or needs to sell or remortgage and then they will find they are obliged to pay you off. Provided the judgment was for at least £5,000, it will be earning interest at the rate of 8% and so a nice investment as you wait to be paid. Once you get tired of waiting you can apply on the back of the charging order for the property to be sold. Enforcement other than by a charging order application can stop interest running (see above).

"But how do I discover what they've got?"

You can apply for an order to obtain information about your debtor's circumstances. Use form N316 if the debtor is an individual or form N316A if the debtor is a company and you want one of its directors to answer questions (£50 fee unless you qualify for remission). The debtor or the director will be compelled to attend at the civil hearing centre local to them and to produce such items as pay slips, bank statements, mortgage statement and any outstanding bills. In the case of a business, production of bills owed to it and two years' accounts will also be required. The debtor or director will be quizzed at court by a member of staff who will complete a questionnaire and get them to sign it. You will then be supplied with a copy. The staff member will be quite competent to do the job properly but you can't expect a Rumpole impersonation. Should you want the debtor or director to produce at court information or documents over and above what will normally be required of them then you can give details in the application form. Should the debt be big enough to make the exercise viable, you can ask for the questioning to come before a judge instead of a staff member and either conduct it yourself or send a lawyer to do it on your behalf.

> *"The judgment creditor requests that the judgment debtor/officer of the company be questioned by the judgment creditor before a judge. The reasons for this request are that (1) the judgment debt is substantial and/or (2) the judgment creditor is seized of certain information which needs to be put to the judgment debtor/director for confirmation and elaboration and/or (3) the judgment creditor submits that the judgment debtor/director is likely to be unhelpful and evasive (consistent with their conduct so far in these proceedings) and expert examination of them is considered to be desirable*

and proportionate."

One of my favourite tricks as a former advocate on these examinations before a judge was to ask the debtor to empty out their pockets. If they decline (and it is doubtful that the judge would force them to do the emptying), you will know you are on to something (like money or property) and they might even stutter out a bit of useful information before they re-establish their equilibrium in response to a supplementary like: "Don't be embarrassed about the car keys, Mr Troublesore, where did you park?" And who knows what might come out of the pockets if the debtor is compliant?

***and a few words to our debtor friends:** Empty your pockets before you get to court! And one other thing. You can ask your creditor for reasonable travelling expenses to get to and from court. You must make this request with seven days of receiving the order to attend.

"But how do I discover <u>both</u> what they've got <u>and</u> what I should do about it?"

There is a special procedure which can be used for enforcement of maintenance orders (as well as orders for the payment of lump sums) arising out of matrimonial and other family cases. This is *an application for enforcement by such method of enforcement as the court may consider*. The form is called a D50K and the court fee is £50. The application is a bit of a secret and is rarely used but it could work well for some. What happens is that the debtor is ordered to attend court on the hearing of the application. They will be questioned about their means much in the same way as they would on questioning in relation to a civil court judgment (see above) but there are two distinct differences. Firstly, the questioning will always be conducted by a judge and, secondly, the judge will effectively point you in the right direction about which method or methods or enforcement (you can use more than one method at a time) is or are right. Different judges will deal with the procedure in different ways. You may find you are required to go on and make a further application for the actual enforcement order you want and pay the additional court fee which is attracted by it...or you may not! If the judge seems disinclined to make an enforcement order of some kind there and then, mention to them the case of *Kaur v Randhawa* and that it can be found at [2015] EWHC 1592 (the judge will know what you are talking about though you won't!) in which Mr Justice Mostyn made a final third party debt order there and then on one of these applications for over £108,000. The one potential disadvantage with the procedure is that it gives the debtor advance notice of what is to be happening so that if they empty their bank account or sell, mortgage or remortgage a property they own before they get to court for the hearing or before appropriate paperwork can be produced to cover the method of enforcement to be followed, you could be left whistling.

The special treat

The *statutory demand* is a very fine demand. It just could get you your money without taking enforcement action through the court and with relative swiftness and little or no expense. But to succeed, you need:

- a debtor who does not want to be made bankrupt;
- a debt of at least £5,000; and
- a debt for a fixed sum so you cannot use the demand for say a claim for damages for restaurant poisoning.

The demand is a prelude to bankruptcy proceedings in relation to an individual or winding up proceedings in relation to a company. The form of demand tells the debtor they must pay you what is owed and that their failure to do so within 21 days of getting the document could result in them being made bankrupt or wound up. The very last thing you want is to have to bring bankruptcy or winding up proceedings because they are expensive and should the debtor (not having been induced by the demand to settle the debt) be prepared to lie down and have the court declare them bankrupt or wound up - see chapter 35), the chances are you will have paid handsomely to recover not a penny. But if you are pretty sure your debtor is solvent (or not hopelessly insolvent) and what's stopping them from settling the debt to you is bloody-mindedness, laziness, cash flow problems, meanness or insanity then bankruptcy or winding up - the ultimate method of enforcement - may be unavoidable. Bankruptcy and so the statutory demand are not available to enforce maintenance orders but there is instead the judgment summons procedure which can lead to the defaulter being potted makes up for it (see rules 33.9 to 33.17 of the Family Procedure Rules 2010).

Whilst the demand can follow a court judgment, that is not essential. It can be used where a debt has been run up and no court proceedings have been brought. But not a good idea to use it in the absence of a judgment if the debtor has some genuine and reasonable ground for disputing the debt or does not quarrel with the debt but maintains you owe them money and that what you owe cancels out what they owe you. In that situation the law expects you to make a court claim rather than speeding down the statutory demand road and the likelihood is that the debtor will apply to the court to set the demand aside and you will be left with a red face, indigestion, a bad night's sleep (maybe seven nights' worth) and possibly a court order for costs against you. The moral is save the procedure for where you already have a court judgment or you have no judgment but the claim is cast iron or as close to that as it gets.

Unless your claim is based on a contract which entitles you to interest on the debt until it is paid, the disadvantage of a demand without a judgment is that the debt will not carry an entitlement to interest and it should not be claimed in the form of demand. You must use a prescribed form of demand (go to www.gov.uk/statutory-demands: form 6.1/2 or 3 for an individual or 4.1 for a company). In the case of a demand against an individual you must insert, where the form invites you to do so, the insolvency hearing centre at which they are entitled to apply for the demand to be set aside. The best way of finding this out is to contact the Insolvency Service's enquiry line on 0300 678 0015 or go to insolvency.enquiryline@insolvency.gsi.gov.uk.

***and a few words to our debtor friends:** You can apply to the insolvency hearing centre identified in the demand for it to be set aside if you contend it is misconceived, unjustified or makes no sense whatsoever or you have a good defence to the claim or a counterclaim. The application should be made within 18 days of getting the demand. Should you be late you will have to additionally apply for a time extension. Or you could actually pay up or put forward settlement proposals to your creditor which are designed to obviate bankruptcy or winding up proceedings. A company cannot apply to set aside a statutory demand which it receives. The appropriate course of challenge then would be an application to the court to restrain the institution of winding up proceedings.

Should the statutory demand be based on a default court judgment which you contest, the likelihood is that the application to set aside the statutory demand will be adjourned to facilitate an application by you to set aside the actual judgment but a tight timetable will be imposed

If the application to set aside the demand is unsuccessful, the court will allow a breathing space before your creditor can petition for your bankruptcy. The norm is seven days. Where you aim to pay off the debt but would require more than seven days to raise the money, ask the judge to allow longer and say why. By paying up before a bankruptcy petition can be issued, you will avoid being condemned to pay the costs that the bankruptcy case would involve and which you would most probably have to pay even though the proceedings were abandoned because you had eventually settled. Beware. It is commonplace for the dodgier creditor to insist on their costs of bringing bankruptcy proceedings being settled as a condition of dropping the case. They can insist on an order for costs against you but not on you producing the money for them before the bankruptcy petition can be dropped. Payment of these costs would be for another day and non-payment cannot stand in the way of the court dismissing the petition on the ground that there is no longer a debt. Not a good idea to refuse forever to settle those costs whether the amount of them has been agreed between you and your creditor or the court has fixed them because of non-agreement. Your creditor could come up with a new statutory demand followed on by a second bankruptcy petition for the costs of the first bankruptcy petition (so long as the costs amounted to £5,000 or more). In fact, it could go on forever. Nice where you have taken a fancy to the court clerk but not nice if you can't afford to take them out for a drink.

Something to watch should you be thinking of agreeing the amount of your costs liability with the creditor. When starting the bankruptcy case, your creditor would have paid over to the court a deposit of a cool £990 towards the expenses of the Insolvency Service which through the official receiver deals with the administration of your affairs post-bankruptcy order. That deposit will be repaid to the creditor should there be no bankruptcy as the case has been dismissed. Therefore, the £990 must not appear in the creditor's costs bill against you. Surprising how often it is.

And a few more words to our debtor friends who haven't paid their taxes

The tax man - more affectionately known as HM Revenue & Customs (HMRC) - has a new and neat way of procuring settlement of your unpaid tax bill introduced by section 51 of the Finance (No 2) Act 2015 (and if you don't believe me go to section 51 and schedule 8). The process is called direct recovery of debt (DRD). It swoops on money you hold in any accounts - typically, with a bank or building society - and after a temporary holding period it settles the tax bill out of the credit and all without any prior court order. Before the swoop, you must owe at least £1,000 with the timetables for appealing having passed and HMRC must leave at least £5,000 across all your accounts after the earmarked tax money has been deducted. Then, you are given the bad news and you have 30 days to object. Grounds include that you have already paid, the action taken is causing or will cause you exceptional hardship or someone else has an interest on one of the affected accounts (for example, your mother-in-law asked you to look after £25,000 for her and you popped it into the account). There is also a right to object on the part of that someone else or a joint account holder. HMRC must consider the objection within the next 30 days and, if they remain unmoved, there is a right of appeal on the same grounds within the next 30 days to the county court.

HMRC is committed to undertake a face-to-face visit with you before considering a DRD (so that's something to look forward to) at which you will be offered a Time to Pay arrangement and they must assess whether you are vulnerable and, if you are they will offer you support from a specialist team. In coming to a conclusion about vulnerability, account must be had not only to a disability or long-term health condition but to temporary conditions which prevent you from putting your tax affairs in order or personal issues that affect you or say an immediate family member (including a bereavement, redundancy, serious illness and domestic or financial abuse). If any account held by a non-vulnerable debtor remains in credit after one of these face-to-face visits, I will be eating yet another of my hats. Nothing personal, you understand.

Chapter 23

Execution

The bailiff strikes

Sounds chilling. It is. Your goods seized to satisfy a debt which is subject to a court judgment or which is due under some other legal process. It's a terrible thing for you but it may be the last resort (or close to it) for your creditor. The seizure is known as execution and is carried out by what, since 2014, are generally known as enforcement agents. They include the good old county court bailiffs who additionally now have the distinction of being family court bailiffs. The enforcement agents who are not county court bailiffs are licensed to execute and are in it for the money about which there is no shame so long as they obey the rules. They take on as part of their business the pleasure of seizing goods under judgments of the High Court and sometimes judgments of the county court which have been transferred to the High Court for enforcement usually because the creditors reckon that the county court bailiffs are too soft and insufficiently aggressive (see chapter 22). There are also certificated enforcement agents who are authorised by the county court to seize goods and will be the guys who go after such debts as council tax.

If you owe money then you should pay it and, if you are not in a position to pay it when required, you should put forward reasonable proposals to pay in the future - probably by instalments - and keep to them so long as that is reasonably possible. When execution is under a High Court or county court judgment you can apply to the court to fend off the enforcement agent. Your creditor will have obtained a *writ of control* in the High Court or a *warrant of control* in the county court. That application would be for the *writ* or the *warrant* to be suspended (halted) so long as you paid up as and when required under the proposals you put forward. But the rules which the enforcement agents must obey are there for your protection. They can only go so far and if they overstep the mark, you the defaulting debtor have legal rights and you can do something about it.

Those rules are in The Taking Control of Goods Regulations 2013 which every self respecting debtor should have under his bed. Depending on the circumstances, your set of the regulations may be protected from seizure and almost certainly the enforcement agent won't be able to make off with the bed even if you are out of it. So let's go to the regulations and see what the enforcement agent cannot take towards the debt and what are the rules of the game.

Can't take

Only goods which you own should be taken for a debt - not, say, those belonging to your spouse or partner or a finance company which are on hire-purchase to you. Some other goods are exempt from seizure. As odious as you are and as much as you owe, the enforcement agent cannot take:

- Items or equipment which are necessary for use by you in your employment, business, trade, profession, study or education (so if you are training to be a law professor you could say that your copy of the regulations under the bed are exempt from seizure on that basis). Included as exempt might be tools, books, telephones, computers and vehicles. The exemption applies only up to goods in this category to the total value of £1,350. Over that figure, the enforcement agent can seize away. This exemption does not apply where the debt is for taxes or non-domestic rates.
- Clothing, bedding, furniture, household equipment, items and provisions as are reasonably required to satisfy the basic domestic needs of yourself and the other members of the household (be they young or old, big or small). What we are looking at here are, for example:
    - ◇ a cooker (but probably not two cookers unless you have 200 people living in your home);
    - ◇ microwave;
    - ◇ fridge;
    - ◇ washing machine;
    - ◇ beds and bedding;
    - ◇ a landline phone or, if no landline, a mobile (but not a landline and a mobile);
    - ◇ a dining table large enough for you and the rest of the household and chairs (ten chairs and only three occupiers would put seven chairs at risk but anything short of solid oak circa 1750 and the enforcement agent is unlikely to be interested);
    - ◇ lighting and heating equipment sufficient to satisfy your basic needs and those of your household;
    - ◇ any item or equipment reasonably required for the care of someone under 18, a disabled person or an older person;
    - ◇ a guide dog (!); and

- ◇ a vehicle on which a valid disabled person's badge is displayed because it is actually used to carry a disabled person or the enforcement agent has reasonable grounds to believe that this is so.

If you are saying that an exempt item has been seized then you must notify this to the enforcement agent as soon as practicable and certainly within seven days of the goods having been removed. You need to give your name and address and state that this address is where you can be sent (served with) documentation about the matter; state the goods concerned; and provide the grounds for saying they are exempt. The creditor will be given an opportunity of admitting or disputing what you say. If there is a dispute, the enforcement agent will notify you of it and you will then need to apply to the court - on form N244 - to resolve the dispute within seven days of receiving the notification. With the application should go a written statement specifying the goods you claim to be exempt and the grounds for doing so and any available documentation to back you up. Where the goods seized belonged to someone else, the owner wishing to challenge their seizure should give notice within seven days of removal.

"I'm coming"

The enforcement agent must give you at least seven clear days' written notice (with prescribed information) that they are coming. In calculating whether sufficient notice has been given, you should ignore Sunday, a bank holiday, Good Friday and Christmas Day. For obvious reasons, most creditors would say that the notice requirement is a bit loopy. That's why the enforcement agent can apply to the court for the period of notice to be reduced (to five minutes?). The court can only oblige if satisfied that your goods will otherwise be moved out or disposed of so as to evade the enforcement agent taking control of them. You haven't had at least seven days' notice? Ask the enforcement agent to show you the court order which reduced the period.

When?

The enforcement agent can do their evil deed on any day of the week and generally only between 6am and 9pm but the court may be prepared to extend that time frame. Should the enforcement agent turn up at 11.30pm you should ask to see a copy of the court order which authorises them to seize after 9pm. Important exceptions coming up. If the goods are on business premises which are open outside 6am to 9pm then the enforcement agent may seize away (two crates of champers and a ton of smoked salmon from a restaurant?) during those extended hours. Generally, if they have started the deed within the permitted period but it is reasonably necessary to take a bit longer, they can finish it so long as the total time taken up is reasonable. Guidance issued to bailiffs in March 2016 tells them to have regard to religious holidays for the debtor when deciding whether to get into seizure mode.

It isn't a condition of the enforcement agent seizing that you are present. However, the agent must not act where the only person present is under 16 or vulnerable. Whether you are present or absent, should the item the enforcement agent wishes to take be in use - by anyone - then the agent should not take if it is likely that this would cause a breach of the peace.

Where?

The enforcement agent may seize goods from where you usually live or carry on a trade or business. They may also enter other premises if they have obtained authority (by a warrant) from the court to do so. That authority will be given where the court is satisfied that there are goods at these premises which can be seized and that it is reasonable in all the circumstances for the authority to be given.

Down the chimney?

No! Generally, the enforcement agent may only enter premises through a door or any other usual means of access such as via a loading bay in respect of trade premises. So apart from the chimney, a window would also be precluded. And the general rule is that the enforcement agent cannot use force to gain entry. This means, for example, that they cannot axe down your front door or push past you. In fact, you don't even need to open the door to them though, of course, it's always good to chat. Two exceptions to the 'no force' rule. If necessary, force can be used by an enforcement agent who is after goods to settle an unpaid criminal fine or income tax or stamp duty. Reasonable force can also be used if the enforcement agent has applied to the court for and been granted a warrant which authorises it. The agent must have explained to the court the likely means of entry and the type and amount of force that will be required.

The motor

Your vehicle might possibly be exempt from seizure (see above). Otherwise, it can be taken. If the enforcement agent comes across your vehicle on the road, they can immobilise it unless you voluntarily surrender the keys. On immobilisation, a warning notice must be fixed to the vehicle with prescribed information including a 24 hour telephone number for enquiries. The vehicle must stay put for at least two hours after which the enforcement agent can have it stored unless you pay the debt in the meantime or reach some arrangement with the agent.

More notices - and more time to pay up

There are strict requirements for the enforcement agent to give you written notice about goods which they have seized and removed for storage. And you must also be given at least seven days' notice before seized goods are sold (with no particular days excluded this time). The agent must achieve the best price that can reasonably be obtained.

Be back soon

The enforcement agent is frustrated. You have nothing on the premises which they can take or what is there is insufficient to pay off the debt. They may return - more than once - if they have reason to believe that since their last visit you have brought fresh goods on to the premises which they can nab. However, you must be given prior written notice of the intention to re-enter. The scheme for this notice is the same as for notice of the initial entry (see above) except that this time only two clear days' notice is required unless the court shortens the period. The guidance issued to bailiffs in March 2016 is that in the course of attempting to get the creditor their money, they should typically conduct three visits to the debtor on different days and at different times and if they have still not scored they should liaise with their manager to consider the prospect of further meetings or seizing goods. Once four weeks are up, the creditor should expect either their money or an interim report.

If the enforcement agent is not frustrated but leaves your premises with nothing except a couple of sheets of paper it is because you have signed a controlled goods agreement. By this, the agent will have assumed control of specified goods on the premises but left them where they are in return for you coming to an arrangement to pay off what is due. In the document you will have agreed not to remove or dispose of the goods or permit anyone else to do so until you have settled up but you can continue to use them. You break the agreement? The agent can remove the goods into storage or sell them. And if say you have sold them or taken them elsewhere "without a lawful excuse" (for example, you were rescuing them from destruction in a fire which you did not deliberately start yourself or a madman invited to the premises by your wayward daughter was about to massacre them) you will be guilty of a criminal offence and risk a fine or imprisonment.

The bill

You give the enforcement agent a hard time at your peril. Of course, if you don't possess a sherry glass to spit in, that may not cause you anxiety. Equally, if you intend to apply for your own bankruptcy or are content for a creditor to bankrupt you, there's not too much to worry about. Otherwise, the more the enforcement agent does the greater their charges and so the greater your debt 'cos you pay those charges though the bill is less painful with the bailiff in the county court and family court. You will find the enforcement agent's price list in The Taking of Goods (Fees) Regulations 2014. Here's an example. With a High Court debt, there are four separate stages which each trigger a separate charge: compliance (all activities from the agent's receipt of instructions up to but excluding the commencement of enforcement) generating a mild £75; first enforcement (from the first attendance at the premises to completion or breach of a controlled goods agreement) generating a fee of £190 plus 7.5% of the sum to be recovered in excess of £1,000; second enforcement (further steps up to but excluding sale of goods taken) generating a fixed fee of £495; and sale generating a fee of £525 plus 7.5% of the sum to be recovered. On top are court fees and other disbursements such as charges for storage, a locksmith and auction.

Enforcement agent gets executed

If an enforcement agent acts illegally - breaches schedule 12 to the Tribunals, Courts and Enforcement Act 2007 or acts under a defective power - you may get back the goods that have been seized and recover damages from the enforcement agent for any loss you have suffered. It is a defence to the damages claim but not to the claim for return of the goods that the enforcement agent acted in the reasonable belief that he was not breaching the law or acting under a defective power. Proceedings relating to a High Court writ of control must be brought in the High Court and relating to a county court warrant of control in the county court. In any other case they may be brought in the High Court or county court but almost invariably only the county court will be appropriate. Where the alleged culprit is a county court bailiff then a claim should be made against the Ministry of Justice which will accept responsibility should the bailiff have erred. The proceedings may be brought by application notice in form N244 which will mean a fee of £255 and be supported by a written statement setting out where the enforcement agent has gone wrong. Where the goods have not yet been sold, you can ask the court to halt any auction or other sale process. Alternatively, you can start proceedings by issuing a (Part 7) claim form. The particulars of claim (and an application notice and the supporting statement can cover the same ground) might go like this:

Case no 970000678

IN THE COUNTY COURT

SITTING AT PEARDROP

BETWEEN

CLIVE TROUBLESORE Claimant

- and -

BERTRAND GRABWELL Defendant

PARTICULARS OF CLAIM

1. This claim is made under paragraph 66 of schedule 12 ("schedule 12) to the Tribunals, Courts and Enforcement Act 2007.

2. At all material times -

a. the claimant was indebted to Peardrop Borough Council ("the council") for unpaid parking charges and penalties ("the debt") in the total sum of £13,546 and

b. the defendant was an enforcement agent instructed by the council to recover the debt and costs by taking control of the claimant's goods under a warrant of control.

3. On 14th July 2016 at about 10.30pm the defendant in the course of seeking to take control of the defendant's goods entered the defendant's premises at 149 Magnolia Crescent, Twickenham, Middlesex KT89 4XZ ("the premises") and took control of and removed cash in the sum of £14,000 and a Ford Escort van registration number CT3 belonging to the claimant ("the van") (together referred to as "the goods").

4. Wrongfully and in breach of paragraph 7 of schedule 12 and paragraph 6 of The Taking Control of Goods Regulations 2013 ("the regulations), the defendant failed to give the defendant not less than seven clear days' notice before taking control but gave him only two clear days' notice.

5. Further and alternatively, wrongfully and in breach of paragraph 10 of the regulations, the defendant entered the premises when the only person present was the defendant's child Clive Troublesore Junior aged 1.

6. Further and alternatively, wrongfully and in breach of schedule 12, the defendant took control of goods the aggregate value of which was more than the debt and an amount in respect of fu-

ture costs calculated in accordance with the regulations when there were goods of lower value on the premises.

7. Further and alternatively, wrongfully and in breach of paragraph 19 of the regulations and in the absence of exceptional circumstances, the defendant removed the goods and secured them in a place which was not within a reasonable distance from the premises, namely at the Dodgy Depository, Poole, Dorset.

8. Further and alternatively, wrongfully and in breach of paragraph 20 of the regulations, the defendant entered the premises through an unsecured ground floor rear window and by applying force to the doors of the garage within the premises.

9. Further and alternatively, wrongfully and in breach of paragraph 22 of the regulations, the defendant entered the premises at a prohibited time.

10. Further and alternatively, wrongfully and in breach of paragraph 28 of schedule 12 and paragraph 30 of the regulations, the defendant failed to give notice of entry to the claimant by leaving such notice in a conspicuous place on the premises or otherwise.

11. Further and alternatively, wrongfully and in breach of paragraph 34 of schedule 12 and paragraph 33 of the regulations, the defendant failed to provide the claimant with a list of goods of which he had taken control as soon as reasonably practicable or at all.

12. Further and alternatively, wrongfully and in breach of paragraph 35 of schedule 12 and paragraph 34 of the regulations, the defendant failed to take reasonable care of the van following its removal from the premises in that he littered the interior or caused the interior to be littered with cigarette butts and damaged the bodywork or caused it to be so damaged requiring repairs at the cost to the claimant of £921 (inc VAT).

13. As a result of the defendant's breaches the claimant has suffered loss.

Particulars of loss

- *cost of repairs to garage doors - £128;*
- *cost of repairs to and cleaning of the interior of the van- £951 (inc VAT);*
- *loss of earnings due to inability to use van - £150 per day as from 14 July 2016 and continuing; and*

- *bank charges incurred in arranging and servicing emergency overdraft - £35 with interest continuing as from the date of this claim at the rate of £x per day.*

Travelling expenses in seeking to recover the goods - £98.

AND the claimant claims-

a. *Return of the cash and van removed by the defendant;*

b. *Damages limited to £20,000;*

c. *Interest for such period and at such rate as the court shall think just; and*

d. *Costs.*

Dated 26th July 2016

Nice execution

The Ministry of Justice has issued national standards which enforcement agents are expected to follow. Their failure to do so will not entitle you to legal redress (though you may well be justified in making a complaint about them which could lead to them losing their certificate to do their job). However, the failure could help you in any claim you do bring along the lines we have looked at: in particular, to rebut a defence to a claim for damages that the agent reasonably believed they were not breaking the law. Here's a taster of these standards. Enforcement agents must:

- not act in a threatening way when visiting a debtor's premises by making gestures;
- always produce relevant identification and, where appropriate, written authorisation to act for the creditor;
- carry out their duties in a professional, calm and dignified manner;
- dress and speak appropriately and act with discretion and fairness;
- as far as practical, avoid disclosing the purpose of their visit to anyone other than the debtor or someone like an advice agency representative assisting the debtor; and
- provide an itemised account of their charges if requested to do so in writing.

Part 7

RIGHTS AND WRONGS

Chapter 24

Interest On Debt, Compensation And Judgments

and now for something completely interesting

If you are entitled to receive money through court proceedings, be it for what you were owed or for compensation, then you are probably entitled to receive interest on that money. The rate of interest and the period for which it is payable will depend on what the money is for. Except for debts payable by one business to another business and for interest payable under the terms and conditions of a contract, it will have been necessary for you to have started proceedings so as to qualify for interest. That's one of the disadvantages of seeking to extract money you are due by serving the debtor with a statutory demand instead of obtaining a judgment (see chapter 22). The statutory demand route limits you to any interest to which the contract entitled you. Whilst there will generally be a right to interest up to the date of a judgment, that right will stop (unless any contract says otherwise) once the judgment is given unless it was for £5,000 or more or enforcement of the judgment has been transferred to the High Court (for which the claimant can apply if the debt is for at least £600). Where proceedings have been started and the defendant coughs up the principal sum claimed but not the interest, the claimant can ask the court to enter judgment for the outstanding interest and the court will normally oblige and do so without a hearing having to take place.

Debt not due from one business to another business

Interest on unpaid debts will usually be awarded at the rate of 8% from when the money was due until the date of judgment and the liability for interest will continue from the date of judgment until settlement on claims for £5,000 or more. The rate could have been adjusted by legislation but as the bank base rate has plummeted the 8% has steadfastly stuck with us since 1993. The interest is generally simple and not compound (interest on interest) except that bankers are able to collect compound interest even though they often don't go for it.

Interest can be very substantial. Despite this, claimants are frequently unaware of their right to claim it or just do not bother. Regard should be had to the possibility that the defendant will defend a claim and it could be many months before a trial takes place and during which the claimant will be out of their money.

Any claim for interest must be made in the particulars of claim when the claimant starts a court case and with online claims (see chapter 9) the claimant will be prompted to state whether or not there is an interest claim and the appropriate calculations will have to go in. The amount of interest up to the date of the claim form will be specified and the daily rate sought after then. The interest figure up to the date of the claim should be added on to the amount of the debt and the court fee for starting the case will be based on the total figure. If no interest has been claimed but the claimant later decides they want to claim it then the claim form and particulars of claim would have to be amended, either with the defendant's consent or the permission of the court where consent is not forthcoming. It is by no means a forgone conclusion that permission would be given. The claimant would be refused permission after judgment. And if the claimant asks for permission at the final hearing (and often the claimant does so, especially on a small claim), the likelihood is that the claimant would be given the thumbs down.

The interest regime can operate harshly against a debtor who has collected a judgment and is struggling to pay it off by instalments. The amount of the instalments may be less than the amount of interest which is accruing on the judgment with the result that the judgment sum is never reduced. There is a possible loophole. The creditor's right to interest comes to an end in the county court when they take action to enforce the judgment - by applying for a bailiff to seize the debtor's goods or for the debtor to be questioned about their financial circumstances (see chapter 22) - and that action produces a payment. Interest will not come to an end if the creditor simply applies for a charging order (see chapter 22). And if the court makes an attachment of earnings (see chapter 22) or administration order against the debtor (see chapter 35), no interest will be clocked up during the lifetime of that order. So it comes down to this. By failing to pay up when they should and thereby forcing the claimant to take some enforcement action (other than applying for a charging order), the defendant can do themselves an enormous favour interestwise so long as they make some payment in response to the step taken by the claimant. Should the claimant attempt to enforce only by bringing bankruptcy proceedings, however, the liability to pay interest will continue to run.

In exceptional cases, it may be possible to persuade the court to cut down on the claimant's interest claim. Where it's an 8% claim, the only real prospect of persuasion is probably where there has been an unreasonable delay in the claimant starting or continuing with their claim which has led to a higher interest liability. Should that be the defendant's only argument, they should put in a defence to the claim which takes this point and the court will in all likelihood then enter judgment in the claimant's favour for everything apart from interest and fix a shortish hearing at which interest can be argued out. The defendant should not lightly embark on this course for it can lead to an increased liability for the claimant's legal costs if the argument fails.

If the parties had come to an agreement that, in the event of default by the defendant, interest should be payable at a higher rate than 8% or on a compound basis then that agreement will prevail unless the defendant can show that what the contract says amounts to a penalty (but see chapter 41).

Losses exceeding interest

The object of interest is to compensate the claimant for being deprived of their money. But it may well be the case that the actual loss to the claimant from that deprivation is far greater than the interest which will be awarded. Mr Clive Troublesore refuses to pay Mr Sucker the £25,000 which is due for building works. As a direct result, Mr Sucker's business collapses, he falls behind with his mortgage repayments, his home is repossessed, his wife leaves him and takes the children and his hair falls out. What can he claim from Mr Troublesore? £25,000 debt plus 8% interest. That's tough on the claimant but in this situation the general rule is that they are limited to recovering interest from the defendant.

Pin back your lugholes for the exception to the rule. Take an agreement by Mr Sucker to lend his best friend Mr Troublesore the sum of £10,000 to be repaid after 12 months. Unfortunately, Mr Troublesore is blacklisted for credit and so can't borrow from a commercial lender. Mr Sucker can only make the loan by borrowing the money himself on the basis that if he doesn't repay within 12 months he will have to pay his lender compound interest as from the expiration of the 12 months until he settles and Mr Troublesore is aware of this. When Mr Troublesore defaults in making the repayment, Mr Sucker could claim the extra interest from Mr Troublesore as damages for his loss on the basis that it was in the contemplation of the parties when the agreement was made that the loss would be suffered if Mr Troublesore defaulted.

Business to business

Where money is due for goods or services from one business to another business and goes unpaid, the Late Payment of Commercial Debts (Interest) Act 1998 says it attracts interest at the rate of 8% above Bank of England base rate presently set at 0.5%. For those of you like me who scored the bottom grade for maths 'O' level, they tell me that adds up to 8.5%. The interest starts to run on the date agreed for payment or, if no date has been agreed, from 30 days after supply of the goods or services or, if later, from the date of invoicing. This is simple and not compound interest and it applies between businesses that are small, large, huge and ugly. It would even apply to businesses run by sole proprietors. On top of the enhanced interest rate, the defaulting business is liable to pay a fixed sum for enforcement costs - £40 for debts of under £1,000, £70 for debts of £1,000 or more but less than £10,000 and £100 for debts of £10,000 and over. The moment the enhanced interest rate is triggered, the entitlement to this office biscuit barrel subsidy is also triggered and the fixed sum is payable on top of permitted legal costs incurred by a claimant who starts proceedings.

This business interest differs from the 8% regime in that the obligation to pay it arises without proceedings having to be started. The defaulting business might, for example, settle an invoice late but fail to pay the interest and fixed sum. The supplier could nevertheless then sue just for the interest and the fixed sum - and if feeling especially cheeky add to the claim interest on the interest (!) and fixed sum at the standard rate of 8% on a graduating basis which it might be left to Archimedes to calculate.

Of course, when a business gets litigious with another business with whom it has been in a contractual bed that's likely to be the end of a beautiful relationship. This has to be borne in mind when a decision is taken about how long should be allowed for an invoice to be paid and how heavy the creditor should get. If there is no serious concern about the long term financial stability of the debtor business and the business owed money is without cash flow problems, why not tarry a while and watch the interest mount up at 8.5% which is better than it is likely to enjoy in a savings account? A court claim for debt though must be started within six years of the date on which the money should have been paid (see chapter 10). The alternative with a claim for at least £5,000 is to obtain a judgment and tarry a while with enforcement as interest on the judgment is clocked up at 8%.

Other cases

In most other cases, the court has a discretion to order interest to be paid on the sum awarded at what it considers to be the appropriate rate and for an appropriate period. This would include a claim for damages for breach of contract (say where duff goods have been sold) and the norm here is for the claimant to ask for 8% interest as from the date on which the loss was incurred in the transaction and take what they get. Where damages for personal injury and financial losses are claimed, for example, against a car driver who has negligently caused a road accident, the court must order interest if more than £200 is awarded unless there are special reasons not to do so. The claimant will normally be entitled to interest at the rate of 2% on the damages they collect for their pain and suffering and loss of amenities as from the date proceedings were started. In relation to compensation for specific sums such as an accident victim's ruined motor cycle helmet, the award could be anything from 0.5% to 3% and, if the loss has accumulated over a period - say, earnings lost through absence from work due to accident injuries - the rate may be halved.

Interim payments

Because personal injury interest rates are relatively low, it makes sense for the claimant who has a strong case which is taking anything from 79 days to an eternity to come on for trial, to apply to the court for the defendant to put hands in pocket of defendant or defendant's insurers and bring out an interim payment so that it can be invested at a superior interest rate which might be available and the interest from the investment would belong to the claimant. The claimant might otherwise find some money handy for a purchase, perhaps even for a deposit on a home purchase. Yes, the court can order a payment on account of what it is satisfied the claimant will probably be ultimately awarded and in fact can do so in any case where money is being claimed. Strict conditions have to be met. The court must have given judgment for the claimant for an amount to be decided or the defendant must have admitted liability - or the court must be satisfied that the claimant will recover a substantial amount at trial. The amount of the interim payment is likely to be anything up to between 75% and 90% of a conservative valuation of what the claimant will ultimately be awarded. And if the court gets it wrong and the claimant gets less or nothing at trial, they will be ordered to pay it back! If on a personal injury case the claimant has a legal representative acting for them (which is likely) then they should insist in an appropriate case that they advise them about an interim payment application.

Chapter 25

Compensation For Hassle And Mental Distress

Inconvenience, distress, disappointment, annoyance, frustration, anxiety, displeasure, upset, vexation, tension, aggravation

A night out with Stephen Gold? How very dare you! When, if ever, are you entitled to compensation for what we can loosely describe as inconvenience or mental distress (or both)? There have been loads of decided cases on the subject and many contradict others. The law could even change with a decision of the Supreme Court but what I recommend is that you ensure it is not your case that goes there as that could be expensive. This is how it looks and the county court and High Court are likely to deal with any claim by (or against) you by applying these general principles.

Inconvenience

In a claim for breach of a contract, you should be entitled to compensation for inconvenience if it is of the physical type such as that suffered, along with discomfort, by a claimant who had to endure living in his defective home because of the unsatisfactory way the damp course system had been installed. And way back in 1875 there was compensation for a man and his family who were put out at the wrong train station on a wet night when it was too late for them to get transport or book a hotel so that they had to walk several miles home in the pouring rain. Otherwise, you may struggle to obtain compensation under this head of loss unless you can show that the inconvenience would have been contemplated by the defaulter if the contract was broken and the contract was related to your personal or family life.

When the claim is not for breach of contract but for what is known as a tort - say for the negligent driving of a car - you will normally get compensation for the inconvenience of having to travel around by public transport instead of using your vehicle because it is off the road due to damage and you have not hired an alternative. And on a claim for what the law calls nuisance - excessive and unreasonable noise from the trombone in the flat above or a disgusting pong from next door - compensation for inconvenience and probably some annoyance thrown in will normally come your way. But courts almost invariably balk at awarding compensation after a road accident for the innocent party's inconvenience in having to deal with insurers, repairers, hirers and the rest, on the basis, as one circuit judge put it, that this was all part of the rough and tumble of being involved in an accident (although this should not eclipse the fact that the innocent driver would be entitled to compensation for the cost of postage, telephone calls and other out of pockets which post-accident arrangements usually involve).

Mental distress

For breach of a contract, you won't generally score compensation for mental distress so if you suffer mentally because the computer for your work was delivered weeks too late, that's no good (although loss of income because you were computerless might be available). You may also be able to recover compensation for alarm, distress or physical inconvenience or discomfort under the Consumer Protection from Unfair Trading Regulations 2010 as amended (see chapter 40). There is a massive exception to this general rule and that is under a contract for what judges call *pleasure, relaxation, piece of mind or freedom from molestation.* They are typically awarded in lousy holiday claims where it all started with the 1973 case of solicitor Mr Jarvis. He paid £63.45 for a fortnight away at a house party in Switzerland over Christmas and the new year with a special resident host and a hotel owner who spoke English. The travel company's brochure promised all manner of delights including a welcoming party on arrival, afternoon tea and cake, a yodelling evening, a bar that would be open several days a week and a great time. In the event, there were only 13 guests in the first week and none in the second. There was no welcome party; no representative for the second week; the tea was dry nut cake and there were some crisps thrown in; the yodeller evening consisted of a local man in his working clothes singing a few songs very quickly; the bar was open on only one evening; and the hotel owner did not speak English. Just a flavour. There was more. The Court of Appeal ruled that Mr Jarvis should have compensation not simply for the diminution in the value of the holiday but for disappointment, distress, upset and frustration. It has since been established that the amount of this compensation should not be linked to the cost of the holiday so, if it was justified on the facts, you could be awarded more for a couple of weeks' hell at Knobbly Knees Holiday Camp than on The Queen Victoria Luxury Floating Hotel.

This massive exception could well also apply, for example, to claims for ruined weddings, chronic wedding photographs, lack of health club facilities and wrongly dyed hair (green instead of black).

For a non-contract case the general position is that compensation for mental distress will not be recoverable. The exception is for some cases (but not those brought by a company) that mainly protect your reputation such as libel and some slanders and breach of confidence along with harassment and assault where compensation for injury to feelings is often collected.

Chapter 26

The Litigant In Person's Bill

And why not?!

Legal costs are not the exclusive preserve of the winning party who was legally represented. Yes, you Mr, Mrs, Ms or Mx Nobody who acted in person - with or without a lawyer in the background - can claim costs just like the winner with a legal entourage. You are known as a litigant in person - some procedural practice directions may call you a self-represented party but that title is out of fashion now - and you can ask for costs if you win (you could ask for them if you lose but you would almost certainly be laughed out of court) and you will get them if a legally represented party would have got them in your shoes. You won't get paid as handsomely as a lawyer. However, your potential is habitually underestimated by lawyers on the other side and it is as well to keep them informed on how that potential is clocking up. As they try and intimidate you with costs budgets and costs estimates going through the roof, offer them a taste of what it might cost their client if they actually lost. It will give them something to think about.

How much?

Steady on. First, let's look at the work you have done and the time you have spent on the case for which you can be remunerated. If a lawyer would have had to do the work and spend time on it then you can claim for it and generally at the set rate of £19 per hour. This, for example, can catch preparing the claim form and particulars of claim, reading and considering the defence, preparing your list of documents and witness statements and considering those sent to you by the other side, preparing for the final hearing and attending at court including getting there and back. We might be looking at 20 hours plus on these items alone. There is one important caveat. You cannot collect more than two-thirds of what a lawyer would have collected if they had represented the loser so if you are a particularly slow reader and claim 480 hours for reading the other side's documents you may run into trouble. You can also claim for the expenses you incurred (we call them *disbursements* in the law) so long as they would have been allowed if a lawyer had incurred them and the two-thirds limitation does not apply to these expenses. This could cover court fees, the cost of medical and other expert reports, travelling expenses and payments you have reasonably made for legal services in the case which might include taking advice from a lawyer and even having a lawyer to advocate for you at court. And you can sling in the expense of getting a lawyer, costs lawyer or a law costs draftsman to help you with your costs claim.

Should the time you have spent on the case have actually lost you more than £19 per hour then you can claim the higher amount. You would need to send to the court and the other side any written evidence you were intending to rely on to prove the loss at least 24 hours before the relevant hearing. This could take the form of a suitable letter from an accountant or employer.

On winning at a fast track trial, in addition to these rules applying to the work you have done up to the trial date, there is a special allowance for the day of the trial. Tell the judge you are claiming it under the Civil Procedure Rules 1998 rule 45.39(5). If you can prove any financial loss for the day, you will collect two-thirds of a sum within the range of £485 and £1,650, depending on what the claim was worth: if you can't prove any financial loss, you will collect £19 per hour. Unnecessarily complicated, I know - but nice.

Statement of costs

If you intend to ask for costs at a hearing, you should complete form N260 (access at www.hmctsformfinder.gov.uk). It is not ideal for a litigant in person but follow it as closely as possible. Ignore the certificate close to the end. The form has changed in recent times. Ensure you use the latest version which has a "schedule of work done on documents" at the very bottom. The party against whom you hope to ask for your costs and the court must have a copy of the form at least 24 hours before the time fixed for the hearing or, if the hearing is a fast track trial, at least two days beforehand. If you fail to comply with these requirements then the amount of costs you are awarded may be reduced - on a bad day to nil!

Small claims

None of this directly applies when you win a small claim (see chapter 18). Nevertheless, it could have some indirect relevance on winning and being able to persuade the court that the loser has behaved unreasonably and so should be deprived of the costs protection which generally applies to small claims cases.

"Judge, I have put a lot of sweat, toil and time into preparing my case before you today. If this was a fast track or multi-track case, I would be entitled to £19 an hour for my time without having to prove I had suffered any financial loss by sitting up to midnight every night for the past two months pouring over 'Breaking Law'. Would you rule that my opponent has behaved unreasonably and*

award me costs against him at the same rate - say £19 an hour for a minimum of ten hours?"

*On second thoughts, better keep quiet about '*Breaking Law.*'

Chapter 27

Court Error Compensation

HMC&TS blunder money

I don't know how to say this.....pause for embarrassment.......further pause for checking nobody is watching or listening.......coast looks clear.......in very soft voice......sometimes court staff make mistakes and the court user (otherwise punter otherwise party to proceedings) suffers financial loss as a result. It happens in the best of organisations. It tends to happen a bit more in the court service for the reasons I have already identified. To be fair, some of you swines can give the staff a very hard time - "I wrote yesterday asking for an order that David Cameron be subpoenaed to attend my trial and for permission to bring my Rottweiler to court to speak on my behalf and for a blanket to be provided just in case he pees on the floor and for an interpreter because swearing is the only language I speak and I haven't heard back yet. What the hell is going on?" - and this can hold them up and make them upset.

When a member of court staff tells you to turn up to the wrong hearing centre for your case or does not notify you of a hearing date for your case or fails to send you a copy of a crucial court order or makes your divorce final when you asked for it to be cancelled because you had become reconciled or wrongly notifies your employer that it must dock your salary for a debt against you when in fact there was no such debt or you attended court for your hearing but the judge wasn't there as they had gone on holiday or loses your case file or or or... And when the result of the error is to cause you loss or just irritation, you can make a complaint and, if appropriate, claim for compensation to Her Majesty's Courts & Tribunals Service (HMC&TS) which makes up for the fact that you won't be able to sue them in the court as you might a commercial organisation for poor performance. You will be relieved and possibly surprised to know that there is no court fee payable when you take the step of complaining. It's useful to use complaint form EX343QA which you can download from www.hmctsformfinder.justice.gov.uk Here's the blow. You can't use this route for complaining about the judge so there. HMC&TS has a leaflet nicknamed EX343 which explains what you can do if you are unhappy with its service. It tells you about the complaints procedure. It does not mention compensation. I think it should.

The complaint and claim should go to the hearing centre at which the case is being or has been conducted. You should get a meaningful response within ten working days or an explanation within that time frame as to why the response will take longer. If you are dissatisfied with the response whenever it comes - and you could make a second complaint if the response does not come within a reasonable period - you may take your complaint to the Communications and Customer Service Team, HMC&TS 1st Floor (1.10), 10 Petty France, London SW1H 9AJ which should come back to you within 15 working days. If you are still doing your nut, the next step should be to make contact with your MP and ask them to refer your complaint to the Parliamentary and Health Service Ombudsman who can recommend to HMC&TS that it pays you compensation. You cannot go to the Ombudsman directly.

You should back up a claim for compensation with documentary proof where available although consideration should be given to making a monetary payment to you where mistakes have had a serious or significant impact on you even though you cannot show that a financial loss has been suffered. This could mean a payment if errors have led to a sustained period of distress or anxiety which has affected your health or severe embarrassment or damage to your reputation. Where you should have received some money from the court and the court has delayed paying it over to you then you may claim for any interest you have lost as a result. In one case, because HMC&TS delayed and generally messed up where it was dealing with the enforcement of maintenance arrears due to an ex-wife from the ex-husband, arrears spanning some three and a half years accrued. Part of the loss made up by HMC&TS was the interest at the prevailing rates which the ex-wife would have earned had she invested the money if it had been efficiently collected. Between £250 and £300 has been paid where a party was extremely upset and concerned as their personal and sensitive information including bank details and pension arrangements had been sent in error to someone else. And again where another party had been turned down for a mortgage because the entry of a judgment at the Register of Judgments, Orders and Fines had not been cancelled when the judgment itself was cancelled and the party suffered a lot of inconvenience. There was delay before a mortgage could be obtained.

Claims by solicitors for work done and expenses incurred by their client because of court maladministration are sometimes made albeit not as often as might be justified. When made they can be substantial. Compensation then will be based on the solicitors' hourly charging according to where they are located, the qualifications of the person who was handling the case in the office and possibly the type of case.

Chapter 28

Money Wrongly Paid To You

Estoppel does you good

"Mavis."

"Yes, Clive."

"My bank statement says I'm three grand in the black. And I thought I would have to tap up Uncle Ted for a grand. Must have been that life policy that paid out. Tell you what. Let's try out that new five star place in the New Forest for a week."

"What with the spa?"

"Yeh and full body massages, stark naked. I'll have some of that."

"You're a dirty beast, Troublesore."

Your bank wrongly credits your account. Your former employer overpays you on your final salary. You were expecting a cheque but it's for a couple of zeros too many. It was all down to a mistake but with computers giving the orders and staff thinking about what time *I'm a Celebrity* is on tonight, mistakes like this are as common as a cup of tea. Do you have to pay the money back? Possibly not.

Enter the defence of *estoppel by representation*. By making the payment, the payer was representing that you were entitled to it and the lot of it and should now be debarred from arguing to the contrary. You relied on that representation. You have altered your position because of the payment and so acted to your detriment and it just wouldn't be 'on' for you to have to make a refund. That's how it goes. In order to escape repayment, you would need to prove that you had spent the money in question or committed yourself to do so in an exceptional and irretrievable way believing that it was yours to do so. Buying this book wouldn't be enough, as commendable as your action has been (and if you're reading this in a library, do us a favour and order a copy, eh?) as I know you would have done that anyway. We are really looking at some expenditure which, but for money in question, you would never have incurred.

Has this defence ever worked? Yes, it has and I'm not teasing. In an 1825 case, a bank fed a customer's account with excessive sums over some five years as a result of which he spent more than otherwise he would have done. Bank lost. In a 1950 case Lloyds Bank over-credited a customer's account. She saw what was going in from her statements, relied on them as being accurate and spent more. Bank lost. In a 1983 case, Avon County Council overpaid a sick employee by £1,007 during an absence from work which spanned nearly two years. Of the £1,007, he spent £546.61 including £53.50 on clothes from *Burtons* and £130 by way of deposit on a car taken on HP. The Court of Appeal ruled that not only was he free from an obligation to repay what he had spent and could account for but the Council had to whistle for the balance too.

And because the recipient may usually be hard put to say precisely where every penny has gone, this all or nothing approach will usually apply. But not always. In 2000 Philip Collins Ltd (*"Yeh, it was him, Mavis. Phil Collins, the singer"*) was after clawing back the royalties it had overpaid two musicians against future royalties they would become entitled to when it was thought they had performed on all 15 tracks of *"Serious Hits...Live!"* whereas they had only performed on three of them. The High Court ruled that just one-half of the royalties - so around £14,000 - and not the lot could be clawed back because the musicians had changed their position by increasing their level of outgoings after they were paid and it would be inequitable to require them to suffer a clawback of the entirety of the money. A defence here of change of position rather than the not dissimilar defence of *estoppel by representation* and being partially successful.

You will fail in your *estoppel* defence if you knew the money had been paid by mistake before you spent it and probably also if you suspected the mistake but turned a blind eye. And where you knew of the mistake and spent away, that could land you in the wrong sort of court - a criminal court and on a charge of theft. The prosecution would need to show you had been dishonest. If you were a jury member at a Crown Court trial in one of these cases, how would you cast your vote? In the 1988 case of a Bristol man who had been earning £100 per week, the jury heard that his building society had wrongly credited his deposit account with a cool £20,000. He protested that the money was not his. Staff insisted it was. So he used about half the money to refurbish his council flat, buy a new car along with a dog and some tropical fish, take a holiday and settle some outstanding bills. When the building society discovered that another investor with the same name should have had the money, the police were brought in and the man was charged with 20 thefts. The jury acquitted him of them all.

In the same year, a sales representative was acquitted of stealing £18,700 from her employers who had increased her wages tenfold thanks to a computer error. She spent it on meals, clothes and holidays. She testified that she believed the money had been compensation for an injury at work.

Now say you have come by money which you thought was yours to deal with but no representation has been made to that effect? Mr Troublesore's brother Cedric steals £10,000 from his boss and loses it at the tables at your casino. Being a philanthropic casino proprietor and hoping this might get you into the next Queen's Honours List you give the £10,000 to charity. Can Cedric's boss get the £10,000 back from you? In this situation you can seek to rely on the defence of *change of position* as in the Phil Collins case (see above) which is more flexible than the *estoppel* defence. You would have to persuade the court that the injustice of requiring you to repay outweighs the injustice of denying repayment.

Case no 97P0000678

IN THE COUNTY COURT MONEY CLAIMS CENTRE

BETWEEN

WHITEWASH LIMITED Claimant

- and -

CLIVE TROUBLESORE Defendant

DEFENCE

1. The defendant admits that between on or about 16 June 2015 and 2 January 2016 the claimant credited his account with Dodgy Bank plc with the total sum of £14,260.18 by the payments ("the payments") alleged in the Particulars of Claim.

2. The defendant denies that he is liable to make restitution to the claimant for the payments or any part of them or that he is liable to the claimant to pay any interest as claimed.

3. The defendant says that by making the payments the claimant was representing to him that he was entitled to them; that the defendant believed he was so entitled; and in consequence and in good faith, he acted to his detriment by changing his position. Accordingly, the defendant says that the claimant is estopped from denying such entitlement and from recovering the payments or any part of them.

4. In the alternative, in the event that the Court decides that no representation was made by the claimant that the defendant was entitled to the payments, the defendant says that at all times the defendant acted in good faith and changed his position in consequence of believing that he was entitled to the payments so that it would be an injustice for him to be ordered to make restitution of the payments which injustice would outweigh any injustice (which is denied) which the claimant would suffer if restitution was not ordered.

5. The particulars of the defendant's change of position are that:

[set out details of payments made which would not otherwise have been made and any other ways in which you assert you have acted to your detriment in believing that the money was yours]

[add, if necessary - "These are the best particulars the defendant can give. The defendant cannot now recall how the balance of the payments was applied but it his case that he generally changed his position in respect of them."]

Chapter 29

Company Down Drain: Directors Laughing

Squeezing money out of the culpable

Enormously gigantic companies: itsy bitsy teeny weenie companies. It makes no difference. The general rule is that the company's directors are not personally responsible for the company's debts or breaches of contract. A notable exception is a director who has been directing at a time when he was disqualified from doing so or had given an undertaking not to do so because they had previously been up to no good. Generally, then, it is pointless claiming against a director for money owed to you by their company no matter how diabolical their behaviour towards you may have been. It is equally pointless to play the common trick of bringing proceedings against a named managing director with whom you have been corresponding about the jar of pickled onions containing a set of false teeth which you bought from their company. You will lose.

Breaking down the wall of immunity

Surely, you say, there must be some situations in which the directors can be made personally liable when the company has gone bust with no hope for you of recovering from its assets what you are owed or more than one new pence of it? Of course there are but you will need tenacity. Here goes.

The phoenix company

If a company has gone bust (insolvent liquidation, should you want to be posh), another company must not re-use the bust company's name or another name which is so similar to that of the bust company as to suggest that the two companies are associated (for example, *Whitewash Ltd/Whitish Wash Ltd*; *Breaking Law Ltd/Broken Law Ltd*; *Air Equipment Co Ltd/Air Component Co Ltd*). Any name used during the 12 months before the first company went down the drain will be relevant. And for five years from the date of insolvent liquidation (alright, I've gone posh), no one may be involved without the court's permission in the management of the second company as a director or in any other direct or indirect way. If they are so involved they will be liable for the second company's debts which have been incurred during that involvement as will someone who allows themselves to be used as a 'front man'. If you are a creditor of the second company you can make a claim against them in their own name. You'll find the relevant law in sections 216 and 217 of the Insolvency Act 1986. A lovely read.

Case no 97P0000678

IN THE COUNTY COURT MONEY CLAIMS CENTRE

BETWEEN

CLIVE TROUBLESORE Claimant

- and -

BERNARD TRYON Defendant

PARTICULARS OF CLAIM

1. The claimant claims against the defendant under section 217 of the Insolvency Act 1986 ("the Act").

2. On 26 January 2015 Whitewash Ltd ("the first company) went into insolvent liquidation. During the immediately preceding 12 months, the defendant was a director of the first company.

3. From 5 January 2016 the defendant has been a director of or has otherwise been involved in the management of Whitish Wash Ltd ("the second company").

4. On 14 July 2016 the second company agreed to sell to the claimant a suite of furniture ("the suite") for the price of £5,500. ("the agreement"). It was a term of the agreement that the suite would be delivered by the second company to the claimant on 20 July 2016 and that time was of the essence. The claimant paid to the second company on 14 July 2016 the full purchase price of £5,500 by cheque which was duly presented by the second company and honoured.

5. In breach of the agreement the second company failed to deliver the suite to the claimant on 20 July 2016 and has since failed to respond to numerous requests by the claimant to make delivery and has refused or neglected to provide the claimant with any explanation for non-delivery.

6. On 2 August 2016 the claimant notified the second company by email that he terminated the agreement for non-delivery of the suite and demanded the immediate return of £5,500. The second company has failed to repay any sum to the claimant.

7. At all material times Whitish Wash Ltd was a prohibited name within section 216(2) of the Act in that it was so similar to Whitewash Ltd as to suggest an association with Whitewash Ltd and on and since 5 January 2016 the defendant has accordingly acted in contravention of section 216(2) of the Act thereby render-

ing him personally liable to the claimant for the return of the said sum of £5,500.

The claimant claims:

a. return of the price of £5,500;

b. interest on the sum of £5,500 pursuant to section 69 of the County Courts Act 1984 from 20 July 2016 to 4 September 2016 at the rate of 8%, the daily rate of interest being £1.21 and thereafter interest at the daily rate until judgment or earlier payment; and

c. costs.

Dated 4 September 2016

(signed) Clive Troublesore

Claimant

Fraudulent and wrongful trading

When a director has been up to monkey business before their company goes into insolvent liquidation, the company's liquidator may apply to the court for them to make a contribution towards its debts. The more money the liquidator can get in, the greater the chances of you and your co-creditors taking a holiday next year. The route to a court order is open only to the liquidator and not to you personally. That's why it is important that you give the liquidator as much information as you can about any company wrongdoings of which you are aware and encourage the other creditors to do likewise. This time you will have to delve into sections 213 and 214 of the Insolvency Act 1986 if you don't believe me.

What's needed is evidence that the company has carried on its business with the intention of defrauding creditors or for some other fraudulent purpose. The court can then order that anyone who was a party to this - it isn't essential that they were a director - should cough up a suitable sum. Alternatively, what will be enough is evidence that a director - and this time it is only a director in the firing line - knew or ought to have concluded that there was no reasonable prospect that the company would avoid going down the drain. For example, the company might have continued to trade and notch up further debts or paid out a fat dividend to the director. The liability of the culpable director would be to pay a suitable amount. However, if the director can show that they took every step they ought to have taken to minimise the potential loss to creditors then they will escape liability.

New law: Big blow

The big blow is to directors who have been disqualified or given an undertaking instead of a disqualification under the Company Directors Disqualification Act 1986 because of their culpable behaviour as directors which makes them unfit for office. It is in the form of sections 104 to 106 and 108 to 110 (among others) of the Small Business, Enterprise and Employment Act 2015 - well they had to find somewhere to stick it all in - which catches director misconduct after 30 September 2015.

The court is given the power to order compensation in your favour where you have been caused loss due to the conduct of a person for which, following a company's insolvency (we are looking at liquidation or administration here) they have been disqualified or given an undertaking that they will not act as such for that period under the 1986 Act. Proceedings may be avoided or compromised if the person undertakes to pay the compensation. To be taken into account are the amount of the loss, the nature of the conduct and whether any other financial contribution has been made in recompense for the conduct. It is the Secretary of State who must take the initiative to go after the compensation and he has two years from disqualification or undertaking to bring proceedings. The new liability may attack non-directors as well as directors. If the conduct of a disqualified director (or a director who has given a disqualification undertaking) came about because they followed the instruction or direction of a third party then the third party may also now be disqualified as also may a director on the strength of an overseas conviction for an office concerning the promotion, formation or management of an overseas company.

The sort of conduct which can lead to disqualification - for between two and 15 years - is obtaining credit when they knew that the company was in grave danger of going down the drain, acting incompetently, trading whilst insolvent and drawing money out of the company for their own benefit when insolvency was staring them in the face.

So to have any hope of getting your loss made good, what you need is misconduct by (usually) a director PLUS that director's disqualification or an undertaking in the place of disqualification PLUS the Secretary of State being persuaded to go after the director for the benefit of creditors like yourself unless, of course, the director agrees to cough up without proceedings. As with fraudulent or wrongful trading (see above), the liquidator should be informed by you and other creditors of all misconduct on a director's part you know about in the hope that disqualification proceedings are brought. The Insolvency Service set up an online tool called the Conduct Assessment Service in April 2016 to facilitate liquidators and official receivers reporting on misconduct by directors so that their disqualification can be considered. The report has to go in within three months of the company's failure so you need to get on with passing on relevant information.

This new law is likely to be impacting. Former directors could be less inclined to put their hands up to a disqualification order or undertaking in its stead for fear that a compensation claim will be the consequence. And we may see aggrieved creditors approaching former directors for a compensation deal off their own bats to which those former directors might accede if they think that pressure will otherwise be put on the liquidator to encourage the Secretary of State to institute disqualification proceedings.

Chapter 30

Protection From Your Creditors

Though shalt not harass me

You owe money. This is because of genuine hardship or because you are a distrustful piece of work, empty of morals and full of Fosters. Either way, the law protects you against the creditor who goes over the top in trying to extract from you what is rightfully due to them. They may be committing a criminal offence or gifting you a claim for damages - or both.

Crime street

The Malicious Communications Act 1988 outlaws the sending of a threatening letter where the purpose is to cause distress and anxiety to the recipient or to anyone else who was intended to read it. It is a defence for the sender to show he believed the threatening letter was a proper means of reinforcing their demand. A separate offence is created by section 40 of the Administration of Justice Act 1970 which criminalises the making of demands which are likely to cause a debtor or their family alarm, distress or humiliation because of their frequency or the way they are made or any threat or publicity which goes with them. And completing this triumvirate are sections 1(1) and 2 of the Protection from Harassment Act 1997 which make it an offence to pursue a course of conduct which amounts to harassment so long as whoever was responsible knew or ought to have known that is what it did. Harassment includes alarming someone or causing them distress. Certain conduct could amount to more than one of these three offences, if not the lot.

Side roads

Your creditor's conduct may well break the rules of any professional body to whom they are answerable, like the Law Society in the case of a solicitor, the Institute of Chartered Accountants in the case of a chartered accountant or a trade association to which they belong. The Financial Conduct Authority would be interested in the malpractice of anyone involved in debt collection and could cancel the authority they need to carry on their business. Banks, building societies and credit card companies which go too far in their efforts to increase bonuses and profits may well be breaching the Lending Code which most of them will have agreed to observe and this would justify use of their internal complaints procedure and, if you are dissatisfied with the outcome, a complaint to the Financial Ombudsman Service which I have utilised (see chapter 7).

Route map

Your creditor is legally entitled to demand the payment of the debt. It would be quite in order for them to write a couple of letters, maybe make a few telephone calls or even knock on your door, always at reasonable hours, and ask you to pay up. The creditor may legitimately warn you of what can or will happen if you don't pay - a county court claim, a credit blacklisting if there is a judgment which goes unsatisfied and what means might be adopted to enforce the judgment. How far the creditor can go is a matter of degree.

If you believe the creditor just won't stop, you should write to them. This may do the trick and at the same time get rid of them for ever. The letter and any response will also be of evidential value should you find it necessary or to your likely financial advantage to make a civil claim against them.

149 Magnolia Crescent

Twickenham

KT89 4XZ

14 July 2016

Dear Creditor

I owe you £2,000 under invoice number 0000000000000000000000698/x. Due to circumstances completely beyond my control and which I have repeatedly and fully explained both to your company and the succession of debt collectors you have sent to my home, I am in no position at the present time to settle the debt or make any proposals for payments by instalments and this is likely to be the situation for some while yet. I am advised that your conduct amounts to harassment under civil law and is also offends the criminal law. Unless you and your agents immediately desist from communicating with me otherwise than by service of properly constituted court proceedings, I shall institute proceedings against you for an injunction to restrain contact and for damages for harassment together with costs. I shall also take steps to report you for prosecution under the Malicious Communications Act 1988, section 40 of the Administration of Justice Act 1970 and the Protection from Harassment Act 1997.

Yours faithfully

Clive Troublesore

And now, ladies and gentlemen, we present a nice little earner

The Protection from Harassment Act 1997 not only makes harassment a crime but gives the person harassed - that could be anyone from the actual debtor to a current or former spouse, civil partner or cohabitee - the right to claim damages from the perpetrator and an injunction to forbid any repetition of their objectionable behaviour.

Ms Lisa Ferguson, a self-employed property investor, used to be a customer of British Gas Trading Ltd for the supply of her domestic gas. She left them. Over the following five months she was subjected to letter after letter and threat after threat to cut off her supply, start legal proceedings against her and report her to credit reference agencies - all without justification. She said this caused her considerable anxiety. She wanted to bring British Gas to book so she made a county court claim for damages against them under the Protection from Harassment Act. They attempted to get the claim thrown out, arguing that it was so weak that it should be killed off before a trial (see chapter 15). The Court of Appeal would have none of it. It ruled in 2009 that the conduct complained of was capable of amounting to harassment and was oppressive and unacceptable. Then in 2013 the Court of Appeal upheld an award of £7,500 damages under the Protection from Harassment Act to a customer of Royal Bank of Scotland plc. She had exceeded her overdraft or credit limit on one or more of her accounts. Although she had made it plain that she did not want to speak to the bank, they spoke or attempted to speak to her over the phone on 547 occasions. The calls constituted intimidation and had been wholly unjustified. The existence of a debt did not give the creditor the right to bombard the debtor with calls. It was the right of the debtor to decide whether they wanted to discuss the matter with the creditor. Good stuff, eh?

Courts are likely to follow the damages guidelines set by the Court of Appeal in a case where a police officer who had been harassed and discriminated against by colleagues was entitled to compensation for injury to feelings (as distinct from compensation for psychiatric or similar personal injury). They said the most serious cases (where, for example, there had been a lengthy campaign of discriminatory harassment on the ground of sex and race) should command between £15,000 and £25,000. The middle band of between £5,000 and £15,000 should be used for serious cases which were not serious enough to fall within the top band. And awards of between £500 and £5,000 were appropriate for the less serious cases such as where the act of discrimination was an isolated or one-off occurrence. These figures would need to be updated to take account of inflation since 2002.

Let right be done

If you make a civil claim for Protection from Harassment Act damages and an injunction or either you will need to complete a Part 8 claim form (see chapter 9) and a written statement in support. If anyone at court tells you that this is not the right procedure then say: "May I respectfully refer you to rule 65.28 of the Civil Procedure Rules 1998" or "Look here, mate, you having a bad day? Take a gander at 65.28." Whichever you are more comfortable with, really. You won't be able to use the money claim online procedure. Unless you are urgently after an injunction - if you are, you must additionally complete an application for an injunction in form N16A in triplicate and include with the rest of your court papers - you should first send a letter to your harasser (see chapter 8). You could even back the letter up with a draft of the documents you will use if there is no settlement and you take the claim to court. That would look quite impressive and ought to convince the harasser that you mean business. Under no circumstances should you falsely suggest you have already started proceedings.

> *"If my claim is not settled by you to my satisfaction then I shall institute proceedings against you and lodge with the court a claim form and supporting evidence in accordance with the draft documents, copies of which I enclose with this letter."*

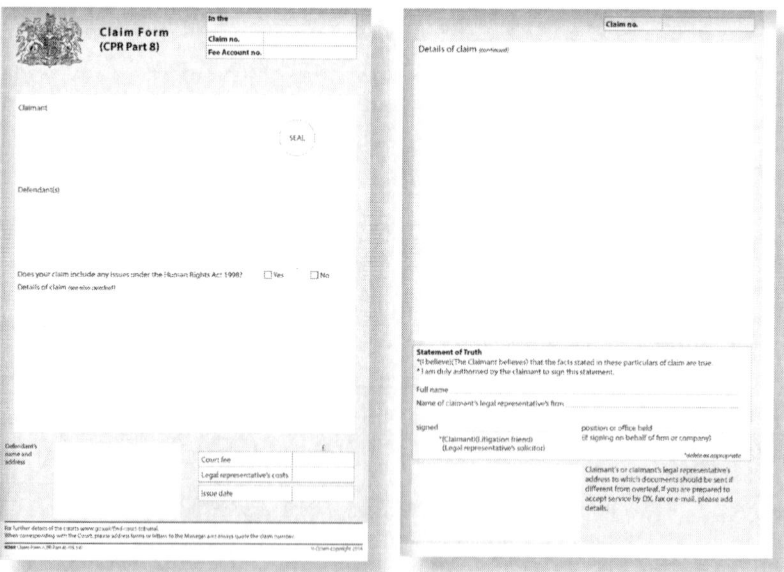

Claim Form
(CPR Part 8)

In the	
Claim no.	
Fee Account no.	

Claimant

SEAL

Defendant(s)

Does your claim include any issues under the Human Rights Act 1998? ☐ Yes ☐ No

Details of claim (see also overleaf)

Defendant's name and address

	£
Court fee	
Legal representative's costs	
Issue date	

Claim no.	

Details of claim (continued)

Statement of Truth
*(I believe)(The Claimant believes) that the facts stated in these particulars of claim are true.
* I am duly authorised by the claimant to sign this statement.

Full name

Name of claimant's legal representative's firm

signed
*(Claimant)(Litigation friend)
(Legal representative's solicitor)

position or office held
(if signing on behalf of firm or company)

*delete as appropriate

Claimant's or claimant's legal representative's address to which documents should be sent if different from overleaf. If you are prepared to accept service by DX, fax or e-mail, please add details.

N208: Part 8 Claim Form

1. At all material times the claimant has been indebted to the defendant in the sum of £7,500 for goods sold and delivered. Due to hardship for reasons beyond his control, the claimant has been unable to discharge the liability ("the liability").

2. Between 1 January and 30 June 2016 the defendant has pursued or caused to be pursued a course of harassing conduct towards the claimant with the intention of thereby forcing him to discharge the liability which has put the claimant in fear and caused him to suffer injury and loss.

The claimant claims:

a. an injunction to restrain the defendant from harassing the claimant and from contacting him in any way whatsoever except for the purpose of serving him with court proceedings brought against him by the defendant and for the purpose of complying with any order, rule of court or practice direction in the course of such proceedings and from instructing or encouraging any person to do so;

b. damages;

c. interest on damages at such rate and or such period as the court shall deem just; and

d. costs.

Dated 4th September 2016

(Signed) Clive Troublesore (Claimant)

Statement in support

Case no 97P0000678

IN THE COUNTY COURT

AT PEARDROP

BETWEEN

Claimant

C Troublesore

1st

CT1-CT3

14 July 2016

CLIVE TROUBLESORE Claimant

- and -

WHITEWASH LIMITED Defendant

I CLIVE TROUBLESORE state as follows:

1. I live at 149 Magnolia Gardens, Twickenham, Middlesex ("the premises").

2. I am a local authority pest control officer.

3. I am the above-named claimant.

4. On 16 December 2015 I purchased building materials and equipment from the defendant for £7,500. I was a long-standing customer of the defendant and it accepted my cheque for the full price. Several days before the purchase I had paid a cheque for £10,000 into my back account which I had received from a relative by way of repayment of a personal loan. I drew the £7,500 cheque against the £10,000 cheque. I had no reason to suppose that the £10,000 cheque would not clear. I was amazed and embarrassed to be informed by my bankers after my purchase and delivery of the goods that the £10,000 cheque had been returned marked "refer to drawer". I have since represented it but it has not gone through. As a result, I am not yet in a position to settle with the defendant although it is my earnest intention to do so.

5. I accept that the defendant is entitled to take reasonable steps to recover what I owe it. However, the steps taken have been excessive and totally unreasonable.

6. Between 1 January and 30 June 2016 the defendant:

a. made numerous telephone calls to my home which often exceeded ten in a single day and which were frequently at unsociable hours;

b. on six occasions made personal visits to my place of employment through its employees or other agents during the course of which they shouted various statements within the presence and earshot of my work colleagues concerning the liability such as that if I did not settle the liability within one week I would be imprisoned and that I would be debarred from following my employment as a pest controller;

c. on twelve occasions made personal visits to my home through its employees or other agents who then threatened me, usually in the presence and earshot of my wife: for example, if

I did not discharge the liability immediately my ears would be cut off , a "heavy" would parade up and down my street with a sandwich board attached to them proclaiming that "Troublesore is a Big Time Con Artist" and the amount of the liability would be quadrupled and carry interest on the increased sum calculated from 1 January 1189 at the rate of 100% compounded with monthly rests until payment; and

d. sent 124 letters to me by post true copies of which I produce marked "CT1" containing demands for the discharge of the liability which were couched in threatening and intimidating terms and 12 of which purported to have come from the Lord Chief Justice of England and Wales.

7. Further particulars of each event or series of events relied on by me as constituting the defendant's harassing conduct are contained in the schedule to this statement.

8. As a result of the defendant's harassment of me, I have suffered injury to my feelings, depression and anxiety. I produce a true copy of the medical report of my GP Dr Goodfor A Sicanote dated 14 July 2016 marked "CT2". I also suffered loss of earnings due to my absence from work because of my state of health attributable to the defendant's conduct in the sum of £648.19 net. I produce a true copy of the letter from my employer marked "CT3" in support of such claim.*

*[*It is worthwhile consulting your doctor whilst harassment persists not only because you may actually need a prescription but because the doctor's report is likely to be of evidential value in any civil claim you may bring. If the harassment is over or your symptoms have ceased, your doctor may still be able to prepare a report recounting what you have told them about the symptoms and expressing a view as to whether they find your account to be credible from a medical standpoint, having particular regard to any relevant medical history].*

SCHEDULE as referred to in paragraph 7 above

[set out under numbered paragraphs and in chronological order, the date of each event or period of any series of events, a short description of what happened and, where applicable, the identity of the defendant's employee or other agent involved: where a very large number of incidents are relied on, a schedule of this kind should assist the judge to separate the various incidents and to quickly get a good appreciation of the facts you assert - you can always seek permission to expand on the schedule with a fuller state-

ment if what you say happened is being denied by the defendant].

No	*Date/Period*	*Event*	*Person involved for defendant*
...	...	...	...
...	...	...	...
...	...	...	...

I believe that the facts stated in this witness statement are true.

Signed

C Troublesore

Dated 4 September 2016

By the way

In response to your protocol letter of claim (see chapter 8) or in their defence, your creditor may seek to shift all blame onto their debt collectors saying, in terms, that they are independent contractors who are required to act within the law and that they did not know and could not reasonably have known they were acting in the way alleged. In any proceedings, you would be entitled to see written communications (or records of them) passing between the creditor and the debt collectors. You could play safe by making the claim against both the creditor and the debt collectors and they can fight out liability between themselves. Otherwise, just claim against the creditor and, if their defence seeks to shift blame, add the debt collectors as second defendant at that stage. The claim form would then have to be amended to name the debt collectors and the particulars on it to state where they come into the picture. You would require the written consent for the amendments from the creditor or, if not forthcoming, you would have to apply to the court (on form N244) for its permission to amend.

In the amended particulars you would wish to add at paragraph 1 that the second defendant was instructed by the first defendant to collect the liability on its behalf. Then at paragraph 2, you would state: ".... the first defendant and/or the second defendant have pursued or caused to be pursued...." Finally, you would make consequential amendments by referring to "the first and/or the second defendant".

"It's your fault, you shouldn't have given me credit"

The argument that a debtor can blame their creditor for extending them credit and so bring about their financial downfall may sound like a crazy one but it has been tried. You would have an uphill struggle to successfully use it to resist a claim or make your own claim. In a 2008 case a greyhound trainer who had been a pathological gambler sued William Hill Credit Ltd for nearly £2m he had lost with them on telephone betting. He had previously reached an agreement with the bookmakers that they would not accept telephone bets from him over a six month period. He wanted to be protected from himself. Because of that specific agreement, it was held that the bookmakers had been in breach of the duty they owed to him not to take the bets but the claim failed because if William Hill had turned him down he would probably have lost the money anyway with other bookmakers. The trial judge rejected the idea that a bookmaker owed a general duty of care to a customer to restrain them from gambling away their money: it was the specific agreement reached in the case that could have made the difference. But the judge did not exclude the possibility that a court might decide a bookmaker was legally responsible where the customer's behaviour had become so extreme as to demonstrate that their gambling was wholly outside their control. There could yet be a case which falls into this category although the gambler would still have to overcome any suggestion that they would have lost the money somewhere else. This "you shouldn't have given me credit" line could conceivably be adopted in a non-gambling context, say by a pathological borrower against a lender who was fully aware of the borrowers' weakness and it might even find favour with a court as part of an *unfair relationship* claim (see chapter 42).

Despite the setback of the greyhound trainer, a not dissimilar argument was put forward in 2015 by a man who had gambled away £2m on the roulette tables at London's The Ritz Hotel casino. He signed a cheque for that amount on one evening in return for gambling chips. The cheque was dishonoured and the casino sued him for the money. His defence included the argument that the casino had owed him a duty to take reasonable steps to ensure he was not harmed or exploited by their provision of gambling facilities. However, the trial judge rejected the gambler's evidence that he was suffering any gambling disorder at the relevant time and there was certainly no evidence that his gambling was outside his control.

If a gambler ever does succeed on this argument they would be highly vulnerable to a finding that they had contributed to their downfall which would lead to a reduction of any damages awarded against the gaming company.

Chapter 31

Claiming On Your Credit Card

The joy of equal responsibility

Imagine a scheme which enables you to go to your lender and saddle them with the sins of the seller of goods or supplier of services who has let you down on the ground that it was the lender's money which was used for the transaction. The engine of the car you have just bought conks out on the drive home. The furniture shop to whom you paid up front for a new suite goes bust. The self-catering chalet owner told you the place was a one minute walk from the sea but it transpires it's a ten second hop from the sewer. The double glazing leaks and the installer never speaks.

There is such a scheme. It's in section 75 of the Consumer Credit Act 1974. Generally, the scheme applies when you paid for the goods and services using a credit card like *Mastercard*, *Visa* and *American Express* or a store card or finance was through a credit agreement for that particular transaction (even a credit sale or hire agreement though not a hire-purchase agreement and debit card transactions will only exceptionally be covered).

And when the scheme applies, the credit card company or whoever else provided the finance is equally responsible with the seller or supplier for any false or fraudulent representation on which you relied in reaching an agreement with them and which has caused you loss or for any breach of contract (including selling goods which were of unsatisfactory quality or unfit for purpose or doing duff work). That doesn't let the seller or supplier off the hook. It means, though, that you can claim against - and, if necessary, sue - whoever provided the credit without bothering with the seller or supplier who may give you aggro by the loads and never satisfy a judgment. Of course, it's sniffle time for the credit provider but they were in the deal for the money, weren't they, and they have a right to reclaim from the seller or supplier whatever they are stuck with having to pay you. As it happens, they will probably try and get a judgment against the seller or supplier in the course of any proceedings you bring against the credit provider alone.

Have I ever used the system? Muggins here ordered a new desk through a newspaper ad and paid for it with his Barclaycard. Desk never arrived. Seller went down the financial drain. I claimed from Barclaycard the price of the desk plus the difference between the price I had paid (which, on the premise that the desk would be delivered, was relatively cheap) and the price I was going to have to pay to another seller for a comparable desk which was at least another £200. Barclaycard came up with the price alright but acted dumb on the rest of the claim. They knew as well as I did that they were liable not only for my direct loss but for what the law calls *consequential* loss like the extra I would have to expend on a comparable desk. For you that *consequential* loss might be distress and disappointment for a ruined holiday because of that no sea but plenty of sewer. Whatever the seller or supplier would have to pay you for the misrepresentation or breach of contract if your claim was against them alone, the finance supplier must pay you. Barclaycard eventually settled the balance of the claim for the extra I would have to pay - and did pay - for the comparable desk on which I am now tapping out this story. Thank you Barclaycard.

I hate to do this but there are some exceptions to the scheme applying. Please don't be hard on me.

* WON'T APPLY unless the cash price for the goods or the service you are complaining about was more than £100. £99.99 won't do. Buying a selection of items which are all individually priced under £100 won't do in respect of any of those items even though the total bill came to more than £100.

* WON'T APPLY if the cash price for the goods or services was more than £30,000 but do not despair because section 75 A may apply (see below).

* WON'T APPLY if your card is in a company's name.

* BUT WILL APPLY although you paid by a mixture of credit card and cash/cheque. So say the price was £1,500 and you paid £5 on your credit card and £1,495 by cheque. The extent of the liability of the credit card company to you will be as great as if the whole £1,500 had gone onto your card.

* AND WILL APPLY even though the transaction takes you over your credit limit or you are behind with repayments to the credit card company.

OK. Take it away section 75A of the Consumer Credit Act 1974. This is for you flash folks. It works like section 75 and covers transactions in which the cash price was over £30,000 and the credit was for no more than £60,260. But that credit agreement must have been directly linked to the transaction so you were being lent money for a particular purchase or service. Either the trader must have dealt with the preparation or making of the credit agreement on behalf of the lender or the specific goods or service must have been explicitly specified in the credit agreement. For example, it would cover a credit loan made to you for the specific purpose of installation of a lift to take you from the ground floor to the third floor of your desirable residence where the trader dealt with the loan paperwork. Then s75A lumbers whoever provided the credit with liability for the trader's breach of contract (not misrepresentation) if the trader cannot be traced, has failed to respond to you after you have contacted them, is insolvent or has failed to satisfy your claim after you have taken reasonable steps to pursue them.

Here's something for you more modest consumers where you want justice - which means money - from your credit card company.

Particulars of Claim

1. On 14 July 2016 the claimant purchased a mattress from Horrorsleep, Hounslow for £102.99. The mattress should have been of satisfactory quality. It was not in that no less than 20 of the mattress springs tore through the upper cover within two days of delivery. The claimant rejected the mattress on 19 July 2016.

2. The claimant paid for the mattress using his credit card number 456791229 issued to him by the defendant. The defendant is equally responsible for the seller's breach of contract under s 75 of the Consumer Credit Act 1974.

Particulars of the claimant's loss

Price - £102.99

Extra paid for substitute comparable mattress - £75.00

Travelling expenses - £30.00

AND the claimant claims:

a. Damages of £207.99.

b. Interest under s 69 of the County Courts Act 1984 at 8% from 19 July 2016 to date of claim of £2.82 and thereafter at the daily rate of 4p.

c. Costs.

Chapter 32

Neglected On Death

Gone but not forgotten

Where there's a will, we at least know what the deceased intended although, as we shall see, they do not always get their own way. And where there's no will, the laws of intestacy kick in and, as we shall see, the court may disapply them. The deceased's like or dislike of what would happen on an intestacy may well have determined whether or not they made a will. One senior figure at the Probate Registry, which deals with issuing authorities to executors of wills and relatives of those who died intestate to wind up the deceased's affairs, once told me he had never made a will because the intestacy laws suited his situation and wishes to a tee. He would have said the very same in a will as the intestacy laws said so no point in wasting the ink and a couple of sheets of paper. You may come to think that the intestacy laws are not for you. Do some cardiac walking, consume a low calorie dinner and read on.

Look, no will

The law changed on 1 October 2014. The deceased is survived by a spouse or civil partner and no children? If yes, they scoop the lot. Formerly, the surviving spouse or civil partner only got the first £450,000 and the rest was shared as to one-half to them and as to the other half to the deceased's parents or, if neither surviving, to the deceased's brothers and sisters. A surviving spouse or civil partner plus children (and not just the under 18s but big and ugly children as well)? The first £250,000 to the surviving spouse or civil partner and then the rest divided as to one half to them and the other half to the children. The law change is that whereas the surviving spouse or civil partner formerly got just a life interest (a right to the income generated by invested capital in the estate) in one half of the rest they now get that one-half outright. In these situations, the surviving spouse or civil partner is also inflicted with the deceased's personal chattels and the new law defines what this means - tangible movable property other than money or securities for money and property which was held solely or mainly for business purposes or was held solely as an investment: pretty wide-ranging.

No surviving spouse or civil partner but children? The children collect 100%. No surviving spouse or civil partner and no children? The parents take the lot and, where neither is still with us, brothers and sisters or their descendants. And so on down to half-uncles and aunts or their descendants and if the only person left is the postman, then the deceased's money goes to the state - and not even a bench commemorated to "a lovely man who spent so many hours sitting in these gardens that he never got round to buying a home made will form."

Incidentally, that £250,000 referred to above is too low. It was set over seven years ago and has been overtaken by a substantial rise in the consumer prices index. The civil servants responsible for drafting the relevant legislation were too pressurised to deal with organising its increase when the other legal changes came in. I would wager my vast collection of Green Shield stamps on the amount being increased before long.

Left out but litigious

Where you are omitted from the will or do you not qualify for a share of the deceased's estate under the intestacy laws, you may still succeed in a claim for something, thanks to the Inheritance (Provision for Family and Dependants) Act 1975.

Who can apply

- Deceased's spouse or civil partner.
- Same sex partner who had not entered into a civil partnership but had been living with the deceased as a civil partner.
- Former spouse or civil partner so long as they have not remarried or entered into a new civil partnership (unless an order for financial remedies made in matrimonial proceedings excludes the right to apply - and frequently it does so).
- A person who lived in the same household as the deceased as if they were the deceased's spouse for at least two years immediately before the death.
- A child of the deceased.
- Any person treated by the deceased as a child of the family in relation to a marriage or civil partnership.
- Any person treated as a child of the family in which the deceased at any time stood in the role of a parent which, for example, would cover a child who was not a child of the deceased but who was brought up by the deceased alone or in the context of cohabitation.
- Any other person who immediately before the death was being wholly or partly maintained by the deceased.

And when

The application for some property or dosh out of the deceased's estate must be made by court proceedings started within six months of probate (in the case of a will) or letters of administration (in the case of an intestacy) having been granted by the probate registry. The court does have the power to extend that time limit but being late is a risky business. A change in the law allows proceedings to be started before probate or letters of administration have been granted which is useful in the situation where say the prospective applicants for the grant are deliberately dragging their feet or they have little incentive to do anything because the deceased's property bypassed their estate (see below). If time permits, a pre-action protocol letter (see chapter 8) should be sent to whoever has probate or letters of administration, actually or prospectively, and efforts made to negotiate a settlement: these cases often do settle by negotiation.

What are your chances?

In every case the court has to take account of the financial resources and needs of you, anyone else who has lost out and is making a claim and all beneficiaries; any obligations the deceased had towards anyone applying and all beneficiaries; the size and nature of the estate; any physical or mental disability of anyone applying and the beneficiaries; and any other relevant matter which can include the conduct of you and anyone else, a promise to see you alright which has been broken or arrangements before death to make a new will which would have benefited you but were never implemented. The court can also have regard to the reasons given in a written statement signed by the deceased with the will and which attempts to justify why some have been omitted and some have been preferred (see below) but the existence of a statement would be far from a cast iron guarantee that it would destroy a claim for provision.

Different rules apply to different classes of applicant. On an application by a spouse or civil partner or former spouse or civil partner, the court must have regard to the age of the applicant and the duration of the marriage or partnership and the contribution made to the welfare of the deceased's family. Where the spouse or partner is applying, the court will look at what would have been awarded if the marriage or partnership had been ended by divorce or dissolution instead of death. A legal change, though, means that the court won't be straightjacketed by this. On an application by a cohabitee, the additional factors to be considered are the age of the applicant, how long the applicant and the deceased lived together and the contributions they made to the family, looking after the home or caring for the family. On an application by a child, the court will additionally look, where appropriate, at how they were being educated or trained. In the case of an old and ugly child, that might involve an investigation into their progress on night school courses in flower arranging and salsa dancing.

What's the prize?

The court can award you a lump sum, maintenance, specific property to be transferred to you or a trust settlement for your benefit. And the court has the power to play around with jointly owned property. Take for example a house which the deceased and his widow both owned as *joint tenants*. The deceased's interest in the house would ordinarily bypass their estate and go automatically to his widow, even if his will stated otherwise. However, the court can claw back into the estate what had been the deceased's interest. Obviously the widow would spit brass tacks if that happened on an application by someone other than her and so would be involved in the proceedings and be heard. Most jointly owned properties are held by their proprietors as *joint tenants*. Otherwise, they are held as *tenants in common* which means the proprietors own in specific shares - say 50-50 - and their respective interests can be gifted by them and, will or no will, those interests count as part of their estates when they die. Owners decide whether they want to be *joint tenants* or *tenants in common* (and, if so, what shares each will take) when they acquire a property and their wishes should be clear from the conveyancing documents and land registry entries. Any owner who holds as a *joint tenant* can easily change over to a *tenancy in common* and, unless there is a contrary agreement with the co-owner, this would have the effect of giving them equal shares. But that's another story, folks.

Which court?

You can bring a claim in the county court and take it or send it to your civil hearing centre. The Part 8 procedure should be used (see chapter 9). You need to put in a claim form and a written statement in support (see chapter 9) and make the personal representatives of the deceased the defendants to the claim. The details of the claim on the claim may go something like this:

> *"The claimant claims under section 1 of the Inheritance (Provision for Family and Dependants) Act 1975 as the spouse of Clive Troublesore deceased for financial provision out of his estate and for the costs of the claim to be paid out of the estate."*

Leaving it late

The will has nothing for you apart from a few raspberries or maybe you scooped the deceased's false teeth and have nowhere to put them. But didn't the deceased tell you close to death that his signed first edition copy of *Breaking Law* was to be yours, or marginally better still, that they would be leaving you their home (paddock land included)? There is an outside chance that such a gift though not in the will is legally effective. But be warned. The law on so-called death bed gifts - gifts made in contemplation of death or *donatio mortis causa* for my Latin readers, is strict. This is because it would be easy to come up with a cock and bull story about what the deceased said and did as the end approached and the deceased cannot readily be called to rebut it. And because of the desirability of preserving a written will as the appropriate means by which we should express our wishes about who gets what when we die.

As it happens, the law has got stricter thanks to a Court of Appeal ruling in 2015 in a case in which four to six months before her death, the claimant's elderly cat and dog loving aunt handed him the title deeds to her home which was not registered at the Land Registry. As she did so she told him; "This will be yours when I go." Her legally effective will gave everything, including the property, to seven animal charities.

Here's a countdown to what you would need to prove to persuade a court to uphold a deathbed (or close to it) gift in your favour.

1. The deceased must have contemplated their impending death - not simply that they were approaching the end of their natural lifespan but that they had good reason to anticipate their death in the near future from an identified cause. The mere possibility of death weeks or months later will fall short of what is required.
2. The gift must only be intended to take effect if and when death occurs so that the deceased can cancel it at any time. When an early death is inevitable the court is likely to relax the need for the deceased to have specifically laid down that the property was to be returned to them if they survived.
3. The deceased must have given you physical possession of the gift or some means of accessing it or documentation showing your entitlement to take possession of it.

In one case the deceased, while dying in hospital, slipped into his partner's handbag the key to a strong box containing the title deeds to his unregistered house. As he did so he said to her: "The house is yours, Margaret. You have the keys. They are in your bag. The deeds are in the steel box."

Margaret got the partner's house.

The nephew didn't get auntie's house. He couldn't satisfy all those conditions.

Ownership of most properties and land is now registered at the Land Registry so there would be no title deeds which the deceased could hand over in order to satisfy condition 3 above. That does not rule out that the handing over of something else would do the trick. A conundrum for a court at some time in the future. Stick around.

FOR THE DECEASED'S EYES ONLY

Don't say we didn't tell you. You worked seven days a week for years, saved a few bob, divorced the first wife after you caught her engaging in sexual commerce with the organic fruit and vegetable delivery man and her Botox refiller and you disowned your son for habitual drugs misuse and profligacy. And now you have kicked the bucket, the divorced wife and the son have made Inheritance Act claims. It's too late now for your voice to be heard except through your personal representatives unless you can get a pass back but you could have put a statement with the will - naturally, signed by you and dated - which set out in moderate yet firm language why those two parasites would not be getting anything from your estate. The statement would have been in the will envelope and so could have been held back when probate was applied for. The judge would have read it and, though by no means could it have been guaranteed to scupper the parasites' claims, it might still have done the trick.

And tell your mate up there that it's no good screaming on about having hidden his will behind the picture of Blondie on the living room wall. Without knowing it is there, one of his relatives will apply for letters of administration to his estate and the intestacy laws will apply - and it's tough that he thinks they stink. We don't have a system of compulsory registration of wills. If a dissatisfied relative rips up a will (a crime so don't try it at home) or the will cannot be found and there is no evidence about what was in it then, again, the laws of intestacy will swoop into action. Your mate could have voluntarily registered the will with the Principal Registry of the Family Division or regional probate registry and that would have totally eliminated the risk of his estate being wound up on the basis that he died without a will. The facility is not widely known. I am not saying that they won't tell you all about it if you ask but they haven't yet taken a full page ad in *The Sun* ("Die Laughing. Make a deposit with us. Hurry."). If your mate is interested for next time around, tell him he can obtain details from the Probate Department, Principal Registry of the Family Division, First Avenue House, 42-49 High Holborn, London WC1V 8NP (telephone 020 7947 6000). The registration fee - a one off - is £20. You'll get a safe custody envelope pack which you can also extract from a regional probate registry and the will can be posted to the London address or the regional probate registry. If you don't trust the post then you or someone on your behalf can take the will inside this impressive envelope to the London address or the regional probate registry. Otherwise, you can keep the will with a solicitor, a bank (watch for a charge) or one of the companies that maintains its own registry (watch for a charge). The Principal Registry of the Family Division is my hot tip for the best location.

Now before you resume living, take a quick look at the law on deathbed gifts (see above). Are you aware of anyone who might show up close to the end and concoct a deathbed gift story? Of course you are. You could put with your will a statement which could go some way to impugning any deathbed gift claim that might be made. You might integrate it into the statement dealing with anyone who has been omitted from the will.

"I have this day executed my last will and testament. I have been advised and fully understand that I can change any of its provisions at any time before my death by way of codicil or revocation with a fresh will. I always have ready access to pen and paper and could easily summon prospective witnesses who could be present and actually witness me making a codicil or fresh will. I also have my solicitor's emergency contact number and she has assured me that I can summon her at short notice in the unlikely event that I should wish to make a codicil to my existing will or make a fresh will.

I assess the prospects of me changing my mind about the provisions of my existing will to be non-existent. I have thought about these provisions with great care before executing the will and I regard it as inconceivable that any event (apart from any gift in my existing will being destined to fail because the beneficiary has predeceased me) could occur to lead me to change my mind about those provisions."

Chapter 33

Adverse Possession

How to become a landowner without really trying

You can steal a paperclip. You can steal a gold bar. But you can't steal land. That's why you never hear anyone up before the local beaks charged with theft of a park or a house. However, you do hear of squatters. This chapter is not about the smelly, scary and unkempt squatters who take over land and buildings for a few months until they are evicted. It is about the more sophisticated and sometimes insidious squatters.

Look, no rent for 12 years

At the start of my days as the BBC Radio Solent on-air lawyer before I became a judge, I was keen to get hold of a good legal story which is how I came to turn up for the first time on national radio. A lady who worked at Gosport Magistrates' Court recounted to me the tale of her parents and their absent landlord. They had taken a monthly tenancy of a house in the town and 12 years previously had stopped paying the rent. They didn't know to whom to pay it. The landlord had disappeared. Enquiries to trace him came to nothing. "Now why don't you get them to write to the Radio Lawyer for advice?" They did. Presenter Jeff Link interviewed me. I opined that thanks to squatters' rights, in the particular circumstances the couple effectively now owned the property. Early next morning in bed and in a semi-conscious state I heard the voice of Jack de Manio on the *Today* programme and then I heard what I thought was my voice and fathomed out it *was* my voice. Having finished recording the interview with me the evening before Jeff Link, unbeknown to me, had packaged the item for *Today*. The postscript to the story is that the landlord never did appear and in due course the couple were registered with the Land Registry as the absolute owners of the house which by then was worth over £150,000.

The squatter at work

The more usual route for gaining land through the squatting laws runs quite differently. The squatter begins using land they have not previously been associated with or moves the fence at the bottom of their garden three hundred metres into the adjoining field and extends the fencing to the sides. They may be less adventurous and erect a wall at the side of their house a quarter of a metre into the next door neighbour's land. They go about their business quite openly for this is one of the essentials to getting the squatting laws to work for them. Where appropriate, they will probably cultivate this land. They will never seek approval from the owner of the new land for what they do because this would be fatal to their enterprise. Should the owner of the new land ask them to desist they will ignore them unless they fear the owner might punch them about the body or bring civil court proceedings against them (as the owner could) for trespass and even damages and costs to boot. Never ever will they sign a written acknowledgment that the land belongs to the owner for that, squatterlawwise, would waste the time they have occupied it. They will reject any offer from the owner to grant a tenancy or a licence to use the land as such a creature would be a killer of their plans. They will exercise some form of physical control over the land. They will be conscious of the fact that when the time arrives (see below), they will need to show that they intended to possess the land and have been dealing with the land as an occupying owner would have dealt with it and that no one else has done so whilst they have been concerned with it. They will not be guilty about their motives for they know that motives do not matter in the jungle of squatters.

Bye bye

Until the time arrives for them to claim that the land in question is now their land, the squatter who is occupying it cannot sell it. But should they sell their own land, they can certainly transfer to their buyer any "rights" they have to the new land because the time the squatter has been occupying the new land can be added on to the time their buyer occupies, having stepped into their squatter shoes, in order to score the time period needed to become the new owner. The prudent buyer will obtain a statutory declaration - a formal written statement signed up in the presence of a lawyer and, indeed, make it a condition of the purchase contract that one is handed over on completion - setting out the squatting history in lurid detail. That's what happened when Christopher Moran bought a house in Dolphin Place, Amersham in 1971. His sellers in the conveyance deed transferred "all such estate right title and interest as the vendors may have in or over ..." a plot of land which had belonged to Buckinghamshire County Council and which it intended to use at some time in the future for a proposed diversion of the A404. From 1967 the sellers whose house adjoined had cut the grass of the plot, trimmed the hedges and from time to time parked a horsebox on it. A statutory declaration was handed over with the deeds explaining the history and Mr Moran carried on where his sellers had left off. He also padlocked the gate to the plot and kept the key. The county council failed in its attempt to have Mr Moran booted out. Because that time had arrived.

When does the time arrive?

The period required for ownership of the land to effectively pass to the squatter depends on whether or not the land is registered at the Land Registry. Most land is registered. If the land is unregistered then the period was and remains 12 years. If it is registered then the period has been reduced to ten years as from the 13 October 2003 by virtue of changes made by the Land Registration Act 2002 unless the squatter had already notched up their 12 years before that date. There is an exception where the squatting is on Crown foreshore. A whacking 60 years of adverse possession is needed there. This embraces "the shore and bed of the sea and of any tidal water, below the line of the medium high tide between the spring and neap tides" and let's hope you aren't too wet to fathom that out (sorry).

The squatter of *unregistered* land with 12 years under their belt as at midnight on 13 October 2003 can apply to the Land Registry for title to the land to be registered for the first time in their name (unsurprisingly called an application for first registration of title). The squatter of *registered* land with 12 years under their belt at midnight on 13 October 2003 can apply to the Land Registry to be recorded as the new proprietor but the existing registered proprietor and certain others will be notified and can put forward objections.

And the squatter of registered land (I know you may be finding this tedious) who notches up the lesser period of 10 years but only after midnight on 13 October 2003 can apply to the Land Registry to be recorded as the new proprietor. Again, notice will be given to the registered owner and certain others who can object. No objections? The squatter is recorded as the new owner. Objections? Generally, the registered owner prevails but if they fail to get the squatter evicted or at least to obtain a court order for the squatter to give up possession within the next two years, the squatter can return to the Land Registry and more or less repeat his application. Second time round the squatter will prevail.

One exception to how things go on a first application. Where the squatter and the registered owner own adjoining land - typically in the moving fence or encroaching wall erection situation - the registered owner will not usually be entitled to object to the application after 10 years of squatting if (a) the exact line of the relevant boundary has not been determined under Land Registry rules and (b) during the time of squatting the squatter reasonably believed that the land they want recorded in their name actually belonged to them.

Dry land

It's all rather complicated, 'aint it?! Should you want more detail, I commend the excellent Land Registry series of guides which you can access on the internet and will guarantee you will never be invited to another dinner party should you mention them at the next one.

The morals

1. Periodically check out land you own.
2. Don't go away for more than ten years less a month or two at a time and as soon as you get back, pop round to *Whiteacres* and check that there's no one there, the grass is longer than you left it, the hedge is reaching for the sky and the next door neighbour does not have a smug look on their face.
3. Avoid any claim of adverse possession by ensuring that when you allow another person to use your land or buildings they acknowledge in writing that they are doing so with your permission. Adverse possession and consent do not go hand in hand.

Chapter 34

Libel, Slander And Malicious Falsehood

Troublesore v Whitecock - Statement in open court

Solicitor for the claimant: "My Lord, I appear for the claimant who is a highly respected citizen. The defendant is a retailer of pedal cycles and their accessories. He is represented today by my learned friend Mr Francis de Lobowalk.

In August 2015 my client purchased a bell from the defendant which fell to pieces when he attempted to fix it to his cycle. It was defective. When he returned the bell to the defendant's shop he was abused by a staff member and denied any redress. The following day the defendant posted a message on the website vexiandvile.com in which he accused the claimant of having made a false claim against him and demanding £10,000 for not reporting him to trading standards. He went on to allege that the claimant was a serial false complainant and urged any shopkeeper who encountered him to evict him from their premises. The website has in excess of 3 million followers and a substantial number of whom hail from the claimant's region.

All these allegations by the defendant were untrue, as the defendant now accepts. In particular, the defendant accepts that the bell was defective and that the claimant made no demands of him or his business other than for a full refund of the price paid for the bell and the expenses incurred by him in travelling by bus to and from the defendant's shop. He also accepts that whilst the claimant has in the past made a number of consumer complaints against other businesses, they have always been well founded and that the claimant is not vexatious.

The defendant appears here today by counsel to apologise to the claimant for the damage, distress and embarrassment caused by the online publication. Further, the defendant has agreed to pay to the claimant a substantial sum in compensation and to deliver to him a lifetime's supply of cycle bells of the highest standard and to indemnify the claimant for his legal costs."

Counsel for the defendant: "My Lord, I confirm everything my friend has said. My client extremely regrets that he failed to give satisfaction to the claimant in the matter of the bell, that the claimant's complaint was not dealt with efficiently but most inappropriately by a very junior member of staff who has since been dismissed and that the defendant in a moment of madness after a very stressful day and completely out of character, should have libelled the claimant as he did."

Solicitor for the claimant: "In the circumstances, my Lord, it only remains for me to ask for permission to withdraw the record."

This is the speak of defamation proceedings - libel and slander - which have settled. The claimant makes a statement in court which has been approved in advance by the court and the defendant usually joins in. The hope is that the statement will be reported on by the media and the public and, in particular, that anyone who knew about the defamation will come to hear of the statement in court and will thereupon realise that the claimant is good and pure. The claimant may turn up at court to hear the statement and pose a little on the way in and out as they insist to their inquisitors that they cannot say how much they are being paid in damages by the erring defendant. Custom has it that actual figures are not mentioned. "Substantial damages" sounds good but they may be only a few hundred pounds. Views differ on whether a statement in court is wise. It effectively repeats the libel or slander and then proceeds to knock it down. Some may think there is no smoke without fire and that the real reason damages are being paid and an apology is being given is that the publisher cannot get the evidence together to justify the truth of what was written or uttered.

Brittan meets Gold

My first experience of an open court statement was when I was despatched off as a naïve trainee solicitor to the Royal Courts of Justice in London's Strand for the making of a statement following the settlement of a libel action brought by the then town clerk of Gosport for whom my principal had been acting. The statement was being read out by a barrister, the late Leon Brittan (pre-MP, Lordship and the rest) who my firm had briefed for the purpose. Back then solicitors from the sticks who had a case in London were required to use a London firm of solicitors for hearings in the capital to act as their agents. So there were Leon Brittan, the London agent and me with the file and one copy of the statement on flimsy paper. Outside court the London agent introduced the naïve trainee to Mr Brittan whereupon he gave him a sneering glance and turned away. An enduring image. The statement having been read out, I was besieged by a multitude of reporters who wanted a copy which taught me - and my principal - always to go to court armed with ample copies to satiate members of the press whose shorthand is not up to scratch.

Cyril Smith apologises

You may wonder why such an array of talent had to be assembled to read from a piece of paper. Good point. The practice was an irritant to solicitor Alastair Brett who in 1985 was senior legal assistant with Times

Newspapers Ltd and, with his employer's consent, was conducting a small private legal practice mainly representing personal friends during the course of which he had been advising Liberal MP Cyril Smith. He along with Radio Trent had been sued for defamation by Leo Abse, Tam Dalyell, Bob Cryer, Dennis Skinner and 21 other MPs over a broadcast Smith had made at the time of the Falklands crisis in which he had adversely commented about their conduct in voting as they did. The case was settling. A few days before a statement was due to be read, Brett telephoned his favourite defamation chambers to retain a barrister to read the statement which was to be made. The last time he had used a barrister to show how well they read, his client had paid out a fee of £50. This time he was being quoted £150 for his choice or £75 for a more junior barrister. "The fees have gone up, sir." For some time Brett had harboured the belief that a solicitor should be able to read out a statement which would make the exercise much cheaper. Generally solicitors were not then entitled to speak in open court unless in hushed tones through the client's right ear. There would have to be a challenge. Brett briefed barrister David Pannick (later Lord Pannick QC) to apply to the High Court for Brett to be given permission to read out the statement. This may not have been an economically viable step in the circumstances but nevertheless, a worthy fight. The High Court judge refused Brett permission. There was only one thing left for it. An appeal to the Court of Appeal. That was proceeded with and failed. But the following year judges announced that mere solicitors would be permitted to appear in formal and unopposed cases in the High Court when sitting openly which would include reading out a statement where a defamation case had settled: something I later did myself. This was the first step in extending solicitors' rights of audience in the higher courts.

"Pass the magnifying glass, please"

It's useful as part of a settlement to seek to extract a commitment by an offending publication to report the statement and to do so in at least as prominent a position as the offending article. I once represented a television presenter who sued a local newspaper for libel. It made a payment into court which he wanted to unconditionally accept but the paper failed to participate in the making of a statement in open court. It reported on the statement but in the most economical of terms and in a position less prominent than that occupied by the local tide times. I thought that the paper deserved a stricture from the now defunct and formerly feeble Press Complaints Commission. But we wanted anonymity. My client would have been guilty of self-inflicted ridicule if he had been unsuccessful in his complaint, having details of it well publicised with him being fully identified. So I asked the Commission's Mark Bolland (who went on to become deputy private secretary to Prince Charles, with no thanks to me) whether anonymity could be afforded. No. We had to forget the complaint.

Gold gets nervous

It was in 1971 that I had begun my weekly broadcasting on the law for BBC Radio Solent. I forgot to stop and was still at it 25 years later when appointment as a judge compelled me to quit. In the event, a regular round up of legal news was sometimes recorded from a small self-operated studio at Portsmouth Guildhall which linked up with the main studios in Southampton. There a producer would deal with matters technical - like starting a recording machine. Fairly early on I was commenting on the outcome of a libel action which had concluded that day with Lady Docker, a bizarre socialite, winning her case and being awarded a halfpenny in contemptuous damages (or possibly a penny or a farthing but let's not fall out over quantum) which would suggest that the jury felt obliged to follow the law and find she had been defamed but didn't think much of her or her reputation. I alluded to her in an uncomplimentary way as I started to chat to producer Jeff Link at the other end. Unfortunately, a presenter had failed to switch the broadcast desk at his end on to Radio 2 resulting in my comments being broadcast live over the sports report. A memorandum was issued from on high. It was not to happen again. It didn't. I could have been on the wrong side of a libel writ but maybe Lady Docker didn't listen in to the sports report on local radio.

Gold gets gazebo

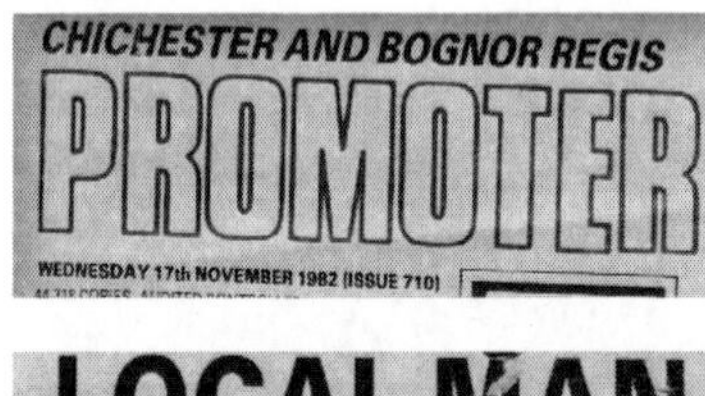
CHICHESTER AND BOGNOR REGIS
PROMOTER
WEDNESDAY 17th NOVEMBER 1982 (ISSUE 710)

LOCAL MAN SUES TVS PRESENTER

"Ouch!"

In November 1982 I was presenting a current affairs programme for the regional television station TVS when the Chichester and Bognor Regis Promoter libelled me. In a lead story on the front page (they must have been hard up for news that week) under the headline "Local Man Sues TVS Presenter" they reported on the issue of a writ against my law firm by a former client who alleged I had been negligent in litigation I had conducted for him. The writ was later abandoned and rightly so. With that out of the way, I sued the paper's publishers for the libel. The report had gravely injured me in my character, credit and reputation and brought me into public scandal, odium and contempt was how the court papers grandly put it. The paper through its insurers put in a defence, not alleging that I had been negligent but, amongst a couple of things, denying that the article had been defamatory. Five years after the article had appeared and sensing that I was not going away, the publishers paid £1,050 into court to settle the claim (the Part 36 procedure did not then exist - see chapter 8) and I accepted. On top, the publishers had to pay my firm's bill covering the work I had done on their behalf in acting for me in pursuing the claim which was all perfectly legitimate. I had a gazebo built in my garden on the strength of the settlement.

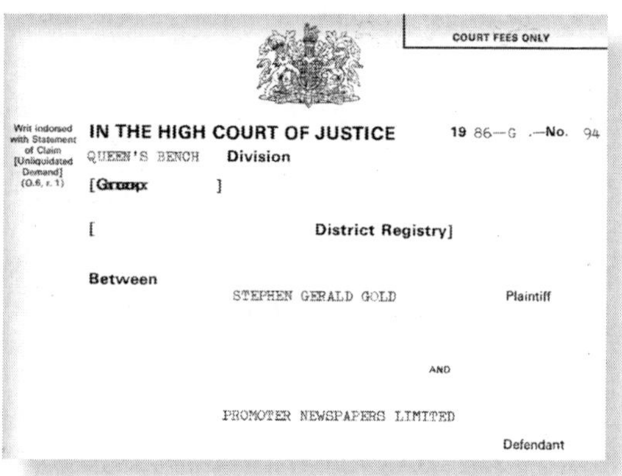

COURT FEES ONLY

Writ indorsed with Statement of Claim [Unliquidated Demand] (O.6, r.1)

IN THE HIGH COURT OF JUSTICE 19 86—G .—No. 94

QUEEN'S BENCH Division

[Group]

[District Registry]

Between

STEPHEN GERALD GOLD Plaintiff

AND

PROMOTER NEWSPAPERS LIMITED

Defendant

"Libel writ"

But what about a statement in open court? I decided against it. On balance, I thought I had more to lose than win by having the libel repeated. After all, you know I couldn't possibly have been negligent.

Hacked off

THE INDEPENDENT

NEWSPAPER PUBLISHING PLC
40 City Road, London EC1Y 2DB
Telephone: 01-253 1222 Telex: 9419611
Direct Line: 01-956 Fax: 01-956 1435

16 November 1989

Mr S G Gold
Donnelly & Elliott
Solicitors
38 Stoke Road
GOSPORT
Hampshire
PO12 1JG

Dear Mr Gold,

Thank you for your letter of 29 September. I have discussed your worry about confusion with your namesake, but I have come to the conclusion that the risk is too small to require publication of a disclaimer.

Yours sincerely,

Andreas Whittam Smith
Editor

"Complaint dismissed"

I have to confess to less success with *The Independent*. In 1989 I was contributing to the paper's Law section. A man with a name not dissimilar to my own had allegedly been involved in a bit of computer hacking and a report of the court proceedings appeared in the paper. I was concerned that readers might think that the report referred to me. I asked the then editor Andreas Whittam Smith to publish a statement which distanced the lawyer from the alleged hacker. I asked for not a penny in compensation, not even for a free subscription to the paper. Liability in defamation can arise in such a situation although a publisher would have a defence when the statement complained of was included in a report of court proceedings which was fair, accurate and contemporaneous. Mr Smith was having none of it. He concluded that the risk of confusion was too small to require publication of a disclaimer. I thought it would be a good idea to carry on writing for *The Independent* so took that one on the chin. I have taken no pleasure in seeing its demise in print form. I liked the paper.

Beware

Should you reckon you have been libelled or slandered and want some compensation then a DIY job will be dangerous. The law in this area is complex, the case would have to be brought in the High Court and the costs there can reach astronomical heights. If your case is strong enough then lawyers will take you on a 'no win, no fee' basis (see chapter 6). If it isn't strong enough for that then you probably ought not to be suing. Maybe you are trying to assess your position through the paperback edition of *The One Thousand Things You Didn't Know About The Law by a Struck Off Solicitor* which your aunt bought you for Christmas 1957. Watch it. The defamation law changed for libels and slanders perpetrated after 31 December 2013. There will now be no defamation unless publication (in a newspaper or on radio or television or whatever) caused or was likely to cause serious harm to your reputation. For a claim by a business (including a company) there won't have been serious harm unless serious financial loss has been caused or was likely. This is a high threshold. Juries in defamation cases (one of the rare categories of civil cases in which they figured) have been virtually killed off which means that a judge alone will now try the case. For an internet libel the one year rule for starting a claim in a defamation case (see chapter 10) is to apply from the date of the first posting and the one year will not rerun from a later publication of the same or substantially the same libel. And a useful power has been introduced which will generally enable the court to order the defendant to publish a summary of its judgment.

Defaming the dead

You can write or say what you like about someone who has died. Or can you? A judgment of the European Court of Human Rights at the end of 2013 suggested that a defamatory statement about a deceased person might, for a relative of the deceased, be a breach of their right to respect for private life under article 8 of the human rights convention. The impact on the relative would have to be pretty monumental for any hope of success on this basis. So if something false has been written or said about late Uncle Jimmy and you've been shunned and avoided by the world since then and have got a couple of hundred thousand to spend on legal costs, have a go, make legal history and get your name into the law reports - so long as the human rights convention is still around for us.

Shut up or else

Perhaps you have been libelled or slandered and have no wish to go near a court of law to do anything about it but want to frighten off the culprit. Never threaten to do that which you are not prepared to do. It will make you look weak and stupid. "Unless within seven days of the date of receipt of this letter you pay me damages of £2,000 and provide me with your withdrawal and unqualified apology for your libel, an irrevocable undertaking that you will not repeat or cause, encourage or permit to be repeated the defamatory statement that I am a raving paedophile or publish or cause, encourage or permit to be published any other statement which is defamatory of me, I shall commence proceedings against you in the High Court for damages, aggravated damages, an injunction to restrain you from defaming me in the future and costs without further notice." Forget it unless you mean it. Instead, adopt an ostensibly stern approach without committing yourself to litigation now:

"At a meeting of Littlecamp Parish Council on 14 July 2016 you stated that I had failed to pay my council tax for seven years, had erected a tablet summarising my marriage vows in the back garden of my property without planning permission and was a serial adulterer. All these allegations are false and amount to the most serious actionable slander of me. You are required to take this letter as formal notice that in the event that these defamatory statements or any of them are repeated by you or any statement which is defamatory of me is made by you in the future or that you cause, encourage or permit any such statement to be repeated or made, I shall, without further notice, institute proceedings against you in the High Court for damages, aggravated damages, an injunction to restrain repetition, interest and costs in respect of the slanders published on 14 July 2016 and the subsequent defamation."

Website libel

If you are libelled on a website and the operator will not remove the statement that causes you concern, you may wish to make a claim against the poster. You know their identity? No problem. You don't know their identity? You can apply to the court for the operator to identify them or consider taking advantage of the Defamation (Operators of Websites) Regulations 2013 because that could be a passport to a successful claim against the operator for publishing the statement which is otherwise likely to be legally difficult. What you do is to send the site operator a *notice of complaint*. This must:

- give your name;
- set out the statement concerned, where on the website it was posted, why it is defamatory of you, the meaning you attribute to it and the aspects of it which you believe are factually inaccurate or are opinions not supported by fact;
- confirm that you do not have sufficient information about the poster to bring proceedings against them;
- confirm whether you consent to the operator providing the poster with your name and email address; and
- specify the email address at which you can be contacted.

Ensure you get all that in. Generally, the operator must send the poster within 48 hours a copy of the *notice of complaint* (with your name and address concealed if you did not consent to disclosure). The poster then has an opportunity to consent or object to the statement being removed. Should the poster consent or do nothing, the statement should be removed. The operator's failure to follow what the regulations require them to do after they receive a *notice of complaint* will rob the operator of the defamation defence otherwise available to them that they hadn't posted the statement.

To vexiandvile.com

Below is my notice of complaint. In view of its contents and, without prejudice to your statutory obligations in consequence of the notice, I call on you to forthwith withdraw the statement referred to in the notice which is highly defamatory of me.

Notice of complaint pursuant to the Defamation (Operation of Websites) Regulations 2013

My name: Clive Troublesore

My address at which I can be contacted: sorebore12@yahooshucks.co.uk

Statement complained of: "Troublesore is a menace and must be stopped. He lies about his purchases being naff and tried to screw my mate out of ten grand for flogging him a bloody bike bell that was a peach saying he was off to trading standards if he didn't pay up."

> *Where statement was posted on your website: Bastard's Corner (on 14 July 2016)*
>
> *Why statement is defamatory: It is untrue and its publication has caused and/or is likely to cause serious harm to my reputation.*
>
> *Meaning I attribute to the statement: I am dishonest; a serial frivolous and vexatious complainant and/or litigant; and a blackmailer.*
>
> *Factually inaccurate aspects of statement: that I am a liar; that I am a menace; that I attempted to extract £10,000 from a bicycle bell seller; that the bell sold to me had been of good or satisfactory quality; and that I threatened to report the bell seller to trading standards if I was not paid £10,000.*
>
> *Aspects of the statement which are opinions unsupported by fact: that I need to be stopped from pursuing any course of conduct which is objectionable or improper.*
>
> *Disclosure of my identity: I consent to you providing the poster with my name and my electronic mail address.*
>
> *Poster's identity: I confirm that I do not have sufficient information about the poster to bring proceedings against that person.*

Malicious falsehood

This is one of my favourites. A claim for malicious falsehood can be made when you have been slagged off and caused financial loss as a result.

> *"Clive Troublesore has retired as painter and decorator. I will be delighted to give you a competitive quote for the sort of job he used to do."*
>
> *"If you want a jar of jam, steer clear of anything made by Clive Troublesore. I've heard he mixes up the strawberries and raspberries in his empty paint pots."*

The recipe for a successful malicious falsehood claim is a written or verbal statement which is not only false but has been communicated to someone else, was made maliciously and generally has caused actual financial loss as was likely to happen. Malicious falsehood differs from libel and slander in a variety of ways. The most striking difference is that you don't have to show that the statement has injured your reputation. Nevertheless, if your feelings have taken a knock as well as your pocket, you could claim damages for both, asking for aggravated damages in relation to the injury to feelings. Libel and slander claims are sometimes coupled with an alternative claim for malicious falsehood.

Here is what makes malicious falsehood such a cutie. Whereas a libel or slander claim cannot be started in the county court, a malicious falsehood claim can be started there. You might even just be able to get an uncomplicated malicious falsehood claim squeezed onto the small claims track although this would almost certainly mean having to limit the claim to £10,000. As to that ingredient of malice which is needed, that may not be as hard to prove as you might think. The defendant must have acted with some improper motive. Normally they will be treated as having done so if they knew that the statement was false or made it recklessly (not caring whether it was true or false). If the statement was made in good faith, don't waste the ink on completing a claim form.

Say you have all the ingredients for a successful claim bar being able to prove the statement has caused you actual financial loss? In certain circumstances, that won't matter. That's when the statement was likely to have caused such loss though it didn't and it was in writing, in a television or radio broadcast or in the performance of a play. You can also succeed without actual financial loss when the statement was likely to have caused actual financial loss in respect of your job or business. Obviously, without financial loss there will be no point in making a claim unless you are after an injunction to prevent a repetition or damages for hurt feelings. The open court statement procedure (see above) is now also available in a malicious falsehood claim that settles.

Particulars of Claim

1. At all material times, the claimant carried on the business of a part-time painter and decorator ("the business") and the defendant was a full-time painter and decorator in competition with the claimant and ordinarily operating in the same localities.

2. Between, on or about 2 to 23 January 2016 the defendant distributed and thereby published in and around Twickenham, Middlesex not less than 200 leaflets ("the leaflets") containing the following words ("the words") relating to the business:

> *"Clive Troublesore has retired as painter and decorator. I will be delighted to give you a competitive quote for the sort of job he used to do."*

3. The words were false and published maliciously. The claimant had not retired as a painter and decorator and was ready, willing and able to take on new contracts. The defendant knew of their falsity or, in the alternative, published them recklessly, not caring whether they were true or false, in order to induce the recipients of the leaflets to contract with the defendant instead of the claimant.

4. In consequence of the said publications, the claimant has suffered loss and damage in that he has lost profit from contracts into which certain recipients of the leaflets entered with the defendant whereas they would otherwise have contracted with the claimant or, in the alternative, the claimant has lost the opportunity of entering into contracts with such recipients. Further and alternatively, the words were likely to cause pecuniary damage to the claimant in the business.

And the claimant claims:

a. Damages limited to £10,000;

b. Interest;

c. An injunction to refrain the defendant from publishing, causing to be published or encouraging any other person to publish the words or any similar words likely to cause damage to the claimant; and

d. Costs.

Chapter 35

Bankruptcy

The ecstasy and the agony

The honourable thing to do is to pay off your debts. Nobody would quarrel with that. Well perhaps they would. Alas, the debts may be so high or your financial position so dire that there is no reasonable prospect of you achieving settlement during the lifetime of your great grandchildren. Or it may be those personal and telephone calls from your more aggressive creditors - and it's the creditors who have bought the debt from the people you originally owed the money to, sometimes for less than the price of a box of ten Woodbines, who can be the most aggressive - are getting you seriously down. Then bankruptcy may be the answer. Let's see what it really involves and, if you find the idea of it to be anathema, are there alternatives?

The nice bits

You can tell your debtors to go to hell. Once you have been made bankrupt, they cannot lawfully chase you for what you owe them. And at the end of one year after you were made bankrupt, generally speaking, the slate is wiped clean. The debts you had are cancelled when you are said to be discharged and the discharge happens automatically without any application to the court or anyone else. That's a pretty good deal, isn't it? The slate cleaning still comes after 12 months even though you have been made bankrupt before although this period can be extended if you have failed to cooperate with the official receiver who deals with your affairs following bankruptcy. I once had the doubtful distinction of making a bankruptcy order against a man who had been through it twice before. Three bankruptcies over a relatively short period. He deserved some sort of medal for finding so many people to extend credit to him.

Before the Enterprise Act 2002 came into force, discharge generally took three years though longer for those who had been bankrupted before within the previous 15 years. The radical change in the law was spearheaded by former PM Gordon Brown when he was Chancellor of the Exchequer with the ostensible purpose of helping struggling entrepreneurs whom it was felt were encumbered by the stigma and restraints which had traditionally been associated with bankruptcy. So the three years came down to one year for entrepreneurs but also housewives on benefits with a string of credit card debit balances, organ grinders, shysters and old hands (none of them being mutually exclusive). The late Labour MP Michael Meacher was once before me as a claimant complaining about how easy it was for debtors to avoid their responsibilities. I told him who he had to thank when it came to bankruptcy!

There are some exceptions to the rule that bankruptcy wipes out your debts. You continue to be liable for arrears of maintenance to a spouse or former spouse and civil partner or former civil partner and, thanks to a change in the law, for a matrimonial order for payment of a lump sum of money or an order for costs as well. Other exceptions (so you will still be liable) are:

- student loans unless the bankruptcy took place before 1 September 2004 and the loan was received or the entitlement to the loan arose before that date;
- fines;
- outstanding child support; and
- money due under most judgments for damages for personal injury.

Creditors who hold security, like a building society to whom you have mortgaged a property or a creditor who has obtained a county court judgment against you and followed it up with a charging order (see chapter 22), can, subject to a suitable court order, dispose of the security and take out of the proceeds whatever they are owed with the remainder being made available for your creditors without any security.

The not so nice bit 1

You lose your assets. Ouch! Ok, so you haven't got any assets. I've always been amazed by the dearth of assets shown in the statements which debtors seeking a bankruptcy order have produced to me. The higher their credit card debts - and it isn't unusual to see someone on benefits having run up liabilities of over £20,000 - the less likely it seems they will have anything to show for it. I do hope, dear debtors, that you haven't been pulling the wool over my bespectacled eyes. Anyway, if there are any assets (and you sure can't hide a house or flat under the bed and if you gave it away in the run up to bankruptcy, it may be retrieved for the benefit of your creditors), you will lose them. That includes your home if you do own it and your interest, with the mortgage debt being deducted from the market value of the property, is worth more than £1,000. Should you jointly own the property with, say, your spouse or partner then it's only your share which will be lost to your creditors. The interest of your spouse or partner will be preserved for them and, when the property is their sole or principal home, the creditors will not usually be after trying to get the property sold until one year from the date you were made bankrupt has elapsed.

The trick in that situation is to buy out the creditors if you can source the money required. You will have to come up with the amount your interest in the home would have raised if it was sold on behalf of your creditors. Perhaps your spouse or partner is in a position to raise the necessary money on a mortgage or you have a relative who can come to your financial rescue - or perhaps released from all those debts which you owed when you were made bankrupt, your financial position is transformed and you can find a willing mortgage lender to come up with the necessary money. Such lenders do exist but criteria are very strict and you'll find yourself having to pay an interest rate way above that which would have been available to the Archbishop of Canterbury (who has never been bankrupt). Although discharge from bankruptcy comes after one year, the official receiver (or whoever has been appointed outside the Insolvency Service to act on behalf of your creditors - either way they are called the trustee in bankruptcy) has three years from the date on which you were made bankrupt to do something about getting hold of your interest in a home by applying to the court for you to leave or for the property to be sold, or both. The court has power to extend the three years but it is rare for this to happen. Subject to this, at the end of the three years, the property will revert to you.

Like virtually everything else in the law, there are exceptions to the rule that you lose your assets on bankruptcy. Your pension is the Enormously Huge exception for bankruptcies ordered after 29 May 2002. Approved personal pensions are safe although the position is not straightforward for certain final salary schemes. Should you take a lump sum under a pension scheme whilst still bankrupt, that lump sum could be treated as income for the purposes on an income payments order (see below). And also excepted are tools, books, vehicles (though if valuable you may be expected to replace the vehicle with a cheaper alternative) and other equipment which is necessary for you to use in your work or business along with clothing, bedding, furniture, household equipment and provisions which are necessary for the basic domestic needs of yourself and your family.

The not so nice bit 2

For the one year you are an undischarged bankrupt (or longer where you haven't been cooperating and the period is extended), you cannot:

- be a director of a limited company or involved in its promotion, formation or management without the court's permission;
- seek credit for £500 or more without disclosing that you are an undischarged bankrupt with the result that only someone out of their mind would then grant it to you;

- manage a business with a different name without telling people with whom you do business that you are an undischarged bankrupt;
- be a member of a local flood defence committee (oh no) but you can be an MP (so that's alright then);
- pursue certain professional careers such as a solicitor or generally work in financial services; or
- work as an insolvency practitioner!

Your immigration status could be affected and any prospective employer might be put off (discriminating against an individual on the grounds of their bankruptcy or former bankruptcy is no more unlawful than whistling in a public place). If your trustee in bankruptcy reckons that you have been in some way culpable for what has happened then they can seek to have certain of those restrictions continued beyond the end of the bankruptcy and for a period of at least two years and a maximum of 15 years. They would be after what is called a bankruptcy restrictions undertaking or order. So you could find that you are no longer bankrupt and are released from your debts but for some period of time you are subject to the same restrictions to which you were subject during the bankruptcy. You will be asked to sign a bankruptcy restrictions undertaking which will bind you not to seek credit for £500 or more without disclosing you are subject to the undertaking and so on and, if you refuse, an application can be made to the court for a bankruptcy restrictions order.

The not so nice bit 3

If you have got some spare dosh after the basic living requirements of yourself and family have been met then the trustee in bankruptcy may seek to have you make a contribution towards your debts by way of an income payments undertaking or, if you won't sign one, an income payments order from the court. The undertaking or order will be limited in duration to three years from when it was made. As a matter of practice, there won't be an attempt at obtaining an order or undertaking unless you have at the very least a spare £20 per month although it is very rare for an attempt to be made at that rock bottom figure. The court might well decline to make an order on the strength of only £20 per month being available.

The not so nice bit 4

Bankruptcy is a good way to alienate family and lose friends who have lent you money and not been repaid, without really trying. Like the rest of your creditors, they will probably have to wave goodbye to their money or place what they are paid out into a partially used packet of salted peanuts. If you favour them over other creditors in the run up to the bankruptcy then they may well find themselves having to pay the money back at the behest of the trustee in bankruptcy.

The not so nice bit 5

Details of your bankruptcy are likely to stay on your credit reference agency file for six years. They will also have gone on the Individual Insolvency Register where they will remain for up to fifteen months (assuming the date of your discharge is not suspended on naughty bankrupt grounds) and will be recorded at the Land Registry against any property you own for five years from bankruptcy but this will not prevent a sale or remortgage of the property where the trustee in bankruptcy confirms they are no longer interested in it.

Easy!

The process of going bankrupt could not be easier. In fact, since 5 April 2016 it's got ridiculously easier. The court is generally no longer involved. You apply for bankruptcy to the Insolvency Service by going online to GOV.UK. A paper application is not available. Initiative and a swear box will be required if you haven't got a computer, tablet, mobile phone or a public library you can afford to get to (and get back from) so as to access a computer. The application will be considered by a so-called adjudicator. It isn't necessary for you to don an Oxfam outfit for the occasion as nobody will be watching unless you are in a public library. I once had a man applying to me for his bankruptcy who was wearing a beautiful sheepskin coat which was so new and stiff that the arms were elevated at an angle of 45 degrees to the legs. He had obviously had a last fling on a credit card with a bit of life in it to buy the garment.

Should bankruptcy be refused you can ask for the refusal to be reviewed and if the decision stands you have a right to appeal to the court. The application will be cheaper than the fee which was payable to the court on issuing a bankruptcy petition - £130 instead of £180 - but the deposit which has to be paid on account of the cost of the work which would be carried out by the official receiver if the application is successful did stay at £525 but has just been increased to £550. The court was able to remit the petition fee. You won't be able to get either the application fee or the deposit cancelled or reduced but you will have the opportunity of paying them by instalments but the bankruptcy application will not be processed until you have scored the full amount required. The court will deal with any issues which arise after bankruptcy and will continue to deal with petitions for bankruptcy by creditors against debtors. If having to stump up both the application fee and the deposit presents a problem for you, borrow from father-in-law ("I said she should never have married him!") or Ken next door or try and get the money from a charity. If all that fails and you remain desperate for bankruptcy, wait for one of your creditors to bring bankruptcy proceedings against you instead of doing it yourself. Anyone owed at least £5,000 (the figure was raised from £750 for bankruptcy proceedings started after 30 September 2015) can do so and they will have to pay the court fee and deposit. If you tell one of your creditors you have just come back from a cheapie in the Bahamas they will probably reckon you good for the debt due to them and bankrupt away.

The adjudicator on a debtor's application for bankruptcy can be expected to watch out for one particular kind of dodgy customer. That's the EC individual who lives in a country whose bankruptcy laws are stricter than ours, wants to take advantage of our crazy laws and is masquerading as domiciled here whereas they arrived yesterday and are going back tomorrow.

Cheers!

Once you have obtained your bankruptcy, it's off for a quick pint and thence to your bank to notify them of what has happened. You can still run a bank account whilst bankrupt so long as the bank (or building society) wants to keep you as a customer. If you owed them money and they don't hold security for the debt then they will lose out and so be pleased to see the back of you. Presentationally, it makes sense to speak to the bank at your own initiative rather than leave it to them to discover from the official receiver that you are bankrupt. It may be you have already opened a basic account with no overdraft facilities in contemplation of the bankruptcy and that you have shared your intentions with the bank. Many do. If an account with a credit balance is frozen the official receiver can be asked to release to you any money you urgently need and also release your partner's share in any joint account you hold with them.

The alternatives to bankruptcy

They all involve coming up with some cash but are worth looking at so here goes.

Debt management plan alternative

You hand over regular instalments out of your future earnings or other income which is shared out to each of your creditors in proportion to what they are owed until they are all eventually paid off. Ideally, you need them all to agree. They won't agree unless they are convinced that you have offered the best they are likely to get. There are a number of companies who make a profit from organising and maintaining plans like this. Beware. Some of them are parasites, charging fees which are knocked off each instalment before it is distributed and are disproportionate to the amount of the instalment and the service they provide. It can also be difficult to extricate yourself from the agreement with the company until the agreement with creditors has come to an end. Payplan (www.payplan.com) is worth looking it. They seem efficient to me and set up and handle the plan free of charge to the debtor. Payplan receives donations from the credit industry.

You can always organise and manage your own plan, seeking an agreement to what you propose from the creditors and then dividing up the agreed weekly or monthly payment among them. When seeking agreement, it is vital that you provide and are seen to provide the fullest information about your financial circumstances and pack this punch that refusal by the creditors to agree will result in bankruptcy and nothing for them.

149 Magnolia Crescent

Twickenham

KT89 4XZ

14 July 2016

From Clive Troublesore

To my creditors

I regret I am presently unable to pay my debts and am in arrears with all payments to you. I am an honourable person and, within reason, I prefer to clear my debts rather than apply for my own bankruptcy which I will be compelled to do if any of you are unwilling to accept my proposals below.

I owe a total of £x. I am prepared to make instalments in the total sum of £y per month to commence on 1 October 2016 and thereafter to be made on the first day of each successive month on the basis that each of you receives the proportion of the instalment which the amount of my debt to you bears to the sum of £x. [My offer is conditional on any creditor who is entitled to claim interest on my debt waiving such entitlement as from 1 October 2016 provided I do not default in instalment payments. It is also conditional on all my creditors accepting my proposal]. Should my financial circumstances improve then I will be happy to increase the amount of the instalments and would provide you with full information about my new circumstances at the time.

Would you please confirm whether or not you are prepared to accept my offer within 28 days of the date of this letter. If you are, a payment book, standing order details or other directions as to the mode of payment you require should be provided to me. I shall be happy to give you any further information you may require. I hope your response will be favourable.

Details of my debts

[insert name of creditor and sum owed]

Details of my financial circumstances

[insert details of assets, income (after tax and national insurance) including benefits and outgoings including travel to and from work and food when working: add income of spouse or partner and state number and ages of all dependants: if you own your home, state the market value after the amount required to pay off any mortgages has been deducted and where you jointly own it give the value of your share after that deduction. Send copies of some recent pay slips and copies of recent bank statements with a view to demonstrating that you are being as transparent as you possibly can].

Individual voluntary arrangement alternative

This is a formal arrangement with creditors to pay something towards what you owe them over a period of several years - it will usually be five years - and which will be set up and managed by a supervisor who is an insolvency practitioner. You may be putting income or capital into the pot to be shared by the creditors, sometimes both. Certainly, if you have or are likely to receive some capital during the lifetime of the arrangement, your creditors would expect it or some of it to go into the pot. The proposals you put forward for the arrangement must be sufficiently attractive to the creditors to get 75% of them to agree which is essential for the arrangement to go forward. That's 75% in value which means that where your total debts come to £100,000, creditors owed at least £75,000 must agree and they won't agree unless they are convinced that the voluntary arrangement would be financially better for them than seeing you made bankrupt. You could end up paying off a small fraction of what you owe and avoid bankruptcy. I have approved voluntary arrangements for substantial debts where the creditors were set to collect as little as 5p and 10p in the pound. The bad news is that the insolvency practitioner who organises things will want their money up front for their service and we are here looking at around £3,500 plus. Future fees for maintaining the arrangement will come out of the money you put in. Should you default under the arrangement, the insolvency practitioner will bankrupt you or you can bankrupt yourself.

Debt relief order alternative

This is an amateur debtor's form of bankruptcy and works in a similar way - Insolvency League Division 4 stuff. It's only available where the amount owed is less than £20,000 (this figure was raised from £15,000 as from 1 October 2015); any car you own isn't worth more than £1,000 and the value of the rest of your assets is £1,000 or less (up from £300 as from 1 October 2015); and your monthly income after tax, national insurance and normal household expenses is no more than £50. There's a fee to pay of £90 so considerably cheaper than bankruptcy and it's the Insolvency Service to which an application for an order is made - through an approved intermediary such as the CAB - and not the court.

Administration order alternative

Available from the county court and for National League debtors who owe a maximum of £5,000. You pay off your creditors by regular instalments and usually over a period of no longer than three years. The court may, and often does, reduce the debts to the creditors you have named - they are all given the opportunity to object - so that you only pay them a percentage of the total bill: in that sense, like an individual voluntary arrangement (see above). Once you have paid off what is required by the order, the creditors named in the order can't touch you.

The dodgy bankruptcy

Here we meet the individual attempting to thwart an application against them for property or money in matrimonial proceedings. Once a bankruptcy order is made, as we have seen, the bankrupt, with a few exceptions, effectively loses their assets. With their assets gone, there is nothing for their spouse or civil partner to share. Apart from a claim for maintenance to be paid out of the bankrupt's future income - and this the court can still order and it would be advantageous to the prospective payee to get an application made before the trustee in bankruptcy gets round to applying for an income payments order (see above) - the spouse or civil partner are stymied. Or are they? Supposing the bankrupt hides some of their assets from the official receiver, avoids an investigation and interrogation about their assets in a financial application because that never takes off as a result of the bankruptcy, enjoys automatic discharge from bankruptcy after 12 months and in due course reunites himself with those undisclosed assets? I have seen it happen. Should the spouse or civil partner discover that the bankruptcy was a ruse, they can apply for the order to be annulled (cancelled). Occasionally, an application to annul is linked up to a financial application in matrimonial proceedings and they are heard together.

Gold rush

It sometimes happens that a marriage (or civil partnership) has broken down and the husband (it could equally be the other party) cannot pay their debts but has assets which they would prefer to see go to the other party rather than their creditors: maybe they are particularly anxious that the family home should be preserved so that any children should have a roof over their heads. What they do is to collude with the other party in procuring a court order which transfers their interest in the home and possibly other property as well with the intention of outwitting the creditors on the bankruptcy which will inevitably follow a few months later. An order like that is highly likely to be successfully challenged by the husband's trustee in bankruptcy and cancelled out once the bankruptcy has taken place.

But should one party get wind of the fact that the other party is heading for bankruptcy, pushing speedily ahead with an application for financial remedies is quite legitimate. Provided there is a court order dealing with financial issues (and the fact that the party heading for bankruptcy has agreed to it matters not) and it is made before the date on which the bankruptcy process has been started, then the likelihood is that the order will stand and the trustee and the creditors will be bound by it. This could mean that the family home and other assets go to the other party and will not be available to be shared out among the creditors towards what they are owed. What is vital to defeat the trustee and creditors, however, is that the final decree ending the marriage or partnership - the decree absolute in the case of divorce (see chapter 48) - has been made prior to the date on which the bankruptcy application or petition was issued. Generally, a period of six weeks and one day must elapse after the date of the decree nisi before the decree absolute can be applied for. Unsurprisingly, a financial order which has been consented to by the bankrupt party should not be mega over-generous to the other party or collusion between the parties may be established which would be fatal to the order.

Chapter 36

Ragbag

Here's a selection of draft particulars of claim (see chapter 9) to go with claim forms for a series of situations - quirky ones, unusual ones, common ones. They would need to be adapted to the facts of any real case. I'm not suggesting for one moment that you should go out and provoke a right to claim. I am suggesting that when you have a legitimate complaint which you make to whoever is culpable and you are met with rejection (and especially rejection coupled with rudeness), you give serious thought to seeking redress where the loss to you is more than trifling. As I have already suggested, you can always produce a copy of the proposed particulars of claim you would use if you started proceedings and send them to the culprit trader. "Look, I'm ready to take this to court. The particulars of claim are ready. Here's a copy. Cough up the reasonable amount I have asked for or it's sue, man, sue." Most of the draft particulars of claim are short enough to facilitate online issue of proceedings (see chapter 9).

Taxi trauma

Some of my best friends are taxi and private hire drivers and I would like to think there will be no impediment to using their services in the future. Yes, some of them do have those wretched highly fragranced packs hanging from the interior rear view mirror to combat passenger armpit aroma and worse and which make me want to vomit but a polite request for them to being taken down has never been refused though the aroma lingers on. And there was this guy who didn't know the location I needed on a pre-booked job in north London the other year and kept going round the same one-way system, to my intense frustration and despair. This led to me walking into a judicial training course late and being dreadfully embarrassed. I'm sorry, but I could not bring myself to tip him.

Anyway, the drivers I've had in the front of my taxis and private hire cars of late assure me that if they or their employer are in breach of contract, it's fine with them for a claim to be made and there's no question of a black listing or any hard feelings so here goes.

Been waiting and waiting

Particulars of Claim

1. On 13 July 2016 the claimant agreed to engage the defendant to convey him from his home at 149 Magnolia Crescent, Twick-

enham (the pick up) to Gatwick Airport to fly to Spain and to collect him at 12 noon on 14 July 2016. The claimant informed the defendant that it was essential that he was collected no later than 12 noon or he would miss his flight and suffer loss. It was implied by these circumstances that time was of the essence of the contract. Despite 12 hastening telephone calls by the claimant to the defendant its collection vehicle did not arrive at the pick up until 12.50 pm on 14 July 2016 in consequence of which the claimant did miss his flight.

2. As a result of the defendant's breach of contract, the claimant suffered the loss of having to pay for an outward ticket with another airline to fly on the same date in the sum of £167 which he claims from the defendant.

Mellor moments

Particulars of Claim

1. On 14 July 2016 the claimant engaged the defendant to convey him by metered taxi from his home at 149 Magnolia Crescent, Twickenham to Eton Avenue, London NW3. It was an implied condition of the engagement that the defendant would follow a route which would render the duration of the journey as short as reasonably possible taking into account road and traffic conditions of which the defendant was or should have been aware. Further and in the alternative, it was an implied condition of the engagement that the defendant would take whichever route which the claimant reasonably required him to take.

2. In breach of the above conditions the defendant, having collected the claimant at 2pm, took a route which was not a short as reasonably possible and was circuitous despite the claimant's protests and refused to take the route which the claimant asked of him thereby trebling the duration of the journey from 30 to 90 minutes.

3. The claimant was charged a fare which was £30 in excess of what he would have been charged had the above breaches not occurred and which he paid to the defendant under protest. The claimant claims its return.

No show

You have advertised for a chief executive, nanny, residential rat catcher or secretary, sifted through 789 applications, interviewed six people on the shortlist and finally hired Mrs Troublesore. She was due to start yesterday. She didn't turn up. Mr Troublesore phoned two hours after you were expecting her, to say she had changed her mind and decided she preferred to stay at home and look after him instead. That is a breach of contract and Mrs Troublesore is liable to you in damages for your losses. She might have found it cheaper to start the job and given notice on the first day. The length of notice would be dictated by the employment contract.

Particulars of Claim

1. On 1 June 2016 the claimant agreed with the defendant to employ her as a nanny to commence work on 1 July 2016 at a wage of £450 pw. In breach of the agreement, the defendant failed to so commence and notified the claimant through her husband on 1 July 2016 that she had decided not to work for him.

2. The claimant has suffered these losses as a result:

- *cost of re-advertising: £35;*
- *difference between defendant's agreed wage and agency wage paid for temporary nanny until new employee started: £1,250;*
- *net loss of income for time spent re-interviewing: £25.*

AND the claimant claims:

a. £1,310;

b. Interest under s 69 of the County Courts Act 1984 at 8% from 23 July 2016 to date of claim of £17.22 and thereafter at the daily rate of 28p;

c. Costs.

Similar principles operate when an employer has been gazumped in that, having accepted an offer of employment, the applicant has secured a better package elsewhere and elected to take the other position. Graduates are especially adept at the practice.

Sue achooer

Why does every person we choose to sit next to or pass by always have a stinking cold and why do they never carry a handkerchief and, if they do, why do they never use it but instead sneeze with the velocity of a tornado directly into our faces and then turn to speak to their companion who has escaped the onslaught as we protest at their disgusting behaviour and why do we never fail to be struck down by their pernicious virus a day or so later? It isn't fair. Until unprotected public sneezing is criminalised, I would like to see some successful claims for damages which might help to reduce the practice at the same time as compensating the hapless sneezee. There are enormous difficulties in the way of the sneezee but are they surmountable?

An assault and battery are known to the civil law as a trespass to the person. "You trespassed my person, you swine. Take this! And this!" You've heard it at the *Dog and Duck* of a Saturday night. If the unprotected sneeze is directed into your face then, in my book, that too is a trespass to your person. And it's probably negligence as well. It could also be either or both when, though not directly aimed at you, the sneezer is aware of your presence and the sneeze is emitted so close to you that they should have foreseen that you might catch something from them.

Proving it was as a result of the sneeze that you were struck down could be the obstacle to a successful claim. Maybe you were already destined for your sick bed from naked dancing in a freezer the night before, maybe you were infected by someone else's virus a day later or maybe your sneezer didn't have an infection to pass on? You must prove it is more probable than not that the sneeze was the cause of your illness. Physical closeness, the absence of prior symptoms, the velocity of the sneeze and the stage at which your symptoms began to manifest themselves will be among the major factors for consideration. The further away from you the sneezer, the weaker your case.

Dr Peter Feldschreiber used to practise in medicine which put him in touch with some of the best sneezers in town. He then decided to qualify as a barrister - possibly because he reckoned that would set him up to sue some of them but I didn't like to ask - and he has stuck with the law in conjunction with being the senior medical adviser to the Medicines and Healthcare Products Regulatory Agency. I got some free sneezing advice from him and it came in language that even I could understand. He tells me that a good sneeze can travel at 60 to 80mph for up to 20 metres and so easily the length of a northern line tube train carriage in the rush hour. However, research published in 2015 by the Massachusetts Institute of Technology suggests that droplets from sneezes - and coughs - may travel 200 times further than we had thought. That's because the drops are accompanied by "gas clouds" which alter their trajectory. The small drops get carried a greater distance while the larger ones drop out.

The incubation period for whatever is to follow the sneeze is around 24 to 48 hours. I get the strong feeling that Dr Feldschreiber would like to see a successful claim by a sneeze recipient (and a sneeze, he says, could quite easily start off bronchitis or even TB) against one of the public transport carriers for causing illness through overcrowded carriages. He has obviously had an unfortunate experience. I asked him whether he would be prepared to take on such a case on a 'no win, no fee' basis (see chapter 6) whereupon he promptly pulled out a handkerchief and it wasn't to sneeze but to hide. I wouldn't recommend it either. But, who knows, this one might work:

Case no 97P0000678

IN THE COUNTY COURT MONEY CLAIMS CENTRE

BETWEEN

CLIVE TROUBLESORE Claimant

- and -

AMELIA SPLUTTER Defendant

PARTICULARS OF CLAIM

1. On 14 July 2016 at approximately 1.15pm the claimant was visiting the ground floor of Z&Y Department Store in George Street, Richmond-upon-Thames, Surrey ("the premises"). The defendant was also a visitor to the premises and walking in the opposite direction to the claimant. When the parties were alongside the spiced nut counter and about 50 centimetres apart, the defendant turned towards the claimant and emitted a loud and powerful sneeze ("the sneeze") directly into his face causing spittle to land on his nose and mouth. As a result of the sneeze, the claimant contracted a virus with which he was ill for a fortnight and suffered loss and damage.

2. The defendant's action amounted to an assault and battery on the claimant.

3. Further and in the alternative, the claimant's illness, loss and damage were occasioned by the negligence of the defendant.

Particulars of negligence

a. Turning towards the claimant when she was close by and, as she must or should have known, was about to sneeze and that such sneeze was likely to infect him.

b. Failing to turn away from the claimant prior to or during the course of sneezing.

c. Sneezing into the claimant's face when she knew or should have known that she was thereby likely to infect the claimant.

d. Failing to carry a handkerchief or to use any handkerchief she was carrying by placing it across her nose and mouth before or whilst sneezing.

e. Failing to stifle the sneeze or take any or any sufficient steps to eliminate or reduce the risk of her infecting the claimant.

f. Being in premises open to the public whilst suffering from a condition which made her susceptible to sneezing and thereby likely to infect any other person with whom she was likely to be in close contact.

4. The particulars of the claimant's personal injury, loss and damage are contained in the medical report of Dr A Kardoma dated 01 July 2016 on which the claimant relies and a copy of which is served with these Particulars of Claim and otherwise -

a. Loss of earnings for period 18 July to 01 August 2016 - £2,480 net;

b. Medication - £13.75.

5. The claimant claims interest on damages under section 69 of the County Courts Act 1984 at such rates and for such periods as the court shall determine to be just.

AND the claimant claims:

a. Damages not exceeding £5,000 to include damages for pain, suffering and loss of amenity not exceeding £1,000;

b. Interest; and

c. Costs.

As meritorious as your case may be, it will not get off the ground unless you can identify the sneezer. Claiming against "the bloke in the green jumper by the cauliflowers in Sainsbury's, Chobham at 1pm on 14 July 2016" is a no-goer. Please don't attempt a private arrest. The chances of persuading a police constable who happens to be standing close by at the red peppers to investigate an assault and battery by sneezing is remote though you can always try. Your best bet is to ask the sneezer for their name and address as you snap them on your mobile before they land you on the ground with blood pouring from your nose at which point the police constable by the red peppers would be more interested. Your even better best bet is to find a staff member who knows the sneezer as a regular and can tell you who they are. Out in the street a direct approach is likely to be the only course open to you. Either way, the less confrontational the better. Under no circumstances should you ape the Carlisle man who in October 2015 was given a six month sentence of imprisonment for assaults and public order offences. He had taken exception to five women, mainly elderly, who had sneezed or taken out their handkerchiefs in public.

Occasion off, Food off, Service off

If you have made a reservation at a restaurant and are turned away, you may be entitled to compensation for disappointment and loss of enjoyment. It depends on the place, the occasion and how things panned out. You would get nothing - from me! - if it was a fast food joint. But if we are talking about a pukka two-star Michelin establishment where dining is an experience or somewhere else down the league table and you or your party were celebrating a special occasion of which the restaurant had been aware, you would have good prospects of success. That's provided you weren't able to get into a comparable restaurant without travelling 150 miles down the road.

Should things be reversed and you be the defaulter by cancelling, the restaurant might have a claim against you. Some restaurants have been known to warn of a cancellation charge in advance and, having already obtained credit or card details, taken the charge on the card. Others have been known to actually make a county court claim against the customer for a no-show and won. The restaurant would only be entitled to their loss of profit. How much would you have spent and what would they have made on that? And, come to think of it, have they lost any profit at all? A few years back I booked into a self-catering 'hotel' in Surrey for two nights but had to leave after the first night. I was assured at 'reception' that if they managed to re-let the room, the charge for the second night's stay would be refunded but on later enquiry was told that a re-let had not been possible. In the room there was a public phone. I had taken the number and on the second night I rang it. The phone was answered by the new occupant! When I challenged the proprietor, he went spare and attempted to deflect blame by outrage at my means of detection. I got my refund.

You can apply a similar detection device following your own cancellation. Telephone the restaurant and ask for a table at the time for which you had made your reservation. If they say they are fully booked, this should be almost conclusive proof that no profit has been lost.

It is conceivable that you haven't cancelled and the restaurant has let you in. It is even more conceivable that the food and/or the drink and/or the service are lousy. If food and drink are not of satisfactory quality (and obviously, fit for human consumption) and, to your detriment, not as described by the menu or waiter and their preparation and the service you get lack reasonable care and skill, there has been a breach of contract by the restaurant. The Consumer Rights Act 2015 (see chapter 39) kicks in. You could ask for replacements of the substandard fare but, as anyone who has ever worked in a restaurant kitchen will tell you, that runs the serious risk of a rather unpleasant liquid or substance finding its way into what you get back. Probably the better options: abandon the meal and decline to pay the price or full price for what you have consumed or, if you don't have the guts for a confrontation or a machete attack by the maitre d' assisted by no fewer than nine waiters, pay up 'under protest' (tell the management that is what you are doing or write 'paid under protest' if you can on any copy of the bill which the restaurant retains) and make a claim later.

There is something of which you need to be particularly careful. It is a criminal offence under section 3 of the Theft Act 1968 to bilk. Do what? That means to make off without having paid as required and with the intention of avoiding payment. You would not be guilty of bilking if you genuinely believed you were not liable to pay up because of the standard of the meal or service. On the other hand, you don't want to run the risk of the restaurant persuading a police constable who has nothing better to do than investigate and, because he is hungry or suffering from station canteen indigestion, arrests you on suspicion of a bilk. Therefore, do not act surreptitiously where you are withholding any part of the bill. Ensure your reasons are explained verbally or in writing.

As to that contentious service charge, it may be discretionary which means you have no obligation to pay it. If it's compulsory, you must have been notified of it before you ordered on the menu or elsewhere: otherwise, you have no obligation to pay it. You could always insist before your order that you will only pay it if you get an assurance from the manager that 100% of it will be distributed to the staff. If that deal is accepted and you don't get the assurance, you don't have to pay (though you could slip 10% cash into the hands of the water as a reward for exemplary attention to your table). If the meal was substandard then you have no greater obligation to pay the service charge than you have to pay for the meal. If the food and drink were marvellous but the waiter's manner and attention were worse than Basil Fawlty's on a bad day, you could refuse to pay the charge.

You can always eat at home.

Drone attack with a touch of Res Ipsa Loquitur

It won't be as big as PPI but litigation over damage to property (or humans) by the operation of drones is an inevitability as the wretched machines proliferate. Operators would be crazy not to see that they are sufficiently covered by insurance for liability to others. Where do you stand as the victim of a drone that has gone out of control and damaged or ruined your property? With luck, your buildings or household insurance policy will see you alright but if you are uninsured, loss or damage by drone is excluded from the insurance risks covered or you just don't want to take advantage of your policy, you can make a civil claim against the drone operator alleging trespass to property. In principle, the same as if I grew a creeper up your wall, dumped rubbish in your front garden or erected a tent in your back garden and planted myself inside it - though more harmful. It would be open to the drone operator to seek to justify the trespass by showing that the loss you claim for was unintentional and without negligence.

You can add on a negligence claim or make one instead of a trespass claim. The probability is that you haven't a clue what went wrong in which event proving the drone operator's negligence could be problematic. There is a special legal approach designed for this situation which shifts the burden from you in having to prove the operator's negligence to the operator in having to prove that they were not negligent. It applies where the facts speak for themselves which lawyers who like to show they know three words of Latin spout off in court and court documents as *Res Ipsa Loquitur* (meaning "the thing speaks for itself"). It's a phrase you can use when in a Roman coffee shop you are asked whether you want to order an espresso or a glass of water. The approach has been successfully applied in court cases where a customs officer was walking in front of a dock warehouse and six bags of sugar which were in the process of being lowered landed on him; where a theatre ceiling fell on the head of a member of the audience; and where a vehicle ploughed into a car which was parked unattended at the roadside. What is needed to pass the buck to the defendant is an unexplained occurrence which in the ordinary course of events would not have happened without the negligence of someone other than them and the circumstances pointing to your defendant rather than anyone else being to blame. Then you can rightly say - altogether now - *Res Ipsa Loquitur* but in Latin and not italics. A very useful rule.

PARTICULARS OF CLAIM

1. At all material times the claimant occupied 149 Magnolia Crescent, Twickenham, Middlesex KT89 4XZ which included a rear garden ("the House") and the defendant was the operator and had control of an unmanned aircraft system ("the drone").

2. On 14 July 2016 at approximately 2.30pm the drone entered the rear garden of the House and struck the claimant's gazebo ("the incident").

3. The incident constituted a trespass to the House and the gazebo. Further and in the alternative, the incident occurred on account of the negligence of the defendant as to which the claimant says Res Ipsa Loquitur.

4. As a result of the incident the claimant suffered loss and damage.

Particulars of loss and damage

a. Cost of repairs to gazebo £x

b. Out of pocket expenses £y

5. The claimant claims interest on damages under section 69 of the County Courts Act 1984 at such rates and for such periods as the court shall determine to be just.

AND the claimant claims:

a. Damages not exceeding £5,000;

b. Interest; and

c. Costs.

Service charges: still waiting

Restaurant misuse of tips, gratuities and service charges collected from customers who wish to reward waiters and staff for what they have received or are embarrassed not to reward them for what they have not received is a national scandal. The government looks to be ready to introduce legislation to outlaw this conduct but it's not here yet and you can't expect it to be retrospective. If a staff contract covers who the money is to belong to then the contract will prevail even if it is morally objectionable except that the employer cannot lawfully use tips and so on to top up an employee's minimum wage. But if the employer does not follow the contractual agreement or if there was no contract or no agreement in the contract covering tips then you the employee may be able to claim the money which has been wrongly withheld from you. In that situation you could claim back in the county court for six years. If your employer has covered up what has been going on, you might be able to claim back even longer (see chapter 10). Before starting proceedings, it would be wise to obtain some expert advice on how you stand in the light of the particular contractual documentation in your case.

The Department for Business Innovation & Skills issued a code of best practice on this topic in October 2009 which could be useful in proving industry custom and practice where you are relying on an implied agreement. The code requires that employees should be fully informed on the distribution and breakdown of tips, gratuities and service charges along with cover charges and the level and purpose of any deductions. Businesses should seek to reach agreement with employees on any change of policy.

A claim for wrongly withheld tips could be brought in an employment tribunal under Part II of the Employment Rights Act 1996 but here a much tighter time limit applies and unless you are eligible for remission, the imposition of fees in employment tribunal cases has removed one of the main advantages of claiming there rather than in the county court.

The particulars of claim in the county court might go like this.

PARTICULARS OF CLAIM

1. Between 1 July 2012 and 14 July 2016 the claimant was employed by the defendant as a waiter at its "Downa Throata Pizzeria" restaurant at 16 Uptown Road, Twickenham, Middlesex ("the restaurant").

2. The terms of the claimant's contract of employment were governed by a written agreement made on 30 June 2012 ("the agreement").

3. It was a condition of the agreement that all tips and gratuities tendered by and service charges added to bills issued to customers served by the claimant would belong to the claimant.

or

*3. It was a condition of the agreement that all tips and gratuities tendered by and service charges added to bills issued to customers served during the period of the claimant's employment would be subject to a TRONC to which the claimant would belong whereby such sums would be paid into a fund administered by the manager of the restaurant who was the TRONC master and distributed among the staff of the restaurant who were in the employment of the defendant at the restaurant on the distribution date which would be each quarter (as from the 1st January in each year) in such proportions as the manager deemed fit. It was implied that the manager would make his distribution on reasonable grounds having regard to all relevant circumstances including in particular the seniority of each member of staff, the number of hours worked by each member of staff during the relevant quarter and the extent of the industry displayed by each such member during the relevant quarter.**

or

3. The agreement was silent on the ownership and application of tips and gratuities tendered by and service charges added to bills issued to customers served during the period of the claimant's employment. In the circumstances, it was an implied condition of the agreement that such gratuities which were paid directly to the claimant by the customer in cash would belong to the claimant and that such gratuities and service charges as were added to the bill would belong to and be paid by the defendant to the members of staff who were on duty for the shift in which the added gratuities and service charges were tendered in equal shares or in the alternative in the proportions which each such member's gross pay for the relevant shift bore to the aggregate of the gross pay of the members of staff who were on duty for such shift. Further and in the alternative, the gratuities and service charges collected by the defendant for each shift for which the claimant was on duty were held in trust by the defendant for the benefit of the claimant and the other members of staff on duty for that shift in equal shares or in the alternative in the proportions which each member's gross pay for the relevant shift bore to the aggregate of the gross pay of the members who were on duty for such shift.

4. In breach of the condition (and/or trust) specified above, the defendant has refused or neglected to account to the claimant for the tips, gratuities and service charges due to him throughout the period of his employment despite the claimant's habitual requests for it to do so.*

or

4. the defendant has refused or neglected to account to the claimant for the full amount of tips, gratuities and service charges due to him throughout the period of his employment despite the claimant's habitual requests for it to do so and the only such payments made by the defendant have been as follows, namely [insert particulars of dates and amounts of the relevant payments].

or

*4. no payments have been made to the claimant under the TRONC.***

or

4. the payments to the claimant under the TRONC which have been derisory and unreasonable in amount having been substantially less than the equal share contended for by the claimant as *above and bearing no relation to the particular criteria alternatively contended for by the claimant as above. The payments have been substantially less than the sums paid to co-employees of the claimant on duty for the same shifts as the claimant and who have been of the same or less seniority as the claimant and have been no more industrious than the claimant during relevant shifts. The only such payments made by the manager have been as follows, namely [insert particulars of dates and amounts of the relevant payments].***

*5. The claimant is unable to provide further and better particulars of the amount of his until disclosure of documents has taken place.***

6. The claimant claims interest on such sums as shall be awarded to him under section 69 of the County Courts Act 1984 at such rates and for such periods as the court shall determine to be just.

AND the claimant claims:

a. An account of all sums due to the claimant as set out above;

b. Judgment for such sums and/or damages limited to the sum of £x;

c. Interest; and

d. Costs.

** delete if the existence of a trust and its breach is not alleged.*

*** The TRONC system is usually an arrangement under which employees decide who is to participate and how distributions are to be made and not the employer. Therefore, in order to succeed in a TRONC claim against the employer it would be necessary to prove that there was a contractual guarantee by the employer when you joined as an employee that you would be a TRONC beneficiary and if there was a guarantee about what share would be paid to you. so much the better: otherwise you would have to rely on an implied condition about how your share would be worked out. Proving an implied condition in a TRONC or non-TRONC case may be difficult where there is insufficient certainty as to what was intended.*

Part 8

GONE SHOPPING: SEE YOU IN COURT?

Chapter 37

At The Supermarket

Lousy plastic bags, parking machine clocks and suspected shoplifting

I spend more time in supermarkets than reading statutes. I know that serving me as your 123rd customer of the day is no joy but the slightest hint of a smile would be ever so nice. Anyway, the contract for the sale and purchase of supermarket goods does not carry an implied term that the cashier will be pleasant so don't even think of claiming for a bad day because the cashier put on a hatchet face. Carrier bags are another matter. I plead guilty to stoking a campaign in my first book *Gold's Law* which proved to be successful for bags to be supplied free which I followed up on a variety of radio and television programmes with the idea that, having reached the cashier, you should refuse to proceed with purchase if the bags were not thrown in and leave it to staff to replace the goods onto the display shelves. I'm not sure that this makes me responsible for global warming though things have turned full circle. You get the plastic bags alright if you have the nerve to ask for them but you pays.

Having recently packed a bottle of wine into a *Waitrose* job alongside a small packet of the lightest feathers, I left the store and as I went to bypass a *Big Issue* vendor, the bag exploded and the bottle rolled onto the pavement. And who brought the bottle's roll to a summary end? The *Big Issue* vendor. This got me thinking about buying a copy of *Big Issue* every time I saw one move - and a bag for life. It also reminded me that I have never succeeded in carrying home a cucumber which has not split through a supermarket plastic bag. The splitting process can be very embarrassing and lead to much pointing and ribaldry by passing students. As with flowers, there should be a conically shaped and strengthened plastic bag which is exclusively devoted to the cucumber.

And a supermarket ticket machine clock got me thinking about innocents being induced to pay parking charges and occasionally penalties which were not actually due though, in fairness, in my case I got customer services to stamp the ticket and the lady smiled - and knew the clock was wrong as other customers had already complained (so why hadn't they fixed the clock or gone over to free parking?).

Been shopping

Particulars of Claim

1. On 14 July 2016 the claimant purchased goods from the defendant's Twickenham store and was provided with (OR sold) through the cashier a plastic bag into which to pack and carry the goods. The bag should have been reasonably fit for its purpose and of a satisfactory standard but it was neither in that although the goods weighed no more than....the bag split within about two minutes of carriage whilst the claimant was on the highway outside the store and most of the goods fell onto the ground and either containers were smashed or the goods were otherwise ruined.

2. The claimant lost the value of the ruined goods and the plastic bag being £50.

OR

1. On 14 July 2016 the claimant purchased goods from the defendant's Peardrop store and was provided with (OR sold) through the cashier a plastic bag into which the cashier packed the goods. It was implied that the cashier would not pack goods of a weight which was greater than that which the bag could bear with reasonable safety and that the bag should have been reasonably fit for its purpose and of a satisfactory quality. The goods were too heavy for the bag and/or the bag was neither reasonably fit for its purpose nor of a satisfactory quality. Before the claimant reached the store's exit doors with the goods, the bag burst open and the goods fell to the ground and were ruined.

2. The claimant lost the value of the ruined goods and the plastic bag being £50.

Been charged 5p for a plastic bag

Whether or not you should be charged 5p for a plastic bag under the new legislation may be less certain than the checkout assistant suggests. If you agree to pay then you may be stuck with the charge. "Bag for 5p?" "Yes, please." But if you paid under the mistake that you were liable when you were not and you would otherwise have been supplied with a free bag then you ought to get your 5p returned. I would not recommend for one moment that you commence county court proceedings for its recovery with interest and costs unless perhaps you are a shopaholic and have shelled out a fortune for 5p jobs. However, you could ask the store to do the right thing and return the money mistakenly paid over or next time make a polite challenge to the cashier who may have to send for the supervisor who may have to send for the assistant manager who may have to send for the manager who may have to telephone head office which isn't open that day but I beg of you not to do it when I am next in the queue or, as tiny and timid as I am, I may try and punch you on the nose.

So when don't you have to pay? Generally, when the business within all its branches employs a total of less than 250 employees but they must be full-timers to count (which is one good reason to patronise a small business) and otherwise:

- when the bag is non-plastic or plastic but more than 70 microns thick;
- when the bag is used;
- when the bag is not supplied for the purpose of enabling your purchases to be taken away, so if the store accepts that you simply want to take the bag home empty or you want to pack purchases from other shops into it and to carry away their goods bagless then they don't have to charge you but, on the other hand, they don't have to give you a free bag either;
- when the bag is to be used only for unwrapped or partly unwrapped food for human or animal consumption - ensure no other item is added to the bag - so there's an incentive to select at least one food item which is not wholly wrapped (but removing part of the wrapping of a wholly wrapped item pre-checkout may earn you a permanent barring from the store and a charge of criminal damage as goods selected in a shop do not become your property until the shop agrees to sell them to you which will usually be when the cashier rings up the price for them on the till);
- when the bag is intended to be used only for uncooked fish or fish products, meat or meat products or poultry or poultry products but, again, ensure that no other non-exempt item is added;
- when the bag is intended to be used only to carry medicine sold under a doctor's or dentist's prescription, live fish in water or only unwrapped axes, knives, knife blades or razor blades (and, frankly, if your store sells unwrapped axes or razor blades, I suggest you take your custom elsewhere or go shopping with iron gloves);
- when the bag has no handles (some of those titchy ones are handleless) or is of woven plastic;
- when the bag is intended to be used to carry goods on board a

ship, train, plane, coach or bus (which could just about be anything and especially a vomit bag and probably not a copy of "*Why I never travel by public transport*").

Been parking

Particulars of Claim

1. On 14 July 2016 at 1.10pm the claimant was automatically issued with a ticket to the defendant's Peardrop store car park at the point of entry and parked his car. Unbeknown to him at the time, the ticket wrongly showed the time of issue as 1.00pm. At 3.05pm on the same date the claimant was compelled to pay £25 into the defendant's exit ticket machine so at to procure a receipt validation in order to leave the park with his car whereas, under the ticket's conditions of issue, the claimant was entitled to free parking because his car had been parked for less than 3 hours and he had spent in excess of £20 in the store. The defendant has refused to make any refund to the claimant.

2. The claimant claims return of the sum of £25.

OR

1. On 14 July 2016 at 1.10pm the claimant parked his car in the car park at the defendant's Peardrop store with the intention of buying goods at the store. It was an implied condition of the parties' contract for parking that the defendant would attend to the claimant at one of its checkouts with reasonable dispatch so as to enable the claimant to depart from the car park when he intended to do so and not incur car park charges in excess of what he had intended. At 2.45pm on the same date the claimant sought to pay for the goods he had selected with the intention of departing from the car park by 3.10pm. At 3.11pm the car park charge was due to increase from £3.60 to £30 on account of a 'penalty' for parking in excess of two hours. Two of the cashier checkout points were unserviced and there were long queues at the other points with three of them being serviced by part-time trainees who were slow. There were no facilities for self-payment (or The Claimant did not have a prior arrangement to use the self-payment facilities OR The claimant did not have the confidence or expertise to use the self-payment facilities for which he has an abhorrence OR the self-payment checkouts were log jammed with customers OR the self-payment machines only accepted credit or debit cards and the claimant wished to pay in cash). In the event, the claimant was not served until 3.20pm thereby compelling the claimant to pay*

£26.40 more than he had intended or wished so as to be able to remove his vehicle from the car park.

2. The defendant, in breach of the above condition, failed to attend to the claimant with reasonable dispatch and should have contemplated that the claimant as a result would be obliged to pay the charge which in fact he did pay.

3. The claimant's loss as a result of the defendant's breach was £26.40 which he claims.

**warning: if there were self-payment facilities of which you could have taken advantage and, had you done so, they would have seen you on your way in time for the football results then the claim might be looking dodgy.*

Not been thieving

If you are wrongfully arrested by a store detective and detained, you may have a claim against their employer for damages for false imprisonment. It is not necessary for you to be carted off to one of Her Majesty's playgrounds: you can be falsely imprisoned in the manager's office. A store detective doesn't have the same power to arrest as a police constable: in fact, no greater power then a private citizen like Madonna or Harry Bloggs next door. The net result is that should it transpire that you had not in fact stolen anything plus the store detective compelled you to go with them plus your free movement was prevented, you should be on to a winner. It matters not that the store detective genuinely thought you had committed a crime. No actual crime means no private arrest permitted. The store detective who has recently been on a training course and remembered everything they were taught will simply invite you to accompany them to the manager's office whilst the arrival of a police constable is awaited. If you agree and go voluntarily then that would end a false imprisonment claim before it had started. But sometimes they jump too early and make it clear by words or action or both that you have no choice but to go with them. Accompanying them when it is obvious you have no real choice would not be counted as a voluntary action. Often the store detective will be in the employ of a security firm which has been engaged by the store and is left to get on with prowling and nabbing without any direction from the store. The law calls the security company an independent contractor and, in this situation, the store would probably deny any responsibility to you and lay the blame on the security firm. So you might have to claim against the security firm and not the store. Should it appear that the store was more involved than it suggests, you may be wise to claim against both and leave it to them to scratch each other's eyes out.

The trend seems to be for shops to refrain from providing a paper receipt for a more modest purchase - usually up to £10 - if they can avoid it. This can only serve to compromise you if you are challenged (as happened to hairdresser Neil Langley at a Richmond, Surrey railway station outlet and hopefully he will buy this book to read about it). The likelihood of a challenge is enhanced by the understandable public response to the 5p plastic bag law in slinging purchases into the trolley without prior committal to any form of bag, to merge with purchases made elsewhere and goods they have just selected but overlooked in the trolley.

I recently took to the internet to ask Marks and Spence about the paperless transactions.

"I am a long-standing and regular customer of yours. I am concerned and perplexed by your new practice of discouraging customers from taking a receipt on purchases. Why are you doing this? Is it to save money? What would happen if I had no receipt and was challenged about whether I had paid? Have you stopped this sort of challenge and, if so, are you not encouraging shoplifting? I would be glad to hear from you.

Stephen Gold"

Here's the reply - and talk about not answering the question?

"Hi Stephen

Thanks for letting us know about your recent visit to one of our stores. I'm sorry to hear you're unhappy the assistant asked if you would like your till receipt.

Our assistants like to give customers the option if they would like the receipt if the total is under £10. I'm sorry this has disappointed you.

I have passed your comments on to our Policy Team as I know they are consistently reviewing customer feedback and will take this into consideration for future planning.

Thanks again for getting in touch.

Kind regards

Lauren C
Retail Customer Services
Your M&S Customer Service"

Incidentally, I have never met my new friend Lauren.

No, I have not been falsely imprisoned by a supermarket (although I have to confess to fantasizing about such an experience) but I did help out two ladies who were stopped by a store detective at House of Fraser in London's Kensington. They had made purchases which the assistant had packed into a store bag and, at the same time and unbeknown to them, chosen to pack a garment from stock to which a security tag was still affixed. The tag activated the alarm system as they left. A claim for damages for false imprisonment was made and judgment entered in default of a defence being submitted in time. The store, through its insurers, then applied for the judgment to be set aside. The ladies made much of the fact that the store would have to demonstrate to the court that it had a real prospect of successfully defending the claim if the judgment went. A settlement was negotiated whereby the insurers paid out £2,000, the judgment was set aside and the claim was dismissed.

Particulars of Claim

1. On 14 July 2016 at about 12 noon the claimant who had been a visitor to the defendant's Peardrop store was about to leave when a store detective employed by or under the direction and control of the defendant apprehended the claimant by seizing him by the right arm and said to him in the presence and hearing of not less than six other members of the public: "I've been watching you, sonny. You've got a packet of razor blades and some sliced smoked salmon in your jacket pocket for which you have not paid and I am arresting you for theft. You will accompany me to the manager's office and the police will be called."

2. Against his will, the claimant was taken to the manager's office in which he was forced to wait until the manager appeared 15 minutes later. He was told to empty out his jacket and trouser pockets which he duly did. They contained neither of the goods allegedly stolen. The store detective said; "He must have dropped them on the way up. The manager said: "We'll let you go this time, Troublesore."

3. The claimant was distressed and humiliated by his ordeal and his feelings were injured.

4. The claimant claims compensatory damages and aggravated damages for false imprisonment. In support of his claim for the latter, the claimant relies on the conduct as set out above of the store detective and store manager and their adherence to the allegation of dishonesty despite no stolen goods being found on his person.

AND the claimant claims:

a. *Damages;*

b. *Aggravated damages;*

c. *Such interest as shall be deemed just;*

d. *Costs.*

Chapter 38

Receipts And Sale Goods And Cheques

and Planes and Boats and Trains

This is my true story as related in my letter to Jaeger's chief executive. I know he probably never saw it but there's always the chance of somebody other than a customer services rep picking up your opening missive.

16 November 2014

Chief Executive
Jaeger
57 Broadwick Street
London W7F 9QS

Dear Sir

Myself and Jaeger

I was in a relatively good mood when I entered your Portsmouth outlet yesterday. My intention was to both make some purchases and return a blue shirt which I had purchased in July 2014 for £25 (less, I think, a percentage discount). Indeed, in July 2014 in the course of three visits to the outlet whilst visiting the area I had spent around £250 - no doubt you will be able to identify the purchases from my account record as I hold a loyalty card with you - and the shirt in question had to be rejected because, whereas the affixed ticket represented that it was sized 16 which is my size, a subsequent sighting of the small label on the shirt itself just before I was about to unwrap and wear it, showed it was sized 15. In view of the fact it was patently obvious that the shirt had come from you and that my case for an appropriate payment was not capable of resistance by any reasonable business or staff member, I had not taken steps to take the receipt with me. In the event, the assistant present remembered me from my previous transactions and could confirm in the presence of the supervisor referred to below that the shirt had been sold to me. I should add here that this was the first time I had been back in Portsmouth and been able to return the shirt to the outlet.

I was confronted by a young lady who, on enquiry, informed me she was a supervisor and adopted the charm of a tyrant. She was economical with words and, judging by her facial expressions, perceived me to be objectionable for complaining about the mistake you had made. No apology. No offer to accept the shirt back. Nothing bar a proclamation that no action could be taken without a receipt. I was amazed and quite upset and forced in due course to leave with the shirt which I now hasten to enclose. Perhaps against my better judgment, I proceeded to buy further garments at the price of £315.20. Fortunately, the supervisor played no part in the further transaction and was absent for most of my additional time in the outlet.

I require you to please pay to me the gross value of the shirt which is £65 plus the cost of the postage which this parcel bears. The gross value is the measure of my loss.

I have since been able to locate one of my July 2014 receipts and enclose a photocopy. It may or may not cover the shirt in question. You will see that I purchased a series of shirts on the date to which the photocopy relates.

Yours faithfully

Stephen Gold

I have not included the shirt or photocopy receipt with this book. So what happened? Jaeger wins the *Breaking Law Inside Leg Award* to retain for the rest of this century. They promptly telephoned and agreed to pay me £65 together with £25 travelling expenses (for which I had not asked) and to gift me a £25 voucher. This is customer relations at its zenith.

The experience is instructive on a couple of counts over and above appraising you of my collar size. Was the Jaeger supervisor correct to insist on seeing a receipt before she would consider any refund? No. When you have a claim against a seller which is legally valid, the absence of a receipt should not prevent you from pursuing it. You would have to prove in court that you made the purchase so it is fair enough that you should prove the same thing to the shop when you complain but there is nothing wrong with your word for proof (although a bank or credit card statement could always be produced as a substitute for the receipt even if it could spoil a good argument). There is obviously scope for deception by a customer so one can empathise with a trader's wish to ensure that they are not being taken for a ride. How empathetic you are may well depend on the attitude of the trader. Mr or Ms Jobsworth may well deserve The Treatment.

"Do you accept I am a truthful person?"

"Yes."

"Well, I as a truthful person am telling you that I purchased this item (a) from you; (b) when I say I did; and (c) for the price marked on it."

"Sorry, sir but our policy is that we must have a receipt."

"Which means I have to sue you and claim the price, interest, court fee and my travelling and car park expenses for today and you will have no defence. What a complete waste of time."

"I'll just get the manager."

The girth of my neck had got me into difficulties before. As I look through my archives of trivia, I see that in 1979 I bought what I thought was a shirt with a 15" collar but mistakenly selected one sized 15.5". From whom? Jaeger. They kindly exchanged it. And this morning, I opened a new shirt I had selected on one of my 2014 visits to them and thought it a little tight. The collar was 15.5" instead of the 16" to which it had grown and, this time, the label had given the correct measurement. My fault entirely. Would you be prepared to take it back for me? Actually, that may not be necessary as I have had the courage to return to Jaeger and the Portsmouth branch to boot. This was on 26 February 2016 (with that false moustache and beard - joking) when I bought a discounted suit and was overcharged £10 for posting on the trousers to me which required shortening by two feet. They quickly made a refund when I raised the overcharge two days later.

The assistant manager of Robert Dyas in Petersfield told me in 2014 when I returned a water filter cartridge which turned out to have been smashed in its box when purchased that I could not have a refund but only an exchange. This was because I could not produce the receipt which I had discarded. I was going to leave it at that but eventually concluded that this would be unfair to you so here are my letters.

2 January 2015

The Manager
Customer Services
Robert Dyas Ltd
Cleeve Court
Cleeve Road
Leatherhead
Surrey
KT72 7SO

Dear Sir or Madam

I have suffered three shattering blows in recent times. In July 2014 I purchased a Brita Classic Single Pack Cartridge (100214) from your Havant branch for £4.29 and when in due course I opened it, I found it had literally shattered. I had not subjected it to any trauma between purchase and opening by way of dropping it onto the ground or throwing it at a wall and so it is as evident as night follows day that the product was in this unhappy state when I had the misfortune to remove it from your shelf as an act preparatory to purchase. This then was the first shattering blow.

The second shattering blow came when I went to return the product to your Havant branch. I found the branch was no more. It had metamorphosed into an outlet vending products at the price of £1 each.

The third shattering blow was when I subsequently took the trouble of calling at your Petersfield store with the product and encountered the assistant manager Damian. I cannot provide you with his surname because he declined to provide it to me although I had no intention of stalking him or holding him up to public ridicule. No doubt you know him. You should be proud of him because he steadfastly held rigidly to what I believe must be company policy, without insulting me or attempting to throttle me. The blow was that although he accepted back the substandard product and offered to allow me to exchange it for a like product without charge, he would not refund the price. I was unable to provide a receipt for the purchase which appeared to be the stumbling block. It is hardly no more likely that I would have retained a receipt for a single Brita cartridge than that I would have done so for using a cubicle at the gentlemen's toilets at Waterloo Station. He said that I could have bought the product at Asda which is perfectly true but the deficiency in his argument was that he expressly accepted I was acting in good faith. My good faith was also implicit in the exchange opportunity and the acceptance back of the product. I pointed out to Damian that it would be appropriate for him to exercise his discretion on this occasion as I would otherwise feel obligated to bring proceedings for the recovery of the price, the court fee payable on this institution of such proceedings and out of pocket expenses. I left him with my contact details when there was no hint of the exercise of discretion so that he could contact you and you would see sense. But I have not heard from you.

The law is against you. I bought the product from you and it was not of satisfactorily quality or reasonably fit for its purpose as it should have been. As a matter of principle, I want my money back. Therefore, I call on you to repay me £4.29 within 14 days of the date of this letter and in the event of you failing to do so I will institute proceedings and seek in them the relief I mentioned to Damian.

It has been several months since my visit to your Petersfield branch. I have been too heavily occupied in writing a legal work on the rights of consumers and apologise for not communicating with you earlier. Fortunately my claim does not become statute barred for another circa five years and six months.

Yours faithfully

Stephen Gold

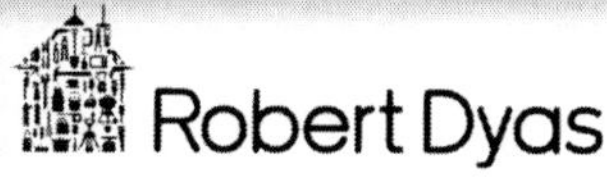

Robert Dyas

Mr S Gold

Dear Mr Gold,

Thank you for your letter dated 2 January 2015 and please accept my apologies for the delay in responding. As I am responsible for Customer Service here at Robert Dyas, this matter has been brought to my attention.

Firstly, I would like to offer my sincere apologies the pack of cartridges became damaged so soon from purchase. As you rightly point out, this does not reflect the standard of products we aim to provide. Whilst I believe this to be a one off I understand it has left you disappointed.

Furthermore, I was sorry to learn our colleagues failed to provide a more suitable resolution. Like most retailers, we encourage colleagues to act in line with our Policy which is designed to protect both customer and the business. However, with this said, we also encourage colleagues to treat each customer as an individual and use discretion where required. Clearly, this experience has left you with a rather poor impression and I would like to give you my personal assurance feedback will be provided to the colleagues involved to improve the service going forward.

In order to bring this matter to a more satisfactory conclusion, I will be happy to provide a refund to the value of £10.00. In order to arrange this, I would be most grateful if you could contact me on 0191 600 0601 at your earliest convenience. I trust this more tangible token of my regret will go some way to restore your faith as I am confident the service you receive from Robert Dyas in future will more closely match your expectations.

Yours sincerely,

"Water cartridge disappointment"

25 January 2015

Lauren P
Customer Services Manager
Robert Dyas Ltd
Cleeve Court
Cleeve Road
Leatherhead
Surrey
KT72 7SO

Dear Lauren P

Thank you for your undated letter received on 23 January 2015. I note all you say and, I will, of course, accept the £10 offered. Please send me a cheque in my favour for this amount to the above address.

I would not wish Damian to miss out on the next Robert Dyas Christmas party or to be in any way disadvantaged by what has happened because, as I indicated in my previous letter, he did very well and was at all times respectful. It is just that I fancy he may not have been blessed with sufficient discretion in the particular circumstances. If I were in your shoes, I would want a bucketful of Damians (provided the buckets were supplied by Robert Dyas).

Incidentally, the cartridge was in a damaged state on purchase which was unbeknown to me at the time.

Yours sincerely

Stephen Gold

I was paid the £10, just a little late but with a suitable apology.

There is an important caveat to this no receipt business. If the goods are perfectly satisfactory but you are after a refund or exchange because:

- you changed your mind;
- you bought the wrong size and that was down to you;
- your boss fired you when you got back from shopping;
- your partner says that green stripes against a pink background with black stars do not suit your complexion; or
- you decided on reflection that Tuesday was an unlucky day to make a purchase,

then you will have to go along with the trader's terms and conditions for making a return. They will probably say.......you must produce a receipt.

Sorry to dance about but I must get back to Jaeger and that shirt and the next nugget to be extracted from the experience. Jaeger asked me to phone them to give them my credit card details.

> *"[in trilly voice] Hello, Jane. Customer Services."*
>
> *"It's Stephen Gold. You left a message for me yesterday."*
>
> *"Oh yes. I have been asked by the customer service manager to deal with this. If you could please let me have your credit card details..."*
>
> *"I'd like a cheque, please."*
>
> *"I'm afraid we don't issue cheques."*
>
> *"So how do you pay your bills? Surely you can send me a cheque."*
>
> *"Could you hold on, please and I'll speak to my manager.............. ....I've spoken to my manager. On this occasion. We can send you a cheque but it will take a little longer."*
>
> *"That's fine."*

And the cheque duly arrived which means that the *Breaking Law Inside Leg Award* to Jaeger has not been forfeited. Could they have insisted that I accept a credit card payment? As the law then stood, no. In so far as I was being compensated for my actual loss, I was entitled to be paid in cash or cheque. Transferring into a credit card account is not always convenient. You don't get the benefit of the credit until your next statement and, for a substantial credit, it may take a while to be able to exhaust it. So Jaeger, thank you. But when a trader is refunding to a consumer on a transaction made on or after 1 October 2015 under the Consumer Rights Act 2015 (see chapter 39) they may be entitled to insist on the same means of refund as the consumer used to make the original payment. The law is not completely clear but, anyway, this would not apply to damages over and above the price refund to which the consumer is entitled or to other transactions outside the 2015 Act.

I should not leave the subject of the receiptless complainant without two little stories. The first concerns some rotting nectarines and Marks and Spencer. Over to extracts from my email exchange with them.

> ***From Stephen Gold On 28/03/2016***
>
> *Message: The box of nectarines I purchased from your Kingston upon Thames store on Thursday last was returned by me to your Richmond upon Thames George Street store today. Each and every one of the four nectarines inside was bad when the box was opened*

on the evening of purchase which must be something of a record. I obtained a refund of £3 but nothing for my trouble although I did not ask for it but expected some small gesture for a breach of the Consumer Rights Act 2015. What concerned me more however is that I was told I would not have been given a refund if I had been unable to produce a receipt - this information was passed on by the manager to the staff member who attended me - and that I should have returned the product to the branch of purchase. I would like your comments on these matters. As to the receipt which I was able to produce, what was explained to me as your company's policy is surely unlawful. Obviously proof of purchase is reasonable and necessary but there is no limitation on the method of proof which is used, the customer's word may be enough. Certainly production of the product - even if it is festering - with the original labelling still affixed as in my case would be pretty good proof of purchase? Does your store manager think I might have robbed a pedestrian of four rotting nectarines so that I could then pass myself off as the buyer and extract £3 from you? As to returning to the branch of purchase, this of course is legal nonsense. Why instruct your staff to utter it?

From: M&S Service Team *<retailcustomer.services@customersupport.marksandspencer.com>*
Date: 29 March 2016 at 11:45:47 BST
Subject: M&S Ref: 334657

Hi Stephen

Thanks for your email. Sorry to hear about your nectarines. I'm concerned to hear that they were rotten and it's really good of you to return them back to store. Please be assured that the store staff will follow this up with the supplier of the nectarines so they will be monitored for any future quality issues.

I was very surprised to hear you were told by the staff at Richmond you should have returned them to the store where they were purchased. There are hundreds of M&S stores in London and surrounding areas. Realistically, we understand that you're not necessarily going to be shopping in the same store all the time. Therefore, as long as you go back to a store which sells food, which you did, this is fine.

The nectarines were clearly not up to standard, so you're entitled to a full refund in accordance with your legal rights. You were right, the fact that you were able to produce the product with its original packaging was more than enough for us and I'm sorry you were told differently.

I've followed this up with our management team at Richmond. Clearly, they need to make sure they're all up to date with the refund policy so that this doesn't happen again.

I'd also like you to have an e gift card for £10 as an apology for what happened. This will be sent to your email address and you should receive this in a few days time. Please also check your junk and spam folders, as it may get directed there. I hope my reply has helped to clear this up, but if you still have any other queries, feel free to email again and we'd be happy to help.

If you'd like to give any feedback about the reply I've sent you today, please feel free to fill in the short survey we've sent on the email separate to this one. I'd really appreciate your comments.

Take care and have a good week.

Anne G
Retail Customer Services
Your M&S Customer Service

For the second little story, please meet Scribbler, the greetings cards people

To Scribbler

3 May 2016

I made a purchase this morning from one of your stores. The receipt with which I was issued stated: "Returned goods will NOT be accepted without a valid receipt." This statement surely falls foul of the law. If, for example, goods are not of satisfactory quality then your customer would be entitled under the Consumer Rights Act 2015 to a refund if they were returned within 30 days. Obviously you would want to satisfy yourself that you had sold the goods and when but there is no legal obligation on the customer to produce a receipt for this purpose. The customer's word might be sufficient, particularly if it was a chief constable, the Pope or Dame J Dench or a credit card statement proving the transaction. Can you assure me that you will immediately alter this misleading statement on your receipts.

Yours sincerely

Stephen Gold

From Gemma R

5 May 2016

Dear Stephen,

Many thanks for your email to customerservice@scribbler.com. I attach a pdf of our returns policy which is on the backs of our receipts. Can you confirm whether or not your receipt stated this. If it doesn't apologies for the confusion.

Kind Regards,

Gemma

Scribbler

scribbler

in store | online | mobile

Visit us at scribbler.com

- Personalise cards with a name or photo
- Send cards anywhere in the world
- Free delivery when buying 2 or more cards

Use code **SCRRWEB20** for **20% off** your next online order!

Keep up to date with the latest news, discounts and fun stuff by signing up to our newsletter.

We love our products and hope you do too, but on the off chance you change your mind...we promise to refund your purchase in full via the original payment method upon production of this receipt within 30 days. Without a receipt we'll give you an exchange. This does not affect your statutory rights.

Registered Office:
9 Harmsworth Street
London SE17 3TJ
VAT. 672405736 Co. No 1863486

From Stephen Gold

5 May 2016

Dear Gemma

Thank you. I have examined the back of the receipt and can confirm that it does set out your returns policy and makes it clear that the policy does not affect the customer's statutory rights. This is all well and good but the words of which I complained were the words on the front and, hence, the more prominently displayed words which are also in bolder type than the words of the policy on the back. There is no indication on the front of the receipt that the requirement for production of the receipt relates to goods returned after a change of mind. "Returned goods" impliedly includes goods returned because they do not satisfy the standards set by consumer legislation. So will you revise those words?

Yours sincerely

Stephen Gold

From Gemma R

10 May 2016

Stephen,

Many thanks for your email. I can confirm the text has been changed.

Kind Regards,
Gemma R
Scribbler

From Stephen Gold

10 May 2016

Dear Gemma

That is excellent news and I commend your company for responding - and so swiftly - to a customer concern and accepting it was in the wrong. I would be very interested to see the new text - before having to buy another card! Perhaps I may?

Yours sincerely

Stephen Gold

From Stephen Gold

13 May 2016

Dear Gemma

You have not come back to me but I could not resist so made a purchase from you on 11 May 2016. The wording on the receipt is exactly the same! That's a blow. Do you suggest I buy myself a condolence card?

Yours sincerely

Stephen Gold

From Gemma R

Stephen,

13 May 2016

Thank you for your email and apologies I haven't been able to re-

spond before now. We're currently going through a companywide upgrade and rollout of our EPOS system which has been requiring the majority of my attention. The text has been changed on sites with the upgraded EPOS. It's unfortunate you have been to a site that has yet to be upgraded. Once all of our sites have come on board to the new system all receipts will reflect these changes. If you can tell me which site it is you visit I can inform you when this shop will be upgraded.

Thank you for your understanding with this matter.

Regards,

Gemma R

Scribbler

Well I gave Gemma the store location and she then came back with the new receipt wording. "If you want to bring something back please save your receipt. This does not affect your statutory rights." This passes the Gold test. If I had been Scribbler, I might have been tempted to tell me to mind my own business so, all in all, I reckons that Scribbler does deserve my continued patronage. Pity they don't sell noodle pots.

Chapter 39

The New Consumer Laws

Buyers' kit to be carried at all times when away from home

You obtained goods before 1 October 2015? Go away! Sorry. There are plenty of good laws to protect you but the new stuff which is in the Consumer Rights Act 2015 only applies to purchases and goods hired or acquired on HP or under conditional sale agreements on or after 1 October 2015. And the new stuff only applies when your supplier is a trader (a person acting for purposes relating to their trade, business, craft or profession) and you are a consumer (an INDIVIDUAL acting for purposes which are wholly or mainly outside their trade, business, craft or profession). It follows that the new stuff does not apply when a trader acquires from another trader or a consumer acquires from another consumer: nor does it apply if when you acquired you were not a crying, talking, sleeping, walking, litigating human being but a limited company because a limited company is not an individual. Again, there are plenty of other laws which would protect you if you have been taken for a ride (even a short one) in one of these other situations but not the new stuff. Incidentally, an individual who acquires goods in the course of their business may still be able to take advantage of the new stuff if the acquisition was made for combined business and personal uses so long as the personal element was the prevalent one. Take the purchase of a computer which is intended for 80% personal use and 20% private use. You would be ranked as a consumer despite the business element and the new stuff would be at your disposal.

The new law - and this is a first for consumer protection legislation - extends to digital content including that supplied free with items purchased and supplied on a DVD. There are some exclusions: for example, the new law does not operate in respect of goods bought at an auction open to individuals who can attend in person or in respect of coins and notes which are to be used for currency which means it would still apply where they were sold as a collector's item.

What you can expect

The old favourites are regurgitated but with knobs on. Goods must be:

- Of satisfactory quality which means they must meet the standard that a reasonable person (not Clive Troublesore) would reckon to be satisfactory. Taken into account will be how they were described, what you paid (though even sale goods with a last day 40% off must still work and for longer than it takes to get them home but a lower standard will usually be expected for second hand goods) and all other relevant circumstances including any public statement which the trader or manufacturer or their representatives have made about specific characteristics of the goods. Particularly relevant will be anything said in advertising (for example, on television, radio, in the papers and on the tube) or on labelling. In looking at the quality, regard will especially be had to whether the goods are up to the job for which they are usually supplied, their appearance and finish, whether they are free from minor defects, and their safety and their durability. But you cannot moan about a defect which was drawn to your attention: "*Seconds - some scratch marks*" or "*I must tell you, Mr Troublesore. The colour of the jumper has slightly faded from the garment being in our window display for a couple of months.*" Where you have examined the goods before you agreed to acquire, you cannot complain about a defect which the examination should have revealed. The moral? If you are going to examine put your specs on and take the item to the natural light but don't walk down the road with it or you might be arrested on suspicion of theft. When you test drive a used car, the bodywork will look immaculate but the defects hidden and an inspection of a dozen scones is unlikely to reveal that they are oozing bacteria so missing what you are complaining about should not be a problem for you. From a legal viewpoint, probably better not to examine goods and then it can't be said that you should have spotted the defect. As a matter of common sense, if the supplier insists on an inspection you may smell a rat and take your litigation elsewhere.

- Reasonably fit for a particular purpose (and there may here be a cross over with the requirement that they are of satisfactory quality). That purpose must have been made known to the trader before the supply was agreed but, more often than not, this will be by implication. If you ask for a bottle of pickled onions it will be implied that you want it to eat the onions inside. If in fact you want the onions for firing out of your son's toy gun, this would be a particular purpose which you would have needed to make known to the supplier. You won't be able to complain about unfitness for purpose where it would be unreasonable for you to rely on the supplier's skill or judgement. *"I really can't say Mr Troublesore whether this lagging is suitable for that sort of job. I've never heard of anyone doing that with it." "Don't worry, my surveyor told me to get it."* Troublesore 0 Trader 1.

- A match with what was described to you by the trader when you agreed to acquire and that extends to any information given to you about the main characteristics of the goods. Generally, this information has to be given by the trader when an agreement is made on or off trade premises or is a distance transaction such as a phone or online sale in compliance with - all together now - the Consumer Contracts (Information, Cancellation and Additional Charges) Regulations 2013. If it could be important in your case, check with the regulations or an advice centre that none of the exceptions to the trader's obligation to give this information applies. One of the main exceptions is day to day sales at the trader's premises where the consumer will be very familiar with what they are getting. *"A rice pudding, The Sun, a bag of spuds and a packet of crisps for the old sod at home today, Cyril, please."*
- A match with the sample you have been shown where you have agreed to acquire on the strength of that sample - except to the extent that any differences have previously been brought to your attention before you agreed to acquire. *"The edges will be slightly rounder, Mr Troublesore and the colour shade will be much darker."*

And what you can do about it when you are let down

Some excited talk about the new laws has clouded the fact that they do not afford you any remedy unless the trader has broken the contract. It may be that you want to be shot of the purchase because Mrs Troublesore doesn't like it or you have changed your mind or you have been made redundant or you have seen an identical item round the corner at half the price and haven't bought from John Lewis. If the trader operates a returns policy and you can comply with it then you gets your money back or an exchange or a credit note but the new laws have nothing to do with this.

The usual rule in the civil law about proof applies so that if you are alleging that the goods or their installation are not up to legal scratch or some specific requirement in the contract has been breached and the case goes to court, it will be your responsibility to show that what you allege is correct. Of course, there are exceptions here which you will like. Where (see below) you are after repair, replacement, price reduction or exercising the right to long-term rejection (but not short-term rejection) on the strength of things being wrong within six months of you getting the goods then it will generally be presumed that things were wrong when you got them. It will be down to the trader to try and show that all was well on delivery and that the goods have met with some misfortune since then. Sounds a bit technical, I know, but important as it puts the trader on the back foot.

"Dear Trader

The idea that the goods were in tip top condition when I took them away from your shop and that:

- *I dropped them on the way home;*
- *My baby must have thrown them out of the cot;*
- *I have wrongly used them;*
- *I have not followed the manufacturer's instructions;*
- *I have submerged them in water;*

is arrant nonsense. I drew your attention to the defects within six months of the goods coming into my hands and section 19(14) of the Consumer Rights Act 2015 treats the goods as not having conformed with my contract with you on (and from) the date I got them.

Yours faithfully

Clive Troublesore"

Now where one of these old favourites has been breached by the seller, you get a right to reject the goods or have them repaired or replaced or have a price reduction - but not the lot! Don't forget that you may well be entitled to compensation as well.

Short term right to reject

Your primary aim could be to get rid of the bloody thing. *"I told you, Clive. I told you it was tat. I told you he was a crook. You wouldn't listen. I told you. Didn't I tell you."* [pause while Clive turns off the record].

There's a long term right to reject which we will come to later but this one is the early right so they call it the short term right (but you cannot use it for digital content). This is how it works. You are entitled to get rid of the bloody thing (do excuse me) and to a full refund when you exercise the right (generally) within 30 days of getting the goods but for perishable goods substitute any shorter period before which perishing would occur. If you agree to or request a repair or replacement and the goods are still not up to legal scratch, you won't be prejudiced. You will be able to short term reject up to seven days after the goods are back with you purportedly repaired or replaced or, if later, up to the original

30 days with the period you waiting for the repair or replacement added on.

The short term right to reject is really valuable. It entitles you to a full refund (plus compensation for any losses) and without a reduction for any use you have had out of the goods before rejection. But 30 days isn't a long time especially bearing in mind that it could take that time, if not more, for the defects to show themselves. Here's the trick. Get the supplier to agree to extending the 30 days. You acquire on condition that they agree and then you will have a right to short term reject throughout that longer period. You will insist on the agreement being recorded on the invoice. The supplier can agree to an extension after acquisition though you are in a stronger bargaining position for that extra time before you have agreed to acquire.

> *We Whitewash Ltd agree that Clive Troublesore's short term right to reject these goods under section 22 of the Consumer Rights Act 2015 is extended from 30 days to X days.*

No vacillation. You cannot exercise the short term right to reject once you have required or agreed to the trader repairing the goods without giving the trader a reasonable time to carry out the repair. *"I'm back. Where is it?" "You only brought it in this morning, Troublesore. Give us a break."* There is an exception. You can change your mind about the repair if giving the trader that reasonable time would cause you significant convenience.

Short term rejection: how to do it

You must sock it to the trader - but not with your fists. You need to make it clear that rejecting is what you are doing and that can be by something you say or do. *"A plague on your shop and you can stick this up your till"* would leave little room for doubt as Mr Troublesore thrusts the goods into the unwelcoming hands of the trader. You can't rule out the possibility of a dispute in the future about whether you did or did not reject so, particularly with expensive items, put it in writing. When you come to reject, you will need to deal with actual return of the goods. If you take them with you and hand them over when you reject, no problem. Otherwise you can reach an agreement with the trader about how they get the goods back and, if no agreement, you must make the goods available for the trader to collect. And as to the price you paid, the trader must refund it to you - in the same form as you paid the price unless you agree otherwise so if you paid in cash you should be paid back in cash and if you paid by credit card then your card must be credited - and do so without undue delay (but see chapter 38). The trader must get on and put hands in pockets rather than pleading a bellyache or a need to send the goods to head office to scrutinise under a telescope. You should also have any return costs. If the trader actually agrees you are entitled to a refund then it must be made no later than 14 days from when they do agree. With a HP agreement, you are entitled to a return of all payments made to date. So let's have a look at what that letter of rejection on a purchase, if you choose to send one, may look like and you can adapt appropriately where rejecting having hired or taken out a HP or conditional purchase agreement.

14 July 2016

Dear Trader

I enclose a copy of my invoice for the goods purchased from you on 7 July 2016. I regret that the goods are:

not of satisfactory quality as required by section 9 of the Consumer Rights Act 2015; and/or

not reasonably fit for purpose as required by section 10 of the Consumer Rights Act 2015: and/or

not as described as required by section 11 of the Consumer Rights Act 2015; and/or

not in accordance with the sample I was shown before purchase as required by section 13 of the Consumer Rights Act 2015; and/or

not in accordance with the model I was shown before purchase as required by section 14 of the Consumer Rights Act 2015.

Details of your breaches of contract as above are that [and here set out concisely what you say is wrong avoiding the use of vulgar abuse and **not** *marking the letter 'without prejudice'* and remembering one sweet day you might have to listen to the letter being read out in court].*

In view of the breaches of contract, I hereby exercise my right under section 22 of the Consumer Rights Act 2015 to short term reject the goods and treat my contract with you at an end and require you to:

a. refund to me without undue delay the purchase price paid; and

b. at the same time, pay to me damages in the sum of £a. Particulars of the damages are £b for travelling expenses and car park charges I estimate I shall incur in sourcing and acquiring *substitute goods; £c for loss of enjoyment of the goods purchased which have not been used and have not been usable for the period of an estimated two weeks from purchase of the goods until when I estimate I will be able to take delivery of substitute goods**; and £d which is the difference between the price I paid you and the price I am satisfied from enquiries I have made that I will be required to pay elsewhere for closely comparable goods***.*

Or

b. note that I reserve my right to claim damages for breach of contract against you and that it is my intention to provide you with particulars of such claim as soon as I am in a position to formulate it.

*I acknowledge that I am under a duty to make the goods available for collection by you. Please let me know when you would like to collect from my address, giving me reasonable notice****. If I do not hear from you in satisfactory terms within seven days of you receiving this letter, I shall be obliged to bring proceedings against you without further notice for the refund and damages to which I am entitled along with the court commencement fee and interest.*

Yours faithfully

Clive Troublesore

**But you could write a separate latter marked "without prejudice" (see chapter 8) which indicates a willingness to accept a lesser sum for damages provided the trader settles with you without undue delay.*

*** These are called damages for loss of enjoyment or loss of amenity which you may be entitled to where an important object of the supply was to give you "pleasure, relaxation or peace of mind" so they could arguably be claimed where, for example, the goods comprised a TV set or luxury food which you had purchased shortly before a carefully organised dinner party (see chapter 25).*

**** You may be able to buy a substitute at the same price which you should certainly take reasonable steps to attempt to do so that there will be no price difference claimable. But you could have a good case for a difference in price where, for example, the goods were originally bought at a discount and the trader could not replace with identical goods which were up to legal scratch and you had to pay more elsewhere for the same goods or goods which were as identical as you could find.*

***** If you prefer to return the goods to where you obtained them then say that is what you will be doing, state the expenses (reasonable) which this will involve if you want to claim them back and add them on to the refund total.*

Repair or replace

Quite why you would want to put up with a repair, I am not sure. Perhaps you are soft, silly or sentimental - or all three. I suppose you might have fallen in love with the kettle having taken it to bed for three consecutive nights or maybe there's just nothing else like it on the market and only the supplier has the necessary parts. Accepting a replacement is understandable if you are convinced that what was supplied to you was an isolated rogue and there isn't something intrinsically wrong with the design or manufacture. Anyway, the general rule is that you can require the supplier to repair or replace and if that's what will turn you on, it makes sense to do so before your time for making a short term rejection is up (see above under **Short term rejection: how to do it**). Having made that requirement, the trader must comply within a reasonable time and without significant inconvenience to you. Whether or not the trader has done so will depend on the nature of the goods (that kettle or sophisticated technological equipment) and the purpose for which you were acquiring them (a toilet or a tin of treacle). The trader must bear any necessary costs involved including in particular the cost of labour, materials or postage. If you have gone for repair, you must give the trader a reasonable time to comply before opting for replacement or short-term rejection unless that would cause you significant inconvenience. Again, if you have gone for replacement, you must give the trader a reasonable time to comply before opting for either repair or short term rejection unless that would cause you significant inconvenience.

But you cannot go for repair or replacement where that would be impossible or disproportionate compared to the other remedies available to you. They will be considered disproportionate if either imposes costs on the trader which are unreasonable compared with the other remedies, taking into account the value of the goods if they had been up to legal scratch, the extent to which they were below scratch and whether you would be caused significant inconvenience. So, for example, if it would cost more to repair than replace, you would probably not be entitled to repair and vice versa.

14 July 2016

Dear Trader

I enclose a copy of my invoice for the goods purchased from you on 7 July 2016. I regret that the goods are:

not of satisfactory quality as required by section 9 of the Consumer Rights Act 2015; and/or

not reasonably fit for purpose as required by section 10 of the Consumer Rights Act 2015; and/or

not as described as required by section 11 of the Consumer Rights Act 2015; and/or

not in accordance with the sample I was shown before purchase as required by section 13 of the Consumer Rights Act 2015; and/or

not in accordance with the model I was shown before purchase as required by section 14 of the Consumer Rights Act 2015.

Details of your breaches of contract as above are that [and as before here set out concisely what you say is wrong avoiding the use of vulgar abuse and ***not*** *marking the letter 'without prejudice' and again remembering one sweet day you might have to listen to the letter being read out in court].*

In view of the breaches of contract, I hereby exercise my right under section 23 of the Consumer Rights Act 2015 to require you to:

repair the goods

or

replace the goods

You should comply with your statutory obligation as above within a reasonable time. I regard this to be within 28 days of the date of your receipt of this letter. You must also bear the necessary costs incurred in you complying with my requirement.

I also require you to pay to me damages in the sum of £a. Particulars of the damages are £b for loss of enjoyment of the goods purchased which have not been used, for the period of five weeks from acquisition to estimated compliance with my section 23 requirement and £c for my out of pocket expenses comprising postages, telephone calls and travel.

I am returning the goods to you with this letter. You should please let me know as soon as possible the latest date by which you expect to comply and as soon as you have complied.

If you do not comply with my section 23 requirement within the time specified above, it is my intention to end the contract and exercise my right to short term rejection and the return of the price paid and to damages for breach of contract.

Yours faithfully

Clive Troublesore

Price reduction or final right to reject

You have a choice: price reduction or final rejection (as distinct from short term rejection). But when? Only after one repair or one replacement have not worked OR repair or replacement are not available because of impossibility or disproportionality (see above under **Repair or replace**) OR the trader has failed to repair or replace as required within a reasonable time and without significant inconvenience to you. It follows that you can't demand a price reduction at the very start. When it comes, the reduction should be for an "appropriate amount" which obviously means the amount by which the value of the goods has lowered because of the contract breach and you will be entitled to a refund of any money you have paid the supplier over and above the reduced value. The reduction could conceivably be 99% of what you paid (I shouldn't spend too long arguing that it should be 100% though you might be right) where the goods are valueless.

Here's the rub with final rejection. Once six months have been clocked up since delivery or installation (where your supplier had to install), what you get back through final rejection may be reduced to take account of your use of the goods and, again, that could conceivably be 99% of what you paid (or the trader might argue for 100% so you don't get back a penny). That's fair enough. Otherwise you could do all manner of things on the duff settee for a couple of years and then demand you had all your money back without a discount. Even Troublesore wouldn't try that one on. Or maybe he would. There won't be any reduction if you finally rejected within six months of delivery or installation. Obviously, there's an exception to the six month rule. You will suffer a discount for use during the first six months where the goods are a motor vehicle other than a mobility scooter or the like.

14 November 2016

Dear Trader

I enclose a copy of my invoice for the goods purchased from you on

7 July 2016. We have reached the end of the road. The goods were:

not of satisfactory quality as required by section 9 of the Consumer Rights Act 2015; and/or

not reasonably fit for purpose as required by section 10 of the Consumer Rights Act 2015; and/or

not as described as required by section 11 of the Consumer Rights Act 2015; and/or

not in accordance with the sample I was shown before purchase as required by section 13 of the Consumer Rights Act 2015; and/or

not in accordance with the model I was shown before purchase as required by section 14 of the Consumer Rights Act 2015;

and you have

attempted to repair the goods but without success in that they still do not conform to legal requirements because [set out outstanding deficiencies]; or

you have replaced the goods but the replacement goods, like the original goods, do not conform to legal requirements because [set out deficiencies]; or

you have refused to repair or replace because this would be impossible; or

you have failed to accede to my requirement that you repair in that you have not done so within a reasonable time and without significant inconvenience to me [give details]; or

you have failed to accede to my requirement that you replace in that you have not done so within a reasonable time and without significant inconvenience to me [give details].

In view of the above and under section 24 of the Consumer Rights Act 2015, I now require you to allow me a price reduction in an appropriate amount which I claim to be £a [give details of how you have reached the reduction figure] and in addition pay me damages in the sum of £b, particulars of which are [set out details and have a look at the short term rejection template letter above to see the sort of things you might be claiming for]; or

take this letter as formal notice that I finally reject the goods and treat our contract as at an end and repay to me the purchase price of £a and in addition damages in the sum of £b, particulars of which are [set out details and have a look at the short term rejec-*

tion template letter above to see the sort of things you might be claiming for].

*Unless the amounts claimed** are paid to me within seven days of the date of receipt of this letter, I shall be compelled to bring proceedings against you for the sums specified along with the court fee and interest.*

Yours faithfully

Clive Troublesore

**If you have allowed more than six months to elapse before final rejection, the trader may well ask for credit to be given to them for the use you have had out of the goods (see above) but you could leave it to the trader to take the point: alternatively you may feel it is fair to take it yourself and say what you are knocking off the claim to reflect use.*

***You could write a separate latter marked "without prejudice" (see chapter 8) which indicates a willingness to accept lesser sums provided the trader settles with you without undue delay.*

Installation

If it is part of your agreement that the trader will install the goods and they are incorrectly installed whether by the trader or on the trader's instructions then that will be amount to a contract breach. The trader is under a strict obligation there. They must do more than use reasonable care and skill: they must install correctly! The result of incorrect installation? All the remedies we have been looking at will apply except the right to short term reject.

Other contract breaches and other remedies

We have been focusing on specific terms that the law says will be treated as included in the contract. There may be other terms which do not have to be treated as such because they amount to specific requirements which the trader agreed to honour. Where one of these has been breached and it is appropriate, you can go for repair, replacement, price reduction or long term rejection (but not short term rejection) under the scheme of the Act as you can with the terms that are treated as included. Tell the trader you are relying on section 19(4) of the Act. You can also go in either case for what the general law has on offer for a contract breach including damages and an order for specific performance ("You shall get on and do that which you agreed you would do or the law says you should have done").

Where is it?

"We'll let you know when it's in, Mr Troublesore and may I say that it's a pleasure to do business and my best wishes to Mrs Troublesore." The answer is to try and pin down the trader about the time for delivery before you commit and have what is agreed written down by the trader on all copies of the invoice or on some scrap of paper or the plaster cast on one of your limbs. Then you can treat the contract at an end and have any deposit you have paid returned to you if the trader fails to keep to the delivery date so long as the importance of the date being kept to was made absolutely clear.

> *"Delivery agreed for 14 July 2016 and this date is absolutely essential; or*
>
> *Delivery agreed within 14 days of today and this period is absolutely essential".*

So you haven't agreed a particular date or period for delivery? In that case, the trader must deliver without undue delay and, anyway, no longer than 30 days after you have reached your agreement. The trader may say they still have every intention of delivering the very second the goods come in and they had spoken to the manufacturer only that morning who are very sorry about the delay but the goods have been so popular that they have got behind with orders and how is Mrs Troublesore. You don't have to wait for ever. Once the 30 days are up, you can specify a period for delivery that is appropriate in the circumstances and require the trader to deliver by the end of that period. Where still no show, you can treat the contract at an end: refund and go order elsewhere. Clearly you won't want to make it too far ahead for your own sake. Equally, you have to be careful not to make it unreasonably soon or you could really come a cropper with the trader being able to effectively force you to accept delivery or pay the price or compensation for loss of profit as you didn't give them long enough. Remember, you have to specify a period which is appropriate in the circumstances and that period is not and cannot be cast in legislative or any other kind of stone. You are unlikely to come a cropper if you have given the trader another 28 days.

> *"I regret that you have failed to deliver the goods ordered in accordance with your obligation under section 28 of the Consumer Rights Act 2015. I need the goods without further delay. Therefore, I require you to take this communication as formal notice that unless the goods are delivered by (insert date). I shall treat the contract as at an end and call on you to reimburse me without undue*

delay for all payments I have made to you and claim damages for my losses arising from your breach of contract. These damages will reflect the fact that I will have been deprived of the use of the goods for an appreciable period of time"*

**You can claim for the same sort of losses you could have suffered where you cancelled the contract because the goods were not up to legal scratch - see above.*

Your bicycle will be delivered next Tuesday between 5am and midnight

If, when you made your agreement, you failed to cater for delivery to your home at a time which did not coincide with the local foxes' investigation of your dustbin, you may be stuck with a wide and unsociable delivery window. But how do you stand when a delivery time or window is fixed, you are twiddling your thumbs awaiting their arrival and the goods don't appear? Unless the trader has allowed for a 'no delivery guarantee' opt out in their terms and conditions, you should be entitled to claim compensation from the trader for any loss you suffer. The most likely loss is a day's or half-day's net earnings. The object of compensation is to put you in the same position as you would have found yourself had the goods been delivered as notified. Strictly speaking, no loss as you were actually intending to take the time off work. Same position: just no goods. The real loss would be in relation to the rearranged delivery date if your salary was docked and it was not reasonably possible or convenient to rearrange delivery for when you or someone on your behalf could have taken the goods in without time away from work. Where you are after compensation for the rearranged delivery, it would be prudent to have your salary docked rather than have the time off in lieu of holiday as some judges take the view that time of in lieu cannot lead to compensation. The small claims rule that a winner can recover lost holiday time on going to court for the hearing of their case (see chapter 18) is a special situation.

"I never have to deliver to you. Go away"

The trader sometimes argues that there wasn't a firm deal to supply: just an agreement to make an agreement and so no contract which was capable of being broken by either side. And that is precisely what the trader said in a case which was decided by the Court of Appeal in January 2016. Kevin Hughes ran two garages and was heavily into Porsches. In 2011 he got to hear that Porsche would be manufacturing a limited edition of the 911 GT3 RS4 model which was the last four litre 911 it was to produce. He wanted one and went for it to Pendragon Sabre Ltd which was a Porsche dealer in Bolton. He rushed to place an order and paid a deposit of a cool £10,000 on the basis that if one of the new model was allocated to Pendragon then Mr Hughes would get it. He didn't. Because they thought Mr Hughes would resell it at a profit they decided it should go to another customer. Mr Hughes sued for damages for non-delivery.

Pendragon contended there was no enforceable contract. When the arrangement was made there was no car, no price agreed and no delivery date agreed, they argued. It didn't matter ruled the Court of Appeal. The Sale of Goods Act 1979 section 5 (which catches contracts made on or after 1 January 1894 so ought to just about be of potential benefit to you if not your great great grandfather) is unaffected by the Consumer Rights Act 2015 and says that there can be a binding contract for the supply of future goods: goods albeit not yet made or acquired by your supplier. Equally, there can be a binding contract for goods to be sold to you although their acquisition may be subject to some contingency which may or may not happen - like the manufacturer allocating goods in demand to your supplier instead of a competitor. And, as to the price, this can be dealt with under section 8 of the 1979 Act (which is also still intact). It says that where the contract does not give it then it may be determined in some manner fixed by the contract or by the course of dealings between the parties and otherwise the buyer has to pay a reasonable price. The law would have required delivery within a reasonable time. On this last point, the Consumer Rights Act 2015 has changed things but it is unlikely that the Court of Appeal's decision would have been any different if reached under the new law. And how much did Mr Hughes get awarded to him? £35,000.

Exclooooooooooooooooooooosion

"Sale goods - no warranty" "We cannot deal with any complaint about the goods unless it is notified to us in red pencil enclosed within a sealed jam jar to be received by us no later than 93 seconds after you have taken delivery" "No short term rejection on our goods as they are so cheap - thank you for buying".

You know the sort of thing. Exclusion clauses is what the law calls them. You might call them small print although it can often be brazenly large print. Not legally worth the cardboard they are scrawled on? When it comes to the contract conditions we have been looking at - and this includes what I have said about when goods should be delivered - these exclusion clauses are totally ineffective and count for nothing although they often mislead consumers into abandoning their rights. Equally ineffective in legal eyes are words that appear to make any rights you have subject to some restrictive or onerous condition that is not in the Consumer Rights Act or allow a trader to put you at some disadvantage as a result of pursuing a remedy.

"Dear Trader

I am advised that the condition you seek to rely on is not binding on me by virtue of section 31 of the Consumer Rights Act 2015 and that you seek to rely on it when you know or should know of its ineffectiveness is a matter I view with considerable seriousness. Hence, I am referring the contract and our correspondence to trading standards."

Here is another no-no. A term in a contract is blacklisted in law where it suggests that a trader who has been negligent as a result of which the consumer has died or been caused personal injury is not liable. It has no legal effect and the position is the same if the trader though not trying to completely escape liability in the contract in this situation does have a go at limiting it. *"The trader will not be liable to the consumer or their estate in the event of death or personal injury for damages exceeding £100,000."*

At your service

If it is a service that you are getting (whether or not some goods are thrown in as with a decorator who provides paint, wallpaper and glue or a vehicle repairer who throws in a new engine or some plugs in which event those goods have to be up to legal scratch in the same way as if you had bought them yourself from a trader) there are mirror type requirements. They are set out in the Consumer Rights Act 2015 as well which will apply, as in the case of goods, where you are a consumer and the supplier of the service is a trader in respect of an agreement made on or after 1 October 2015 and this is in place of the Supply of Goods and Services Act 1982. The service is to be provided with reasonable care and skill. If you haven't agreed when the service is to be performed then it must be within a reasonable time. What's reasonable? Good question, reader. Depends on the facts of each individual case, says the Act. Crikey.

"Dear Trader

You said you would start as soon as you could. I am advised that you were obligated to perform our agreement within a reasonable time by virtue of section 52 of the Consumer Rights Act 2015 and you have failed to do so. I require you to take this letter as formal notice that unless you commence work within 14 days of the date of receipt of this letter I shall treat the agreement at an end and* *claim from you the deposit I have paid you and damages reflecting losses I have and will have suffered as a result of your breach of contract to include any sum I have to pay to another contractor to do the work you had agreed to carry out over and above our contract price. Of course, you will also be required to complete the contract if and when you commence it as promptly as possible and in any event within a reasonable time which I consider to be 28 days of the date of receipt of this letter.*"*

**These deadlines may be too long or too short. As we have seen, what is reasonable depends on the facts of each individual case. If in doubt, err on the side of caution and allow a bit longer.*

If you agreed a time for the work to start and the words of the agreement or circumstances made it abundantly clear that it was vital for this date to be adhered to and the trader has defaulted, you can tell the trader you are treating the agreement as at an end. Your remedy would again be recovery of whatever money you had paid over plus damages along the lines set out in the threatener above.

How much are you obliged to pay for the service? Generally, whatever you agreed to pay and if you made a bad bargain then I'm afraid that's tough on you. Sometimes the price or at least the means by which it is to be calculated - £50 call out charge plus £40 for each 30 minutes of service or part thereof (to include talking about the weather and looking out of the window) plus £10 in lieu of a tea break - will not have been agreed in advance. In that case, you have to pay a reasonable price and no more. What is reasonable again depends on the facts of each individual transaction. If you are being swizzed, pay what you say is the reasonable price and explain how you got there. You will not usually be legally justified in paying nothing on the ground that an excessive amount has been demanded.

"Dear Trader

You have invoiced me for £1,568.75 for unblocking my drain. We did not agree the price in advance. The job took 45 minutes. The amount of the invoice is exorbitant. My legal obligation under section 51 of the Consumer Rights Act 2015 is to pay you no more than a reasonable price for the service. I have made enquiries of several other drains specialists in the area and none of their estimates for the work exceed £250 inc VAT. I am satisfied that £250 inc VAT is more than a reasonable figure. I enclose my cheque for £250 in satisfaction of your entitlement and await your VAT credit note. If you are misguided enough to bring proceedings against me for the balance then I can assure you here and now that such proceedings will be defended. I am reporting you to your trade association whatever your response to this letter as I am convinced that your conduct justifies such action. In future, I shall be taking my drains elsewhere.

Yours faithfully

Clive Troublesore"

Where the trader told you something about the service, verbally or in writing, and you took it into account when deciding to give them the job, that something is now treated as a term of the agreement and must be complied with. These somethings include information provided under regulations 9, 10 or 13 of the Consumer Credit Regulations which we met above in respect of goods.

Duff service remedies

The new Act establishes a regime for dealing with a trader who has not used reasonable care and skill. The general law which applies to contract breaches may well entitle you to other remedies: in particular, to throw the trader off a job but you should be confident that the law is on your side before taking such a drastic step or you could be in trouble with a trader's claim against you for damages including the profit they have lost from not being able to see the contract through. Perhaps not too much to worry about if it's the gardener you are dispatching who had a penchant for mistaking your delphiniums for weeds. It's when we come to big money building contracts, for example, that the order of the boot could be a bit risky.

So what's this new Act's remedy regime for services then? You have a right - if you want to exercise it and it's not an impossibility - for a repeat performance and that doesn't mean messing up again. The trader would be obliged to make right what they have done wrong and to do so within a reasonable time and without significant inconvenience to you. Any costs in doing so including labour and materials would have to be borne by the trader. Should a repeat performance be impossible or the trader has failed to repeat within a reasonable time and without significant inconvenience to you then you have a right to a price reduction which could be up to 100%. A price reduction is also available where the job has not been done within a reasonable time.

"Dear Trader

You have failed to carry out our contract using reasonable care *and skill so that you are in breach of section 49 of the Consumer Rights Act 2015. I attach a separate list of 169 deficiencies in your work. I hereby require you to remedy these deficiencies by way of repeat performance under sections 54 and 55 of the 2015 Act. It will be your obligation to bear all costs involved in the repeat performance and I consider that the remedial work should reasonably be completed within 7 days of your receipt of this communication.* If you fail to repeat within this time frame, I intend to instruct another builder to do the work and to claim their bill against you together with damages for breach of contract which will reflect the stress and disruption we are suffering and will continue to suffer until things are put right.*

Yours faithfully

Clive Troublesore"

** The time allowed should be reasonable. Longer than seven days may well be appropriate. It depends on the particular circumstances. Err on the side of allowing more rather than less time than may be needed.*

Where you are supplied with goods along with a service - say bricks by a bricklayer - then as already noted the goods must be up to the same legal scratch as a computer bought from a shop and the service must be performed with reasonable care and skill. This means, for example, that you could exercise the short term right to reject the goods along with the right to a repeat performance of the service.

"Dear Trader

Certain of the materials supplied by you under our contract were not of satisfactory quality as required by section 9 of the Consumer Rights Act 2015 (the Act) and/or reasonably fit for purpose as required by section 10 of the Act. I enclose a separate list of the relevant defects. Further, you have failed to carry out our contract using reasonable care and skill so that you are in breach of section 49 of the Act. I attach another list of 169 deficiencies in your work. I hereby require you to replace the defective goods under section 23 of the Act. In addition, I require you to remedy the defects specified in my second list by way of repeat performance under sections 54 and 55 of the Act. It will be your obligation to bear all costs involved in the repeat performance and I consider that the materials should be replaced and the remedial work should reasonably be completed within 7 days of your receipt of this communication. If you fail to replace and repeat within this time frame, I intend to treat our contract as at an end, reject the materials under section 24 of the Act and instruct another builder to make the replacements and redo the work and to claim their bill against you together with damages for breach of contract which will reflect the stress and disruption we are suffering and will continue to suffer until things are put right.

Yours faithfully

Clive Troublesore"

Excloooooooooooooooooooooosion

In the same way as a trader's attempts at excluding or restricting your rights under the Act in relation to goods will be in vain, so it is in relation to the provision of a service. You have similar safeguards under section 57 of the Act.

Present prescience

Supposing that instead of popping up to the attic and dusting off the cherry stoner or smart phone overcoat to gift to Auntie Vera for her birthday, you actually dip into your pocket and buy her a present. And, worse still, supposing the present falls to pieces in Auntie's hands. We have an awkward contractual situation. When Auntie identifies the trader who supplied the present from the tiny sticky label on the box and takes a trip to their premises, she could legitimately be sent packing. *"Push off, Auntie. Our contract was with your nephew. You have no status to make a complaint, let alone a claim. Goodbye - unless you want to pay for something yourself rather than moaning about somebody else's purchase."*

There are two ways round the problem which avoid Auntie Vera suffering the embarrassment of telling you that you gave her rubbish and please could you take it back for her or pretending that the cherry stoner was a better invention than underpants or that her smart phone looks ever so cute in its overcoat but she can't find it at the moment.

First way round is using the Contracts (Rights of Third Parties) Act 1999. Tell the trader that the goods you want to buy are a gift for Auntie Vera. You are sure she will be delighted with them but, in case they turn out to be defective, you want her to be able to enforce the same rights against the trader as you would have been able to do as the purchasing consumer. If the trader agrees then they must write some magic words on the invoice or till receipt and then you can go ahead and buy. This would satisfy the requirement of the 1999 Act that the contract expressly states that a named third party can enforce it. Put the invoice or till receipt in with the birthday card which will have the bonus of Auntie seeing how much you have spent and being extremely impressed.

Magic words: *These goods are being bought for Vera Troublesore and we agree that she shall be entitled to enforce all terms of the contract for their sale as the third party.*

The second way round is to assign - transfer - your rights to enforce the contract to Auntie Vera when you hand over the gift or subsequently. This would not involve any concurrence or action on the part of the trader.

> ***Assignment*** *To Auntie Vera Troublesore: I Clive Troublesore hereby assign to you the benefit of all rights and remedies including those treated as applying by the Consumer Rights Act 2015 to which I am entitled under my contract for the purchase of this gift, namely a cherry stoner which I made on 14 July 2016 from The Ridiculous Kitchen Utensil Store, Macclesfield under invoice/till receipt number 679WQZ16. Many Happy Returns. Love Clive.*

If Auntie Vera decides to follow through a complaint or claim she will need to give the trader a copy of the assignment.

Incidentally, despite the general rule that a person who is not a party to a contract cannot enforce it, there are exceptions in relation to holiday contracts. In the case of a package holiday (within the Package Travel, Package Holidays and Package Tours Regulations 1992), a claim can be pursued by members of a party on whose behalf a single individual has made the booking. And in the case of a non-package holiday, a claim can be pursued by the person who made the booking on behalf of themselves and the other members of the party.

Distance sales cancellation

We have already met in another context the Consumer Contracts (Information, Cancellation and Additional Charges) Regulations 2013 which now incorporate the law on cancellation of goods, services and digital content such as music and software downloads and streamed films contracted for DISTANTLY on or after 13 June 2014 by a consumer from a trader. Cancellation (because you changed your mind or for whatever reason which may have nothing to do with the fault of the trader) will apply to the vast majority of deals which do not involve you going into a shop (including a pop up shop) or other business premises of the trader and making your agreement to buy or have some work done there and then - or to use what you may find to be the indigestible words of the regulations, cancellation will apply to distance contracts and off-premises contracts. This means that the most usual deals to be caught are those fixed up on the internet, by phone, by mail order or at your home. Distance selling requires some organised scheme for transacting with you so if you ring a bookshop and ask them as a one-off to send you six copies of *Breaking Law* (you fool) you will be stuck with them once they arrive even if the picture of the author turns your stomach. Not an organised scheme.

The right to cancel, wherever the deal was done, is excluded for:

- medical products and services;
- passenger transport services such as bus, rail or flight tickets;
- personalised goods;
- perishable goods ("liable to deteriorate or expire rapidly");
- urgent repairs or maintenance where you have specifically called out the trader;
- the supply of accommodation, vehicle hire and leisure activities for specific dates;
- goods bought at auction but eBay and other online auctions are caught where a trader is involved; and
- some others so check regulations 27 and 28 to ensure you are not ruled out before getting too stroppy when the trader has not told you that there is a right to cancel.

For deals which were done off the trader's business premises - so generally we are not here looking at internet and other distance situations - there is no right to cancel unless you had to pay more than £42.

There's no doubt that reaching a deal with a right to cancel often gives you an advantage over going into a shop which does not offer a returns policy because then you have no such right. Against that, you will be denied the opportunity of being coughed or sneezed at in the face by other shoppers (see chapter 36) and to fully examine goods and even try them on or try them out.

How long do you have in which to cancel? Generally, 14 days starting the day after you made the contract. But with goods it's generally 14 days after the day on which they came into your possession or the possession of someone else to whom you asked them to be delivered. There are special rules for multiple or regular deliveries. The time for cancelling is extended if the trader has not supplied you in the prescribed way with prescribed information about your right to cancel (see part 2 and schedules

1 and 2 to the regulations). The extension is to 14 days from the date on which you get the necessary information from the trader. However, once 12 months from the date on which the trader should have come up with the information are up, the right to cancel disappears.

How do you cancel? You can use a template cancellation form which you will find in schedule 3 to the regulations. You don't have to. Instead, you can use an online form provided to you by the trader - but again you don't have to - or you can just communicate with the trader using you own words (or mine!) and you don't have to give any reasons for cancellation.

> *"I require you to take this communication as formal notice that in accordance with regulation 29 of the Consumer Contracts (Information, Cancellation and Additional Charges) Regulations 2013 I hereby cancel my contract with you numbered 000001XB4 made on 14 July 2016."*

So long as you have sent off the cancellation communication before the end of the cancellation period you will be treated as having cancelled in time even if the trader does not receive it until outside that period.

What next? You get back any money you have paid to the trader including any original delivery costs. If you had asked for an expedited or otherwise enhanced form of delivery which was more expensive than the trader's basic form on offer then only the cost of the basic form is refundable. You cannot lawfully be charged a cancellation fee. If you have damaged the goods - diminished them by any amount "as a result of handling...by the consumer beyond what is necessary to establish the nature, characteristics and functioning of the goods" - the amount may be deducted from your refund. In the case of services, the trader can deduct the cost of any supplied at your request during the cancellation period.

You must return goods to the trader within 14 days of notifying cancellation at any address they have specified unless the trader has offered to collect them. If no address has been specified, you can use a trader's contact address and, if none, any address at which they carry on their business. The cost of return is to be borne by you unless the trader has agreed to pay it. But when giving you details of your cancellation rights, you should have been told that the responsibility for bearing the return cost would be down to you if the trader was not intending to meet it or where the goods could not normally be returned by post (because, for example, they were too large) what the return cost would be. If the trader failed to give you this information then they must pick up the bill for return.

The refund due to you is to be paid without undue delay and within 14 days of cancellation unless you have to return goods. Then, you should be refunded within 14 days of the goods arriving back or, if earlier, within 14 days of the trader receiving proof that you have sent the goods back. Unless you have agreed otherwise with the trader, the refund is to be made using the same payment method as you originally used.

Chapter 40

Unfair Trading

The price (and possibly any one of a dozen other things) is wrong

You cannot compel a trader to sell to you. In legal eyes, when the trader displays goods they are inviting you to make an offer to buy them. You make that offer once you present the goods to the cashier or to the assistant manager or to the big shot down from head office who is checking out the cashier and the assistant manager or to whoever happens to be standing or sitting at the purchase point and they decide whether they will accept the offer. It matters not that you have been queuing all night to bag the rug or tin of silver plated baked beans marked down by 90% and nobody else wants them. Because you have no right to insist on a sale to you it follows that you have no right to insist on a sale to you at a particular price.

But say the goods were mistakenly marked at £10 when they should have been marked at £100 and the shop won't sell to you at the lower price despite you having travelled 26.3 miles to get them? It makes no difference. The same principle applies although the conversation at the purchase point - by which time you have been joined by the store manager and six other shoppers who are pretending to be inspecting the nearby itching powder or staring at the fascinating white ceiling - could go something like this:

> *"I accept I can't make you sell them to me but you do know you have broken the law, don't you?"*
>
> *"We never break the law. We pride ourselves in discharging our legal obligations to the letter."*
>
> *"You are conversant with the Consumer Protection from Unfair Trading Regulations 2008, I am sure. They make it an offence for a trader to mislead customers about the price of a product and lots of other things like the existence of a specific price advantage if that misleading would lead them or would be likely to lead them to purchase the product or simply go into the shop. It's in regulation 5."*
>
> *"Would you like to sit yourself down and partake of some refreshment."*

Now it would be quite improper for you to use a trader's commission of an offence as a device to harass or intimidate them into bending to your demands. However, where it is brought home to the trader that what they have done amounts to an unfair commercial practice and constitutes an offence, they may well be only too pleased to relax their attitude towards you. After all, you are giving them the opportunity to avoid a visit by trading standards and possible prosecution. The trader has a defence if they can show that they made a mistake, the offence was due to an accident or another cause beyond their control but also that they took all reasonable precautions and exercised all due diligence to avoid an offence - and this is where they may come unstuck.

Where do you stand where you have actually been charged for goods at a higher price than the displayed price? In a strong position. As chance would have it, I had a bit of bother along these lines myself. I was after 96p, an apology and greater care.

From: STEPHEN GOLD
Sent: 30/12/2015 18:26
To: customersupport@waitrose.co.uk
Subject: Overcharging

Did you know it can be an offence to display goods at a price less than that which you intend to charge? On 22 December 2015 I purchased from your Richmond, Surrey store goods for which I was charged £146.24 (till 003 seq no 126436). These included four Kabuto ramen noodle pots which were on display at £3.50 for two. I was charged and paid £1.99 per pot which was 96p in excess of what I should have been charged. I did not notice the overcharge until I had arrived home. If this had been the one and only occasion this had happened to me at Waitrose, it would have been one thing. But it has happened before and it is presumably resulting in a host of customers who need to count their pennies being deceived where they are less diligent than I was (belatedly) on this occasion. I am fed up with this happening and equally fed up with having to waste the time and take the trouble to return to the store and queue up to complain. Would you please take greater care and would you reimburse me the overcharge?

Whilst writing, may I point out that your displayed bananas are habitually soft and/or black and/or blacken within a couple of days of purchase. This is no doubt due to them being frozen or over refrigerated before display. I am advised that consumption of overripe bananas is not conducive to good health because the sugary content is increased.

Yours faithfully

Stephen Gold

On 2 Jan 2016, at 16:26, Waitrose Customer Service *<customerserviceteam@waitrose.co.uk> wrote:*

Thank you for your email Mr Gold.

I'm sorry to hear of your disappointment on your recent visit to our Richmond store.

I have double checked our product database and I'm afraid the Kabuto Noodle range has not been on offer since January 2015. The selling price is £1.99.

Mistakes at our tills are thankfully rare, but I can understand that your confidence in us has been dented. Following your feedback, I've made the Richmond branch management team aware. They will discuss this with their cashiers and we're confident this won't happen again.

As a gesture of our goodwill for the disappointment caused, I'd like to send you a gift voucher. Please can I ask you to provide us with your full postal address and I will be happy to arrange this for you.

Thanks again for telling us about this and I hope we can look forward to seeing you again soon.

Kind regards

Katie S

Waitrose Customer Service

Case Reference: 01361887

From: STEPHEN GOLD
Sent: 02/01/2016 17:28
To: customerserviceteam@waitrose.co.uk
Subject: Re: Overcharging [ ]

Thank you for your message.

I am very concerned - indeed irritated - by your third paragraph. I care not what your database discloses. The display of the product in question was accompanied by a prominent and unequivocal notice to the effect that two were available for the price of £3.50. I had this independently verified the following day. That is why I purchased four. If you made the mistake of allowing the notice to be in position when you intended otherwise then please say but do not insinuate as you are doing that I have given you a false account or that I was suffering from some hallucination. I expect an apology and an acceptance that you were in error. I will address your offer of a gift voucher when I have heard from you in more satisfactory terms. You may also wish to say something about my banana comments which you have ignored.

Yours faithfully

Stephen Gold

On 4 Jan 2016, at 08:18, Waitrose Customer Service
<customerserviceteam@waitrose.co.uk> wrote:

Thank you for your email Mr Gold.

I am sorry you are dissatisfied with my previous response and I am sorry for any upset caused.

I'm afraid I cannot comment as to the location of the sign at the time of your visit as this may have been moved since. I have spoken to the branch and I have asked that they double check all of the offers to ensure that the shelf edge tickets are clear and accurate so we do not mislead any of our customers.

I'm also sorry to hear of your disappointment with the bananas purchased from our store. I'd really like to look into this for you. So I can do this, please can you reply with as much of the following information as possible:

- your full name, address and phone number;
- product barcode/product name;
- cost of the product;
- use by/best before date;
- packer's/batch code (this is usually printed near the use by/best before date).

Once we have this, we'll pass this matter on to our merchandise complaints department for full investigation and then we will write to you.

Thanks again for letting us know and I look forward to hearing from you.

Kind regards

Katie S
Waitrose Customer Service
Case Reference: 01361887

From: STEPHEN GOLD
Sent: 04/01/2016 18:19
To: customerserviceteam@waitrose.co.uk
Subject: Re: Waitrose Customer Feedback [ ]

Thank you for your further message from which it seems you accept you were in error. Is this so?

The mischief is in failing to update your tills with offer data and, incidentally, in failing to display reduction notices in a way that does not confuse customers into thinking they relate to goods immediately by them or to all goods immediately by them when they do not. I cannot see how cashiers can be blamed as you previously suggested. You should be apologising to them for having to suffer protests about wrong pricing.

In the matter of the bananas, my complaint was of habitual problems. I fear I would have to go to the refuse tip to answer most of your questions.

I give my contact details below.

Yours faithfully

Stephen Gold

The exchange continued with my new best friend Katie who responded to each of my messages with commendable speed and never lost her cool. I accepted a voucher for a fiver and let matters rest after an acknowledgment that she was not suggesting that my complaint was false or indeed that I had suffered a hallucination BUT *"however as previously mentioned, without any evidence of the ticket in branch, I cannot confirm or deny what was on display at the time of your visit."* I regard the acknowledgment as tantamount to an admission that *Waitrose* had been at fault, albeit I accept this had been due to a human error. Why not have the grace to say so in the first place? There are drawbacks for the trader in going overboard with open contrition.

The fiver was more than adequate compensation for me. What I didn't know at the time was that, within a matter of weeks, I should have a spot of similar trouble at *Tesco* over the matter of an overcharged cucumber. I will let the emails tell the story.

To: "Customer Service
Subject: Tesco Customer Service Enquiry Call Form

Sent: 23/01/2016 20:16
Title: Mr
First Name: Stephen
Surname: Gold

I today made purchases from Tesco Metro, George Street, Richmond (till receipt no 309700710344043) including two cucumbers: one organic at £1 and one non-organic at circa 45p. I now notice from the receipt that I have been charged for two organic cucumbers. I have the cucumber labels which are available for inspection by appointment. I do not have the time at the moment to return to the store. Would you please make me an appropriate refund to the address at the bottom and be more careful in the future because overcharging albeit by mistake is an offence when lack of care is involved. It might also be a good idea for you to advise your customers to check their receipts for instances of overcharging because I fancy that not all shoppers are as vigilant as me.

Yours faithfully

Stephen Gold

From: customer.service@tesco.co.uk
Date: 24 January 2016 at 11:02:54 GMT
Subject: Re: Tesco Customer Service Enquiry Call Form

Dear Mr Gold

Thank you for your email.

I was very sorry to learn that you had paid more than you expected for one of your cucumbers at your local Tesco Metro in Richmond and I can appreciate how disappointed you must be.

It is very disappointing that the product was incorrectly scanned and as a result of this you were overcharged. Our overcharge policy is to refund double the difference.

Whilst there is little more that can I say to alleviate the disappointment this situation has caused you, I'd like to thank you for taking the time to bring this matter to our attention. I do hope that despite this incident, you will give us the chance to restore your confidence in our operation.

As you are unable to return, for me to issue a Tesco Moneycard please could you provide a copy or a photo of the receipt and the labels you have available?

Finally, thank you for bringing this to my attention: I eagerly await your response so I can resolve this issue for you.

Kind regards,

Ryan K

Tesco Customer Service

To Customer Service

Sent 24 January 2016

From Stephen Gold

Dear Mr K

Thank you for your message. I congratulate you on its promptness. I regret what has happened although I would not say I was as disappointed as you suppose.

I have sent to you by separate message copies of the till receipt and labels. I have no problem with your request. Whilst I would not expect my request to materially affect your company's share price, I can understand that you must protect yourself against what could in theory be an attempt at obtaining money by deception. Should you wish to send the branch manager along to authenticate the copies against the original documents then I would be happy to see him by appointment and perhaps he would care to partake of some organic cucumber sandwiches whilst he is here although I can see that his bus fare may exceed the sum of money in issue.

In passing, I am particularly impressed by the freshness of your bananas.

Yours sincerely

Stephen Gold

From: customer.service@tesco.co.uk
Date: 25 January 2016 at 06:56:36 GMT
Subject: Re: Overcharge

Dear Mr Gold

Thank you for your email and for the photo provided.

I think maybe my colleague in store presumed they were both organic based on the other items purchased but we can't be caught making assumptions as in this instance it's caused you to be overcharged.

As requested, I've issued a Tesco Moneycard for £5.00 so that you can make some extra sandwiches. This will be with you in 7 to 10 working days.

Finally, thank you for taking the time to bring this to my attention. We value your custom very highly and we always do our best to put things right. I hope you give us another chance to deliver and provide the service you expect and deserve. If you have any further questions please don't hesitate to contact us again.

Kind regards,

Ryan K

Tesco Customer Service

Poor Ryan K. Does he never go to bed? That matter was settled in less than one and a half days and for the first time in my experience someone from a customer services department displayed a sense of humour. I can overlook that my suggestion was not addressed. Well done *Tesco*. Well done Ryan K who gets the Breaking Law Life Award for Services to Sliced Cucumber Sandwiches with a Pinch of Salt. Incidentally, legal pedants would be quite correct to point out that I could have insisted on a cash refund of the overcharge which would not have committed me to return to *Tesco*. But I love them - and their bananas.

And legal pedants really on the ball would also point out that in this situation the changes to the 2008 regulations now kick in. They are a gem. Previously, the erring trader could face a prosecution but not a county court claim simply on the basis that they had breached the regulations. The changes can give you the consumer the right to redress in a noodle pot situation - as indeed with a multitude of misleading actions and also aggressive practices - which has occurred since 30 September 2014. You will need to show that you entered into a contract with the trader or you made a payment to the trader PLUS that an average customer would have been likely to have done so (an objective test and, therefore, we are not concerned with what a very weird customer would have done) PLUS the action you are complaining about was a significant factor in your decision to enter into that contract (which is a subjective test).

So prove those things where the trader has done something misleading under regulation 5 of the 2008 Regulations, and you can get out of the deal within 90 days from when you received the goods or service (yes, services and even digital content are also covered) so long as you haven't fully consumed the goods or fully received the service. It's called a right to unwind. You must return the goods and you are entitled to your money back.

Alternatively, and, possibly of more interest, you can keep the goods and enjoy a discount where you have paid the price or some of it. How much? For a minor transgression, 25% of the price; if it is significant, 50%; if it is serious, 75%; and if it is very serious, 100%! The degree of seriousness will be judged according to the trader's behaviour, the impact on you and the time that has elapsed since the transgression. There is an inevitable exception where the purchase price is over £5,000, the market value of the goods was less than you agreed to pay and there is clear evidence of the difference between the two figures. Then, you are entitled to the same percentage of the price as market value bears to what you agreed to pay. In certain circumstances you may also be entitled to damages.

In addition to an unwinding or a discount or instead of them, you can claim damages for any financial loss you have incurred which, but for the trader's misleading you, would not have been suffered as well as for any alarm, distress or physical inconvenience or discomfort you have been caused. These rights do not affect any other rights you may have under the general law for breach of contract or misrepresentation but you cannot collect duplicate compensation. Unlike the position with a prosecution, it is no defence to a civil claim under the regulations to unwind or for a discount for the trader to say that what happened was due to a mistake, accident or somebody else or was beyond their control and that they took all reasonable precautions and exercised all due diligence but that defence can be put forward for a claim for damages.

The new rights do not apply to house and flat sales; property lets apart from assured shorthold tenancies and holiday accommodation; pensions, mortgages, insurance, banking and other financial services though there is plenty of other protection there; or generally to credit agreements (but again, plenty of protection elsewhere).

A claim can be brought in the county court. I have yet to come across one despite this being a valuable right.

PARTICULARS OF CLAIM

1. The claimant brings the claim under regulation 5 ("regulation 5") of the Consumer Protection from Unfair Trading Regulations 2008 as amended ("the Regulations").

2. At all material times the claimant was a consumer and the defendant was a trader within the Regulations.

3. On 14 July 2016 the claimant entered into a contract with the defendant ("the contract") for the purchase of a 'Brain Scramble' laptop computer ("the computer") for the price of £1,250 ("the price"), paying the price and taking delivery of the computer on the same date.

4. The defendant engaged in a prohibited practice ("the prohibited practice") in relation to the computer within regulations 5 and 27A(4)(a) of the Regulations (or the manufacturer of the computer engaged in the prohibited practice within regulations 5 and 27(4)(b) of the Regulations of which the defendant was aware or could reasonably be expected to be aware as at the date of the contract).

Particulars of prohibited practice

[Set out the false information relied on which must relate to any one or more of the matters referred to in regulation 5 - for example, the amount of the price or how the price has been calculated; the existence of a price advantage (for example, "50% off"); the extent of the trader's commitments (for example, saying the trader gives a full guarantee when it turns out to be only for parts and not labour); indicating by a statement or symbol that the goods or the trader are sponsored or approved (for example, "By Appointment to Dame Barbara Windsor" or "Approved Platinum Member of He'salrightmate"); the need for a service, part, replacement or repair (for example, "All parts last for life"); the attributes of the trader (which includes their qualifications, status, approval, affiliations and connections and awards and distinctions); and information on the main characteristics of the goods which includes among a long list their benefits, risks, composition, after-sale customer assistance, method and date of manufacture, results to be expected, fitness for purpose, usage and specification - ***you will detect some crossover with the Consumer Rights Act 2015 and we touch on this below: alternatively, you may be able to rely on a misleading omission - omitting or hiding material information or providing it unclearly, unintelligibly or ambiguously etc under regulation 6****].*

5. Pursuant to regulation 27E of the Regulations, on 20 July 2016 the claimant exercised the right to unwind the contract on account of the prohibited practice by indicating to the defendant that he rejected the computer and informing the defendant that the computer was available for collection from his home subject to 24 hours' prior notice to the claimant of the defendant's intention to call in order to collect.

6. The defendant has neither refunded the price to the claimant nor collected the computer from the claimant.

7. The claimant claims the return of the price.

Or

5. The defendant has not exercised the right to unwind in respect of the contract.

6. Pursuant to regulation 27I of the Regulations, the claimant claims a discount in respect of the contract.

7. The relevant percentage discount within regulation 21I of the Regulations which the claimant says is just and appropriate is:

25% on the basis that the prohibited practice was minor;

Or

50% on the basis that the prohibited practice was significant;

Or

75% on the basis that the prohibited practice was serious;

Or

100% on the basis that the prohibited practice was very serious.

Pursuant to regulation 27J of the Regulations, the claimant further claims damages for financial loss incurred by him and for distress and physical inconvenience or discomfort suffered by him which he would not have respectively incurred and suffered if the prohibited practice had not taken place.

Particulars of financial loss

[insert particulars]

Particulars of distress and physical inconvenience or discomfort

[insert particulars]

And the claimant claims:

a. return of the price of £1,250;

or

a. a discount limited to £x;

b. damages limited to £y;

c. interest at such rate and for such period as the court shall deem just; and

d. costs.

Dated 4th September 2016

(signed) Clive Troublesore

Claimant

Crossover with Consumer Rights Act 2015

The new laws in the 2015 Act do the consumer proud (see chapter 39). Sometimes you will have a remedy under both the 2015 Act and the 2008 regulations. If goods are not reasonably fit for purpose and the trader has convinced you that they are reasonably fit, for example, that could amount to a breach of both pieces of legislation. You may be too late for a short term rejection under the Act but in time for an unwinding under the regulations. Or you may get a better result by going for a discount (especially in the case of a very serious case of misleading) under the regulations than a price reduction under the Act. Provided that your case falls within both pieces of legislation, there is no shame in making claims as alternatives which rely on both and relying on the general law to boot if that is justified although do not over complicate the claim if you can avoid it. You would need to appropriately adapt the particulars of claim in this chapter and chapter 39.

Oh, I almost forgot

Having tested out customer relations on price at *Waitrose* and then at *Tesco* it would have been ungallant to have neglected *Marks & Spencer*. My sentiments are genuine.

Sent from my iPad

Begin forwarded message: On 20/02/2016 22:34,

Message: I bought a packet of five "Happy Easter" cards from you today. The product reference is T21/7790/3428E. The price label appeared to be £2. When I got to the checkout the cashier pointed out that the price was in fact £2.50 and on the closest inspection I see that there this is so. But the 50p is a small fraction of the size of the £2 and is in less bold print. Since 50p is more than I ordinarily spend on my afternoon tea, I consider that giving it so little prominence is very misleading and that many of your customers, particularly the elderly with poor eyesight, will be deceived. I would welcome your observations. I can send you a copy of the packaging. Alternatively you may be able to source a packet of the cards at your end but I should put on a pair of strong specs first.

***On 22 Feb 2016, at 19:52, M&S Service Team** <no_reply@customersupport.marksandspencer.com> wrote:*

Hi Stephen

Thanks for contacting us about the Happy Easter cards you bought from us today. It sounds like I'd need my super strong glasses on to see how small the pricing was on the packaging of these cards. This is quite unusual as normally the font size of the numbers on the price is the same.

I've passed your feedback onto out Stationary/Card team, they'll be keen to look into this further and to see if this is just a one off on this particular pack of cards. They'll also take your comments into consideration when discussing this with our supplier as we want to make sure all of our customers are happy with our labelling.

Thanks again for getting in touch, we look forward to seeing you in store again soon.

Kind regards

Karen B
Retail Customer Services
Your M&S Customer Service

From: STEPHEN GOLD
Date: 22 February 2016 at 21:56:21 GMT
To: M&S Service Team <no_reply@customersupport.marksandspencer.com>
Subject: Re: M&S

Dear Ms B

Thank you for your prompt response. However, I see from a revisit to the store that this misleading practice is being adopted with a number of other cards - including cards on display for what appear to be £1 but which an inspection with one's nose almost touching the packaging reveals are priced at £1.50. Can I have your assurance that all these cards will be immediately removed from display and relabelled. This may have sounded a trivial complaint from a lunatic but it really is a serious matter. I await your early response.

Yours sincerely

Stephen Gold
Sent from my iPad

From: M&S Service Team *<retailcustomer.services@customersupport.marksandspencer.com>*
Date: 25 February 2016 at 21:17:56 GMT
Subject: M&S

Dear Mr Gold,

Ref: 310957

Thank you for getting back in touch.

I hope you don't mind me replying on behalf of my colleagues Karen and Paul. I can appreciate your frustration as I've also noticed the labelling has changed when purchasing a Mother's Day this weekend and I found it very hard to read the notably smaller decimal and 50p.

My colleagues have passed your comments and feedback onto our Stationary Team along with our Marketing Team who will evaluate your comments along with any further feedback we receive on our label pricing.

I'm afraid I'm unable to say whether the cards with the current labelling will be removed from sale as this is something our teams will review and they will do this by using the feedback we've received. Your comments are incredibly important and will play a part in this review.

Thank you again for getting in touch and for your valued feedback.

Kind regards
Lucy M
Retail Customer Services
Your M&S Customer Service

Waitrose revisited

You'll never guess what happened. Or perhaps you might.

From: STEPHEN GOLD
Sent: 02/04/2016 17:25
To: customerserviceteam@waitrose.co.uk
Subject: False representation as to price

Dear Team

I have had to complain to you in the recent past on the above subject. I regret I have to return to you on the very same subject.

Today at your Richmond branch I selected two bags of creme eggs which were displayed as having been marked down from 37p to 19p each. At your till, however, I was asked to pay the original price. This is another instance of reduction data not having been input into the till. Fortunately, I was alert to the possibility of an overcharge attempt being made on this occasion and was able to draw your assistant's attention to the error before the transaction was closed. You really must be more diligent or I fear that sooner or later you will face prosecution for this practice (although you may have a defence) independently of any claim for compensation that may be made as a result of breach of statutory duty. Can I have an assurance that you are going to be more careful for I shall otherwise find shopping with you too much of a nervous experience.

Yours faithfully

Stephen Gold

On 5 Apr 2016, at 09:11, Waitrose Customer Service
<customerserviceteam@waitrose.co.uk> wrote:

Thanks for getting in touch with us Stephen, though I'm sorry to hear what happened when you were shopping in our Richmond branch recently.

From looking at our records, the reduced price of 37p came into effect on the 31st of March. Could I ask if the 19p price was on a reduction sticker on the product? I'm unable to see this further reduction.

Once I've heard back from yourself I'll then investigate this for you and then once I've gathered all the information I need, I'll then respond to you in full.

Thanks again for getting in touch, I look forward to hearing from you.

Kind regards

Kieran D
Waitrose Customer Service
Case Reference: 01784361

From: STEPHEN GOLD
Sent: 05/04/2016 11:48
To: customerserviceteam@waitrose.co.uk
Subject: Re: Waitrose Customer Feedback (Case No. 01784361)

Thank you. The reduction to 19p was clearly notified on the shelf by the product display although not on the selected products. You do not usually mark products with their price, do you?

Stephen Gold

From: Waitrose Customer Service *<customerserviceteam@waitrose.co.uk>*
Date: 5 April 2016 at 14:08:18 BST
Subject: Re: Waitrose Customer Feedback (Case No. 01784361) [ref:_00D20laeb._50020xiZDX:ref]

Thanks for your reply Stephen and for confirming those details for me.

We may on occasion have a reduced sticker on a product to indicate a further reduction.

As I can't see this on our system, I'll speak with the buyer and highlight to them about this. It may have been a change that was not communicated to the relevant team to put the price into action on our checkouts, if so they'll review the way they communicate such changes for the future to avoid such issues.

I'm sorry that we've let ourselves down in regards to the service provided, but I hope that knowing this will be reviewed by the right Partners shows you how we're dedicated to getting things right and improving our customers experience when shopping with this.

Thanks for giving me the opportunity to look into this for you Stephen, I hope this doesn't deter you from shopping with us and that we'll see you in our Richmond branch again soon.

I hope my response has been helpful today and if you'd like to provide feedback we have a link to a short survey. It'll only take a few minutes and as a thank you for your time you'll be entered into our prize draw where you could win £500 in gift cards.

www.waitrose-cs.com/?certcode=011

Kind regards

Kieran D
Waitrose Customer Service
Case Reference: 01784361

We'd love to hear your thoughts on your contact with us. If you'd like to take a couple of minutes to fill in our survey you could win £500 of vouchers - www.waitrose-cs.com/?certcode=011

From: STEPHEN GOLD

Date: 9 April 2016

To: customerserviceteam@waitrose.co.uk

Subject: Case number 01784361

Thank you for your last communication. I note what you say but the misleading continues at the same branch. Please see photo of display at the store today. Does the money off notice not imply that it relates to the product immediately above it (which I selected and for which I was charged the higher price). This is the third complaint I have had to make as to misleading pricing in rapid succession. Once is careless. Twice is reckless. Three times is a scandal.

Sent from my iPad

Stop the press!

I promise that I do not go out with mischief on my shopping list. But they've done it again.

From: STEPHEN GOLD

Sent: 11/04/2016

To: customerserviceteam@waitrose.co.uk

Subject: O1784361

Please see extract below from the relevant receipt. I was charged

£1.99 for the displayed Unoco coconut water. You will appreciate that the shelf label indicated that the reduction applied to this product by virtue of its proximity to the Unoco display. This was misleading. Would it be wise for you to warn customers to carefully check their till receipts as there is a good chance they will be overcharged? I would welcome your particular comments on this suggestion.

Yours sincerely

Stephen Gold

"Shelf snap"

CUCUMBER
2 @ £0.45 0.90
V UNOCO COCONUT WATER 1.99
OYSTER MUSHROOMS 1.80
V KALLO CHOC RICE CAKE 1.49
V KALLO ORG R/CAKE CHC
3 @ £1.49 4.47

** kallo get 1 1/2 ** -0.75
** kallo get 1 1/2 ** -0.75
** Cake 2 For £4 ** -0.80

myWaitrose card
************3125

mW money off shop -£2.70
mW 10% off wine -£1.00

46 items
BALANCE DUE £107.56

"£1.99? How dare you!"

From: Waitrose Customer Service [customerservicet-eam@waitrose.co.uk]

Sent: 14/04/2016

To: Stephen Gold

Subject: Waitrose Customer Feedback (Case No. 01784361)

Thanks for the photo of your receipt Stephen.

I'll contact the branch management team to investigate why this keeps happening. Once I've looked into each of your concerns I'll then be back in touch to respond to you in full.

Kind regards
Kieran D
Waitrose Customer Service

On 14 Apr 2016, at 15:37, Waitrose Customer Service <customer-serviceteam@waitrose.co.uk> wrote:

Thanks again for getting in contact with us Stephen.

Further to my last email as discussed, I've contacted the branch management team at our Richmond branch.

I've spoken with Liam, branch manager, who would like for me to pass on his apologies.

Having discussed this we agreed that it was quite clear that we've clearly let ourselves down on delivering excellent customer service. Liam can't provide any reasons for this shortfall in standards, however it is a Partner error and should not have happened. Going forwards Liam and his management team will be speaking with Partners and offering refresher training to those who they feel may not be completing any tasks given to them correctly.

If you'd like to speak with Liam regarding this, he's more than happy for him or his assistant managers, Kate or Vicki, to sit down and discuss what the branch are doing to resolve these issues and what they'd like to do for you as our customer. Please do ask for Liam, Kate or Vicki upon your next visit to the branch if you wish to do so.

Thanks again for bringing this to my attention, I hope that the above goes some way to showing you how we want to get it right and deliver brilliant customer service.

Kind regards

Kieran D

Waitrose Customer Service

Case Reference: 01784361

From: STEPHEN GOLD

Date: 14 April 2016 at 21:07:16 BST

To: Waitrose Customer Service <customerserviceteam@waitrose.co.uk>

Subject: Re: Waitrose Customer Feedback (Case No. 01784361)

Dear Keiran (if I may)

Thank you for your message. As delightful as a meeting with Liam, Kate or Vicki (in whatever combination) might be, I feel I must plead the hair washing defence. However, I would be prepared to police the pricing practice at the branch for a limited period on your behalf if that might help - I do not think that I am known as the troublemaker so would not be rumbled - and could report back to you. What do you think? Also, I would appreciate your view on the suggestion I have already put forward about warnings to customers. It could be watered down a bit if you thought that appropriate by reference instead to the slight possibility of an overcharge.

Yours sincerely

Stephen Gold

From: Waitrose Customer Service <customerserviceteam@waitrose.co.uk>

Date: 15 April 2016

To: Stephen Gold

Subject: Re: Waitrose Customer Feedback (Case No. 01784361)

Thanks for your reply Stephen.

We'd recommend the best course of action is to speak with the branch management team. As they're at the branch and focused on delivering the best service possible, it's always good to feedback directly to the branch. As previously mentioned, Liam is more than happy to meet with you and discuss whatever you might find in the branch, if he's not available then Kate or Vicki would be able to assist.

In regards to your suggestion, we wouldn't use this at the checkout, we empower our Partners and put our faith in them to ensure that they carry out their duties to the best of their ability. Again, if you do find something that isn't right, please highlight this to a branch management team Partner who'll be more than happy to help.

Once again I'm sorry for the service you've received but hope we can welcome you into branch again soon and show you that the branch is turning things around.

Kind regards

Kieran D

Waitrose Customer Service

Case Reference: 01784361

And M&S revisited.

On 01/05/2016 21:16, STEPHEN GOLD *wrote:*

I regret that I am back but to report a different transgression. In your George Street, Richmond branch today you were displaying bottles of Oudinot medium-dry rose champagne at a price of £21. However, the price programmed into the till just a few feet away was £23. Your assistant sought to charge the higher price - "The till is always right," she said - but when I pointed out the representation of the lower price she dealt with the matter properly and courteously, taking the lower price. I have lost nothing but how many customers had been charged the higher price believing they were purchasing for the lower price? I have had to tackle your good friends at Waitrose about this practice. I hope it is not going to catch on with you and that you will be more careful. Do you realise it could get you into deep trouble?

Yours sincerely

Stephen Gold

Good afternoon Stephen

Our ref: 355048

I am sorry that you were charged the incorrect amount for our Oudinot medium-dry rose champagne in our store.

It is never our intention to let our customers down but clearly an error occurred within our system on this occasion. It is a new offer at the moment with £2 off selected wine products and this had not been programmed into the till.

I have forwarded your experience to the Store Management team who will review how this offer could have been missed. The store will ensure this does not happen again.

I do apologise and thank you for highlighting this error and ensuring we rectify it.

I hope this won't deter you from shopping with us and that you'll enjoy your next visit. Thanks again for getting in touch.

Kind regards
Julie R
Retail Customer Services
Your M&S Customer Service

Chapter 41

Small Print

And bigger print

We have seen how a trader's attempts at wriggling out of legal responsibility for breaching their specific obligations to a consumer which are treated as part of the contract under the Consumer Rights Act 2015 can be thwarted (see chapter 39). That same Act may well thwart attempts at doing you down in a multitude of other ways where you are a consumer and your contract was made with a trader on or after 1 October 2015. There are similar rules for contracts made before then which you will find in the Unfair Contract Terms Act 1977 and the Unfair Terms in Consumer Contracts Regulations 1999 but the new laws are an improvement for the consumer.

Having a laugh

A contract term that the law now says is unfair will not bind you. Yes, you can laugh in its face unless for some reason it suits you to rely on it. If it looks unfair and smells unfair, the probability is that it will be unfair under the law. It must not cause a significant imbalance in the rights and obligations of each side but to your detriment. If the term is ambiguous so that it could have different meanings then the meaning which is the most favourable to you as the consumer will prevail.

Train tickets and car park notices

The fairness law applies not just to written contracts but to verbal contracts too and not just to standard form contracts which are offered to one and all on a 'take it or leave it' basis but to contracts which have been individually negotiated. And it applies to what are called *notices* which catch a written or verbal announcement or other communication which creates a contract. This would typically include a car park sign proclaiming that by leaving your car there you will be agreeing to pay 50p per 15 minutes or part thereof, mortgage your home if you stay longer than two hours and kill yourself if you lose your ticket. However, the law does not catch an employment or apprenticeship contract (although there may well be other laws which can come to the rescue of a downtrodden employee or apprentice).

Core law

You have a problem when it comes to *core terms* of the contract because the general rule is that you cannot challenge them as being unfair. A *core term* is one that goes to the core of the contract. I know, I know! It will specify the main subject matter of the contract. What it is you are buying or hiring or what service you are getting. What you are paying. This means that if you decide you don't like the goods or services involved or you have paid more than they are worth, you cannot use the unfairness law to effectively escape from or reopen the deal.

But you could still challenge a term that allowed the trader, without your consent, to change the goods or services you were due to be getting. Also, there are certain price terms which would be susceptible to challenge. A term which provided when and how the trader might increase the price you agreed to pay would be one or a term which said you had to pay an administration charge but no service was being performed by the trader in exchange for it because the challenge would not be based on value. Similarly, a term in an agreement made by a landlord with their property letting agency that if the landlord came to sell, they would have to pay commission to the agency even though they offered nothing and did nothing to achieve the sale. And if the object or effect of a core term is to allow the trader to get away with something that the law says is probably unfair (see below) then it can be challenged.

Ok then. Whether or not the term is a *core* job might involve a head scratch. If it is *core* then weep not quite yet. There may still be hope. A *core term* will not be binding on you unless it is transparent and prominent. It has to be in plain and intelligible language and, if in writing, it has to be legible but remember that verbal contracts must also be fair. And it must be prominent so that an average consumer who is reasonably well-informed, observant and circumspect would have been aware of it. Nevertheless, the reality is that we do not read every single word which appears in a contract and most judges would not expect you to do so. In deciding whether a term is transparent and prominent the court will look at such things as technical mumbo jumbo, long sentences, killer text the size of a pinprick and whether, though it is burdensome on the consumer, it appears at the bottom left of the 126th page of the contract. Hidden extras could well be successfully challenged. The more onerous on you the consumer, the clearer the meaning and the greater the prominence that the law would expect to be given to the term. Beware, however, of the trader trick of surrounding a detestable term which appears in giant flashing light text with other terms equally prominent with the intended result that you ignore the lot of them.

Grey talk

In the Consumer Rights Act 2015 you will find a list of terms which may be considered by the court to be unfair. It's called the *grey list* and you will find it in schedule 2 to the Act. I suppose we could reproduce schedule 2 here and now but that could add another £1.50 to the price of this book which you might be buying on the internet for 1p plus postage so I'll tell you what. Let's have a look at the juiciest terms in the list which is the Act's way of giving guidance on how it works and at some examples of terms that would fall foul of the guidance. Some of them have actually appeared in contracts and traders have been forced to delete or change them. If one or more of the terms with which you reckon you have been stitched up is described in the list or is similar to the description then you may well be onto a winner. These are potentially unfair terms which the court could say were not binding on you. Some may be blacklisted and automatically unenforceable against you although deft word play by the trader may disguise the fact that they fall into this category.

Some are patently and blatantly unenforceable: some are unenforceable because the trader has gone too far with terms that are too wide and exclude or restrict liability for every conceivable eventuality whereas exclusion or limitation in certain eventualities might have been ok.

Grey (nasty) list

(and note that some of the terms could fall into more than one category).

A term that has the object or effect of limiting the trader's liability if you die or are injured because of some act or omission on their part

Like:

"If we kill you due to our cock-up we won't have to pay your estate more than £10,000."

A term which has the object or effect of inappropriately excluding or limiting the legal rights of the consumer in relation to the trader in the event of total or partial performance or inadequate performance by the trader of any of the contractual obligations including the option of offsetting a debt owed to the trader against any claim which the consumer may have against the trader

Like:

"Sold as seen."

"This car wash is used entirely at the customer's own risk and we will not under any circumstances be liable if it damages your property while on these premises."

"The company does not accept responsibility for any fire protection equipment it has supplied in the event of fire." [really!!!]

"We will not be responsible for any injuries to pregnant passengers."

"No guarantee is given as to the use or mileage of the vehicle and any information provided on these matters is without prejudice."

"The hirer shall not make any claim for loss or damage to any property left in the vehicle."

"No complaints can be accepted after the carpet has been cut."

"It is the customer's responsibility to make sure that goods have been tried before delivery and that they are fit for the purpose for which they were intended."

"Your signature constitutes acceptance that you are 100% satisfied with the goods."

"The company will not be responsible for consequential losses due to damage caused by the installation."

"The company will not be responsible for damage or theft of clothing or other possessions brought into the gymnasium."

"We will not be liable for any monetary loss."

"Payment is due on completion. The buyer shall not be entitled to withhold payment by reason of any minor defect."

"You must pay the balance due under this contract without any deduction."

A term which has the object or effect of permitting the trader to retain sums paid by the consumer where the consumer decides not to conclude or perform the contract, without providing for the consumer to receive compensation of an equivalent amount from the trader where the trader is the party cancelling the contract

Like:

"If the customer falls into arrears for not less than two monthly instalments, this agreement shall stand automatically cancelled and the deposit held by the trader shall be forfeited. If the company cancels this agreement for reasons beyond its control, it may retain the deposit it holds."

A term which has the object or effect of requiring that, where the consumer decided not to conclude or perform the contract, the consumer must pay the trader a disproportionately high sum in compensation or for services which have not been supplied

which we will look at in conjunction with:

A term which has the object or effect of requiring a consumer who fails to fulfil his obligations under the contract to pay a proportionately high sum in compensation

A host of dodgy terms are covered here like requirements to:

- pay excessive interest on arrears such as a rate well over and above what the trader is paying its bank on a loan or overdraft;
- pay the whole contract price if you cancel without grounds to do so but the trader could find another customer to fill your shoes;
- when a contract runs indefinitely (say, from month to month instead of for a fixed period), to pay an excessive amount of money to the trader for not having given them the amount of notice they were looking for; or
- pay on ending a contract an excessive disconnection fee (which is a disguised penalty).

Terms such as this are loosely called penalties and until recently courts would disapply them both under general contract law and under the consumer fairness law which applied before the Consumer Rights Act 2015 came into force. If the defaulting consumer was being told to pay the trader an amount which was over and above the trader's genuine advance estimate of the financial loss they would suffer because of the default then the courts would say this amounted to a penalty and was unenforceable.

There has been a shift in the law in this area with the decisions of the Supreme Court in November 2015 in two cases including that of Barry Beavis who overstayed his welcome in a parking bay. Courts will in future be asking themselves whether a term which costs money to the consumer who defaults is simply to punish them or whether it has a legitimate purpose, and, if so, what the purpose is. If the consequences of the term are extortionate or extravagant in relation to that purpose the term will be struck down and the consumer will be off the hook. The fact that the trader has come up with a term which gives them more money than they will lose as a result of the consumer's default whilst relevant will not of itself make the term a penalty and so unenforceable and unfair.

We can see this test at work in the car parking case. Let's go to the Riverside Retail Park in Chelmsford where visitors could park for free for up to two hours but if they stayed put for longer they would be charged £85. Mr Beavis left his car for a total of 2 hours 56 minutes. He subsequently received a demand for the £85 although he was told this would be discounted to £50 if he paid up within 14 days. Reckoning that £85 for a 56 minute overstay was ridiculously steep, Mr Beavis decided he would pay neither the £85 nor the £50 and when he was sued in the county court he defended the case. He lost there and lost again when he appealed to the Court of Appeal. It was a case of general public importance and thousands of other claims involving the same legal issues were dependent on its outcome. That is how the case ended up in the Supreme Court.

The Supreme Court ruled that the £85 was not a penalty and was fair under the law which was in operation when Mr Beavis was 56 minutes late. The result would be the same now as that part of the law has been replanted in the Consumer Rights Act 2015 which we are now enjoying (aren't we?). The £85 had two objects: to deter drivers from staying for too long and so depriving other shoppers from being able to park, and to provide an income stream to the company which ran the park so that it could operate the scheme and make a profit. This did not give the company a licence to charge what it liked but there was no reason to suppose that £85 was out of all proportion.

A term which has the object or effect of enabling the trader to alter the terms of the contract unilaterally without a valid reason which is specified in the contract*

Like:

"If for any reason the company is unable to supply a particular item it will notify the customer. It will normally replace it with goods of equivalent or superior standard."

"The company may at any time vary or add to these terms as it deems necessary."

*The trader can legitimately vary in this way if the contract is not for a fixed period and requires the trader to give you reasonable notice of their intention to do so and leaves you free to escape from the contract if you are unhappy.

A term which has the object or effect of limiting the trader's obligation to respect commitments undertaken by the trader's agents or making the trader's commitments subject to compliance with a particular formality

Like:

"The company reserves the right to sub-contract any of its obligations under this agreement without the consent of the customer and the company shall not in the event of doing so be liable for the acts or omissions of any agent so sub-contracted whether or not the company would be liable to the customer if the acts or omissions were those of the company and whether or not loss may be incurred by the customer."

"Proceedings for breach of this agreement must be brought within 12 months of delivery of the goods."

"You must give written notice of any claim within three days of receipt of the goods."

A term which has the object or effect of excluding or hindering the consumer's right to take legal action or exercise any other legal remedy, in particular by:

a. requiring the consumer to take disputes exclusively to arbitration not covered by legal provisions;

b. unduly restricting the evidence available to the consumer; or

c. imposing on the consumer a burden of proof which, according to the applicable law, should lie with another party to the contract.

Like:

"Although this contract was entered into in England and Wales, the customer is resident in England and Wales and the goods and services supplied hereunder were so supplied in England and Wales, any claim by the customer for the alleged breach of any provision of this contract on the part of the company must be brought in France and the law governing such claim and this agreement shall be the law of France."

"Any dispute between the parties under this agreement must be referred to arbitration* by an arbitrator selected by the company before whom the customer shall not be entitled to legal representation and the decision of the arbitrator shall be binding on the company and the customer and shall be final."

*The drive is relentless to persuade warring parties to take their disputes to an arbitrator (or for some other form of alternative dispute resolution such as mediation or adjudication) (see chapter 7). But it may not be on to force arbitration down a consumer's throat and deny them the right to take their case to court instead. Any attempt to do so may be branded as unfair and so unenforceable. In fact, section 91 of the Arbitration Act 1996 automatically outlaws anything in a contract which says that arbitration is compulsory where it relates to a claim for £5,000 or under. It is blacklisted and so it does not have to be shown that it is unfair.

"The company shall not be under any obligation to provide any records, data or documentation relating to any dispute between the parties which was created more than 12 months before the customer gave notice of the dispute to the company."

"The meter reading shall be conclusive proof of its accuracy and of the volume of gas/electricity/water consumed under this agreement."

"The company shall not be under any obligation to entertain any claim against it by the customer unless the customer proves beyond any doubt that the company is in breach of any of its obligations under this agreement."

And some miscellaneous other terms which have been regarded as unfair

"The company shall not be responsible for any assistance given with measuring."

"If a staff member assists you without our written authority we will not be responsible."

"We will accept liability for defective goods only to the extent that we can make a corresponding claim under the manufacturer's warranty in our favour."

"The customer agrees it is fair and reasonable to exclude liability for negligence."

"Your installation is guaranteed for five years provided the invoice is paid in full upon completion of the work."

"The management reserves the right to refuse access to the member without giving any reason for doing so."

In court

The outcome of a court claim against you may well depend on whether certain wording of the contract passes the fairness test or is automatically blacklisted. The judge is now obliged to consider fairness whether or not you, as the consumer, have raised it as an issue in your defence to the claim. But this obligation will not apply unless the judge has before them sufficient legal and factual material to enable them to consider fairness. There is a very real danger that the judge will not have sufficient factual material to come to a sensible conclusion on what can be a difficult matter. Then the judge could adjourn the case to another day and direct each side to put in evidence on the subject. Otherwise, the judge could decide that, because sufficient material is absent and you haven't take any point on fairness, the question of fairness will have to go out of the window. So don't take a chance. Raise fairness in your defence. And unless it is plain that the term is not automatically blacklisted, it may be prudent to start off by alleging blacklisting. That way, if the court is with you on blacklisting that would make the term automatically unenforceable and it would not need to trouble with deciding on fairness.

Case no 97P0000678

IN THE COUNTY COURT MONEY CLAIMS CENTRE

BETWEEN

WHITEWASH LIMITED Claimant

- and -

CLIVE TROUBLESORE Defendant

DEFENCE

*1. In so far as the claimant relies on clause 16(3) (clause 16(3)) of the contract between the parties referred to in paragraph 2 of the particulars of claim (the contract), the defendant says that clause 16(3) is not binding on him because it excludes or restricts the claimant's liability as covered by section 31 of the Consumer Rights Act 2015 (the Act) and, further and in the alternative, it is unfair within the meaning of section 62 the Act.**

2. If (which is denied) clause 16(3) is a core term of the contract within section 64(1) of the Act, the defendant says that it is still assessable for fairness under section 62 of the Act because it is not transparent within section 64(3) or prominent within section 64(4) of the Act.

3. Further and in the alternative, the defendant says that clause 16(3) is ambiguous in that it could mean either that notice by the defendant that he did not wish to renew the contract had to be given so as to expire within the initial fixed period of the contract or it could mean that such notice could expire outside such fixed period so long as the defendant made a pro rate payment for the period of the notice which so fell outside the fixed period. Therefore, and in accordance with section 69 of the Act, the defendant says that the latter meaning should prevail.

4. For the purposes of the matters alleged at paragraphs 1 and 2 of the defence, the defendant relies on the subject matter of the contract and all the circumstances existing when clause 16(3) was agreed and to all the other terms of the contract and in particular (but not exhaustively) on the following factors:

a. *the claimant neglected to explain clause 16(3) to the defendant before the contract was concluded notwithstanding that, as the claimant well knew or should have known, the defendant had no experience of contracts of this nature or of the operation of contract renewal terms and conditions.*

b. *the language of clause 16(3) is highly technical and complicated.*

c. *the font size of clause 16(3) is small.*

d. *clause 16(3) is not in a prominent place and appears among other terms and conditions which are of less and/or little importance.*

e. *the defendant was given no indication by the claimant in the contract document or otherwise of the importance or significance of clause 16(3).*

f. *the claimant neglected to afford the defendant sufficient opportunity to read and/or to attempt to understand clause 16(3) or the other terms and conditions of the contract in that the claimant's representative tendered a biro to the defendant so that he could sign the contract at the same time as he presented the contract to him and told the defendant that he was in a hurry and he had 20 other customers to see that day who wanted to "sign up with us for this great deal before it is withdrawn."*

g. *the period of notice of non-renewal required of the defendant was too long.*

h. *the deadline fixed by the contract on the claimant's interpretation of the meaning of clause 16(3) for the giving of notice of non-renewal was too early.*

**adapt if you are not alleging that the term is blacklisted under section 47 of the Act.*

The next defence could be suitable in a Barry Beavis type car parking claim or any other claim involving the consumer being required to make a payment to the consumer for terminating a contract early.

Case no 97P0000678

IN THE COUNTY COURT MONEY CLAIMS CENTRE

BETWEEN

WHITEWASH LIMITED Claimant

- and -

CLIVE TROUBLESORE Defendant

DEFENCE

1. In so far as the claimant relies on clause 16(3) (clause 16(3)) of the contract between the parties referred to in paragraph 2 of the particulars of claim (the contract), the defendant says that clause 16(3) is not binding on him because it is void at common law as a penalty in that-

a. its sole purpose was to punish the defendant if he defaulted under clause 16(3); and

b. there was no legitimate purpose for the imposition of the payments the defendant would be liable to make under clause 16(3) if he defaulted under it or, if (which is denied) there was such a legitimate purpose, the consequences so imposed were extortionate and/or extravagant in relation to such purpose.

2. The defendant says that the following factors in particular are relevant to the matters alleged at sub-paragraphs 1 (a) and (b) above-

a. the payments the defendant would be liable to make under clause 16(3) if he defaulted under it were in excess of the loss the claimant was likely to suffer as a result of such default;

b. the payments the defendant would be liable to make under clause 16(3) if he defaulted under it were in excess of any estimate, genuine or otherwise, which the claimant made or might have made if he had conducted an estimate of the loss the claimant was likely to suffer as a result of such default;

c. upon entering into the contract the subject of the claim, the defendant had no bargaining power in that the provisions of clause 16(3) were not open for negotiation and the defendant was obliged to 'take it or leave it' if he wished to take advantage of the service or facility available to the defendant under the contract; and

d. the matters set out at paragraph 5 of this defence.

3. Further and in the alternative, the defendant says that clause 16(3) is unfair within the meaning of section 62 the Act.

4. If (which is denied) clause 16(3)is a core term of the contract within section 64(1) of the Act, the defendant says that it is still assessable for fairness under section 62 of the Act because it is not transparent within section 64(3) or prominent within section 64(4) of the Act.

5. For the purposes of the matters set out at paragraphs 3 and 4 of the defence [continue as at paragraph 4 of the draft defence above, adapting appropriately].

Who claims

So far we have assumed that the trader has claimed against you on the basis that you have not paid up under a blacklisted or unfair contract term. As it happens, you don't have to wait to be sued before you take the point that the term is not binding on you. You can always ask the local authority's trading standards department, the Competition and Markets Authority or the Consumers' Association to help you - they are among a group of regulators which can take enforcement action against a trader who flouts the Consumer Rights Act 2015 - but it could be that circumstances demand some swift and definitive action in your particular case which might not be achieved through a regulator so that you know where you stand. For example, when you are anxious to escape from a contract, do you risk ignoring a term which calls for you to give what seems to be an interminably long period of notice to end the contract in the hope that it is unenforceable or do you honour it? So long as you reckon your case is a good one, you can bring your own county court claim against the trader and ask the court to make a declaration to the effect that the term does not bind you. But beware: if you do this and lose, you could have to pay the trader's legal bill. Your ability to take the initiative could give you a useful bargaining tool with the trader, especially if they twitch at the prospect of a court declaring the term to be unenforceable, possibly in a blaze of publicity, and so run the real risk that thousands of other customers, displeased like you, will get to know that the term is useless.

"Dear Trader

It is my misfortune to have entered into contract numbered XBF1239555666/yx with your company dated 14 July 2016. I wish to bring the contract to an end but I am unwilling to make the payments specified under clause 16(3) which suggests that they would be due upon me doing so. I now have the benefit of expert advice on clause 16(3) which is that no payments as specified could be lawfully demanded of me because the clause is not binding on me. The reasons for this are that the payments amount to penalties at common law and that the clause is unfair within section 62 of the Consumer Rights Act 2015. The advice given to me takes account of the judgments of the Supreme Court in Parking Eye Limited v Beavis and another appeal on 4 November 2015.

In the above circumstances, I require you to confirm to me within seven days of your receipt of this letter, that your company will release me from the contract as from the date of your confirmation and that your company will not make any claim against me for any moneys allegedly due or allegedly to fall due under the contract at any time. In the event of receiving that confirmation within the period mentioned, I agree not to publish to any third person that this confirmation has been given save and except as I might be compelled by law to do so. If I do not hear from you as required and within the period specified, I shall institute proceedings against your company in the county court for a declaration that clause 16(3) is not binding on me and for an order that your company should pay the costs of the proceedings."

"But I'm not a ruddy consumer, Gold"

Calm down. If, as a non-consumer, you have signed up to the other party's standard terms of business - maybe you are a professional property owner and apparently saddled with an estate agent's standard contract - then any term which excuses the other party for a contract breach has to be reasonable before it can be used against you. That's the Unfair Contract Terms Act 1977 at work. It's down to the other party to prove that the condition under attack is reasonable. The court will look at such factors as the strength of each party's bargaining position; whether you had the opportunity of transacting with another business without being bound by the same sort of condition; and whether you knew or ought to have known of the existence and extent of the condition. On that last point, previous dealings with the people you contracted with will be taken into account.

One of my all times favourites

Be you a consumer or a trader there is always one of my favourite cases you might be able to fall back on where, for whatever reason, the legislation we have been looking at doesn't cover your situation. Alternatively, perhaps you simply want to demonstrate how senior judges were prepared to do justice and how your judge might try and follow in their footsteps. Over to *Interfoto Picture Library Ltd v Stiletto Visual Programmes Ltd* decided by the Court of Appeal in 1987. Interfoto ran a photographic transparency library. Stiletto were in advertising. Stiletto telephoned Interfoto and asked whether they had any 1950's transparencies which were wanted for a presentation. The same day, Interfoto sent them round 47 transparencies which were packed in a bag. Also in the bag was a delivery note. It specified the return date and included nine prominently printed conditions set out in four columns. Condition 2 required the return of the transparencies within 14 days and imposed a fee of £5 plus VAT per day per transparency for every day of lateness. Stiletto went over the return date and so received an invoice for .... £3,783.50! You guessed it. They refused to pay and were sued. The Court of Appeal knocked the invoice down to £350. It was felt that Stiletto could not have known of the "very high and exorbitant charge" as their attention had not been drawn to Condition 2. That should have been done. This ruling reflected the words of Lord Denning in a previous case. The more unreasonable was a condition, the greater the notice of it that had to be given to the customer. "Some clauses which I have seen," he said "would need to be printed in red ink on the face of the document with a red hand pointing to it before the notice of it could be held to be sufficient."

Part 9

HOME UNDER ATTACK

Chapter 42

Behind With The Mortgage

Keeping out the lenders

I made my first repossession order against a borrower who owed more than a million in 2011. Now that level of mortgage indebtedness comes without shock. Many fail to treat mortgage repayments with the priority they command: many just don't have the cash to pay. Either way, the lenders' repossession of your home can more often than not be avoided if you keep your head above the sand. And more often than not there's hope right up to the nanosecond before you and your family are evicted. What needs to be appreciated by every borrower is that the lenders need an order of the court to evict through the bailiff or a High Court enforcement agent and it is the judge who decides whether you must go and not the lenders.

Talking to the animals

Well, actually, not all lenders graze in the zoo and even some of the aggressive ones have been obliged by regulatory control and media publicity to temper their attitude with a modicum of reasonableness. What has also helped is a pre-action protocol in residential mortgage cases and which was revamped in April 2015. It contains rules which lenders are expected to follow before they ask the court to evict. If the lenders have failed to comply, you can legitimately ask the judge at the hearing of any possession claim that is brought to put off the case for a period. "Please adjourn the hearing so that the lenders can do what have should have done and have failed to do - follow the protocol. They have jumped the gun." This will not give you a defence which could lead to the case being thrown out but it could earn you valuable time.

Under the protocol (which does not apply to buy-to-let mortgages) and before any court proceedings are started, the lenders must provide you with information about where you can get help, the amount of the current monthly instalments and what you have paid over the last two years and the amount of the arrears (including an estimate of any interest or charges that may be added). A reasonable request by you to change the day of the month you make your payment or how you pay must be considered and, if refused, you are to be given written reasons for the refusal within a reasonable period. The lenders must respond promptly to any payment proposal you make. If they are rejecting a proposal then you should have their written reasons within ten business days of making the proposal (that excludes weekends, bank holidays, Good Friday and Christmas Day). Where the lenders make a payment proposal to you there should be sufficient details to enable you to understand its implications and you are to have a reasonable time to consider it. You have made an agreement to pay off the arrears and then broken it? Before starting a possession claim, the lenders are to give you written warning at least 15 business days beforehand.

And there's more. The lenders must consider not taking you to court when you can demonstrate to them that you have submitted a claim to the Department for Work and Pensions for mortgage interest help or universal credit, a mortgage protection policy insurer or a local authority mortgage rescue or other homelessness prevention support scheme and have provided all the evidence needed to process that claim. But there must be a reasonable expectation that you will be eligible for the assistance you have sought and that you can cope with what has to be paid which will not come from the DWP or elsewhere. The lenders should also consider waiting where you have a specific personal or financial difficulty and need time for debt advice or you have a reasonable expectation of an improvement in your financial circumstances and, where possible, can provide evidence of this. Again, the lender should consider holding on for a realistic period if you can show you have or will put the property up for sale at an appropriate price based on reasonable estate agents' or other professional advice. You are then expected to take reasonable steps to actively market the property. If, despite it all, the lenders decide to press on to court they must give you written reasons for their decision at least five business days before starting proceedings.

You have made a complaint about the potential possession claim to the Financial Ombudsman's Service? If it is a genuine complaint, the lenders must consider postponing starting proceedings until the Ombudsman has decided it. Where the lenders are not prepared to wait, they must tell you that they intend to start proceedings and their reasons for not waiting.

More of the protocol later.

You are taken to court

You will receive a claim form telling you where and when the case is to be heard. Along with the claim form will be a defence form. Complete it and return it to the court. It will ask whether you want the court to consider allowing you to pay the mortgage arrears by instalments and how much you can afford to pay in addition to the monthly instalments.

More talk - and pay

Before the hearing, keep up or start up a dialogue with the lenders.

There's nothing to stop you trying to reach an agreement with them even at that stage and even though you may believe them to be the biggest parasites in the financial services market. Not only talk, pay as well even though the payment may fall substantially short of the monthly instalment due and not even address the arrears. To say to the judge that you didn't pay a penny because you could not afford the amount required or because you were coming to court never goes down well.

Though shalt turn up

If there still remains any dispute between you and the lenders come the day of the hearing, you stay away from that hearing at your peril. At the court, there will be an advice desk with a solicitor or Citizens Advice Bureau or some other expert adviser at hand to help you. Where necessary, they should be prepared to speak on your behalf to the judge. You can take advantage of this help which will be free and independent even though you may have done absolutely nothing in response to the case up until then and the judge will listen to your proposals notwithstanding that you failed to return a defence but could be disgruntled because of that failure.

Getting technical

There are various rules to be complied with and steps to be taken by the court and the lenders before the hearing. If they have not done as required and you would welcome the extra time that an adjournment of the hearing would afford you - perhaps to get a job or borrow from friends or family or progress your own marketing of the property for sale - that's when you can go for it and ask the judge to adjourn so that things can be put right. You ought to get a four week breather out of it at the least. Here is when you can go for it:

- when the lenders have not followed the protocol (see above);
- when the lender's representative does not have with them at court a completed form - it's called form N123 - which shows what they have done to comply with the protocol;
- when the hearing date is less than four weeks after the lender issued their claim;
- when you have not been sent the court paperwork (the claim form and particulars of claim) at least three weeks before the hearing;
- when the particulars of claim omit some compulsory information such as:
    - ◇ the amount needed to pay off the mortgage at a stated date no

more than a fortnight after the claim started and showing how much in solicitors' costs and administration charges has been included;

  - the rate of interest payable when the mortgage started, immediately before arrears arose and when the proceedings were started; and
  - whether anyone who is claiming a right to occupy the property (we are effectively looking here at a spouse or civil partner with whom you have fallen out) has registered that claim at the land registry or land charges registry;

- when the lenders have left compulsory information out of the court papers originally sent to you and they are intending to rely at the hearing on written evidence to plug the gap and to update what has been happening and that further evidence has not been sent to the court and you at least two days before the hearing;
- when within five days of receiving notice from the court of the date fixed for the hearing, the lenders have not sent details of the proceedings including the hearing date, to the mortgaged property addressed *"to the tenant or occupier"* (the property may be a buy-to-let or you may have unlawfully let in a tenant without the lenders' consent and, in either event, you are living elsewhere); the local authority's housing department; and any other lender (there may be a prior lender, this being a second mortgage or a subsequent third etc mortgage); or
- when before or at the hearing, the lenders do not produce a land registry or land charges registry certificate - positive or negative - about any registration of a right to occupy the property (see above); official land registry documents showing what information about the property is on the land register (these are called *office copy documents*); a copy of the mortgage deed; and copies of the notices to *"the tenant or occupier"* etc (see above) and evidence that they have been sent.

The judge does have the power to shorten the time limits I have mentioned. It is more likely that you can persuade the judge not to shorten and to adjourn the hearing because of the lenders' non-production of essential information or documentation if you can show that you will be prejudiced in some way by the rules not being kept to. If you can throw in some detail about oppressive behaviour towards you by the lenders then more strength to your elbow. Don't be frightened to ask at the hearing to see any document or be given any information which you think is missing and should have been provided.

What the judge can do

The judge will usually have the option to take a course which would save you from eviction if that would be justified in the circumstances whether you have a repayment or interest only mortgage or a mixture of the two or are in arrears with a first, second or 11th mortgage. Alas, the judge will not be able to save you where the mortgage required you to repay the lender *on demand* (for example, a mortgage securing a bank overdraft) or a mortgage has come to an end (where, for example, you had an endowment mortgage for 25 years and, at the end of the 25 years, the policy has matured and what has been paid out by the life company falls short of the amount you need to pay back to the lender). Here, your position will be weak though if you need just that little bit of extra time to vacate the property under a possession order or to repay the lender pretty quickly, the judge might just be prepared to grant it.

The lenders may have accepted your proposals but want them incorporated in a court order and that is why they have started or continued the proceedings. This will happen where the lenders are after a suspended order for possession which would involve the court ordering you to leave by a specified date and then to go on to paralyse the order: suspend it so long as you keep to the agreement which, no doubt, would be to pay the monthly instalment plus something each month off the arrears.

Should you have made no proposals or any proposals made been rejected then the lender will almost certainly ask you to be ordered to leave at the end of 28 days from the hearing, allowing them to sell the property, take for themselves the amount required to pay off the mortgage and hand over any surplus to you. Any shortfall would be your liability and where it is one you cannot reasonably tackle then bankruptcy might be a sensible escape route (see chapter 35).

The case for the lenders will be put by someone with legal qualifications or training whose mouth has been hired for the outing and, more often than not, a specialist in mortgage possession claims. Before the hearing, they may want to chat to you or any adviser you have helping you out: no harm in going along with that as it may be possible to negotiate a settlement even at the court doors. Some of these representatives have a heart and will not oppose (or only do so in a token way) any fair proposals you put to the judge whereas others follow to the letter the written instructions they have been given to secure an order ousting you after 28 days so that they can report back to the lenders that they have won and they would like to do loads more cases for them, thank you very much. Occasionally, they only get paid for the outing if the court makes the very order they were instructed to obtain. Do not be intimidated by what they say to the judge. Again, it is the judge who decides on the court order, not the lenders or their court representative.

Faced then with a demand for that 28 day order for possession, you put forward your proposals to the judge. The last thing the judge wants to see is somebody booted out of their home. But they do have to apply the law and take account of the interests of both sides.

"Please let me stay put with a suspended order"

To achieve a suspended order, you must be able to demonstrate not only that you can pay the monthly instalments but that you can clear the arrears by regular payments as soon as reasonably possible and certainly before the mortgage is due to come to an end. Say you have a mortgage which was granted for 25 years, there are five years left and the arrears are £8,000. In that event, the very least the judge would find acceptable would be a commitment to pay the monthly instalments plus £8,000 divided by five years (60 months) = £133.33 per month. With a second or subsequent mortgage there may be greater flexibility.

"But I can't afford monthly payments and £133.33"

Then you must set out to persuade the judge that what you cannot afford today, you may be able to afford tomorrow - or at some time in the foreseeable future. Perhaps your wife will be taking a part-time job, your son is going to get off his backside and obtain a job and make a meaningful contribution to the household finances or you are expecting promotion - whatever. The judge might still make a suspended order for possession and fix a hearing at which the position will be reviewed when the change in your circumstances is likely to have materialised.

When you have no or only a meagre income and any help towards the mortgage from the Department for Work and Pensions or elsewhere will fall short of what is required to address the monthly payments let alone the arrears, the judge may still be prepared to adjourn the hearing for a short period if satisfied that there is a good chance of you obtaining a job offer (but not a bequest under the will of your aged uncle who you are intending to murder). The lenders' representative will hit the roof at the idea of current monthly instalments not being met for any period at all. "Judge, you cannot interfere with my client's contractual right to receive the monthly instalments as and when they fall due. If the borrower cannot afford to pay these - and he accepts he cannot - then you have no alternative but to make a possession order today." Should the judge look like wavering, pitch in fast with this:

"With respect, I am advised that under section 36 of the Administration of Justice Act 1970 you can allow the monthly instalments to go unpaid for a period ***if it appears likely that the borrower will be able within a reasonable period to pay those sums.*** *I also submit that you can adjourn today's hearing under your Civil Procedure Rules case management powers. I am told that these cases are regularly adjourned or suspended possession orders made under which monthly payments are allowed to be missed for a little time so long as the court is satisfied the borrower will be able to make them up within a reasonable period. There is nothing in the 1970 Act or anywhere else to say you cannot do this. On the contrary, the Act says you can. Only the lender says you cannot. What is the lender's authority for this?"*

Or you may have decided you cannot afford the mortgage and the property must be sold. A private sale by you will almost invariably generate a higher price than a forced sale, often at auction, by lenders who have obtained possession through the court. Pin back your lugholes. Unless and until you have lost possession to the lenders, it is your legal right to market the property for sale yourself. The lenders' representative at the possession hearing might well sneeringly say to the judge: "There's no buyer. There's no offer. It could be months before a buyer is found and even then the sale could fall through. My client's cuddly general manager will cry if you give the borrower more time. The borrower isn't paying a penny at the moment. You MUST order a sale." Now there's a challenge!

Judges are increasingly more ready to consider allowing the borrower time to sell themselves so long as they are satisfied that the borrower is genuine about wanting to get rid of the property, would accept a realistic price and there is a good chance of a sale within a few months. More time for finding a buyer can be achieved by the judge making an order for possession on a date later than the conventional four weeks - eight weeks is popular - and should a buyer surface within that period and at the very least, be close to commitment by an exchange of contracts, there would be an excellent chance of procuring an extension either with the lenders' consent or by referring the case back to the court yourself via an application for the time for giving possession to be extended.

What to take to court

- ***Accompaniment number 1*** - the joint owner be it your spouse, civil partner or mother-in-law because it demonstrates the seriousness with which the household is treating the predicament. It also establishes that the co-owner is in the loop and so should ensure that any proposals you put forward will be kept to. It is commonplace for an owner to hide the co-owner's court papers which would normally have been sent in the post and to stay mum about what is going on. Perhaps they have drunk or gambled the mortgage money? In one sad case I dealt with, the husband was an honourable man who had suffered a series of misfortunes leading to financial difficulties, had kept from his wife that the mortgage was not being paid and destroyed her court papers. He turned up at court alone and without the wife's knowledge. I was obliged to make an order for possession. He left the court and it transpires he then tried to take his own life. All then came out and, whilst he was in recovery in hospital, the wife put together an emergency plan and made an application for the possession order to be set aside. I was eventually able to approve her proposals and the order for outright possession was changed to a suspended order.

- ***Accompaniment number 2*** - a valuation of your property which can be an estate agent's assessment (not simply of the suggested asking price but what the property would actually go for) which you should be able to obtain free of charge should you be contemplating putting the property on the market with them. The object would be to show, hopefully, that there is a comfortable equity in the property - its market value less the aggregate of what it would take to pay off the mortgage and selling fees and expenses. That could make the difference between being ousted and being allowed to stay put as a comfortable equity removes or diminishes any possible prejudice to the lenders in the judge acceding to your proposals to stay on or be given more time. Of course, if the valuation would establish an equity of a tenner or less, you would be better off leaving the valuation on the bus. Where you are resisting an order for possession in favour of lenders with a first mortgage and you have a second mortgage, the amount required to pay off the second mortgage can be ignored for the purpose of calculating the equity. The reason is that the first lenders would pay themselves out on a sale if they repossessed before handing over any balance to the second lender. If no balance or a balance insufficient to pay off the second lender then that's tough on the second lender. The sale would still go ahead. But the judge may want to know if you are behind with a second mortgage and, if so, what the second lender is doing about it. A second lender can itself go for repossession if you have defaulted though the first lenders have not brought proceedings and is bound to be more aggressive or proactive about doing so because, being second in the queue, it would be more exposed should the equity be small. On a sale by a second lender which has repossessed, it would have to pay back the first lenders before taking any money for itself.

- ***Accompaniment number 3*** - where the property is already on the market, a letter from marketing estate agents to confirm that they are marketing the property, the asking price, the likely actual price which will be achieved and the prospects of an acceptable offer and within what time frame. Please, please, please put the property on the market sooner rather than later if you cannot afford the mortgage. Doing so five minutes before the hearing will raise the suspicion that you are not in earnest. And it may sometimes be prudent not to put all your eggs in one basket and if you have proposals for a suspended order which are shaky, put the property on the market as an alternative. Then you can say to the judge: "I would like to stay and this is my plan but just in case you are going to be against me, this is what I have done about selling." You can't get more responsible than that.
- ***Accompaniment number 4*** - up to date details of the household income and expenses backed by wage slips or business accounts (even if you have completed a defence and given figures there).
- ***Accompaniment number 5*** - if you are relying on a loan or other financial help from a friend or family member, that friend or family member should be at court so that they are available to be questioned by the judge. Should their attendance not be possible without frogmarching them to court with a gun in their back, obtain a letter from them explaining their connection with you, what help they are willing to give and on what terms and setting out some information which will satisfy the judge that their own financial circumstances allow them to help and when the money will be available.

Second, third etc mortgages

The court usually has broader powers to assist you where the lender has granted you a second or subsequent mortgage provided it was not taken out with a bank or building society to buy your home. It is by way of a magical *time order* under section 129 of the Consumer Credit Act 1974. We are looking at secure loans for such things as home improvements and the facilitation of spousal or partner extravagance. The powers may not exist if the mortgage was taken out before 6 April 2008. For loans before 1 May 1998 the amount borrowed must be less than £15,000 and for loans between the 1 May 1998 and 5 April 2008 the amount must be less than £25,000. There is no limit for loans taken out on or after 6 April 1998. The court can assist to cater for temporary difficulties. It can reduce the monthly payments and refrain from obligating you to make a contribution to the arrears for the time being. It can even allow payments to be made after the mortgage term has come to an end. Regard will be had not only to your interests but to those of the lenders. You won't get anywhere unless you can satisfy the court of the likelihood that you will be able to resume payments at some stage at the rate you originally agreed.

You don't have to wait for your lenders to take you to court for a possession order before going for a time order. You can make your own application to the court but only after your lenders have sent you an arrears notice, a default notice or a termination notice. One of these titles will be on the document so you should realise you have had it! Use form N440. It will strongly indicate to the judge how seriously you regard the situation and puts you into a tactically advantageous position. Back up the application with a written statement.

Case no 97P00000678

IN THE COUNTY COURT

AT PEARDROP

BETWEEN

CLIVE TROUBLESORE Applicant

- and -

DODGY BANK PLC Respondent

I CLIVE TROUBLESORE state as follows:

1. I live at 149c Magnolia Buildings, Twickenham, Middlesex KT89 4XZ.

2. I ordinarily work as a double glazing salesman and painter and decorator but am presently unemployed due to injuries sustained in an assault.

3. The facts referred to in this statement are of my own knowledge.

4. On 14 July 2014 I entered into a mortgage agreement with the defendant for a principal loan of £30,000 with interest payable at the rate of 12% per annum which was repayable over a term of 20 years by monthly instalments of £429.83. The loan was raised to pay for my engagement party, a car, a home cinema and a ten day cruise with Gerry and the Pacemakers and other 1960's bands.

5. On 3 January 2016 I was wrongfully arrested by a store detective at the High Street, Peardrop branch of Farthing Universe who alleged I had stolen three toothbrushes. I attempted to free myself from the store detective's hold and in an attempt to restrain me he kicked me in the groin and I fell to the ground and exacerbated a long standing back condition which has since incapacitated me from work. My present financial circumstances are particularised in my form N440.

6. Up to the date of the assault I had paid all instalments due to the respondent regularly and punctually. However, since the assault I have been unable to comply with my obligations in full. I have made what payments I could afford but have fallen into arrears in the sum of £y which represents three monthly instalments.

7. I have kept the respondent closely informed of my situation. However, I have found it hostile and totally lacking in empathy. On 1 July 2016 the respondent served me with an arrears notice.

8. I am advised by my GP that I should be fit to return to my-pre-assault work in about six months time. In the meantime I am having regular physiotherapy.

9. I have instructed Piranha Hector & Co on a claim for damages against the store detective and his employers on a conditional fee basis and am advised that I have a good prospect of recovering damages of not less than £8,000 including loss of earnings.

10. In the circumstances, I ask that the court should make an order under section 129 of the Consumer Credit Act 1974 which reduces the monthly mortgage repayments to £z, and suspend the payments of interest on the basis that I pay all arrears in full within 12 months from the date of this statement and against my undertaking to make such payments earlier should I recover damages arising out of my assault claim at an earlier date. I would keep the respondent fully updated on the progress of my damages claim. I accept it is appropriate that these terms should be incorporated in a suspended order for possession of the property.

11. I submit that the conduct of the respondent has been totally unreasonable and that the court should debar it from adding its costs of this application to the security and order it to pay me my costs of the application to be summarily assessed on the litigant in person basis. I will provide the court and the respondent with a statement of those costs before the hearing**.*

I believe that the facts stated in this witness statement are true.

(signed) Clive Troublesore

13 July 2016

**Mortgage agreements invariably entitle the lender to recover its legal costs and expenses in taking any action or doing any work arising out of the borrower's default by adding those costs and expenses to the secured mortgage debt. In exceptional cases, the court has the power to veto this.*

*** See chapter 25.*

You can make a similar application to the court if your lenders have brought repossession proceedings against you and the application and the lenders' proceedings would then be heard together. Even without a specific application, you can ask the court when it comes to hear the lenders' proceedings to make a *time order* but this could lead to an adjournment because longer than has been allocated would be needed for the court to consider the application. Make the application in advance if you possibly can. Otherwise, in the most unlikely event of the judge going red in the face with fury and gnashing their teeth when you put forward your proposals, you might gently say: *"May I respectfully draw attention to the fact that it is a second mortgage I entered into and humbly ask you to consider exercising the special powers you possess to make a time order to cater for my temporary difficulties?"*

Time orders are not restricted to mortgage agreements. They can be made in respect of any agreement which is regulated by the Consumer Credit Act 1974 such as a hire-purchase agreement.

"But it was unfair"

If you have been taken for a ride by your lenders you may be able to persuade the court to reopen the agreement's terms and do you some justice. This is an option for second or subsequent mortgages where your lenders have started proceedings against you because you have defaulted or you can start your own proceedings against them. You have up to 12 years from when the agreement was made. Your legal peg is section 140A of the Consumer Credit Act 2014 relating to agreements made since 5 April 2008. There are not dissimilar but narrower laws for earlier agreements. You would be alleging that there was an unfair relationship between you and your lenders. Steady on. This is nothing about the lenders' rep taking you out for a *Babycham* and making indecent suggestions. It is about things such as ridiculously high interest and secret commissions. The fact that the lenders have the upper hand will not itself be sufficient. That's usually the position and will not of itself give rise to a relationship that is rendered unfair. What you are complaining about really needs to offend against the ordinary principles of fair dealing. The lenders have the job of justifying the fairness of the point under attack. The court can do all sorts of things to remedy the unfairness: most notably, change the interest rate and order the lenders to refund you money. That would certainly get the arrears down and so, where you have good grounds, the unfair relationship argument is well worth a try.

In the most recent leading case on an unfair relationship decided by the Court of Appeal in June 2016, a consumer paid Northern Rock (now NRAM plc) an arrangement fee of £22,320 for a substantial loan and the consumer's broker was to collect a procuration fee from Northern Rock of £11,160. Even I can calculate that as one-half of the arrangement fee. Trouble is that nobody told the borrower about the fee split. Acceptance of the fee by the broker was a breach of its duty to the borrower and had been brought about by Northern Rock. The borrower had been deprived of the disinterested advice of the broker which made the relationship between the Northern Rock and the borrower an unfair one. The fact that undisclosed commissions of this known were not uncommon at the time made no difference. The borrower was to have the £11,260 handed over to him with interest.

Where you intend to allege an unfair relationship in the course of the lenders' proceedings against you then you should let the court and the lenders know about this within 14 days of getting the claim form.

Case No 97P00000678

IN THE COUNTY COURT

AT PEARDROP

BETWEEN

DODGY BANK PLC Claimant

-and -

CLIVE TROUBLESORE Defendant

NOTICE OF INTENTION TO SEEK REOPENING OF CONSUMER CREDIT AGREEMENT

TAKE NOTICE pursuant to Civil Procedure Rules 1998 Practice Direction 7B that I CLIVE TROUBLESORE, the above-named defendant, intend to seek an order in these proceedings under sections 140A and B of the Consumer Credit Act 1974 relating to an unfair relationship between myself and the claimant in respect of the mortgage agreement the subject of the claimant's claim and will rely on the following matters:

a. the contractual rate of interest which I contend is exorbitant or alternatively grossly excessive;

b. the excessive and otherwise unjustifiable amount of administration charges debited to my mortgage account when I have defaulted with repayments or sought short extensions of time for complying with the terms of the agreement when due to circumstances beyond my control I have been short of money; and

c. the Claimant's failure to disclose to me the fact that it received or would receive substantial commission as to the amount of which I shall seek disclosure upon my taking out a payment protection policy incidental to the mortgage agreement which policy was mis-sold to me by the claimant (but for which such mis-selling I have been compensated).

Dated 14 July 2016

(signed) Clive Troublesore

To the Court

And to the claimant

The chances are that the hearing of the claimant's claim which will have been listed for up to ten minutes will be adjourned on the day and the court will give directions for that claim and your attempt to get the court to reopen the mortgage agreement to be heard together at a later date.

Taking a shtum powder

Because you can legally sell your property at any time before you are evicted, you can market it and carry on marketing it even after an order for possession has been made by the court. Not a good idea to mention the order for possession to any viewers or prospective buyers for they may just get it into their heads that it would be a good idea to capitalise on your situation and offer a stupid price or reduce the price they have agreed. Bearing in mind that all is fair in war and home transactions, they might - and I have seen it happen - delay exchanging contracts and withdraw at the last moment with the result that you are evicted and they subsequently purchase from your lenders at a substantially reduced price. Keeping quiet about the possession proceedings is perfectly legitimate. I wouldn't mention it to the marketing agents either. They have the habit of leaking confidential information to applicants like a gigantically holed sieve.

"How long do I have?"

You are expected to vacate the property - family, furniture, back editions of *Radio Times* and cats included - by the date for possession specified in the court's order. You won't be committing a criminal offence by staying on. Once your lenders realise that you remain in residence they will apply to the court to arrange for the court bailiff to evict you. The bailiff will fix an appointment to come and evict you and must give you at least one week's prior notice of when that will be. The likelihood is that this process will add a fortnight on to the date you were given to leave. It could be longer. You can issue a court application to extend the time you were given to go before you hear anything about the bailiff or wait until you hear from the bailiff with an eviction date and then issue a court application for the bailiff's warrant to be suspended. Either way, an urgent hearing of the application will be fixed by the court and your lenders will have an opportunity of attending the application. Many borrowers wait for the very last moment and apply for the warrant to be suspended the day before the bailiff is due to evict: sometimes on the very day of the eviction. The judge may construe this as playing the system and take an adverse view of the borrower's conduct. Two key points: firstly, try and ensure that when you make your application your case for earning time is at its strongest and, hopefully, that there have been developments in your favour since the case was last before the court; and, secondly, that you make the application before the bailiff has evicted.

More time refused

You can seek to appeal against a judge's refusal to grant you more time (or the original possession order itself). You will have to proceed at hare type speed should the refusal come on the day of eviction or very close to it. You will want to get before the appeal judge before you are evicted although if you happen to be evicted and then go on to win the appeal, you would be let back in but just think of the upheaval and you may miss *Coronation Street*. The appeal would be to a circuit judge (see chapter 21). You need permission to appeal either from the judge who refused the application or from the circuit judge. So, if you want to appeal:

- Tell this to the judge who refuses the application immediately they have done so and ask the judge for permission to appeal and, whether or not permission is granted, ask the judge to "stay the warrant of possession pending the appeal" which means halting the eviction so that you can get the appeal under way. If the judge seems reluctant, invite them to do as requested on condition that you issue your notice of appeal that day.
- Issue your notice of appeal which will include an application for

permission to make the appeal if it was refused by the first judge. Because you will be under intense time pressure, you might have got hold of the form of notice of appeal from the hearing centre's office before your application was refused and, even more cheekily but practically, you might have already completed it or most of it. If you are going to need to apply for remission of the court fee on the application (see chapter 13), well get the application for that too and complete it in readiness to lodge with the notice of appeal.

- If permission to appeal has been refused by the judge who refused the application for more time, you must get before the circuit judge and ask them to "stay the warrant of possession pending the appeal". The court staff should put you in front of a circuit judge as soon as humanly possible and hopefully on the same day so that you can do this. A particular problem arises where, as is often the case, there is no circuit judge sitting at the hearing centre where your hearing took place. You will be told at what centre a circuit judge can be found who can urgently hear you. You might even be told that you have to take the appeal papers to that other hearing centre. What is essential is that the bailiff who may be waiting outside the property ready to carry out the eviction process is aware of the steps you are taking because they will probably be prepared to hang fire to allow you to take them. A lack of liaison between staff at the hearing centre and the bailiff outside the property has been known to lead to the eviction being carried out whilst the borrower is waiting to see the circuit judge.

Chapter 43

At War With Your Landlord

Home attack

There are many advantages to residential renting. No risk of escalating mortgage interest which you are unable to pay. Many essential repairs down to the landlord. The chance for the kids to draw Bugs Bunny on the hallway stairs (in red), the dog to foul the living room carpet and you never to clean the cooker and then to argue when the deposit comes up for return time that the drawing (red) was fair wear and tear to be contemplated from any reasonably normal brat, the dog has been permanently constipated since the letting began and the oven was like that at the start of the tenancy - and that your mother-in-law came in on the last day of the tenancy with four of her friends and they spent 47 hours between them scrubbing and vacuuming and shining and scraping and hosing and the place looked like a museum when they had finished.

The one gigantic disadvantage is that you may have to leave the house or flat which is your home earlier than you would have wished. Generally, your landlord can't evict you without a court order. To be precise, he can do so but if he does, you'll be in the money as the eviction will be unlawful and entitle you to damages. If the landlord takes you to what will be the county court to get you out, you will have the opportunity to put forward a defence or ask for more time to go than the landlord would like. Much of our guidance given to mortgage borrowers who are taken to court by their lenders (see chapter 42) applies to tenants who are taken to court by their landlords. If you would prefer to stay put, obtain advice about your legal rights, if it's only on the day of the court hearing when free professional help will be available at the court hearing centre.

Before you sign a tenancy agreement, check whether the landlord has a mortgage and, if they do, that their lenders have consented to the tenancy. Where a mortgage exists, it is virtually certain that it will preclude the landlord from granting a tenancy without the lenders' prior approval. Should the landlord let on regardless, the tenancy will be regarded as unlawful and the lenders will not be bound by it (unless they subsequently find out about it and acquiesce in the way they act towards the tenant). The knock on effect of the lenders not being bound is that, should the landlord default with payment of the mortgage instalments and a possession order be made against the landlord, you will be stuffed and evicted. True that the Mortgage Repossessions (Protection of Tenants etc) Act 2010 would give you some protection - a breather of up to two months to go if you follow the procedure it sets up - but that's it.

That you had a two year tenancy which is still running and you paid six months' rent in advance and you paid a dilapidations deposit and you spent a grand on improving the place count for nothing as between you and the lenders. Of course, it's another matter as between you and the landlord but if the landlord has effectively lost the property the prospect of you squeezing any compensation out of them would be as good as getting the mother-in-law to the moon by next week.

So how do you check? Ask the landlord or the letting agents to see the lenders' written confirmation that they are ok with the tenancy and if the landlord says there is no mortgage, check this out at the Land Registry: you could make an online search. I have seen countless evictions where the tenancy has been unlawful and the lenders have legitimately swooped. I have also seen a number of cases where the tenancy has been granted between the start of mortgage repossession proceedings and the hearing of those proceedings with the landlord mercilessly pocketing the up-front rent and deposit well knowing that a couple of months later, the tenant would be thrown out.

FOR TENANTS' EYES ONLY

Private tenancies

We are looking here at non local authority and housing association tenancies. Things to watch out for if you want to stay put - for a while or longer than a while.

- Is the landlord trying to get you out too early? Check what the tenancy agreement says about how long the tenancy is to last. If the tenancy was granted for 12 months and only six months are up and **provided you have behaved**, the landlord cannot generally call for you to go until the entire 12 months have expired - unless, that is, the agreement contains what is called a *break clause*. Many agreements are for 12 months but go on to say that the landlord can bring the tenancy to an end following the first six months by giving the tenant two months' notice that their time is up. This is lawful. Before ever signing a tenancy agreement you should scrutinise it for any mention of what amounts to a *break clause*. It could be buried among several pages of smallish print. Why have to go before your two eggs are hard boiled?
- The landlord will generally only be able to get you out if your time is up under the tenancy agreement or you have broken the tenancy plus, in either case, they have presented you with a written notice to go. Most private tenancies these days are *assured shorthold* tenancies so I'll restrict myself to these. If you have an

assured shorthold tenancy then the agreement will probably say so but not necessarily so. Whatever the agreement does say, it will not be an *assured shorthold* if granted to a company or at a rent of £100,000 per annum or more where granted after 30 September 2010 (and, if that's what *you* are paying, go and hire a QC for advice instead of sponging on this book). There are a couple of other exceptions.

- Assuming the *assured shorthold* landlord is not after closing the front door permanently behind you before the end of the fixed period of your assured shorthold tenancy, you must have at least two months' notice (judges, lawyers, professional landlords and letting agents who have a language of their own - no, not Polari - call it a section 21 notice) and it does not have to be in a prescribed form unless the tenancy began after 30 September 2015. Giving the notice can be down to the whim of the landlord. Perhaps you have won the Ms Wonderful Tenant of the Year Award for each successive 12 months of the tenancy. Perhaps the landlord has broken a tenancy condition by say failing to repair the premises. It generally matters not. The landlord's whim gives you no defence to a claim for possession though, in the event of the landlord's breach of a tenancy condition (for example, by failing to repair), you may still have a valid claim for damages against them. But if the landlord is after your exit before the fixed period is up on the ground of a tenancy breach, the notice period is usually shorter at a fortnight and the use of a prescribed form of notice (which was revised in April 2015 and again in April 2016) is essential. Judges and the rest call this a section 8 notice. The shorter notice may also be relied on by your landlord if the fixed period is up and the tenancy is continuing as a monthly tenancy but the landlord says you have broken its terms and prefers not to have to give you a full two months' notice. A notice which is too short is not worth the paper on which it is written.
- The grounds on which the landlord can rely are limited where they seek possession during or after your fixed period and they want to give you less than two months' notice. The most common ground is that the rent is two months' in arrears (or eight weeks where payable weekly or fortnightly) both when the notice is given and at the date of the court hearing. So long as all the necessary procedural requirements have been met by the landlord, possession would then be mandatory. The trick then is to reduce the arrears to less than two months' (or eight weeks') worth before the hearing although the court might even then have a discretion to

boot you out because of persistent delay in paying the rent but you would be unlucky for that to happen if it looks to the judge that the arrears still left will soon be cleared and you are good for future rent. No, I can't lend you the money. And, no, the judge should not adjourn the hearing simply to enable you to come up with the arrears or a sufficient part of them to bring the figure down to less than two months (or eight weeks) - though you can always try it! - unless there are exceptional circumstances such as you having left the cash on the bus on the way to court. Where rent arrears are relied on by the landlord as a ground for possession and the landlord has broken their repair obligations to you then you may be able to escape a possession order by defending and, at the same time, making a counterclaim for damages for breach of repair which could be set off against the arrears and bring them down to less than the magic two months (or eight weeks).

- Check that the notice makes sense. If it is confusing about when the landlord would like to see the back of you, it might well be legally ineffective.
- Where your landlord is relying on a section 21 notice there is an evens chance that they will mess things up. That's because the law has come up with an almost unintelligible set of rules for them to follow. If they have gone wrong, be it innocently or deliberately, then the section 21 notice will probably be invalid. This would result in them having to restart court proceedings once they had taken corrective action by giving you a fresh notice and any court proceedings based on the invalid section 21 notice would be thrown out or abandoned.
- The most likely area in which your landlord will have come a cropper is over any deposit paid when the tenancy was taken out. The deposit protection legislation was well meaning. However, unfortunate statutory wording and various technical amendments have turned it into a sick joke for landlords and a sweet respite and moneyspinner for many tenants. The deposit must have been protected with one of the three government approved schemes which are Deposit Protection Service, MyDeposits and The Dispute Service - Capita Tenancy Deposit Service provided a scheme for a short period only and any deposits paid to them have been transferred over to MyDeposits - and with you being notified of protection information unless your landlord is a *resident landlord* in that they live in the premises, the rental is over £100,000 a year (cool), the tenancy has been taken by a company or you have rented student accommodation from a university or college.

That protection information is formally called *prescribed information* and is set out in the Housing (Tenancy Deposits) (Prescribed Information) Order 2007. You would be doing yourself a great favour by checking whether you have had each and every item of information. Failure to protect or to give you the protection information where required will mean that the section 21 notice is ineffective and the windfall for you of a penalty entitlement from the landlord which might sweeten the ultimate eviction (see below). You may feel that it would be unfair to cane a good landlord with a penalty where they have innocently failed to protect on time and remedied their default as soon as they realised what they should have done. The only escape route for your landlord who has not protected the deposit and provided protection information in time is to do both late - this should have been done within 14 days of receipt or within 30 days for deposits received from 6 April 2012 - but prior to giving you the section 21 notice or to return the deposit to you before giving you the section 21 notice. Whilst enabling the landlord to proceed to get you out, this belated action will leave them exposed to a successful penalty claim by you. The deposit protection regime originally caught only tenancy agreements granted after 6 April 2007. However, it now even impacts on deposits paid before then. If you have moved on to a monthly tenancy prior to 6 April 2007 (say you went in with an agreement for 12 months which expired on 1 February 2007 and you have stayed put as a monthly tenant since then) the landlord must return your deposit or protect it now before they can give you a section 21 notice but you will not be entitled to make a penalty claim. If your original tenancy started before 6 April 2007 and you did not move on to a monthly tenancy until after then, your landlord cannot give you a section 21 notice until they have returned the deposit to you and you will have an entitlement to a penalty claim - UNLESS the landlord protected the deposit and provided protection details to you late but by 23 June 2015. See what I mean!

- The deposit will probably be the money you paid over which your landlord could use at the end of the tenancy for redecorating and repairing the premises after you had wrecked them. But it could be something else. The definition of a deposit for the purposes of this protection law is "money intended to be held (by the landlord...) as security for (a) the performance of any obligations of the tenant, or (b) the discharge of any liability of his, arising under or in connection with the tenancy." This would extend to a sum paid at the start of the tenancy as security for rent: not advance rent for say the first month or two of the tenancy but a sum to be set aside into which your landlord could dip if you missed a rental payment which fell due (sometimes called a *deposit security fund or agreement*).

- If you haven't heard from the landlord about deposit protection the chances are that they have broken the law. You should check out with the three schemes whether any of them is holding the money. All the schemes allow you to make the check online, if you wish.
- You can still claim a penalty if the tenancy has come to an end but you must do so within six years of the landlord having defaulted.
- If it wasn't you but Mummy or Daddy or Uncle Russell who to the landlord's knowledge shelled out the deposit then they instead of or in addition to you may be able to claim a penalty.
- OK then. Your landlord has scored full marks for their performance over the deposit? All is not lost. If the premises are in multiple occupation, the local authority probably required them to be licenced for it. If unlicenced, a section 21 notice will be invalid. Where appropriate, check with the council whether they should have been licenced and, if so, whether they were licenced. And for tenancies granted after 30 September 2015 (and the recent changes we will look at now have no application to Wales which is doing its own thing and why not) landlords cannot give a section 21 notice within the first four months of the original tenancy and they must follow up giving a section 21 notice with the commencement of a county court claim for possession within six months. A notice given too early will be invalid and a county court claim started too late will be thrown out. And there's more but this more only applies where the tenancy was granted for a property in England after 30 September 2015. Instead of being written out on the back of a bus ticket, the section 21 notice must follow a prescribed form. It has a very sexy title does this form - form A - and if you want to see what it looks like - and I suggest you do check that the correct form has been used - feast yourself for a couple of minutes on the Assured Shorthold Tenancy Notices and Prescribed Requirements (England) Regulations 2015 and you'll find it at the back. The landlord hasn't used the correct form? Notice invalid.
- Also for a tenancy granted after 30 September 2015 you must have been provided with an energy performance certificate and gas safety certificate before being given a section 21 notice as well

as the then current version of the eight page checklist published by the Department for Communities and Local Government called *How to rent: the checklist for renting in England.* It's available free (and there's a money making opportunity lost) on www.gov.uk/government/publications/how-to-rent. It was revamped for tenancies granted on or after 1 February 2016. The landlord is to provide it - so it's not good enough for the landlord to rely on the copy you picked up in the street - and to do so in hard copy or by email where you have given an email address for receiving documents. This obligation in relation to the checklist does not extend to social landlords such as local authorities and housing associations. Once provided, any revised version published during the same tenancy need not also be provided. The landlord (or someone on their behalf such as the letting agent) hasn't come up with all these documents before giving you the section 21 notice? The notice will be invalid.

- Hell hath no fury like a landlord scorned. Just in case you have been complaining about the state of the premises and the landlord has decided you would be better off on the street than in the hovel they have rented out to you, the law now comes to your rescue so long as you didn't cause the damage yourself. Any section 21 notice may be invalidated where you have complained to the landlord about the condition of the premises, then complained to the local housing authority after the landlord has failed to respond to you adequately or at all or served a section 21 notice and the authority has sent the landlord an improvement or emergency action notice. And your landlord is in any event prevented from giving you a section 21 notice within six months of them receiving from the local authority an improvement notice or a notice to take emergency remedial action concerning the state of the property, whether or not this has arisen from your complaint. Unhappily, they don't seem to have thought about invalidating a section 21 notice if it was triggered by the tenant claiming a deposit protection penalty from the landlord during the currency of the tenancy. That would have been of much wider benefit.

- The nightmare scenario for you is that your landlord has done everything according to the book and you have no defence to the possession claim. You will usually be ordered to give possession within 14 days of the hearing. Often there is no hearing because the landlord is relying on having given you two months' notice and is asking for the case to be accelerated and dealt with by the judge on the papers and in the absence of the parties. Where this has happened the 14 days will run from when the judge has looked at the papers and decided that you must go and you should receive a copy of the judge's order through the post a couple of days later. The maximum period the judge can allow for you to go is 42 days but they will only allow more than 14 days where you can show you would otherwise suffer exceptional hardship. You can ask that you be allowed more than 14 days and up to 42 days to leave in your defence - you will receive the defence form with the claim form and you should complete it and send it back to the court - and state why you want more time. What will then happen is that you will get an order to give possession within 14 days of the date of the order and, at the same time, details of a court hearing at which the judge will decide whether to extend the 14 days to anything up to 42 days (as from the date on which the order for possession was made). Occasionally, the landlord would have stated on the claim form that they would be content for the judge to decide whether to grant more than 14 days if asked for, without fixing a hearing on that one matter. Then the judge could allow anything up to 42 days in the original order.

- What happens once the 14 or 42 days (or something in between) are up? Do you get locked out whilst up at the chippie? No. The landlord requests the bailiff to evict you and the bailiff gives you details of an appointment for eviction which will be at least seven days later. All in all, you are likely to have around 14 days plus from the expiry of the date by which you should have given possession before being actually forced out by the bailiff.
- If ordered to give possession within anything less than 42 days, you could apply to the court for the time to be extended for up to 42 days from the date of the possession order should circumstances amounting to exceptional hardship have arisen since the order. Remember, the longer the period you are allowed within which to give possession, the longer the landlord has to wait before they can ask for the bailiff to get to work.

A bit more on one of those penalty claims - or how an estimated 284,000 landlords are holding an unprotected £500,000,000*

(*The estimates were made by the Centre for Economics and Business Research in a report published in January 2016).

Alright then. I can't resist it. If you have a claim you should notify it to the landlord before rushing into court proceedings. Once upon a time, the defaulting landlord could be ordered by the court to repay the unprotected deposit to the tenant or pay it into a scheme and to stump up for the tenant a penalty equal to three times the amount of the deposit. The law has now gone softer on the landlord. They can still be ordered to repay the deposit or pay it into a scheme where the tenant is still renting but the penalty may be mitigated. It will be a minimum of an amount equal to the deposit and a maximum of three times the amount of the deposit. It could be the deposit x 1.5! Judges are alive to the harshness of the deposit protection law and only in the most diabolical case - say your landlord was fully aware of the law but steadfastly refused to do anything about complying with it, ripping up your letters pleading with them to protect and returning the tiny pieces in an unstamped envelope dipped into horse manure and treated the previous tenant in exactly the same way - is it likely that the maximum penalty would be imposed. You would be lucky to achieve a triple penalty. Your letter to the landlord might go something like this:

Dear Landlord

Re 61 Trinoble Close, Peardrop

You are in breach of your obligations under the Housing Act 2004 (as amended by section 213) in relation to the deposit of £500 which I paid you on entering into my tenancy agreement with you of the above premises dated 14 July 2015 in that:

as I have established on enquiry of the three approved schemes for deposit protection, you have failed to protect my deposit.

or

you have failed to provide me with the prescribed information as to deposit protection.

I hereby claim against you the return of the deposit and a statutory penalty of £1,500 representing three times the deposit sum. If you do not pay me the total sum claimed of £2,000 within 14 days of receipt of this letter, I shall be obliged to commence proceedings against you in the county court in which I shall claim that total sum together with interest and the costs of the proceedings.

Without prejudice*

With a view to obviating court proceedings I am prepared to accept the sum of £1,250 from you inclusive of the deposit return in full and final settlement of my claim against you provide I receive payment from you within 14 days of the date of this letter. Otherwise, I will institute proceedings against you without further notice in which I shall seek the full £2,000 plus and interest and costs as set out above.

Yours faithfully

Clive Troublesore

**see chapter 8*

On the other hand, you may be under pressure to get out. Different tactics are then required. You may wish to advance a penalty claim in response to receiving a section 21 notice from your landlord or later if your landlord starts county court possession proceedings against you. Those proceedings could be based on the fact that you have stayed put when the section 21 notice expired or you have clocked up rent arrears.

Why would you want to respond then and how would you do it? If you have had a section 21 notice and been a good tenant - or you haven't been too bad - and you want to stay on in the premises, the landlord may be dissuaded from following up the section 21 notice with possession proceedings by the legitimate threat of deposit protection proceedings.

Dear Landlord

*Without Prejudice**

61 Trinoble Close, Peardrop

You have served me with a notice under section 21 of the Housing Act 1988. If I am obliged to vacate then, of course, I shall vacate but do so with regret. I would prefer to continue in possession. I have been a good tenant. Unfortunately, you have not complied with the Housing Act 2004 in relation to my deposit. Even though it was protected and I had been given the prescribed information when the notice was served:

the deposit was protected late;

or

the prescribed information was sent to me late.

I am advised that I am entitled to claim or counterclaim for the return of the deposit and a penalty equal to three times the amount of the deposit and interest. However, if you are prepared to withdraw the section 21 notice and to grant me a new tenancy for 12 months on the same terms as my last fixed term tenancy then I am prepared to forgo any claim for relief on the ground of your breach. This offer shall be treated as withdrawn if I do not receive written confirmation that you accept it within 14 days of the date of this letter.

Yours faithfully

Clive Troublesore

**see chapter 8*

Should your landlord not accept your kind offer but bring proceedings because you are still in occupation, you could counterclaim for the deposit return, penalty and interest when you answer the proceedings. This would enable you to request the court to set off any money awarded to you against the order which would probably be made in your landlord's favour for their costs of the possession proceedings and to collect the balance awarded. There is one technical difficulty with this approach. The landlord will probably have used the accelerated procedure for gaining possession and the defence form for your completion sent out with the court papers does not cater for a counterclaim. The solution is to draw up your own form of counterclaim, staple it to the defence and send both documents in to the court. You may wish to wait and see if you are asked to pay a counterclaim fee. Otherwise, you can refrain from counterclaiming and bring your own claim (see below on procedure) which the court will probably deal with separately to the possession claim but may link up with the possession claim.

The alternative scenario is that although there are rent arrears, the return of the deposit and a penalty would wipe out those arrears or would at least reduce them and possibly bring them down to less than the equivalent of two months' rent so that the court would not be forced to order you out where relying on a tenancy breach but would have a discretion as to whether or not to do so. With this scenario, you should put in a defence to the claim.

I set-off against the arrears in the sum of £z which I admit, the amount of the deposit of £y and a penalty for three times the amount of the deposit (or such sum as the court shall think fit) and interest thereon at the rate of 8% from the date of the claimant's breach until judgment on the grounds that the claimant has:

failed to protect my deposit;

or

failed to give me the prescribed information;

or

has protected my deposit late in that it was only protected on 2 January 2016;

or

has given me the prescribed information late in that it was only given on 2 March 2016.

Insofar as the amount of the claim is less than the aggregate of the deposit, penalty and interest, I counterclaim the difference.

And another bit more on one of those penalty claims

If you decide to take your landlord to court for some deposit penalty cash, you cannot - or, at least, you should not - do it by claiming online. There is considerable confusion about the procedure to be followed and some of it is fuelled by internet advice websites. You should start proceedings in the county court at the civil hearing centre for the district covering the premises in question. If you don't they will be sent on there. You start them by using claim form N208 which is for what is known (to judges, lawyers, court staff and anyone who has already had a go) as a Part 8 claim (see chapter 9). This form is different from the one used for claims for money to be paid to you and the procedure is different from that which applies to money claims. You pay a flat fee of £355 (see chapter 13) when you kick off unless you qualify for fee remission and you don't quantify the precise amount you are after on the front of the form. Also, although some particulars of the claim must be given they may not be as comprehensive as the particulars of claim in say a money claim and, at the same time as you issue the claim form, you must put in a written statement of your evidence. These documents should be presented to the court in triplicate.

Should court staff query whether you are in need of mental treatment because you have used form N208 and are attempting to start the proceedings at their hearing centre, tell them to have a gander at the Civil Procedure Rules 1998 rule 56.1(1) and Practice Direction 56 paragraph 2.1 - and don't be cocky.

Where your landlord contests the claim and it looks as though the case could be protracted in view of the lengthy, complex and boring points they take, write to the court and ask that the judge reallocate the case to the small claims track (see chapter 18). You have a very good chance of that happening. The different procedure means that you cannot obtain a default judgment against your landlord should they do nothing about contesting: there must be a hearing.

Let's just see how the details of your claim on the claim form might go.

1. At all material times, the claimant was the tenant of 61 Trinoble Close, Peardrop ("the premises) and the defendant was his landlord. The premises were let to the claimant by the landlord under a written assured shorthold tenancy agreement dated 14 July 2015 ("the agreement") for a term of 12 months.

2. On 14 July 2015 the claimant paid the defendant the sum of £1,000 ("the deposit") which was a tenancy deposit within the definition contained in section 212(8) of the Housing Act 2004 ("the Act").

3. The defendant has failed to pay the deposit into an authorised scheme in compliance with section 213(3) of the Act.

or

3. The defendant paid the deposit into an authorised scheme on 2 November 2015 which was outside the period of 30 days beginning with the date of its receipt and, accordingly, the defendant failed to comply with section 213(3) of the Act.

or

3. The defendant paid the deposit into an authorised scheme in compliance with section 213(3) of the Act but failed to give the claimant prescribed information in compliance with section 213(5) and (6) of the Act and the Housing (Tenancy Deposits) (Prescribed Information) Order 2007.

or

3. The defendant paid the deposit into an authorised scheme in compliance with section 213(3) of the Act but did not give the defendant prescribed information until 2 November 2015 which was outside the period of 30 days beginning with the date of receipt of the deposit and, accordingly, the defendant failed to comply with section 213(5) and (6) of the Act and the Housing (Tenancy Deposits) (Prescribed Information) Order 2007.

or

3. The defendant paid the deposit into an authorised scheme in compliance with section 213(3) of the Act and gave the claimant what was purportedly prescribed information but such information was insufficient so as to comply with section 213(5) and (6) of the Act and the Housing (Tenancy Deposits) (Prescribed Information) Order 2013.

or

3. The claimant has been notified by the defendant that the X [insert scheme name] authorised scheme applies to the deposit but has been unable to obtain confirmation from its administrator that the deposit is being held in accordance with such scheme.

4. In the above circumstances the claimant claims:

a. an order that the defendant repay the deposit to the claimant.

or

a. an order that the defendant pay the deposit into the designated account held by the scheme administrator under an authorised custodial scheme.

and

b. an order that the defendant pay to the claimant a sum equal to three times the amount of the deposit.

and

c. interest under section 69 of the County Courts Act 1984 at the rate of £8 per centum per annum on such sum and for such period as the Court shall deem just.

and

d. costs.

And the statement that has to go in? If there are relevant aggravating facts of which you are aware then they should go in as they could make the difference between a penalty of the deposit x1 and the deposit x3. Evidence, for example, that your landlord knew of what the law required of them; that they had "form" with regard to breaking this particular law; that you repeatedly reminded them that they must comply; and that you were prejudiced in some way by their default. Something along these lines but depending, of course, on which of the alternative grounds you are resting on.

Case no 2015P00068

IN THE COUNTY COURT

AT PEARDROP

BETWEEN

Claimant

C Troublesore

1st

CT1-CT"

1 December 2015

CLIVE TROUBLESORE Claimant

- and -

WHITEWASH LIMITED Defendant

I CLIVE TROUBLESORE state as follows:

1. *I live at 61 Trinoble Close, Peardrop ("the premises").*

2. *I am a local authority pest control officer.*

3. *The facts referred to in this statement are of my own knowledge.*

4. *The premises were let to me by the defendant under a written assured shorthold tenancy agreement dated 14 July 2015 ("the agreement") for a term of 12 months. Immediately before the agreement was completed I paid the Defendant's lettings administrator Mr Archibald Daredevil the sum of £1,000 in cash of which receipt was acknowledged in the agreement. This sum was intended as a deposit to secure my performance of the obligations to maintain the premises in a state of good repair as set out in the agreement. I produce a true copy of the agreement marked "CS 1". Mr Daredevil told me when I handed over the deposit to him that although he and the directors of the defendant regarded the law of tenancy deposit protection to be "bloody mad", he would personally see that the deposit was protected and that I would receive details of this as soon as he could get them to me. He said that the defendant has already had its fingers burnt with a previous tenant of the premises and it would not happen again.*

5. *I took up possession of the premises on 14 July 2015.*

6. *By 28 July 2015 I had heard nothing from the defendant*

about deposit protection and so on that date I telephoned Mr Daredevil on six occasions. On each occasion he told me he could not speak because he was tied up on urgent company business but that he would write to me.

7. I waited about one week and heard nothing from Mr Daredevil or anyone else on behalf of the defendant and I then began telephoning the defendant's office. Over a period of three weeks I made about 79 telephone calls to the office. I was never able to speak to Mr Daredevil. I was given a variety of excuses for the non-availability of Mr Daredevil by the series of staff members I spoke to ranging from him being crippled with stomach ache and unable to converse to him being in conference with the defendant's managing director and not to be disturbed. Each time I gave my name and address and asked that Mr Daredevil contact me urgently about the protection of my deposit.

8. On I August 2015 I wrote to the defendant about the deposit demanding a reply within seven days and warning that I would bring proceedings against the defendant if I did not have a satisfactory response within seven days. I produce a true copy of my letter marked "CT 2". I heard nothing back.

9. The amount of the deposit is substantial to me and I can ill-afford to lose it. Not only have I had been considerably inconvenienced by the time wasted in chasing the defendant but I have been worried that my deposit may have been dealt with improperly or may in some other way be in jeopardy.

I believe that the facts stated in this witness statement are true.

Signed

C Troublesore

Dated 1 December 2015

Tenancies from social landlords

Here we are looking at tenancies granted by councils and certain other social housing sector landlords. As with private tenancies, there are specific grounds which the landlord must establish to obtain a court possession order but, generally, the landlord must go on and prove that it is reasonable to order possession (though not with an *assured shorthold* tenancy but see below). Because of this, the court has considerable scope to allow the tenant who has broken a tenancy condition to stay put by:

- dismissing the claim (rare but possible where say you got into arrears only because the housing benefit people lost your documents and wrongly ceased payments);

- ordering possession but suspending the order (effectively, paralysing it) so long as certain conditions are observed by you (for example, paying off the arrears in addition to paying future rent as and when it falls due or no longer using the back garden to cultivate cannabis); or
- adjourning the possession claim for as long as you keep to agreed terms (for example, where there are rent arrears but they are modest);
- or postponing possession.

A few words on postponement. This is an alternative to a suspended order and involves the court making a possession order but not fixing a date for you to go. Instead, the court leaves it to the landlord to apply for an order fixing the date should you break any of the terms of the order which will usually relate to payment of the arrears by instalments and payment of current rent. A postponed order would be better for you than a suspended order. The reason is that the landlord needs an additional court order before requesting the bailiff to evict when you breach a postponed order but, with breach of a suspended order, the landlord can go straight to the bailiff. Social landlords hate postponed orders: many judges love them.

The tenant is sometimes stumped because they lack the security given to the so-called conventional secure tenant who rents from a council. Or do they? A homeless person who has been granted temporary accommodation by a local authority under a licence instead of a tenancy can be evicted without a court order. But take a homeless person who has been put into temporary accommodation by the council as a tenant or a council or housing association tenant who has an assured shorthold tenancy. They won't have the same security as the conventional council tenant: in short, it's easier for the landlord to get them out through a court order. Still, for such a non-secure tenant there might just, just, just be a modicum of hope in defeating the landlord who has overstepped the mark with a (drums roll, trumpets fanfare, George Clooney and his wife enter stage left)....**public law defence or human rights (or both) defence**.

The public law defence involves arguing that the landlord's actions are irrational or disproportionate. The human rights defence is along the lines that the landlord has breached article 8 of the human rights convention. That says everyone has the right to respect for their private and family life, their home and their correspondence and that there is to be no interference with this right by a public authority (such as a council landlord) except where it is in accordance with the law and is necessary in a democratic society in the interests of national security etc etc. Often, both defences are run. If the landlord has called a meeting at the request of the tenant to review its decision to bring possession proceedings and sat with cotton wool in their ears and laughter on their faces as the tenant addressed them or the tenant owes only £25 in rent and they have mental health problems then the landlord may well be denied possession. The defences are usually raised - and stand the best chance of succeeding - where the tenant is vulnerable as a result of mental illness, physical or learning disability, poor health or frailty. Incidentally, that public law defence will never be available to the tenant of a private landlord so there is no scope for the private tenant to argue, for example, that their landlord's decision to have them ousted was disproportionate. The idea that this defence could be successfully run was put to bed by the Supreme Court on 15 June 2016.

The social landlord is obliged to follow a pre-action protocol which was revamped in April 2015. If they fail to do so, the court may order them to pay any costs you have incurred whether or not you have been represented by a lawyer. It may also be persuaded not to order you to pay the landlord's costs in making the claim which you would otherwise almost certainly be stuck with and it can take the landlord's naughtiness into account in deciding what order to make when it has a discretion about what to do. And where the landlord is solely relying on one of those grounds we have been looking at where you are normally stumped because you lack the security of a conventional tenant, the court can adjourn the hearing to give the landlord the opportunity to take the protocol steps it should already have taken - or even throw out the claim!

When you have run up rent arrears, the social landlord must:

- contact you as soon as reasonably possible to discuss the case, your financial circumstances and any entitlement you may have to benefits or other help;
- try and agree a plan for you to pay off the arrears;
- send you quarterly statements showing the rent due and the sums received for the past 13 weeks;
- arrange for the arrears to be paid by the Department for Work and Pensions out of your benefit, if you meet the appropriate criteria;
- offer to assist you in claiming housing benefit, discretionary housing benefit (where you have been hit by the bedroom tax) or the housing benefit element of universal credit; and

- withhold taking you to court if you can demonstrate a reasonable expectation of eligibility for housing benefit or that element of universal credit and you have provided all the evidence required to process an application for it so long as you have paid all sums not covered by the benefit. The landlord should inform you of the date and time of any court hearing and advise you that, because your home is at risk, you should attend.

Lodgers

Most lodgers can be required to leave without a court order so long as they have been given reasonable notice to go and the notice period has expired. This applies provided that the landlord lived on the premises as their only or principal home when you moved in and they are there on this basis when your time is up. You must also be sharing some living space with the landlord: bathroom, kitchen or whatever. Notice period? 28 days is the norm but more could be needed where you have been in the accommodation for a very long time and less could be sufficient where you have been there for five minutes. Should you have beaten up your landlord then very short notice might suffice. In one case I tried, I decided that a lodger who had kicked and bruised his elderly landlady in the course of a dispute could be required to go the next day.

FOR PRIVATE LANDLORDS' EYES ONLY

"I smell trouble"

Your *assured shorthold* tenant misses one month's rent. Unless the premises are unfit for human habitation so that you will never find another mug to move in or you are having a passionate affair with the tenant, consider very carefully whether to serve notice requiring possession (provided, of course, the law gives you the grounds to do so at that stage), even though you do not follow it up with a court claim for possession. More often than not, one month missed means further trouble down the line.

A notice will concentrate the tenant's mind on their obligation to pay and if further arrears accrue and you have already served a notice then you may be able to start a claim immediately or very soon. If it's say a monthly tenancy (either because it always was a monthly tenancy or the fixed term has come to an end with the result that the law treats the tenant as staying on as a monthly tenant) you can serve a two months' notice under section 21 of the Housing Act 1988. If a fixed term is still running then there may be a break clause in the tenancy which you can invoke and the section 21 notice may well be sufficient to trigger the break - or it may not. Study the tenancy wording. That's one good reason to have a break clause in a fixed term tenancy: ideally, one that entitles the landlord to end the tenancy by giving two months' notice. The prohibition against the landlord ending an *assured shorthold* tenancy during the first six months of its life does not apply to lettings after 27 February 1997. But for a tenancy granted on or after 1 October 2015 there has been a prohibition on an end within the first four months of the tenancy. The section 21 route will entitle you to utilise the accelerated possession claim regime and you can seek the arrears in a separate online claim.

You can explain your point of view to the tenant without prejudicing your legal position.

"Dear Mr Troublesore

I very much regret that you have failed to pay your rent due on 14 July 2016. I am hopeful that this is due to some unexpected difficulty and that you will shortly clear the arrears and not default again as I would prefer to keep you as my tenant and not be compelled to take steps to recover possession of the premises from you. However, I am sure you will understand that I must protect myself as I am heavily reliant on receiving the contracted rent from you regularly and promptly. Accordingly, I enclose a formal notice under section 21 of the Housing Act 1988 and ask you to please acknowledge receipt. If I am able to withdraw the notice, I will let you know but, subject to this, its terms must stand.

Yours faithfully,

P Rachman"

Section 8 v Section 21

Where two months'/eight weeks' arrears are already outstanding you can serve a 14 days' notice under section 8 of the Housing Act 1988 during a fixed term or monthly tenancy. But in that situation you will not be entitled to use the accelerated possession procedure and there will have to be a court hearing leading to a slower process. Against this, you will be able to make a claim for the arrears in the same proceedings. Should the arrears be cleared or brought down to less than the equivalent of two months/eight weeks before the hearing then your right to a mandatory possession order will have been lost. You can always serve a section 21 notice when the law permits it at the same time as the section 8 notice (telling the tenant that each notice is without prejudice to the other). Once the time for giving possession under the section 21 notice has expired, you can restart proceedings on the strength of it should you still be on a quest for possession and the section 8 notice not have led to it.

Accelerated possession no-show

The normal order in an accelerated possession claim is that the tenant must leave the premises within 14 days of the court order which will be made without a hearing provided the judge is satisfied with what they have seen on the papers. But the tenant may have asked for more time: up to 42 days instead of 14 days. The claim form will have invited you to say whether you consent to a request for more time being decided on paper. It may be a bad idea to give that consent. At a hearing on whether there should be more time, there may be matters you can bring to the judge's attention which will have a bearing on whether the tenant would suffer exceptional hardship in having to leave within 14 days. Where there is a hearing devoted to whether more time should be given the initial order on the papers will still have been for possession within 14 days.

Friends for breakfast

When the eviction is through the county court the bailiff will do the deed and the same procedure will apply as for the eviction of a mortgage borrower. There is a trend for some persons facing eviction to invite 50 or so friends for breakfast to coincide with the eviction appointment and for the friends to gather in the front garden before the baked beans are heated, possibly with a drum or two and some trumpets and maybe an accordion and some flags and notices unflattering to the bailiff and the claimant and some menace. When this happens, the bailiff who has respect for his physical health and pension takes fright although the accompanying claimant or their representative on hand to board up the property once possession has been achieved is occasionally up for some muscle power. The process is frustrated. With a view to outwitting the claimant and their friends - and, more often than not, the friends are part of an organised group who are heavily into this nonsense - a new scheme came into operation in October 2014.

Where the bailiff has been frustrated first time around, the claimant will be given the opportunity of agreeing to a second eviction to be set on a date and at a time which will not be notified to the defendant. A new form has been created: the N54A which is otherwise to be known as the notice of further attempt at eviction. It will be served on the defendant by a minimum of two bailiffs no less with appropriate protective equipment at least seven days before the date of the intended eviction date. It informs the defendant that bailiffs will re-attend at any time without further notice after a stated date to enforce the warrant. With gritted teeth, it gives the unfriendly defendant user friendly guidance. It will be accompanied by a scary warning to occupier that their home is at risk if they ignore the notice and provide details of the usual agencies who can help. Before the secret eviction attempt, bailiffs who have been specially trained will conduct a risk assessment and formulate an action plan to mitigate any noted risks. The police will not become involved in the eviction but may attend to deal with any breach of the peace. If there is reason to believe that the defendant has got wind of the second eviction date then that will be aborted and a new date set although no further notice will be served on the defendant.

Here's the rub. Bailiffs are advised that they must withdraw from enforcement if there are risks of threats of harm or violence. They must assess the risk throughout the eviction. This new procedure is a commendable attempt at avoiding an organised protest but it is no panacea. There are alternatives for the obstinate defendant. One is to seek to have them evicted by an enforcement agent who is likely to be readier for some bother and almost certainly will be able to give an earlier eviction date than a county court bailiff. To achieve this you have to get the case transferred to the High Court. It is by no means a forgone conclusion that the county court judge considering the matter will agree to transfer. Some judges feel that the trusted county court bailiff should be left to get on with enforcing a county court judgment. You can apply orally to the judge at which you obtain the possession order for an order that the case be transferred to the High Court for enforcement by a writ of possession or you can apply subsequently on paper using an application notice in form N244 and accompanying it with a request for a certificate of judgment in form N293A. Attempts by enforcement agents acting for landlords to bypass the county court because it was taking too long to process the form N244 by applying directly to the High Court without notice to the tenant for possession to be dealt with there have now been thwarted: any such application must in future be made on notice to the tenant. On the N244 to the county court you should apply for an order that *the claim to be transferred to the Central Office of the Queen's Bench Division of the High Court for enforcement of the order for possession dated 14 July 2016*. You will need to support the application with a written statement giving viable reasons for transfer.

The defendant is making no payments to me for his occupation of the property and is currently £4,560.72 in arrears of rent. I have a mortgage on the property and am reliant on rental income from it. I have been unable to service my mortgage since the defendant's default began and I am in grave danger of possession proceedings being brought against me imminently if I cannot re-let to a new tenant.

I am informed by the bailiff's clerk at this hearing centre that a bailiff cannot offer an appointment for eviction for at least five weeks. I have been in touch with an enforcement agent who assure me that he could act immediately on a High Court writ of possession subject to giving appropriate notice to the defendant of an eviction appointment.

The defendant has informed me that if I seek to enforce the possession order he will do everything in his power to prevent the bailiff from getting near the property. He says that bailiffs are the scum of the earth and he would rather punch them into a pulp than lose his home.

A copy of any N244 should be attached to the N293. The county court may impose a condition that the enforcement agent gives a minimum period of notice to the defendant of the eviction date and time. There is a feeling among some judges that enforcement agents can be a little too quick off the mark.

And the other alternative? Apply for the defendant to be committed to prison for their contempt of court in not obeying the court order for possession. A prison sentence for contempt will get them out of the property. But the enforcement agent is probably the fastest route if you can persuade the county court to transfer the case to the High Court.

Beware letting agents

Many letting agents offer their landlord clients an all-in service which includes serving a section 21 or section 8 notice and dealing with a subsequent court claim for possession. Though some of these agents try it on, they do not have the legal status to conduct proceedings on the landlord's behalf and very often they blunder over the timing and form of notice used and completion of the claim form. The consequences of a blunder for the landlord could be monumental. I beg of you, take legal advice if only to check over the documentation which the agent has prepared and ensure that any claim form prepared by the agent is signed by you and has your contact details down and not those of the agent. That is what the court rules require if a lawyer is not involved and that way you know what is going on. I have seen many instances of agents' cock-ups which have been hidden from the landlord for ages because court documents have been sent out to the agents.

Deposited!

That's what you will be if the tenant's deposit has not been protected when it should have been or you have protected but failed to give the tenant the necessary protection information in time and you serve a section 21 notice. It will be legally ineffective and any possession claim you make on the strength of that section 21 notice will fail. You will have to protect late and serve a fresh section 21 notice and then start a new possession claim. Excellent for blood boiling and internal combustion. Fast fix? Refund the deposit to the tenant before you serve the section 21 notice though it won't work as a barrier to a tenant's claim to a penalty for non-protection (see above). Calm down. We know there are rent arrears and the tenant has taken a hammer and saw to the double wardrobes and telly and the deposit was your only realistic hope of gaining some recompense. But the alternative is a delay of around at least three months before you can secure a possession order.

Part 10

RELATIONSHIPS: BEFORE AND AFTER

Chapter 44

Domestic Violence Damages Claims

Bill for battery

A spouse, civil partner or cohabitee who assaulted you can be sued for damages as well as forbidden to repeat the exercise. This is quite independent of any criminal proceedings that may be taken against them and in which the criminal court might order them, if convicted, to pay you some compensation, though probably only a token amount.

You also have an option of making an application for compensation (not through any court) under the Criminal Injuries Compensation Scheme which you can be sure will be paid should it be awarded 'cos it's state money. You will need to be patient and have a reasonable expectation of a few years' life since the process would embarrass a snail. An application has to be made as soon as reasonably practicable and, anyway, within two years of the incident but this time limit may be extended in exceptional circumstances. Compensation may be refused where you have not reported the incident to the police as soon as reasonably practicable. Nevertheless, consideration will be given to whether the effect of the incident on you would explain any delay. There is a knock out condition which could scupper you before you have posted the application form. You will be ineligible for compensation if, when injured, you and your assailant were both at least 18 and were living together as part of the same family. However, you will be OK should you and your assailant be apart when you make the application provided you are unlikely to live together again. You will also be ruled out if your assailant may benefit from the award.

A court claim for damages can be made under the Protection from Harassment Act 1997 or (and this would be more appropriate for a claim based on a single incident) you can simply allege an assault and battery which comes under the umbrella of what is called the tort of *trespass to the person* ("If you trespass my person again, I shall punch you up the bracket.") The claim can be linked to an application for an injunction or be made separately. The alternative to seeking an injunction under the 1997 Act is to do so under the Family Law Act 1996 (when it is called a *non-molestation* order) which is more commonly relied on by someone associated with the assailant such as a cohabitee or former cohabitee. A damages claim cannot be made in 1996 Act proceedings but can be made separately, relying on allegations of assault and battery.

Small bills and big bills

What might a claim for damages be worth to you? This depends on the nature of the injury, the extent of the pain and suffering you endured and whether you have a continuing disability and, if so, how long it will last. These are some of the considerations. Guidelines followed by judges (last updated in October 2015) suggest that a transient eye injury from which complete recovery is made within a few weeks is worth between £1,840 to £3,300; a very minor wrist injury requiring a plaster or bandage for a matter of weeks with a full or virtual recovery within a year is worth between £2,940 and £3,960; the fracture of a finger has a value of up to £3,960 (depending on the recovery time); and moderate post-traumatic stress disorder following a serious incident from which you have recovered or largely recovered could earn an award of between £6,850 and £19,360; and trivial scarring could bring in £1,430 to £2,940. At the other end of the scale, if you had the extreme misfortune to lose an eye, the court would most likely say that the compensation had a value of between £45,840 and £55,000. On top you would be entitled to be compensated for specific losses flowing from the incident - they are called *special damages* - such as medical expenses and loss of earnings and any future losses which you expect and can establish.

Another route to compensation

It may be possible to get the court to convert your assailant's violent behaviour into money for you when it comes to deal with a financial application in matrimonial proceedings (such as divorce). It should be prepared to do so when it would be inequitable to disregard it (see chapter 49). But what the hell does that mean? These days it means that the conduct in question must have been pretty diabolical to affect the outcome of the capital share out. Judges are keen to discourage what can become an acrimonious and very time consuming and so potentially costly investigation into the reasons for the relationship breakdown with a view to increasing the innocent party's pay out, not only because of the expense of it all but because both parties may well have contributed to the breakdown. Nevertheless, such investigations are sometimes permitted and sometimes they work. In one case, the husband's share of the capital was reduced to 25% where he had attacked the wife with a bread knife in front of the children and been sentenced to 12 years' imprisonment for the attack. In another case the husband's share in capital was reduced from 50% to 33.33% where he had struck the wife in the chest with a kitchen knife and then attempted suicide. The wife had suffered deep psychological damage along with a superficial wound.

Should the seriousness of your assailant's conduct fall short of what is required to cut down their share of the assets in matrimonial proceedings then you might be well advised to bring a civil claim for damages against them and, if that claim is contested, it can be linked up to the matrimonial application and heard at the same time. That way, whilst the violence may not be serious enough to enable the court to reflect it in the matrimonial application award, it can deal with the damages claim in the same way as if you had been assaulted by a complete stranger. Then, the damages you are awarded in the civil claim might be ignored in the matrimonial application with you being treated as not about to receive the damages and your assailant being treated as not having a liability to pay them. Get it?!

How does your assailant's bankruptcy affect any unpaid lump sum or damages? With both, you can now chase any assets they may have along with their other creditors by putting forward a claim to their trustee in bankruptcy. If some of the lump sum still remains outstanding then your assailant will not be released from the obligation to pay when the bankruptcy order comes to an end and they are discharged: they remain liable to you until you have received payment in full. With a damages award, however, anything unpaid will probably be lost at the end of the bankruptcy.

It is possible that your assailant is a maniac. If making a claim for damages might promote more trouble from them in the future from which you do not feel a court injunction can adequately protect you, this is a factor which you will obviously consider when deciding what to do.

A claim under the Protection from Harassment Act 1997 must be brought under Part 8 of the Civil Procedure Rules (see chapter 9). You should drop off or post the papers to a county court civil hearing centre instead of the County Court Money Claims Centre but it must be the hearing centre which serves the address at which either you or your aggressor reside or carry on business: otherwise there will be delay whilst it is sent on to the right place. With the claim form must go statements of your written evidence and the evidence of any other witnesses you intend relying on (see chapter 14). Your own statement will put flesh on the allegations in the claim form and your witnesses will corroborate where necessary. This is what the claim form may look like.

Case no 97P0000678

IN THE COUNTY COURT

SITTING AT PEARDROP

BETWEEN

MAVIS MAGNOLIA Claimant

- and -

CLIVE TROUBLESORE Defendant

Details of claim

1. The claimant claims for relief under section 3 of the Protection from Harassment Act 1997.

2. At all material times the parties cohabited together.

3. Between, on or about 31 December 2013 and 14 July 2016 ("the period") the defendant pursued a course of conduct which amounted to harassment of the claimant and which he knew or ought to have known amounted to such harassment.

Particulars of harassment

4. Throughout the period the defendant bombarded the claimant with texts, emails and telephone calls which were abusive and/or insulting in content and refused to heed the claimant's request that he desist. The claimant would hear from the defendant by one or more of these media on most days and not less than 20 times a day: sometimes as many as 120 times a day or thereabouts. He would frequently telephone her in the early hours of the morning thereby disturbing her sleep.

5. On 1 January 2016 the defendant posted a message on his Facebook page calling the claimant a "whore" and a "fat cow".

6. On 4 January 2016 at 149 Crescent, Twickenham the defendant assaulted the claimant by slapping her across the face with force using his open hand five times causing her to fall to the ground whereupon he kicked her on both legs not less than six times using both feet whilst wearing heavy boots. He then placed his hands around her throat whilst she remained on the ground and squeezed tightly for about 25 seconds so that she thought she might die and only withdrew them and departed when the next door neighbour rang the front doorbell.

7. By reason of the defendant's conduct as set out in paragraphs

4 to 6 above, the claimant has suffered personal injury, distress and anxiety and loss and damage.

Particulars of personal injury etc and loss

8. The claimant relies on the medical report of Dr A G Ramakin dated 2 June 2016, a copy of which is annexed hereto.

9. The claimant incurred prescription charges of £13 and loss of earnings from her employment of £614.91 net.

10. The claimant claims interest on damages under section 69 of the County Courts Act 1984 at such rates and for such periods as the court shall determine to be just.

AND the claimant claims:

a. An injunction restraining the defendant from pursuing any conduct which amounts to harassment in relation to her until further order;*

b. Damages in excess of £5,000 but not in excess of £15,000;

c. Interest; and

d. Costs.

**If you are wishing to obtain an interim injunction pending the full hearing of the case, you should issue an application in form N16A indicating where asked, towards the top, that you are applying in pending proceedings. Where you feel that you need some protection when your assailant receives the court paperwork, you can ask the court to grant you a temporary injunction before they come to know anything about the proceedings. This is known as an ex parte (pronounced party) injunction. Your written statement would need to set out why you say this is necessary. The reasons would need to be pretty compelling.*

The one-off

You won't get anywhere with a Protection from Harassment Act claim, be it for an injunction or damages or both, unless your assailant has been responsible for at least two incidents. You can still go for an injunction (and one which is temporary and, in a serious case, one obtained ex parte) and damages in an assault and battery claim on the strength of just one incident. This time your claim should be brought under Part 7 of the Civil Procedure Rules (see chapter 9) and so you would need to prepare a claim form and a separate document called *particulars of claim*. They might go something like this.

Case no 97P0000678

IN THE COUNTY COURT

SITTING AT PEARDROP

BETWEEN

MAVIS MAGNOLIA Claimant

- and -

CLIVE TROUBLESORE Defendant

PARTICULARS OF CLAIM

1. On 14 July 2016 at 149 Magnolia Crescent, Twickenham whilst the parties were cohabiting together at that address, the claimant was assaulted and beaten by the defendant. The defendant slapped the claimant across the face with force with his open hand five times causing her to fall to the ground whereupon he kicked her on both legs not less than six times using both feet whilst wearing heavy boots. He then placed his hands around her throat whilst she remained on the ground and squeezed tightly for about 25 seconds so that she thought she might die and only withdrew them and departed when the next door neighbour rang the front doorbell.

2. By reason of the assault and battery, the claimant suffered personal injury and loss.

Particulars of personal injury

3. The claimant relies on the medical report of Dr A G Ramakin dated 2 June 2016, a copy of which is annexed hereto.

Particulars of loss

4. The claimant incurred prescription charges of £13 and loss of earnings from her employment of £614.91 net.

5. The claimant claims interest on damages under section 69 of the County Courts Act 1984 at such rates and for such periods as the court shall determine to be just.

AND the claimant claims:

a. An injunction restraining the defendant from pursuing any conduct which amounts to harassment in relation to her until further order;

b. Damages in excess of £1,000 but not in excess of £15,000;

c. Interest; and

d. Costs.

The clock

There are usually time limits for bringing civil proceedings (see chapter 10). A claim under the Protection from Harassment Act must relate to conduct within the previous six years and a claim for damages for personal injury arising out of an assault and battery to an incident within the previous three years (so it may be that you will be too late to claim damages for the latter but in time to do so for the former). Raising your assailant's conduct in the course of a financial application in matrimonial proceedings is possible, however long ago it occurred, although its likely impact on the result will be minimal, if non-existent, where it is very stale.

Chapter 45

Cohabitation

The scandal

Don't be fooled. The rights of cohabitees on the breakdown of their relationships are rubbish. The Law Commission would have it otherwise as would many politicians and marchers: the talk about reforming the law to strengthen rights has been incessant for some years. But the law 'aint going to be reformed yet. As the talk goes on, many are obliged to walk away from the relationship with...nothing. The law treats cohabitees in an entirely different way - a substantially inferior way - to the parties to a marriage or civil partnership when the end comes about. Cohabitees have no entitlement to maintenance in respect of themselves although the party who has the main care of a child of the relationship is likely to score child support, if not more, for the child's benefit. And the courts lack the ability to do what is fair between the parties by dividing up their assets. As a general rule, what they own is what they can keep. The message is clear. Marry or enter into a civil partnership and take advantage of the matrimonial laws if the relationship fails. Bully them (though not duress, dear and please no violence), trap them, humiliate them in front of their parents or propose on network radio or television so that they dare not embarrass you with a refusal. All is fair in love, war and getting hitched.

But if, despite it all, cohabitation is your fate, let's see what we can do for you as, in this book, there's always hope.

The home - on the deeds

If both parties are registered as owners - this would be at the Land Registry where registration takes the place of those lovely old parchment title deeds written out with a blotchy quill pen and making perfect lamp shades - then both can expect the law to deal with the property more or less in the same way as with any other joint owners. It will be evident from the Land Registry documentation whether each party owns one-half of the property or they own it in different shares. One of them may have stumped up a large deposit against nothing from the other when the property was bought and so, by agreement, taken a larger stake in ownership.

If the home was acquired as, or later became, the home of the couple and their relationship is over then the likelihood is that the court will order it to be sold at the instigation of one of them when the other is resisting a sale or just dragging their feet. Again, the likelihood is that the court will go on to direct how the property should be marketed, by which agents and at what price; which of the parties is to organise the sale (frequently, this will be both of them); and that the sale price after deductions for what is required to pay off the mortgage, any estate agent's commission and the legal costs on the sale be divided in accordance with the parties' respective shares in ownership.

Now you might think that what the title deeds say about the shares in which the property is owned is conclusive. Most certainly this is the most powerful evidence that could be available and will usually carry the day. However, it is still open to one of the parties to say that the other has practised some fraud on them (for example, got them to sign the deed which shows the shares pretending it was a request for tickets to attend the recordings of six back to back editions of the *Jeremy Kyle Show*) or that they (or the lawyer who drew up the deed) simply made a dreadful mistake.

The law does recognise that a couple's intentions about those shares may change over the course of time. Pin back your lugholes for this case which was decided by the Supreme Court in 2011. Ms J and Mr K were cohabiting and bought an Essex property in their joint names in 1985 for £30,000. In 1993 Mr K moved out. Ms J stayed put with the couple's two children and took full responsibility for the mortgage and other outgoings. In 1995 the couple cashed in a joint life policy and split the proceeds between them. Mr K used his money as the deposit on a new home for himself. By 2008 the value of the Essex property had increased to £245,000. The Supreme Court decided that by then the couple's intention about how they shared had changed from a presumed 50-50 to 90-10 in favour of Ms J! As you might say, you never can tell.

The home - off the deeds

Constructive trust

It may well be possible to establish an interest in property despite the fact that only one person is registered as the owner - that swine of a former cohabitee. If you are out to establish that interest then you will have to prove that you both intended you should have the interest - there was an agreement, arrangement or understanding between you to this effect, usually before the property was bought but sometimes later on - and that you acted to your detriment in the reasonable belief you were acquiring it. This is known to the law as a *constructive trust* claim.

Let's look at what is needed to prove the intention you should have the interest. The fact that the swine used to call the property "our house" won't get you far unless, say, it was to lawyers or accountants and evidence of discussions between the two of you may be crucial. *"You're going through a divorce right now. I won't put your name on the deeds as this could mess up the financial case between you and your hubby." "As you're 21 you'll have to stay off the deeds at the moment."* This sort of comment by the swine would be very useful and they will be taken to have been telling the truth even though they now say they were palming you off with a pack of lies. Nice one, eh?

A financial contribution by you towards the purchase price would be particularly strong evidence of an intention that you were getting an interest. And so might some other financial payment such as conveyancing or survey fees or mortgage instalments (under a repayment mortgage with interest payments only usually being insufficient) or bearing the cost of substantial improvements to the property.

Where a financial contribution has been made, the payment should additionally serve to prove that you have acted to your detriment.

Proprietary estoppel

This, I agree, sounds painful. To Ms B two years ago it was anything but painful. She couldn't prove a constructive trust, though she tried. Nevertheless, she could prove she had an interest in the home in which she had cohabited with Mr T, through the doctrine of proprietary estoppel. This is how it works. You score by proving that the property owner has made a promise to you relating to the home - usually, it's that you can live there until whenever- and that you relied on it to your detriment (which has to be not insubstantial) plus that the owner has acted unconscionably.

In Ms B's case, she had come out of a failed marriage with about £25,000 of which she spent some £15,000 fitting out and furnishing a housing association property she had secured for herself and two daughters in Manchester. Then she met Mr T who was a single man working as a claims manager. The trial judge found him to be "by nature, shrewd, cautious and guarded." But he was to come a cropper. He was against the idea of marriage but wanted to live with Ms B and her daughters. They found a house in Droitwich which was purchased in his sole name. He used £140,000 from the house he had previously owned and otherwise financed the purchase with a mortgage. He reassured Ms B - here comes his downfall - that she would always have a home and be secure in this one. On the strength of that assurance she gave up her Manchester tenancy and moved into the Droitwich home with the girls. She spent £4,000 to £5,000 towards setting up the new home although Mr T paid the mortgage and never suggested that he regarded or intended Ms B to be a joint owner. Around nine years later after a breakdown in the relationship Ms B and her daughters found themselves homeless. That promise was broken.

The Court of Appeal upheld the trial judge's ruling that the doctrine of proprietary estoppel applied and in relation to the argument that Mr T's behaviour had not been unconscionable, it regarded the repudiation of his promise as unconscionable. That was enough. Ms B was to be compensated for the prejudice to her by Mr T's failure to honour his promise. She had been awarded what the £25,000 she had shelled out on Manchester and Droitwich would be worth when the case was heard - £28,500. The award would stand.

And in March 2016 the Court of Appeal upheld a trial judge's decision that a cohabitee in a 15 year relationship with the man who owned the home in which they lived had acquired an interest in the property thanks to proprietary estoppel. She had contributed £200 per month towards the mortgage instalments. They were said at the time to be "towards the house" and all the evidence showed that meant "towards ownership of the house".

Equitable accounting

You could conceivably be laughed out of court on all your main arguments but still leave court with some money in your hands. If, say, you have shelled out money towards substantial improvements or repairs or paid or contributed to the mortgage instalments without, in law, earning a proprietary interest in the property, the court might say it was only fair and equitable that the swine should pay you back. It's called *equitable accounting*.

It's litigation time

The party after sale or compensation should send a pre-action letter to the other party (see chapter 8) and, if that results in no shift or a brick though the letterbox, it's off to court. A claim should be made under the Trusts of Land and Appointment of Trustees Act 1996 which lawyers call a *TOLATA* claim so that, as usual, nobody else will know what they are talking about. In such a claim, sections 14 and 15 of the 1996 Act say that the court is to take account of all relevant matters (when shouldn't it?!) effectively including the intentions of the person you will be claiming against, what the property is being used for and the welfare of anyone under 18 who is occupying it or might reasonably be expected to occupy it.

Any moment you will see *TOLATA* particulars of claim with some mix and match paragraphs which can guide you on the sort of argument you could advance in your case. The particulars would be used in conjunction with a Part 7 claim form (see chapter 9) to start the case in court. If you are not expecting what the law calls a "substantial issue of fact" (and I call "a punch up") to have to be decided in the case then you can use the Part 8 procedure (see chapter 9) but in that event you would need to put in a witness statement (see chapter 14 for how to set it out) instead of particulars of claim. The statement can follow the drift of what would have been in particulars of claim but give more factual detail and, of course, be in the first person ("I left the defendant..." etc).

Case no 97P0000678

IN THE COUNTY COURT

AT PEARDROP

In the Matter of the Trusts of Land and Appointment of Trustees Act 1996

BETWEEN

MAVIS BULWARK Claimant

- and -

CLIVE TROUBLESORE Defendant

PARTICULARS OF CLAIM

1. Between 12 August 2006 and 1 November 2016 the parties cohabited together.

EITHER

2. On 14 July 2007 the parties purchased the freehold property 149 Magnolia Crescent,, Twickenham, Middlesex KT89 4XZ ("the property") registered at HM Land Registry with title absolute and which on that date was transferred to them as joint tenants. On the same date the parties entered into a charge of the property to Parasite (No 3) Building Society ("the Building Society") for the principal sum of £240,000 ("the mortgage") and the claimant contributed one-half of the mortgage instalments and buildings insurance premiums in respect of the property as from acquisition of the property until on or about 1 November 2016.

3. The property was purchased by the claimant and the defendant with the intention that it should be their home for the subsistence of their relationship. On 1 November 2016 the defendant left the property with the intention of bringing cohabitation with the claimant to a permanent end.

OR

2. On 14 July 2007 the defendant purchased the freehold property 149c Magnolia Buildings, Twickenham, Middlesex KT89 4XZ ("the property") registered at HM Land Registry with title absolute and which on that date was transferred to him in his sole name. On the same date the defendant entered into a charge of the property to Parasite (No 3) Building Society ("the Building Society") for the principal sum of £240,000 under a repayment mortgage ("the mortgage).

3. The property was acquired by the defendant with the intention that it should be the parties' home and at all material times such intention has subsisted. Further, between 14 July 2007 and 1 November 2016 the parties occupied the property as their home. The defendant holds the property on a constructive trust for the benefit of the parties in equal shares. Further and in the alternative, the claimant has an interest in the property by virtue of the operation of a proprietary estoppel.

Facts relied on by the Claimant in support of her claim for a constructive trust

a. Immediately before the purchase the defendant said to the claimant: "You won't be on the title deeds. The only reason is that the solicitor told me it would delay the conveyancing if you had to sign up too."

b. At the request of the defendant, the claimant organised removal to the property of the contents of the defendant's previous home.

c. At the request of the defendant, the claimant paid one-half of the fee for the survey on the property requisitioned by the Building Society and one-half of the conveyancing charges and disbursements on the purchase.

d. Shortly after the purchase, the defendant suggested to the claimant that the property be called 'Chez Magnolia-Troublesore'.

e. Between 14 July 2007 and 1 November 2016 the claimant almost invariably made payments out of her earnings as a mobile hairdresser and pedicurist towards the mortgage and the premium for the buildings and insurance cover on the property and, more often than not, such payments were for one-half of the sums due. Further, during the same period the claimant purchased numerous household items for the property and thereby freeing the defendant from any obligation to purchase them and facilitating his payments or contributions towards the mortgage and insurance premiums.

f. The claimant assisted the defendant in internally decorating the property shortly after its purchase and again in 2014.

g. In 2011 the claimant asked the defendant to construct a patio area at the rear of the property whereupon the defendant said to her; "If you want a bloody patio, stick it down yourself." The claimant did thereafter construct the patio with her own labour and using materials for which she paid in excess of £1,000.

h. At all material times the claimant acted to her detriment in believing that the defendant was to hold and/or held the property on trust for herself and the defendant.

Facts relied on by the Claimant in support of her claim for a proprietary estoppel

a. The claimant relies on the facts set out in support of her claim for a constructive trust in addition to the facts set out at sub-paragraphs (b) to (d) below.

b. The claimant met the defendant in or about April 2007. By then, she had acquired the tenancy of 689 St John's Wort Parade, Southend, Essex which had been granted by the local authority and following the breakdown in a long-standing relationship with a man who had subjected her to domestic violence. She had spent £10,000 on furniture and household equipment for the accommodation and had done so with the intention and expectation that her occupation of it would be permanent, She had also established a network of clients for her business as a mobile hairdresser and pedicurist.

c. In July 2007 the defendant told her that he loved her and wanted to live with her for the rest of his life. He further stated that he wanted the claimant to move into a property with him to be purchased in Twickenham, Middlesex and that, if she did so, she would be secure in it, would never have to leave and could give up her tenancy without having any qualms about her future. The claimant relied on these statements and, in consequence of them, she surrendered her tenancy and ceased carrying on her business in the Southend area, losing her clients, and moved in to the property with the defendant on 14 July 2007.

d. On 1 November 2016 the defendant locked the claimant out of the property and thereafter barred her entrance so that she was rendered homeless and has had to return to the Southend area where she is living with relatives and is currently unemployed.

PLUS

4. The relationship between the parties has irretrievably broken down and the object of the trust claimed by the claimant has failed. The defendant has remained in the property and currently has exclusive possession of it.

AND the claimant claims:

a. A declaration that the defendant holds the property on trust for the claimant and the defendant in equal shares or in such other shares as the Court shall determine.

b. An order for the sale of the property.

c. Such other relief as shall be just.

d. Costs.

And when there are children

We have seen that one of the considerations for the court on a *TOLATA* claim is the welfare of an under 18 year old occupying the property. If the claim is against a parent of the child then it may be prudent for the claimant who is the child's main carer and who either wants to stay put or to get back into the property or, alternatively, is after buying another property, to make a separate claim under schedule 1 to the Children Act 1989. This is a family law claim and is procedurally governed by the Family Procedure Rules 2010. The *TOLATA* claim and the Children Act claim would almost certainly be linked together by the court and heard at the same time (it being necessary to ensure that the judge is qualified to deal with both civil and family cases). A mother, for example, might fail to persuade the court that the father holds the home on trust for her or that there is any merit in her proprietary estoppel argument but succeed in getting the court to allow her to live in the property or in another property which he must provide until the child has completed tertiary education up to and including first degree.

For swines only

The time: approaching midnight.

The place: a romantic French bistro (though part of a large chain) in Clapham Junction.

Clive Troublesore has wined and dined Mavis Bulwark. Unbeknown to her, whilst Mavis pops to the ladies, he proposes to pay the bill with a selection of vouchers and a 'two for the price of one after 10pm weekdays only' coupon torn out of the *Pet Fanciers Weekly*. It is possible that the bistro may end up owing him money.

The verbal intercourse:

> *"Mavis."*
>
> *"Yes, Clive."*
>
> *"We get on well don't we?"*
>
> *"Yes, Clive."*
>
> *"I've got my rambling place 149 with all that space and you are cooped up in that matchbox next to the station. Come and stay at my place. You can help towards the Xs and we will make music together. You can sign a piece of paper so that you can't take me to the cleaners. As if you would (laughs nervously)."*
>
> *"Ooooh, yes, Clive."*
>
> *"That's settled then."*

Let's leave the bistro and go over to the agreement I have devised for you. I've kept it short and uncomplicated. It gives the prospective cohabitee a licence to occupy the property into which they are to move and should eliminate or reduce the risk, if and when the music stops and the relationship ends, of any allegation being made that you made promises which would enable them to advance a case of proprietary estoppel (see above).

THIS AGREEMENT is made on 2 November 2016 BETWEEN CLIVE TROUBLESORE of 149 Magnolia Crescent Twickenham Middlesex KT89 4XZ ("the House") ("Mr Troublesore") and MAVIS BULWARK of Upper Flat 62 Estuary Lane Clapham Common London SW4 XET ("Ms Bulwark") (together called "the Couple")

BACKGROUND

1. Mr Troublesore owns the House.

2. The Couple are in a relationship.

3. Mr Troublesore is desirous of Ms Bulwark living with him at the House and she is desirous of doing so.

4. Ms Bulwark acknowledges that her present living accommodation is unsatisfactory and that in relation to her employment base and the locations of her family and friends it would be as convenient if not more convenient for her to live in the House instead of remaining in her present accommodation.

5. Mr Troublesore does not intend that Ms Bulwark should acquire any legal or beneficial interest in the House beyond the terminable right to occupy it as hereinafter granted or to become entitled to a tenancy or the right to exclusive possession of the House or any part of it and Ms Bulwark acknowledges and accepts that this is the position and further that this is fair and reasonable.

6. Ms Bulwark acknowledges that she has read this agreement and fully understands it and has either obtained independent legal advice on it or that she is aware of her right to do so and of the preparedness of Mr Troublesore to pay the cost of her obtaining such advice.

7. Ms Bulwark acknowledges and accepts that should during the currency of this agreement she make any payments in respect of the House and/or for the entire or partial benefit of Mr Troublesore which she is not obligated to make by the terms of this agreement then she shall nevertheless not be acquiring a beneficial interest in the House or any rights relating to the House to which she would not otherwise be entitled by the terms of this agreement by making such payments.

8. The couple intend and acknowledge that this agreement shall be legally binding on each of them.

IT IS HEREBY AGREED THAT in consideration of the above matters and the mutual acknowledgements and concessions made by them:

1. Mr Troublesore grants to Ms Bulwark the personal licence to live with him in the House and to use the fixtures fittings furniture and equipment in the House with Mr Troublesore and in common with any other person whom Mr Troublesore may from time to time permit to live in or otherwise occupy the House.

2. Ms Bulwark agrees with Mr Troublesore that during the currency of this licence she will:

a. pay to Mr Troublesore the sum of £100 per week payable weekly with the first payment to be made seven days after the date of this agreement or such other weekly sum as the parties may from time to time agree in writing towards the living and other expenses arising out of her occupation of the House.

b. not cause or permit any other person to occupy the House without the prior consent of Mr Troublesore.

3. This licence shall come to an end:

a. forthwith upon Mr Troublesore giving Ms Bulwark written notice that he revokes the licence and why so in the event that Ms Bulwark fails to comply with paragraph 2(a) and/or (b) of this agreement; or

b. forthwith upon Ms Bulwark permanently vacating the House with the intention of never returning; or

c. at the expiration of not less than one month's written notice by Mr Troublesore or in the event of his death by his personal representatives.

IN WITNESS whereof the parties have executed this instrument as a deed on the day and year first before written

SIGNED AS A DEED BY

CLIVE TROUBLESORE in

the presence of:

SIGNED AS A DEED BY

MAVIS BULWARK in

the presence of:-

Pet time

If you have or may have a pet while living together then you can deal in this agreement with what is to happen to them on separation. You will find some suitable wording in our pre-nuptial agreement at chapter 46. It will need some tweaking to suit the different type of relationship.

Dead or alive?

Should one cohabitee expire with either the survivor inheriting nothing under the will or, there being no will, inheriting nothing under the intestacy laws, then the survivor could still be smiling, of course after a suitable period of mourning (see chapter 32).

An alternative cohabitation agreement

You will find another template for a cohabitation agreement - trendily called a *living together* agreement - along with a checklist, both of which you can download free, on www.advicenow.org.uk. It covers every conceivable situation which could arise during a relationship but you can pick and choose the bits you want and disregard the rest. For couples in for the long haul, I commend it. The difficulty is that if one of you produces it to the other before a relationship is given a cohabitation try out it could frighten the other off unless one of you is a forensic accountant and the other is an actuary. Some of my best friends are forensic accountants or actuaries so please do not take umbrage if that happens to be your calling.

Chapter 46

Pre-Nuptial Agreements With What Should Happen To Fifi Thrown In

"I loves you but..."

And it's a big but. It's the but about being terrified your hard grafted dosh and that fat inheritance Aunt Dora left you could go down the drain if and when you marry or enter into a civil partnership and the relationship later fails. Not quite down the drain but to your partner, though the drain would be the destination of your perception. Personally, I don't know how you could do it: how you could be so smitten as to want to spend the rest of your life with this man or woman and at the same time contemplate the destruction of the relationship and that they would then want to take you to the matrimonial bleed-dry cleaners? How could you seek their signature to a pre-nuptial/partnership agreement - the agreement that dare not speak its name? There must also be a modicum of risk that your partner will tell you to get on your bike. There are special, exceptional situations of course. The couple in the late summer or autumn of their lives who have children may be desperate to preserve a good chunk of their assets for them when it's mortal coils time. He or she who has been married before and after bitter proceedings has saved the matrimonial home at great personal expense and is apoplectic at the idea of losing it should the new relationship come to a summary end. For them I can have some sympathy.

Still, it has nothing to do with me. If you want a pre-nuptial agreement, have one. As a solicitor-advocate, I represented plenty of defendants who pleaded 'not guilty, my Lord' when I was convinced in my heart that they were guilty. It wasn't for me to decide on guilt or innocence. It was for the court. And so it is not for me to pass judgment on you (well not now, anyway). It is for you to decide whether to go pre-nuptial and I'll do my best to give you a reasonably digestible agreement which you can use.

There's something you need to understand about a pre-nuptial agreement. It won't be watertight. It could go wrong but, on the other hand, it could go right so it has the potential to save you a fortune. It could go wrong when your partner decides to challenge it in court in financial proceedings which are allied to the nullity, divorce, partnership dissolution or separation case. The court may uphold it or reject it.

Here are the ground rules:

- The agreement must be freely entered into by both sides with a full appreciation of its implications. Duress (gun to the head or as good as) or fraud or misrepresentation by one party to the other aggrieved party will secure the consignment of the agreement to the matrimonial court waste paper bin. Undue pressure ("I know it's all happening tomorrow and you've got two hundred members of your family coming and Neil Diamond is doing the cabaret and we are honeymooning in the Bahamas but if you don't put your signature where I am pointing, you can count me out") will tarnish the agreement and may well render it worthless. The court may take into account a party's emotional state, what pressures they were under to agree, their age and maturity and whether they have been married or in a partnership or a long-term relationship before. To ensure that appreciation of the agreement's implications exist, each side should obtain independent advice from a lawyer. Sorry, but you can't jeopardise the whole enterprise by going lawyer-shy.
- The agreement must be fair to both sides. It is likely to be unfair if it leaves one side in a predicament of real need, while the other enjoys sufficiency or more. If, for example, one side has been incapacitated during the marriage or partnership and thereby incapable of earning a living, this might justify not holding them to the full rigours of the agreement as it would be unfair to do so. It is also likely to be unfair where the devotion of one side to looking after the family and the home has left the other free to accumulate wealth which the agreement says they can keep for themselves.
- There must have been full disclosure of financial information by each party to the other.
- The agreement cannot be allowed to prejudice the reasonable requirements of any children of the family (that is to say children of the union or other children who have been treated as such).
- Respect should be accorded to the decision of a couple as to the manner in which their financial affairs should be regulated particularly where the agreement addresses existing circumstances (especially where it seeks to protect property acquired before the start of the marriage or partnership) and not merely the contingencies of an uncertain future (for example, a term of the agreement which says: *"The Husband's business may or may not win very substantial contracts at some point in the future, which if won could earn him an additional annual income of in excess of £69,000,000 and which could even reach a figure which is double or triple that but in that event the Wife shall not been entitled*

to enjoy any part of such income by way of periodical maintenance, a capitalised sum or otherwise.")

So here's the sort of agreement that can be entered into which would need to be adapted according to the circumstances of each individual case. It can also be the model for an agreement between a couple who are contemplating entering into a civil partnership in which event revisions to the agreement should record that it is intended that the agreement should still hold good and be effective if the civil partnership is followed by a marriage and it is the marriage which fails. And as a special treat, the agreement deals with what is to happen to the family pet on breakdown. Judges will be eternally grateful to parties who can reach an agreement on such a subject as pet disputes are about as judicially popular as cases involving a determination on who keeps the sugar tongs. Even the Law Society recommends that parties address pet care in the event of a breakdown. For pet haters, please tweak the agreement suitably and perhaps take in a human but check their teeth first.

THIS DEED is made on 14 July 2016 BETWEEN CLIVE TROUBLESORE ("Mr Troublesore") and MAVIS BULWARK ("Ms Bulwark") (together called "the couple") both of 149 Magnolia Crescents Twickenham Middlesex KT89 4XZ

BACKGROUND

1. The couple intend to marry one another no later than 31 December 2016.

2. The couple have the earnest hope and expectation that their marriage will last for the entirety of their joint lives but have decided after the most careful consideration and with the benefit of the legal advice referred to below to enter into this agreement with the wish that its provisions shall govern their financial affairs in the unfortunate event that the marriage breaks down and it is annulled, dissolved or the subject of a judicial separation upon a decree in favour of either or both of them.

3. It would be anathema to the couple to face the potentially heavy cost and, in particular, the unpleasantness of contested financial proceedings following a breakdown of their marriage. It is a matter of comfort to the couple to know in advance albeit without absolute certainty how they would financially stand following a breakdown of their marriage and they perceive this to be one of the many advantages of this agreement. Whilst they recognise that this agreement cannot prevent a court from examining this agreement and that the court's discretion to depart from its terms, wholly or in part, cannot be excluded, it is the couple's strong wish that the court should uphold it in its entirety.

4. The couple are in no doubt that it is and would continue to be fair to them both and to any children of the family for this agreement to govern their financial affairs should the marriage break down. This conclusion is based on all the relevant circumstances including the disclosure of the present financial circumstances of them both as referred to below and the legal advice they have obtained which is also referred to below.

5. The couple accept that the other of them has acted honourably in wanting this agreement and in their discussions and conduct preceding the agreement and are satisfied that its terms not only satisfy the legal test of fairness but are morally fair and right.

6. The couple acknowledge that neither of them has been put under any pressure by the other or by anyone else to enter into this agreement and that, for example, neither of them has threatened or indicated by themselves or anyone on their behalf that they would not proceed with the marriage if this agreement were not made.

7. The couple have each received legal advice on the draft of this agreement (which was in exactly the same terms as the agreement itself). The advice was in plain English which each of them fully understood. The advice was given to each of them independently of the other and was given to Mr Troublesore by Mr Freeman Hardy-Willis of Speakeasy, Solicitors of Twickenham and to Ms Bulwark by Ms Amelia Doughty-Fighter of Sodscrews Law, solicitors of Richmond-upon-Thames.

8. Mr Troublesore declares that (a) he owns or has some interest which he specifies in the capital assets which are set out in Part 1 of the schedule to this agreement; (b) he has done what has been reasonably possible to provide an approximate figure as to the open market value of those capital assets where their actual value cannot be readily quantified; (c) he is satisfied that all values are reasonably accurate; and (d) he is entitled to the income particularised in Part 2 of the schedule to this agreement.

9. Ms Bulwark declares that (a) she owns or has some interest which she specifies in the capital assets which are set out in Part 3 of the schedule to this agreement; (b) she has done what has been reasonably possible to provide an approximate figure as to the open market value of those capital assets where their actual value cannot be readily quantified; (c) she is satisfied that all values are reasonably accurate; and (d) she is entitled to the income particu-

larised in Part 4 of the schedule to this agreement.

10. The couple accept and agree that the terms of this deed cannot and shall not affect the rights of any child of the couple or treated as a child of the couple as at the date of the marriage or who shall hereafter be born to Ms Bulwark by Mr Troublesore or become a child of the family and that the jurisdiction of the courts to order provision for any such child is preserved and shall not be ousted or in any way affected by the terms of this deed and the couple further accept and agree that the birth of any such child or the fact that a child shall come to be treated as a child of the family is not intended to be a circumstance which would justify Ms Bulwark becoming entitled to any financial or other provision from Mr Troublesore over and above that set out in the hereinafter mentioned Part 5.

NOW THIS DEED WITNESSES as follows:

1. This agreement is conditional on Mr Troublesore and Ms Bulwark being lawfully married to one another no later than 31 December 2016 and shall come into full force and effect forthwith on the celebration of such marriage.

2. In the event of the marriage being annulled, dissolved or the subject of a judicial separation upon a decree in favour of either of Mr Troublesore or Ms Bulwark (a) the financial and any other provision that Mr Troublesore shall make for Ms Bulwark shall be as set out in Part 5 of the schedule to this agreement ("Part 5") and subject to clause 4 of this deed; (b) in respect of the couples' pet dog Fifi ("Fifi") or any other dog which the couple may own in succession to Fifi as at the date of such annulment, dissolution or judicial separation ("the pet") the provisions set out in Part 6 of the schedule to this agreement ("Part 6") shall apply; and (c) the couple shall take all steps that are reasonably possible if called upon by the other of them to do so to cause an order of the court to be made incorporating the provision set out in Part 5 and the provisions of Part 6 and subject thereto dismissing all claims for capital property and maintenance by each of them against the other (the dismissal of Ms Bulwark's maintenance claims to take effect upon her entitlement to maintenance under this deed coming to an end) and debarring each of them upon the death of the other from applying for provision under the Inheritance (Provision for Family and Dependants) Act 1975 as amended and in the event that the court is precluded from dismissing any such claim in proceedings for a judicial separation the couple shall take all such steps that are reasonably possible if called upon by the other of them to do so to cause an order of the court to be made in subsequent proceedings for annulment or dissolution dismissing all such claims that have not already been dismissed in like manner as hereinbefore specified.

3. In consideration of the financial and any other provision as set out in Part 5 Ms Bulwark agrees that she will make no financial claim of whatsoever nature against Mr Troublesore or any company and/or business in which he shall have an interest arising out of the couple's relationship or the marriage save and except for the purpose of complying with her obligations under clause 2 of this deed.

4. The couple acknowledge and agree that (a) in the event that, contrary to their understanding and intention, any part of this deed shall be void or otherwise invalid and/or unenforceable then the remainder of the deed shall remain fully valid and enforceable; (b) the provisions of this deed shall remain in full force and effect notwithstanding the annulment or dissolution of the marriage or the grant of a judicial separation to either or both of Mr Troublesore and Ms Bulwark; and (c) in the event that the marriage is annulled or dissolved or a decree of judicial separation (or the equivalent thereof) is granted to either or both of Mr Troublesore and Ms Bulwark by a court outside the jurisdiction of England and Wales then the provisions of this deed shall nevertheless have full force and effect and if unable to take the steps set out at clause 2 of this deed for lack of jurisdiction within England and Wales they shall take equivalent steps in the appropriate court outside England and Wales.

5. The couple agree that neither of them shall on the death of the other make any claim for provision against the estate of the other under the Inheritance (Provision for Family and Dependants) Act 1975 (as amended).

THE SCHEDULE referred to above

Part 1

149 Magnolia Crescent Twickenham Middlesex KT89 4XZ - open market value with vacant possession £950,000 less outstanding mortgage of £60,000.

Land adjoining 149 Magnolia Crescent as above (including allowance for development potential for 12 detached dwellinghouses) - £3,750,000.

Back editions of 'Radio Times - £3,000.

Copy of 'Gold's Law' published in March 1989 - £1,500.

Copy of 'Gold's Law' published in March 1989 signed by the author - £1.50.

Collection of antiques - £150,000.

Building Society investments - £1,750,000.

Stocks and shares - £3,000,000.

Part 2

£750,000 per annum.

Part 3

Wet Wet Wet CD - 5p.

Jewellery (Primark) - £2.50.

Part 4

Nil.

Part 5

A: Upon nullity, dissolution or judicial separation decree within two years of the date of the marriage

Mr Troublesore shall pay Ms Bulwark a lump sum of £750,000 within 28 days of decree absolute or decree of judicial separation.

Mr Troublesore shall pay Ms Bulwark maintenance for herself at the rate of £5,000 per annum during their joint lives for a term of three years as from the date of decree absolute or decree of judicial separation.

In the event that there is a child or there are children of the family the lump sum shall increase from £750,000 to £850,000.

B: Upon nullity, dissolution or judicial separation decree within two to six years of the date of the marriage

Mr Troublesore shall pay Ms Bulwark a lump sum of £1,500,000 within 28 days of decree absolute or decree of judicial separation.

Mr Troublesore shall pay Ms Bulwark maintenance for herself at the rate of £7,500 per annum during their joint lives for a term of six years as from the date of decree absolute or decree of judicial separation.

In the event that there is a child or there are children of the family the lump sum shall increase from £1,500,000 to £2,000,000.

Mr Troublesore shall transfer to Ms Bulwark his interest in his signed copy of Gold's Law.

C: Upon nullity, dissolution or judicial separation decree after six years of the date of the marriage

Mr Troublesore shall pay Ms Bulwark a lump sum of £3,000,000 within 28 days of decree absolute or decree of judicial separation.

Mr Troublesore shall pay Ms Bulwark maintenance for herself at the rate of £10,000 per annum during their joint lives for a term which shall end upon Ms Bulwark attaining the age of 65, as from the date of decree absolute or decree of judicial separation.

In the event that there is a child or there are children of the family the lump sum shall increase from £3,000,000 to £3,500,000.

Mr Troublesore shall transfer to Ms Bulwark his interest in his signed copy of 'Breaking Law'.

Part 6

Fifi is owned by the couple in equal shares.

Any pet acquired by the couple or either of them in succession to Fifi shall be owned by each of them in equal shares notwithstanding how as between the couple the cost of and incidental to acquisition and the cost of maintenance and care have been borne.

Subject to any contrary agreement which the couple may make from time to time:

- *the pet shall live with each of Mr Troublesore and Ms Bulwark for alternate weeks save and except that when for any period ("the period") it is not reasonably possible or convenient for the pet to be in their care Mr Troublesore and Ms Bulwark shall give the other of them the first option to care for the pet during the period and in the event of such option not being taken up Mr Troublesore or Ms Bulwark (as the case may be) shall ensure the pet is cared for at the expense of the one of them who should have been caring for the pet by a responsible adult in their stead during the period and shall notify the other of them of the name and address of the carer and the other of them shall be entitled to contact with the pet during the period.*

- *The parties shall during the lifetime of the pet take out annually a pet insurance policy in standard terms to include cover for veterinary fees and expenses and neither of them shall do or omit to do any act or thing which may invalidate the insurance.*

- *During each and every period that the pet is living with Mr Troublesore and Ms Bulwark each of them shall (a) use their best endeavours to ensure the safety and welfare of the pet including complying with the requirements of the Animal Welfare Act 2006 ("the Act") and all regulations and codes of practice made thereunder and any other legislation from time to time in force relating to the safety and welfare of animals and shall not commit any offence under the Act or any other such legislation or any such regulations; and (b) pay for the cost of feeding and otherwise maintaining the pet save and except that all fees and expenses of veterinary surgeons and the premiums on such polices of insurance as the couple shall from time to time take out in respect to the pet shall be borne equally by them.*

IN WITNESS whereof the parties have executed this instrument as a deed on the day and year first before written

SIGNED AS A DEED BY

CLIVE TROUBLESORE in

the presence of:-

SIGNED AS A DEED BY

MAVIS BULWARK in

the presence of:-

Chapter 47

The No Sex Agreement

A customised marriage or civil partnership

This is positively not an early April Fool. There *are* couples who wish to marry or enter into a civil partnership without the sex. More than you may think. This can be for a variety of reasons, the most likely to be age, incapacity, repugnance or simple disinterest in sexual activity. Companionship may be quite sufficient.

The courts have recognised that some degree of sex is the norm in a marriage between parties of the opposite sex and there is no reason to suppose they would take a different view with a same sex marriage or civil partnership.

In a 1964 case on the ground of cruelty - the precursor, and less onerous ground, of the modern unreasonable behaviour - the parties married when the wife was 18 and the husband 33. They had a child soon afterwards but sexual intercourse ceased about one year later. After 15 years of the husband refusing intercourse, the wife left home. She alleged her health had suffered. She was refused a divorce and her appeal was thrown out. "I'm not satisfied," said the appeal judge, "that the husband was guilty of inexcusable conduct. In view of his natural disinclination for sexual intercourse, to find him guilty of cruelty is rather like beating a dog because it will not eat its food."

And in a 1977 case, the wife was refused a divorce because of her husband's alleged unreasonable behaviour which was based on an unsatisfactory sex life. She said he had been cold and indifferent to intercourse. This had taken place about once a month and, when it did, the husband quickly withdrew. There were upsets and the wife also left home. Even though her word was accepted, the judge hearing the case decided that unreasonable behaviour had not been proved and an appeal court came to the same conclusion.

In 1980 the Court of Appeal ruled that sexual intercourse once a week over a three month period did not amount to unreasonable behaviour when the 30 year old husband used this as the foundation for his divorce petition against his 31 year old wife. The couple had two children during a ten year marriage. The couple had had sexual difficulties over the years and the husband had undergone a vasectomy. The wife's rationing had followed that procedure. Lord Justice Ormrod said: "I find it wholly unreasonable to say that she (the wife) was behaving unreasonably."

If these first two cases were to be rerun now, I would be surprised if the results would be the same. So it is that the party for whom sex is off the matrimonial agenda is vulnerable to their spouse or partner using this as justification for seeking a marriage annulment, a divorce or a partnership dissolution (see chapter 48) and to the financial consequences which could follow. It all depends on the circumstances of each individual case but vulnerability does exist.

My no-sex agreement can be adapted to a civil partnership and to cater for some sex between opposite sex parties which falls short of intercourse. It could scupper an attempt at an annulment of an opposite sex marriage or divorce or civil partnership dissolution on the basis of no-sex. However, in some situations it might not work. Take this one. A healthy and young opposite sex couple enter into an agreement and marry. Later, the wife changes her mind about sex and wants a child through intercourse. The husband though perfectly capable of the act refuses her. The court might well say that the husband's conduct amounted to unreasonable behaviour despite the agreement. There is also a risk that the court would say that the agreement had to be ignored on the ground that it was contrary to public policy and unreasonable. Be that as it may, in the right circumstances, worth a try and, at the least, the agreement could well deter both parties from bringing the bedroom into their matrimonial dispute. That cannot be a bad thing: bedrooms are better left as places of privacy.

THIS AGREEMENT is made on 14 July 2016 BETWEEN CLIVE TROUBLESORE of 149c Magnolia Buildings Twickenham Middlesex KT89 4XZ and MAVIS BULWARK of Upper Flat 62 Estuary Lane Clapham Common London SW4 XET (together called "the parties)

BACKGROUND:

1. The parties are engaged to be married to each other and this agreement is made in contemplation of such marriage taking place by 31 December 2016.

2. The parties intend to display their love and affection for each other during the marriage but have agreed that this shall not extend to engaging in sexual intercourse (or any form of sexual commerce) with each other (or any other person).

3. The parties are desirous that their agreement as described in sub-paragraph (2) above and on incidental matters shall be formally recorded as set out in this document.

4. The parties have each obtained independent legal advice on this agreement and fully understand its terms and its legal implications.

NOW IT IS HEREBY AGREED as follows:

1. This agreement shall come into full force and effect forthwith upon the celebration of the marriage of the parties.

2. During the subsistence of the marriage, neither party shall require or expect the other party to engage in sexual intercourse (or any form of sexual commerce) with them.

3. In any proceedings during the subsistence of the marriage or after its dissolution between the parties or their personal representatives in which the conduct of the parties or either of them may be relevant:

a. neither party to the proceedings shall rely or seek to rely on the abstinence of either party to the marriage from sexual intercourse (or any form of sexual commerce) with the other or the refusal to engage in sexual intercourse (or any form of sexual commerce) with them; and

b. the parties to the proceedings shall invite the court concerned to refrain from taking such abstinence and/or refusal into account in determining any question or issue which shall be relevant to the determination of the proceedings between the parties to the proceedings.

4. Neither party to the marriage nor their personal representatives shall bring any proceedings against the other or the estate of the other of any nature whatsoever during the subsistence of the marriage or after its dissolution which rely wholly or partly on either party to the marriage having abstained from sexual intercourse (or any from of sexual commerce) with the other.

5. Each party shall affirm this agreement in writing if required by the other to do so at any time after the celebration of the marriage.

IN WITNESS whereof the parties have executed this instrument as a deed on the day and year first before written

SIGNED AS A DEED BY

CLIVE TROUBLESORE in

the presence of:-

SIGNED AS A DEED BY
MAVIS MAGNOLIA in
the presence of:-

Chapter 48

Divorce, Judicial Separation, Nullity And Dissolution

That's 'yer lot!

I do solemnly declare that I know of no lawful impediment why I Clive Troublesore may not be joined in marriage to...

Hold on a mo, Mr Registrar. If this goes badly tonight, can I cancel and have my money back?

This is most unorthodox, Mr Troublesore. No cancellation.

What about with six months' notice?

The law does not provide for any notice period.

For a fixed term of 12 months with an option to renew the marriage exercisable no later than half an hour before the first wedding anniversary?

No option.

So how long would I have to wait for a divorce?

12 months, Mr Troublesore, before you start the divorce proceedings and then a few months before you are legally free. That's so long as you have grounds, of course, and your wife doesn't defend the case.

Blimey, grounds as well! Irreconcilable differences, that would be enough.

This isn't California. For a divorce after a year, you would have to prove your wife's adultery or unreasonable behaviour.

What about my adultery?

You can't bring your own divorce case on the grounds of your own misconduct. That would be novel.

I need time.

The bride doesn't. She walked out three questions ago with the engagement ring still on her finger. She can almost certainly keep it. The law presumes it was a gift but Clive can always have a go at showing the contrary was intended. I don't rate his chances. There's no hope of damages on a claim for breach of promise of marriage. That quaint route to some appeasing lolly was abolished years ago. As for engagement and wedding presents, the law presumes them to belong to the person whose relatives or friends gifted them but the court might be persuaded in a particular case that the couple intended an equal sharing. That's another story. This story is about getting unlocked from a marriage or civil partnership that has broken down - or keeping the lock on!

The registrar was right. There can be no divorce unless the party who brings proceedings has grounds and so it is with same-sex marriages as well. Two of the grounds require proof of the other party's misconduct and the other grounds depend on a period of separation. Dissolution is a civil partnership's version of divorce and this works in a similar way.

Adultery

The other party's adultery is the first ground so long as the party asking for divorce finds it intolerable to live with them. The intolerability does not have to arise out of the adultery. You could have the situation in which the adultery does not trouble you - because, say, you had had 149.5 affairs yourself - but you could not tolerate living with your spouse by reason of their incessant snoring. That's good enough. Once upon a time, those after a divorce had to personally attend court to give evidence. There I was having a pre-hearing discussion with a petitioner at court on the day - the case had been prepared by an executive in my firm and I was dealing with the advocacy - and I was running through the evidence they would be required to give.

> *So, madam, do you find it intolerable to live with your husband?*
>
> *No.*
>
> *I beg your pardon.*
>
> *I could tolerate living with him.*
>
> *But he has committed adultery, is living with another woman by whom he has had a child and you have chosen to bring divorce proceedings against him.*
>
> *Yes, I know but I could still tolerate living with him again.*
>
> *Is there any chance of a reconciliation? Would he ever come back to you?*
>
> *No, but I could still tolerate living with him again.*

This candour was admiral albeit coming rather belatedly. It could have been overcome by the lady changing her grounds to unreasonable behaviour on the basis of an improper relationship on the husband's part - she would in effect have been saying that she could not reasonably be expected to live with him in view of the behaviour although she herself would have been prepared to do so if he was prepared to come back which he wasn't! - though this would have involved an adjournment. In the event, after, I must confess, a few table thumps and some eyebrow raising (on my part, not hers) plus a reminder of how much the lady had spent on the case so far, she decided she could not tolerate living with her husband again. I gave four internal cheers when she said so in the witness box.

Should you have committed adultery yourself and have brought divorce or judicial separation proceedings, you can lawfully keep quiet about what you have been up to. Under the old law, it was otherwise. The eyebrows of the judge at Portsmouth County Court (as it then was) before whom I was appearing shot up to the rafters as his mouth simultaneously dropped open in disbelief. He has just read my client's discretion statement. Eh? The law was that if you were relying on your spouse's adultery to get a divorce or judicial separation and you yourself had committed adultery then you had to confess that in a statement to the court which would then have a discretion to refuse you what you were asking for. The confession had to be in writing and lodged with the court in a sealed envelope when the case was started. At the court hearing, the envelope would be opened with a flourish by the court clerk and be shown to the judge. On this occasion, my client had confessed to committing adultery during the marriage with 24 different women over a period of three years. He was mighty proud of it. It would have been a paradigm case for the judge to have refused a divorce but he was obviously impressed at the client's prowess - and honesty - and a divorce was duly granted.

Some other points on adultery:

- You are not obliged to name the person with whom adultery is alleged. If you do, they must be made a co-respondent - man or woman - and served with the court papers. It is rare for the person to be named: instead the petitioner usually alleges adultery with "an unnamed person" or "an unknown person". Why would you want to name them? Because you want them to pay the costs of the case. You could apply for costs against your spouse or the co-respondent or both. Your quest for costs against the co-respondent would probably fail if you could not prove they knew your spouse was married when adultery occurred or the court decided that the marriage was dead and buried well before the co-respondent came onto the scene. Or you might want to name them so as to cause them maximum discomfort. Any prospective co-respondent would be well advised to carry a mock-up of a summons for jury service or a county court claim form in their back pocket so that they can do a quick swap should a divorce petition land on the breakfast table over toast and coffee with their spouse.

- Adultery is not a ground for divorce in a same-sex marriage or for civil partnership dissolution (which is the civil partnership version of divorce) and when you come to think of it, that makes pretty good sense.
- There's no adultery without sexual intercourse.
- If actual intercourse cannot be established by direct or circumstantial evidence but it is possible to prove a romantic relationship then a divorce could be sought on the ground of unreasonable behaviour (see below), relying on an "improper relationship".
- Not so many years ago, when there was an actual hearing of even an uncontested divorce case, the practice was to prove the adultery with evidence from an enquiry agent who had taken written statements from the other party and the co-respondent in which they confessed to adultery. The statements were often obtained in a seedy hotel room and the agent would have observed items of male and female attire in close proximity. I sometimes wondered whether the very same items of attire were featuring in all the cases and if they were ever washed. As a solicitor, I once instructed a firm of private enquiry agents run by ex-police officers to attempt to gather adultery evidence against a wife who was denying to her husband a relationship with another man. This wasn't hotel room stuff but overnight bungalow close encounters stuff and called for discreet observations. Having spotted the other man's car parked close by at around 3am, two agents commenced observations and waited for the man to emerge. Some eight hours and about £200 later they got a bit peckish and decided - both of them! - to make a quick visit to the local chippie. By the time they had got back, the man had gone. I never instructed them again. Nowadays, the norm is for the other party to confirm in the form of receipt for the divorce papers - the *acknowledgment of service* it is called - that they admit the adultery alleged and for the petitioner to say why adultery is alleged and that will be quite sufficient proof.
- And what pain can be inflicted on the co-respondent? There's that order for costs. Sometimes there's a punch on the nose or a spiking of mascara (depending on the co-respondent's gender) though that could lead to a criminal charge so do not go there. There used to be a right for the petitioner to claim damages for adultery against a male co-respondent. Such claims were only occasionally made. I once negotiated settlement of a claim where the wealthy co-respondent had lured the wife away from her hapless husband

with gifts of jewellery and crispy bank notes. The co-respondent paid up what in today's money would amount to around £20,000. Damages for adultery are no more.

Unreasonable behaviour

We are talking here about the respondent having behaved in such a way that you cannot reasonably be expected to live with them. This ground is a substitute for the former ground of cruelty though less onerous to prove. Sometimes the most ludicrous behaviour is relied on and if the respondent does not defend, the divorce goes through but you can never be sure how relaxed the court is going to be about allowing a weak petition to succeed. The trick is to particularise sufficient unreasonable behaviour in the petition but not go over the top because that could provoke the respondent into defending. After all, he wouldn't want his mum or new girlfriend to see that he is in to black eyes and blue moods more than once a month, would he? Some general allegations and then some examples of specific incidents including the most recent one are recommended.

Respondents are often hesitant about allowing an unreasonable behaviour petition to go through undefended because they fear this could prejudice them in the financial aspects of the case. They should fear not. It is only in the most extreme and rare cases that the respondent's conduct which has founded the petition will increase the money or property the petitioner will be awarded when the court comes to decide on the finances (see chapter 49).

Mrs Troublesore might be particularising Clive's unreasonable behaviour like this:

a. Throughout the marriage the respondent frequently used abusive and insulting language to the petitioner and made hurtful remarks to her about her appearance and mother.

b. Throughout the marriage the respondent frequently embarrassed the petitioner by making in her presence unjustified and vexatious complaints to firms with which he had contracted about the quality of goods and/or services supplied to him.

c. Throughout the marriage the respondent refused or neglected to provide an adequate allowance to the petitioner for the household food and other necessaries he expected her to buy.

d. Throughout the marriage, the respondent made excessive sexual demands of the petitioner well knowing that this distressed and tired her.

e. On 31st July 2014 the respondent slapped the petitioner's face, falsely complaining that the dinner she had prepared for him was "a plate of shite".

f. On 14th July 2016 the respondent locked the petitioner out of the matrimonial home for 12 hours having falsely alleged that she had winked at a leaflet distributor in an encouraging way.

g. These particulars are not exhaustive and the petitioner reserves the right to amend this petition to add further particulars if the respondent defends.

The separation grounds

The remaining grounds depend on the parties having lived apart for a minimum set period. The most straightforward of these is that there has been a separation lasting at least two years and that the respondent consents to divorce or dissolution of a civil partnership. Potential problems are that the court will not usually be prepared to order the respondent to pay the petitioner's costs on a two-year separation petition unless the respondent agrees to do so and, for a variety of reasons, the respondent may not wish to actively consent to the divorce or partnership dissolution. Here's a suggested way round these problems.

Dear Clive

Sued anyone lately?! There is no hope for our marriage and you know I have decided to divorce you. It is regrettable that you have so far been hostile to the idea but, be in no doubt, I will not be deterred. I can divorce you on the ground of unreasonable behaviour on which I have a very strong case. However, I am prepared to refrain from having to make allegations in the divorce papers about the disgusting way you have treated me throughout the marriage and instead to divorce you on the ground that we have been separated for over two years and you consent to the divorce. My conditions are that you confirm to me within the next week that you will consent and also that you will agree to the court ordering you to repay my divorce costs which will be the court fee amounting to £550.

Yours

Mavis

If the other party has deserted the petitioner for at least two years then consent to divorce or partnership dissolution is not needed. Desertion occurs when one of the parties walks out on the other against their will.

Say the other party will not consent to a divorce or partnership dissolution on the ground of two years' separation and there's no desertion because the party after divorce or dissolution was the one who walked out, threw out the other party or was overjoyed to see the back of them? In the absence of the respondent's adultery or unreasonable behaviour, the party after divorce or dissolution is in a bit of a jam. The tactic sometimes adopted is for them to start their own proceedings in which they make puerile allegations of unreasonable behaviour against the other, not with the intention that they will be the party obtaining the divorce or dissolution but so as to provoke the other into action.

"Look at this Maude. That b......d Clive has started a divorce against me! He says I distressed him by refusing to support him in meritorious civil proceedings he instituted during the marriage, failed to fan him in hot weather and forbade him from having sexual relations more than twice a week. I'm not having it. He's not having a divorce against me. I'll defend and divorce him. You mark my words!"

And that has been known to work. If it doesn't then the party after divorce or partnership dissolution will have to wait until the separation has lasted for at least five years. Divorce or dissolution then is almost certainly assured no matter how diabolical their own conduct may have been. *Almost* certainly assured? That's because the party hostile to divorce or dissolution can scupper it if they can satisfy the court that divorce or partnership dissolution would result in grave financial or other hardship to them and that it would be wrong to end the marriage or partnership. It's a notoriously difficult defence to succeed with. Where the financial implications of divorce or dissolution are relied on by the respondent - for example, a wife may be saying that she would lose out on a substantial amount of money under the husband's pension scheme in the event of him dying before her as she would no longer be his widow, if divorced - the petitioner may have to come up with some proposals for compensation so as to combat the defence. Otherwise, the respondent may be saying that divorce or dissolution is contrary to their religious beliefs or would make them a social outcast.

I once represented a man whose wife steadfastly refused to cooperate in bringing an obviously moribund marriage to a respectable end all because she could not accept that it was over. To reinforce the point, with weekly regularity she washed and rewashed the husband's shirts he had left behind and dried them on the garden clothesline. When five years of separation were finally clocked up, the husband issued his divorce petition relying on that lengthy separation as his solitary ground. After some initial resistance, the wife caved in and the case went through as undefended. Hopefully, the wife's washing powder bill dramatically fell.

Separation trap

A spouse or civil partner against whom a divorce or dissolution petition has been presented on the grounds of either two years' separation with their consent or five years' separation can hold up the decree absolute. They do so by relying on section 10(2) of the Matrimonial Causes Act 1973 which requires a specific application. This allows them to apply to the court to consider what will be their financial position after divorce or dissolution. Then the decree absolute will be postponed until the court has either decided that financial provision for them should not be required or that the financial provision made is reasonable and fair or the best that can be made in the circumstances. There is one route out of the decree absolute blockage. The party after the divorce can give an undertaking to make financial provision for the other party - concrete and specific proposals must be put forward - and if the court reckons they are not too far wide of the mark and it is desirable that the decree absolute should be made without delay, it has a discretion to allow the decree absolute to be issued. The application for the court to consider the post-divorce financial position is more often than not coupled with the more usual financial remedies application for maintenance, property transfer etc though it is a useful device to get the best deal out of the petitioning party whose tongue is hanging out for liberation and remarriage. The section 10(2) device is not available where one or more of the other divorce grounds are relied on.

Two households: one roof

It is legally possible for parties to live apart under the same roof so long as they are running separate households in the property. For the purposes of the two and five years' separation grounds, there could be divorce or civil partnership dissolution though the parties have been at the same property for the entirety of the separation period. Likewise, carrying on living at the same address for over six months after adultery was discovered by the petitioner or after the final incident of unreasonable behaviour will not prejudice the petitioner if separate households under the same roof can be established. And why the hell not? The fact that the marriage or partnership has irretrievably broken should not have to mean that the parties sell up or that one of them moves out. I have come across cases where the divorced parties are living at the same property many years after marriage breakdown as it suited them to do so for financial reasons or because they thought this was better for their children. Nevertheless, the court tends to be a little suspicious in these same address situations so deal with the point when you make your statement in support of the petition: otherwise, the court will probably raise queries which would lead to delay. Whatever happens, do not answer the question posed in the statement form about whether you have lived with the respondent since you became aware of their adultery etc in the affirmative. The correct answer will be 'No'. And you might be saying something like this:

"I have continued to live at 149 Magnolia Crescent, Twickenham since 14th July 2014 to the date of this statement. Throughout this period, the respondent has also lived at the same address. However, we have not lived together but in separate households under the same roof. The reason for this is that neither of us was in a position to obtain what would have been a necessary mortgage advance to buy alternative accommodation for single occupancy. At all times, we have slept in separate bedrooms and no sexual relations have taken place. We have prepared our own meals and eaten them separately. We have been responsible for our own washing and ironing and the cleaning of the parts of the accommodation we have separately occupied. We have maintained separate bank accounts and contributed equally to the mortgage repayments and other outgoings on the property. We have not socialised together or taken holidays together. We have not entertained our respective friends at the property on any joint function. We have behaved civilly towards each other but in all respects have led our own lives for the whole time and in contemplation that one of us would bring divorce proceedings against the other when the law permitted."

But there's no irretrievable breakdown

A respondent implacably opposed to their marriage or partnership coming to an end could say to the court; "Yes, I have committed adultery. Yes, I have behaved unreasonably. Yes, I deserted the petitioner. Yes, we have lived separately for over five years. But I love her, I want her and I know it can work." I doubt that William Hill would take any bets on that defence succeeding but it is theoretically possible for a respondent to admit to what is alleged against them but still contend that there is still hope for the marriage or partnership.

Reconciliation attempts

The law encourages parties to try and mend their relationships but a party after divorce or partnership dissolution is under no legal obligation to enter into mediation or counselling with a view to doing so. Either party can begin divorce or dissolution proceedings without going within a square mile of a mediator or counsellor or mentioning what they think about reconciliation prospects to the court (although there are different rules when it comes to financial applications within matrimonial proceedings and cases involving children under the Children Act 1989). Curiously, the procedure changes when a lawyer is acting for a petitioner for divorce or civil partnership dissolution for they must notify the court when starting the case whether they have discussed the possibility of reconciliation with their client and given them the names and addresses of people qualified to help over a reconciliation. However, they don't have to discuss and give this information but simply say whether they have done so and the court will not bat an eyelid even if they say they have not done it!

Where the law is active about reconciliation is in permitting parties to live together for certain periods without destroying the grounds for divorce or partnership dissolution. So it is that if parties have lived together for up to six months (in one go or in the aggregate) any adultery of which the respondent was aware beforehand can still be relied on. As we have seen, after six months, it cannot. But if the adultery is wiped out because they are together for more than six months, any fresh adultery, even with the same person, which occurred after the reconciliation attempt began may afford a fresh ground. Similarly, in an unreasonable behaviour case, the parties can live together for up to six months after the final incident being relied on without the ground being destroyed but if the respondent returns to kicking and beating or whatever after the six months, the old behaviour will be revived and the petitioner will be able to rely on the old and the new stuff. And in calculating whether there has been desertion for two years or a separation which has lasted for two or five years, living together for up to six months after the separation started will not destroy the grounds but neither can it be reckoned towards the two years or five years.

Divorce/partnership dissolution v nullity

A thumping enormous away win when it comes to this match. If the marriage or civil partnership is ended by nullity instead of divorce or dissolution then the parties are treated as though they had never been in the marriage or civil partnership. You could have twenty marriages annulled and advertise yourself as new goods. Among the nullity grounds for opposite sex marriages are non-consummation due to the incapacity of either party (so that the petitioner can rely on their own incapacity) or the respondent's wilful refusal to consummate. For all marriages, a nullity could be secured on the grounds that at the time of the marriage the respondent was suffering from venereal disease in a communicable form or that the respondent was pregnant by someone else but in both these situations the case must be started within three years of the marriage. And with all the nullity grounds mentioned it is a defence that the petitioner led the respondent to believe that they would not bring nullity proceedings when they knew it was open to them to do so and that it would be unjust to the respondent to grant an annulment.

Is anybody there?

Usually no, when it comes to undefended matrimonial cases. Nowadays, the petitioner's evidence will be given in a written statement and, generally, the only hearing will be when the judge pronounces a decree in court. Then the parties can attend if so inclined but the entertainment factor is minus 1,000,000. A generic "I hereby pronounce the decrees in these cases to which the relevant parties are entitled in accordance with the certificates which have been given" (or words to this effect) will be declared in relation to thirty or so cases at a time. If anyone turns up it will probably be a respondent to argue about whether they should have to pay the petitioner's costs or one of the parties after the decree absolute being expedited (see below). The application for the decree absolute when made by the petitioner is again a paper exercise.

I have fond memories of attending matrimonial hearings as a trainee solicitor when the petitioner had to turn up to give evidence in support of their petition for divorce or whatever. Judges could find the endless repetition of substantially the same stories a tedious business and many a yawn was stifled. At Southampton one afternoon the judge who was a crusty and mature part-timer playing the part of a High Court member of the judiciary enquired, with a jolt, of the petitioner's barrister: "Mr Field-Fisher, where am I?" to which Mr Field-Fisher calmly responded "Your Lordship is sitting in Southampton." Come to think of it, there was not much else he could have said.

The race is on

An undefended divorce, partnership dissolution or nullity case will take anything from around three to six months from start to finish depending on pressure of work at the regional centre at which the case is being handled and the level of efficiency there. Procedural changes which came about in 2015 have resulted in a faster process with cases being started out of one of the six national centres which have been established. That estimate includes the six weeks and a day which must elapse from the date of the first decree - the *decree nisi* or, in the case of partnership dissolution, the *conditional order* - until the petitioner can apply for the second decree which is called the *decree absolute* or, in the case of partnership dissolution, the *final order*. Not until the second decree will the parties be legally liberated and free to try it again. Should the petitioner fail to promptly apply for the decree absolute then the application can be made by the respondent once three months have elapsed from the earliest date on which the petitioner could have applied: effectively after six weeks and a day plus three months.

But is there a way of accelerating progress to the first decree? Yes. For a start, ask the court to send you the papers which have to be delivered to the respondent instead of the court posting them. Arrange for the respondent to have them - you are not allowed to personally serve them yourself but you can get a responsible adult to do the job for you - and to complete and return to the court the form of acknowledgment of service of the petition which will be included with the papers and, at the same time, send you a photocopy. Whilst waiting for that to be done you can be drafting out the statement of your evidence in support of the petition - you can get the form of statement from the court or online at www.hmctsformfinder.gov.uk - so you are ready to pounce and apply to the court for the first decree with your statement the moment the court has notified you that the acknowledgment of service sent in by the respondent has been received by them. In suitable circumstances, you could apply to the court when lodging your statement to expedite the pronouncement. Then you could turn up at court when the decree is due to be pronounced - the time, date and venue will have been notified to you - and ask the judge to expedite (cut down on the six weeks and one day) the making of the second decree. A letter from the respondent consenting to expedition would be most valuable. An application for expedition can also be made after decree nisi but this would involve a fee and a special hearing for the application. You wish to ensure that the child you or your partner is expecting can be born legitimate or to remarry a terminally ill person? This may be sufficient reason but expedition is the exception and not the rule.

And now for something a little different

Judicial separation is available on the same grounds as divorce and partnership dissolution (though it is simply called separation in the case of a partnership). *Irretrievable* breakdown of the relationship is not alleged. The legal effect of a decree is that it is no longer obligatory for the petitioner to cohabit with the respondent. Big deal! The attraction of judicial separation in practice is that it can be sought, unlike divorce and partnership dissolution, within one year of cutting the cake - within five minutes if you like - and a decree empowers the court to grant the same financial remedies like maintenance, lump sums and sales and transfers of property (but not dismissal of claims for financial remedies or pension sharing) as on divorce and partnership dissolution. There is nothing to prevent either party going for divorce or partnership dissolution at a later date. The petitioner who has obtained a judicial separation can rely on the same grounds for the subsequent divorce or partnership dissolution.

For the party who, for whatever reason, does not wish to give the other freedom from the marriage or partnership and prefers to see them sweat out five years' separation before they can start their own proceedings as they have no other grounds, judicial separation tends to do nicely.

Defending

So you don't fancy the idea of the petitioner obtaining the decree they are after? You can defend by putting in an *answer* which is a defence to the petition. Relatively few cases are defended. The reason is that the grant of a decree to one party no longer has any impact on what the other party is going to be paying or receiving when finances are decided (see chapter 49). But if say your wife has falsely alleged that you are a paedophile arsonist who murdered his mother, I can understand you might not be prepared to let that go uncontested. Frequently, a respondent to an unreasonable behaviour petition will negotiate with the petitioner for particular allegations in the petition which they find obnoxious or highly embarrassing to be deleted in return for not defending the case.

In addition to defending, the respondent who has grounds could issue their own petition in the same proceedings seeking a divorce, partnership dissolution or judicial separation. And there's an alternative course that could be taken. The respondent is able to issue their own petition in the same proceedings without defending the petition against them. Then, for example, you might have the wife asking for a divorce on the ground of the husband's unreasonable behaviour and the husband asking for a divorce on the ground of the wife's adultery. In fact, it is common for both parties to ask for a divorce on the ground of the other's unreasonable behaviour! The court will generally go along with an arrangement which involves the grant of a divorce to each party. An order from the court will be needed converting what is technically a defended case because of the two petitions into an undefended case with double decrees. Then both parties can justifiably brag that they got the divorce.

Wallets out

To start off the matrimonial cases we have been looking at (and there will be a separate fee for any financial application made in the course of the proceedings), you will have to shell out £550 to the court or £365 if you are after a judicial separation. Though it's consoling to weigh against that what you will be saving in anniversary and birthday presents but less consoling to ponder on how much you spent on the wedding. Presenting your own petition in response to the petition against you will set you back the same amount. Putting in an answer (defence) to a petition against you will cost a court fee of £245. Should you both defend with an answer and put in your own petition, you will be looking at a court fees bill of £795 (with a little less when you go for judicial separation). For getting any of these fees remitted, see chapter 13.

Chapter 49

After The Breakdown

The anti-stitch up guide

The marriage or civil partnership has broken down. That phase of your life is over. How the next phase progresses is likely to be deeply affected by how you financially come out of the relationship. The law strives to achieve fairness for both parties. However, there are no scientific formulae to be applied to how income and capital are to be shared for the future. The range of fairness can be very wide indeed: ten different judges may give you ten different ideas of what on a specific set of facts is fair to them. "Please may I not be stitched up." This should be your prayer.

This is a massive topic. My aim is to give you a taster of what orders the court can make and how they will approach these financial cases with some tips on dealing with the slippery customer who is worth chasing for that fair deal.

The menu

The court can make orders against your opponent which cover both income and capital. So far as income is concerned, it can order maintenance for you by way of *periodical payments* which will normally involve equal monthly amounts and, where the payments are temporary and ordered in an emergency type situation (see below) they are called *maintenance pending suit* or *interim periodical payments*, depending on whether or not the final decree has yet been made. It will not usually make an order for maintenance in respect of a child except if you and your opponent agree that there should be an order and how much is to be paid. Child maintenance is otherwise dealt with through the Child Maintenance Service (see chapter 50).

If your opponent is patently untrustworthy and they have some capital to their name, the court might be persuaded to secure the maintenance (for example, by charging a property owned by your opponent) so that, come default in maintenance payments, you can get what you are owed out of the security.

Maintenance for you will last for a period which the court will set: for so many months or years or until you cohabit or remarry but never beyond the grave so that an order will automatically lapse on the death of you or your opponent. If you want maintenance to continue to be payable after your opponent's death out of their estate then they will have to agree and you would need a commitment on this through a deed which would bind their estate. Where the maintenance has lapsed on your opponent's death and they have not made acceptable provision in a will to take the place of the maintenance then you may be able to successfully claim against their estate under the Inheritance (Provision for Family and Dependants) Act 1975 (see chapter 32) unless the right to do so has been excluded by the court when it made a final order in the financial proceedings. A maintenance order can be varied by the court or cancelled where circumstances change.

The court does not like to see a party who has the responsibility or the main responsibility of caring for the children giving up a claim for maintenance before the children have say reached 18 unless they are faring particularly well on capital to compensate for this. Remember that the court will not make an order unless it is satisfied that it is reasonable to do so. The court is no rubber-stamper.

So far as capital is concerned, the court can order your opponent to pay you a lump sum; transfer property to you (like the family home); alter the basis on which property is owned (perhaps say that property should be transferred from your opponent's sole name into your joint names so that you become equal owners); postpone the sale of property (perhaps say that the family home should not be sold until your death, cohabitation, remarriage or the youngest child attains a certain age or finishes full-time education). And the court can give you a share of your opponent's pension (a pension sharing order) or direct that maintenance should be paid to you out of the pension (a pension attachment order).

When it makes its order, the court can be asked to dismiss certain claims of either party or both parties. For example, if one party is scoring over the odds with the capital share they are to walk away with, it might be appropriate for their claims for maintenance to be dismissed. This is known as the *clean break*. Where one party has a good chance of obtaining a sizeable maintenance order but still has a bit of life and hormone activity about them, it may be prudent for them to take a larger slice of the capital and forgo maintenance because any maintenance order could have a short life on account of good cohabitation or remarriage prospects. The capital would not be repayable on remarriage or cohabitation. Conversely in that situation, the other party would be well advised to suffer the maintenance order and keep the capital at a more modest level.

Match rules

In deciding what is fair, the court must have as its first consideration the welfare of any child of the family who is under 18 but look at all the circumstances of the case so that, for example, if it is especially important to one party to have adult children of the family still living with them, the court may be prepared to factor this wish into its decision. Of particular importance to the court will be:

- The income, earning capacity, property and financial resources of the parties - now and in the foreseeable future.
- Their financial needs, obligations and responsibilities - now and in the foreseeable future.
- The standard of living enjoyed by them before the breakdown.
- Their ages and the length of the marriage or partnership.
- Any physical or mental disabilities they may have.
- Their contributions already made or likely to be made to the family's welfare including looking after the home or caring for the family.
- Any benefit they may lose on account of a divorce, dissolution or nullity.
- Any conduct of the parties which the court reckons it would be "inequitable to disregard".

The court will always look to see how equal the parties will be in terms of capital if it makes the order it has in mind. In fact, in a large proportion of cases the court will use equality as a starting point when it comes to the division of the property and the judge will say to themselves: "Let's calculate what a 50-50 split would give the parties and how that can be achieved and then see if there is any reason to depart from that equal split." The parties' lawyers will be fully alive to this sort of approach and set out to persuade the court that there are sound reasons for it to depart from equality. The most common arguments used are that the other party should not have the benefit of:

- property which one party has brought into the marriage or partnership and to which the other party has not contributed;
- property which one party has inherited during the marriage or partnership; and
- property acquired after the breakdown.

However, the longer the marriage or partnership has subsisted (and the shortness of a marriage or partnership may of itself justify a departure from equality but, for the purpose of the arguments, usually add the cohabitation period to the marriage or partnership period and stop when the parties separated), the more likely that all property (except for post-break up wealth) will be reckoned and particularly when the needs of one of the parties so dictate. In what judges and lawyers call a *needs case*, the court will depart from equality so that it can ensure that one of the parties - especially the party who has the responsibility or the greater responsibility for caring for the children - has enough to satisfy their needs.

Your own cohabitation should not deny you the fair share of the assets you would have enjoyed had you not been cohabiting. You have earned it. However, where the cohabitation has materially improved your financial position and your opponent might suffer hardship if you got that full share then you might just suffer a reduction in the share, especially if there are children under 18 or continuing their education who are living with your opponent.

"Darling, let's keep out the lawyers and sort it ourselves."

Now there are some decent people around (or so they tell me) who want to do the decent thing on breakdown. If the expense, acrimony and stress of contested proceedings can be avoided, then go for it. You may be able to settle heads of agreement between yourselves or through out-of-court mediation. After all, if the case goes to court and through to a contested hearing, the legal costs of both sides effectively come out of the matrimonial pot. It is rare for the 'winner' (in so far as anyone ever *wins*) to have to pay the costs of the loser (in so far as anyone ever *loses*) and so each side will generally have to bear their own legal costs. This makes anathema the prospect of running up heavy legal bills and is the main reason that both parties should be sensible in their demands and responses and be prepared to give and take. Does it matter that much if the dog spends half its time with your husband or your partner keeps the David Hockney? A good precursor to negotiations is for each side to complete the comprehensive statement of financial information which they would be compelled to do if the finances went to court. It's called a Form E and you can access it on www.justice.gov.uk . Parties are encouraged to comply with what is called a pre-action protocol for the exchange of information before financial proceedings are ever started. The protocol can be found as an annex to practice direction 9A with the Family Procedure Rules 2010 (see the same website). If your opponent has a lawyer and you do not, the chances are that the lawyer will do the running in respect of the protocol. There is no immediate sanction for non-compliance with the protocol and the court will not refuse to accept a financial application because the parties or one of them have failed to follow it. The worst that can happen is that non-compliance will be taken into account by the judge when the costs of the proceedings come to be decided should there be no settlement but a contested hearing and the non-complying party has generally behaved unreasonably over the proceedings.

With both sides lawyerless, the chat may go something like this:

> *"I'm more than happy to keep the bloody lawyers out. Just complete this form which I downloaded. I'll do the same. Then we'll both know everything we need to know about the numbers and when we reach an agreement, neither of us will be in jeopardy of the other trying to wriggle out of the agreement in a year's time because we were hoodwinked on the numbers."*
>
> *"For goodness sake, I'll have to give up work if you expect me to fill this lot out. Statements for every bank account for the last twelve months and the cash equivalent value of every one of my pension policies and do I expect to be cohabiting. I want a settlement, not a Spanish Inquisition."*
>
> *"Well don't worry about all the documents right now. Just fill out the form so I can see what you are worth."*
>
> *"No wonder this marriage never worked. No trust. Well, if you think I'm a trillionaire, instead of trying to scratch a living running a back street used car business, go ahead and prove it. See you in court."*

This attitude doesn't bode well for a productive mediation, does it? Even so, the court does expect whoever starts a financial application to have attended a short meeting with a trained mediator who will provide them with information about possible settlement through mediation and assess suitability for mediation. Nevertheless, you cannot be compelled to mediate even though your opponent is keen or willing to do so. You will have to accompany any financial application you make with a form stating whether or not you have attended this meeting and, if not, why so. For help finding a mediator, go to www.familymediator-council.org.uk. There are a large number of exemptions from attending. If you were to wrongly claim to be exempt, it is possible - but more unlikely than likely - that this will be picked up by the judge on the first appointment and that they will adjourn so that what should have happened does happen.

And there is the option of using a financial arbitration scheme run by the Institute of Family Law Arbitrators (www.ifla.org.uk). It has a pool of around 220 lawyers (but do remember my dodgy maths) from which a couple can select an arbitrator to decide their dispute in much the same way as it would be decided by a family court judge. You could call it a private court. I am looking at the list of arbitrators now. They are all impressive and some more so than others. There are even a couple of retired High Court judges here trying to supplement their pensions.

The scheme's main advantage over actual court proceedings is that it is private so you won't be appearing in the papers walking a poodle away from the hearing having poured a jug of water over counsel for the other side and if it was not much faster than going through the court then I would be eating my slightly dented cap (again). If you can cope with the cost, it could be of especial use when there are only a couple of issues and time is of the essence. On top of any lawyers' fees, the arbitrator has to be paid by the two of you and a sum well in excess of the court fees that would have to be shelled out if the case took a conventional course.

A number of the arbitrators on the panel have been prepared to tell me their charging rates. Barristers were higher than solicitors. The barristers first. One QC expects £5,000 for Day 1 and £1,000 per half-day thereafter but on a five-day arbitration he would be looking for £32,500. He regards his fees at the higher end "but perhaps Europa League rather than Champions' League." Duncan Brooks charges £2,500 for a one-day arbitration or £2,000 per day for an arbitration lasting longer than one day. There is a charge of £200 per hour for writing up his decision and an extra charge if the paperwork occupies more than one lever arch file. Rhys Taylor wants £3,000 to £3,500 for a two day arbitration including writing up his decision. David Walden-Smith is after £2,500 for Day 1 and £2,000 per day for each successive day.

Now the solicitors. Malcolm Martin asks for £1,500 for Day 1 and £750 for each half day thereafter plus £500 for writing up his decision. The arbitrators at national firm Mills & Reeve charge £1,750 for a one day arbitration or £1,000 for a half-day arbitration plus something for writing the decision as to which a quote will be given when the nature of the case is known. For more complex cases, preparation time and preliminary hearings will be charged at £300 to £385 per hour. Tim Melville-Walker might be able to deal with a straightforward case for £500 and would not expect a 'medium asset' case to cost more than £2,000.

VAT has to be added to charges and there may be extra charges for directions hearings where they are necessary. I fancy that in most instances the arbitrator will throw in the facilities of their chambers or office at which the arbitration can take place but otherwise the venue would have to be organised and paid for by the parties.

Although the scheme has had the blessing of senior judges - yes, there is no lack of judicial enthusiasm for parties settling their differences out of court and, no, this has nothing to do with an urge to get an early lunch at *The Wig & Pen* - take up has been relatively slow so far. The arbitrator's decision can be appealed if they make a mistake of law unless you both agree their decision shall be final. And an order from the court in the matrimonial proceedings incorporating the arbitrator's decision will need to be obtained to ensure everything is legally watertight but only in the most exceptional of cases will the court interfere with the decision and there is a special fast track procedure for securing the order from the court.

Finally, if you are desperate to agree a settlement by negotiation, there is a process called collaborative law whereby each party appoints an independent legal representative to try and thrash out an agreement. I have never been an enormous fan because it can be costly and if no agreement is ever reached that's money down the drain. In one case I tried, the parties had expended over £18,000 on the process by which time they had agreed...nothing. The court had to decide after all. Nevertheless, I have come across a number of cases where it has worked. You want to be satisfied that the other side is genuine about trying to reach a settlement and is being completely open about what they have got. In the same way as an arbitrator's decision has to be okayed by the court so does an agreement reached through the collaborative law process.

But if you are faced with an oily spouse or partner who you cannot trust further than you can throw them, going to court is probably the only feasible option carrying with it the mechanism for forcing out the truth about their financial circumstances. And if advice comes too late and you have already come to an agreement when the relationship was on the rocks or finally broke down, can you be held to it? Depends! The agreement may well be effectively torn up by the court if you press ahead with a financial application despite its existence where you had no legal advice (and possibly where you had legal advice but it stank), where the other side has subjected you to undue pressure to sign up, where there has been an important change in circumstances which was either unforeseen or just overlooked when the agreement was made or in a *David v Goliath* situation with an inequality of bargaining power (say, the other side has been in a dominant position which they have abused). Then the court may divide capital and income in a way which bore no relation to what you had agreed.

Getting ready for court and being ready to pounce

This isn't getting ready in the conventional way. It's getting ready to grab the realisable assets and plead poverty. It involves your spouse or partner emptying the joint bank account and paying off the loan their brother supposedly made to them in the previous century and the repayment of which has taken on an extreme urgency which could irredeemably damage the sibling relationship if it went unheeded. It involves transferring a couple of a buy-to-let properties to a distant cousin on the pretext that they had paid for them and were always regarded as the true owners. It involves a sudden cessation of overtime, an increasing debit balance on the current account, a threat of redundancy, and the rewriting of the in-laws' wills to disinherit their son or daughter "because on no account is that bitch/bastard (please delete, as appropriate) going to get their hands on my hard earned money when I kick the bucket."

If you get wind of planned monkey business on the part of your spouse or partner, it may be wise for you to pounce before the deed is done. The court has the power to prevent them from disposing of assets where their intention is to reduce what you might be awarded on a financial application, if not totally frustrate your application, or frustrate or impede any enforcement action you might be taking in respect of a financial order you have already obtained. Should you be too late to prevent the disposal, the court can be asked to set it aside. These powers are contained in section 37 of the Matrimonial Causes Act 1973 where the parties are or have been married, schedules 5 and 7 to the Civil Partnership Act 2014 where they are or have been partners and section 24 of the Matrimonial and Family Proceedings Act 2004 which relates to financial proceedings here following an overseas divorce. The court application form to be used is the cuddly entitled D50G (see www.justice.gov.uk) and this would need to be supported by your witness statement.

In very urgent cases the court may be prepared to make an order preventing disposal of any property - it could be money in the bank, an antique, a house - even before you have had an opportunity of making a financial application to the court. The asset at risk of dissipation might also be a pension entitlement where the pension holder may seek to draw a lump sum which is available under the pension conditions or to take advantage of the newish right to trade in an annuity for cash. If the judge was with you, a temporary order would be made which would last until a further hearing soon afterwards at which time your spouse or partner would be heard and have the right to ask for it to be revoked. A temporary order might also be wise where there is a real danger that the disposal would otherwise be made at some stage between the court papers for a preventative application being served and the hearing of that application.

Obtaining a preventative order is not a doddle. The evidence must be there. The court will not make an order in your favour unless satisfied it is more probable than not that your spouse or partner intends to dispose of assets to do you down in your financial application. If in fact the disposal would have the effect of frustrating or diminishing what you are claiming, the law presumes that this is what is intended with the result that the task shifts to the spouse or partner to show otherwise.

Where the evidence justifies it and usually only in really big money cases, the court can prevent a spouse or partner from removing assets from England and Wales and dealing with them wherever they may be by way of a so-called 'freezing order'. There is also power in exceptional cases for the court to order that the applicant's legal team may go into the other party's premises to search for and seize documents and to remove computer records - without any prior warning. Wow! This is called a search order. They used to call it an '*Anton Piller*' order. If you are divorcing the head of a global organisation who eats his fish and chips out of twenty pound notes, mention 'Anton' as he is eavesdropping on you speaking on the phone to your girlfriend and watch the blood drain from his ruddy face. Or perhaps don't. The stuff of dreams.

"What have you done with my gold studded toothpick?"

Here's a gem that is property specific and should ensure that the property comes to no harm before the court decides on its ownership. Pray silence and welcome your uncomplicated saviour. Ladies and Gentlemen, I give you section 4 of the Torts (Interference with Goods) Act 1977. This effectively provides that the family court has the power to order any goods which are or may become the subject of litigation to be handed over pending a final court decision about them. We could be looking at chattels of monetary or sentimental value to you, jewellery, motor vehicles: any goods. The court might order that the goods be held by your lawyer or some independent third party and you could possibly take the sting out of strong opposition to an order by offering to pay into court a sum of money approximating to the value of the goods where it would remain until the dispute was resolved. The procedure is governed by Part 20 of the Family Procedure Rules 2010.

Fings 'aint what they used t'be

What did a spouse do in the old days when they sensed that, sooner or later, there would be matrimonial proceedings and the court would be dealing with the finances? They did the obvious thing. Rifled through the other spouse's personal papers, photocopied those which related to foreign bank accounts and the land in South Africa bought in a false name and kept them up their sleeve until the other spouse hanged themselves with a pack of lies about what they possessed. When the spouse was techno-savvy enough to use a computer, even a file or two might be invaded. So long as what was copied did not include correspondence passing between the other spouse and their solicitor and the possession of the copy documents was disclosed to the other spouse at a specified time in the proceedings, nobody except the other spouse would be troubled. The documents could be used in evidence and, faced with that prospect, the less-than-honest spouse would frequently bow to the inevitable and do a deal which well suited the vigilant spouse.

This all changed six years ago with the Court of Appeal ruling out that sort of conduct as usually breaching the civil and criminal law. Gird your loins for new tactics. The least contentious course to follow is, immediately after the honeymoon - actually you could start this on the honeymoon itself - take as deep an interest in the financial affairs of your other half as they will permit. Become their personal assistant, if they will wear it. That way, surreptitious raids will be unnecessary. You will have all the information you need at your fingertips in the unhappy event that the relationship breaks down.

Catering for cuties

If the other half has accumulated substantial wealth, they will be too cute to fall for that one. The action plan to cater for cuties demands the greatest care. The crux of the legal objection to what used to be commonplace rifling and hacking is that they amount to breaching confidence. Now, the other party can recover copies or the originals of unlawfully obtained documents under court order which could also forbid use of the documents without their consent and the court might even compel the party who has copied or removed them and then shown them to a legal adviser to dis-instruct that adviser and go elsewhere for legal representation.

But do not be too downhearted. What you have obtained in breach of confidence might just turn out to be of some use. If you can establish that the documents reveal that the other party has committed some unlawful conduct or intends to do so which could include holding back from the court information about their finances then the court might say that you can rely on them after all. And the court could reach the same decision in relation to very important documents if, taking into account a host of matters, it reckons it is fair to do so. The alternative course which the court might follow before deciding whether to order the other side to produce confidential documents which you have seen is to allow you to give evidence about the nature of the documents and their contents. So if you happen to innocently come across tasty documents, remember what you have read but leave the documents in place and perhaps recite the details before you retire at night so that they are well implanted in your memory.

> *"Darling, why do you keep saying account number AXD45669209888 sort code 14-78-04?"*

But it's not confidential!

That's another matter. If the documents are not confidential then they can be copied, if not 'borrowed', and used in evidence. Confidentiality, though, is not dependent on a lock and key. And, as the Court of Appeal has put it, if a husband leaves his bank statement lying around open in the kitchen, living room or the parties' bedroom (they actually called it the marital bedroom - *"I'm tired, darling. Let's repair to the marital bedroom." "Oh. Let's and no conjugal rights tonight"* - the statement may not be confidential so far as the wife is concerned. If the statement was kept by the husband in his study, it is more likely to be regarded as confidential and even more likely if in a drawer in his desk and even more likely still if kept locked in his desk.

"No rush, darling"

or "Let's talk about it ..... for the next 30 years"

There's a trap here. If you remarry or enter into a civil partnership after a divorce or annulment without having applied for financial remedies against your former spouse then it will be too late to do so, except for a pension share. You must ensure that the application has gone in first. Your new status may have some impact on what you will be entitled to from your former spouse but you can nevertheless pursue the application which could, for example, be for an order for transfer of property or its sale and split of the sale proceeds. Maintenance for you would no longer be payable. An application in the petition or answer would do or a later application in the prescribed form. Just the right words in the document is looked for and not a court hearing.

Provided you have not remarried or entered into a civil partnership, there is no time limit for making a financial application against your former spouse or partner. The court might be unsympathetic if you left it for ages and then suddenly pounced when your former spouse had thought they were out of the woods.

A Supreme Court case where the wife had delayed making a financial application for 19 years after divorce hit the headlines in March 2015. The publicity was manic and innocently deceptive. When they separated the parties were leading a nomadic lifestyle and there was nothing about the husband's circumstances to excite court proceedings. But how things changed with time. When the wife ultimately made her application the husband was alleged to be worth £107m. The appeal judges gave the wife the green light to pursue her belated application though the husband had fought to have it chucked out on the ground that after all this time there were no reasonable grounds for making it. But that green light was switched on because the Supreme Court ruled that there was no legal ground in this situation to summarily kill off a financial application before a ball had been kicked. The wife was entitled to have her case heard. This was an exceptional case. While a substantially belated application will be afforded a decent hearing, unless there are really compelling grounds, it will then be afforded a decent burial and the applicant could end up paying the other party's costs if the court reckoned the applicant had behaved unreasonably in making and persisting with the application.

The very peculiar payer

You can't afford to pay but desperately yearn for legal representation, especially when the opposition is blessed with high powered and higher charging lawyers. Please discount the idea of abducting a barrister from their chambers. That leaves the courses we have looked at previously (see chapter 6). And something else I have saved up for you. The court can now order your spouse or partner in war to pay for YOUR lawyer as the case progresses under a *legal services order*. I know it is hard to believe but it really can be done and the prospect of having to shell out not only for their lawyer but your own could well induce 3-D nightmares for your opponent and enhance the chances of a decent deal for you. (Who said this was licensed blackmail?). You won't find securing such an order a walkover but they are regularly being made in the family court for finance cases so it's worth looking into. Obviously, the court will have to be satisfied that your spouse or partner can afford to pay and won't want to stifle their ability to get a lawyer for themselves.

To succeed, it is essential for you to prove that you cannot reasonably obtain representation without the opposition dipping into their pockets to help you. Don't you have assets you could sell to pay for a lawyer yourself? The court is unlikely to expect you to sell or mortgage your home or deplete a modest fund of savings. Can't you raise a litigation loan from a bank or some other lender? The court may look for evidence of two rejected loan applications. If you can only borrow at a very high rate of interest, you probably won't be expected to have taken up the loan unless your opponent were to offer to pay the interest or, at least, cover the 'excess' element of it.

Won't solicitors be prepared to act for you in return for a mortgage in their favour over any assets you recover in the case? This is known as a *Sears Tooth charge*? Not that many solicitors will be happy with such an arrangement. Can't you tap up family or friends?

Your spouse or partner may have the benefit of financial support from a family member of friend. When they contend that the support has been withdrawn but the position is ambiguous or unclear, the court may well treat the support as likely to continue for the time being.

The *legal services order* will more likely than not provide for monthly payments to be made rather than a lump and can reflect your legal costs up to and including the financial dispute resolution appointment (see below) after which a further order could be made. Any intransigence by you in negotiations with the opposition or other unreasonable behaviour in the proceedings will go down badly on an application for an order. Whether or not your opponent has legal representation will be a relevant factor. An order can be made to cover not only costs already incurred under solicitors' unpaid bills but future costs. Your solicitors may be saying: *"We love you and feel for you, little clientipoo, but you owe us £15,000 and we just can't afford to continue to act for you unless you settle what you already owe us and something more for future work. We have rent to pay, mouths to feed and law books to buy".*

If you are after legal representation for arbitration or mediation (see above), the court can still oblige you with a *legal services order* and will approach your application in the same way as for an order to cover a court hearing.

Getting to the truth

There are three possible stages to a financial application. You may be able to reach a settlement at or before any of them. They are the first appointment, the financial dispute resolution appointment and the contested final hearing. The sooner the truth emerges the earlier a settlement becomes a possibility. The first lap of the journey to the truth runs from when you make your application up to and including the first appointment. A lapse of 12 to 16 weeks. Both sides will be expected to attend at court on the first appointment - with lawyers, if they have them - and this is likely to last around 45 to 60 minutes. At least five weeks beforehand, you will each have completed a comprehensive statement of your financial circumstances (even if you have voluntarily shared information prior to the application). This is the famous Form E. E doesn't stand for Edith or Edgar or anything in particular but they thought it was a good idea because it slotted nicely between Forms D and G.

The completed Form E must be sent to the court and the other side at least five weeks before the first appointment. You and your opponent should actually swap your completed forms - that is what is meant by exchanging them - so that neither of you has seen the other's statement before you have parted with your own or you might just be tempted to modify what you disclose in the light of what you read from the opposition or rant on about what they have said and raise the temperature. Guidance is available on completing Form E (or, in the case of an application for variation of an earlier order, Form E1) in a leaflet *Form E notes* from https://hmctsformsfinder.justice.gov.uk. The opposition may be late with their Form E or go into paralysis mode. Where this happens, send your own completed Form E into the court and tell the court and the opposition that you will withhold sending the opposition a copy of your Form E until they are ready to exchange with you.

The questionnaire

Let's assume that you have both done as required and that your opponent's Form E is overflowing with fiction instead of fact. The tool for digging out the truth (and exposing the fiction for what it is) is *The Sizzling Juicy Questionnaire*. It needs to be compiled and sent to the court and the opposition at least a fortnight before the first appointment so that you may have just three weeks to do what has to be done. In practice, you may have much less time because of frequent delay in Forms E being exchanged. Your opponent may be deliberately late so as to shrink the time available to you to compose those searching questions. If you feel that you have insufficient time - particularly if you want to obtain legal help and advice with your questionnaire - you can legitimately seek more time even if this would result in the first appointment having to be postponed. Ask your opponent to agree. If they refuse or won't answer, write to the court and ask for more time and, if necessary, for a postponement of the first appointment without any court attendances being necessary on the hearing already listed. Where the court refuses or fails to respond, turn up on the day and ask again at the hearing. You can also ask the judge to order your opponent to reimburse you any expenses you have incurred on the abortive hearing. The court ought to be with you.

This crucial questionnaire should set out all the further information and documents you want from your opponent. One of the other documents to be produced by each side and to accompany their questionnaire is a concise statement of what they are arguing about - the issues between them. For example, should the family home be sold and, if so, how should the sale proceeds be divided up; should your opponent pay you maintenance and, if so, for how long (for a fixed number of years, until the youngest child has ceased full time education or indefinitely so long as you are both alive and you have not remarried or entered into another civil partnership); and whether you claim that your opponent has assets or income or both which they have failed to disclose in their Form E. The further information and documents you go after must be linked to the issues: something often forgotten. The judge who scrutinises the questionnaire at the first appointment should be on alert for questionnaire requests which are irrelevant or disproportionate. Your questionnaire should positively not be used merely to draw out admissions from your opponent which you think might be helpful to your case (for example, "Does the respondent accept that the applicant worked her guts out for the entirety of the marriage and in 1989 during the course of a streaming cold she single-handedly laid the foundations for a rear extension at the matrimonial home?"). Here's what your questionnaire might look like.

Case no 2016F2016

IN THE FAMILY COURT

SITTING AT PEARDROP

BETWEEN

MAVIS TROUBLESORE Applicant

- and -

CLIVE TROUBLESORE Respondent

APPLICANT'S QUESTIONNAIRE UNDER FAMILY PROCEDURE RULES 2010 RULE 9.14(5) (c)

QUESTION 1 *The respondent has failed to answer 1.8 of his Form E ("Are you living with a new partner?") and 1.9 ("Do you intend to live with a new partner within the next six months") and, if appropriate, 4.6 (as to the financial circumstances of a cohabitee or intended cohabitee). These questions are repeated.*

QUESTION 2 *If the respondent does not intend to live with a new partner within the next six months but does intend to live with a new partner outside that period, when does the respondent intend this should happen?*

QUESTION 3 *The respondent has failed to attach to his Form E at 2.3 statements for the last 12 months with Dodgy Bank. He should produce these statements.*

QUESTION 4 *In respect of the respondent's current account with Barclays plc numbered X49701B7 disclosed at 2.3, he should provide details (including payer or payee where not evident) of every credit and debit entry for a sum of £500 or more for the period of three months prior to separation (on 14 July 2015) and since separation.*

Or

QUESTION 4 *The respondent should produce statements of his accounts disclosed at 2.3 where not already attached to his Form E for a period of 12 months prior to separation (on 14 July 2015) to date. He should further provide details (including payer or payee where not evident) for every credit and debit entry on all state-*

ments for this period for a sum of £500 or more.

QUESTION 5 *The respondent has failed to disclose at 2.3 (or elsewhere) his accounts with Dodgy Bank numbered 2866421/3/4. He should state the reason for non-disclosure and produce statements for the accounts for the last two years.*

QUESTION 6 *The respondent should produce a full and complete copy of his passport and state the purpose of each trip abroad in respect of which an entry has been indorsed since separation (on 14 July 2015).*

QUESTION 7 *The respondent should produce copies of his tax returns, forms PIID (as to benefits and expenses not put through the payroll) and all notices of assessment to tax issued by HM Revenue & Customs in relation to him for the last three complete tax years.*

QUESTION 8 *The P60 produced by the respondent for the last tax year does not indicate the receipt of any bonus from his employer and the respondent is silent on bonus entitlement at 2.15. The respondent should (a) produce a copy of his contract of employment and any variations of the contract and other documents issued to him by his employer relating to bonus entitlement; (b) explain the non-receipt of a bonus for the last tax year; (c) state when he expects any bonus referable to the last tax year to be paid to him and how much he expects to receive; and (d) state what future bonuses he expects to receive.*

QUESTION 9 *The respondent should state his current mortgage capacity, support the figure with a letter from a financial adviser; and produce a copy of his letter of instruction to the adviser.*

QUESTION 10 *The respondent should produce a copy of his application to the Halifax for the further advance on the family home which he raised in 2012.*

QUESTION 11 *The respondent should produce particulars of properties which he asserts would be suitable for occupation by the applicant and the respondent respectively in the event of a sale of the family home, limited to six properties in each category.*

QUESTION 12 *The respondent should particularise all private cash transactions into which he has entered in the course of his part-time business as a property development adviser during the last 12 months.*

QUESTION 13 *The respondent should state what he believes his employment promotion prospects to be and the likely impact of* *promotion on his salary and benefits and should produce copies of all correspondence passing between himself and his employer in the past 12 months relating to these matters.*

(signed) M Troublesore

Dated 14 July 2016

Bank, credit and store card statements may reveal sources of income which the respondent has failed to disclose in their Form E and a level of expenditure and style of living inconsistent with the penury being suggested. However, the judge at the first appointment may be reluctant to allow you to embark on a fishing exercise which could involve the respondent in time consuming and potentially costly enquiries to answer your questions. Be prepared, therefore, to substantiate your line of enquiry by reference to the contents of the statements of issues and to highlight to the judge some choice examples of the respondent's apparent high living or suspicious transactions close to and since the separation. "Madam, he has been on three holidays abroad this year alone, his Dodgy Bank statements show he withdrew £12,000 in the three months before he left me and when he came to collect his son last week, he pretended to be on foot but he had parked a brand new Ferrari with a personalised number plate round the corner."

The threshold for explaining debit and credit entries on statements is usually a matter of contention. Better to pitch for a higher threshold - like £500 as in our specimen questionnaire - than one which is too low and might lead the judge to assess you are being unreasonable and so disallow the request entirely or restrict the number of entries for which an explanation is ordered and raise the threshold, to boot.

Armed for the first appointment

There could be a settlement at court on the day of the first appointment. Pressure on you to settle may come from the lawyer for your opponent. The majority of lawyers will treat an unrepresented litigant on the other side fairly and courteously but there are others who are bullies and ready to intimidate so as to achieve the best result for their client. Even the judge who is conducting the first appointment may urge you to seize the opportunity of attempting to come to an agreement that day. It is not uncommon for the judge to allow more time for negotiations between the parties and any lawyers who represent them to take place throughout the rest of the court day in the court building. In fact, the judge may decide - whether or not you and your opponent agree - to convert the first appointment into a financial dispute resolution appointment which is the next stage of the application and which, with no settlement, would otherwise follow several months later. Watch it. You cannot be forced into a settlement against your will and the judge will not allow this to happen but, with the combination of pressure from the other side and judicial urging along with the attraction of an end to what has probably been a long period of contention, you might just find yourself highly tempted to settle on terms that you come to regret. Negotiate in haste and repent at leisure.

If a settlement is agreed without qualification on the day of the first appointment, you will find it hard if not impossible to extricate yourself from it later. Obviously, where the settlement is too good to be true - whether this be due to keenness on your opponent's part to avoid an investigation of their finances by paying over the odds to get off the hook or for some other reason - you would be wise to accept it. Otherwise, refuse the offer *or* say you would be happy to continue with the negotiation process after the conclusion of the first appointment *or* say that you want to take legal advice on the offer and ask for the first appointment to be adjourned to a later date so that you can do so. When there is a settlement between the first appointment and the financial dispute resolution appointment, the court can be asked to make an order encompassing what has been agreed without a further hearing and for the financial dispute resolution appointment to be cancelled. So:

- if you are without a lawyer at the first appointment and you are unsure whether or not to accept an offer there and then, don't accept; and
- if possible, hire a lawyer for the first appointment (so at least you are on a level playing field with your represented opponent when it comes to any negotiations which may take place) and even though you may have been acting for yourself up to that stage and intend to act for yourself in the future (see chapter 6).

The financial dispute resolution appointment

You may have thought that the first appointment scored high points on negotiation talk. Well, you 'aint seen nothing yet. There should have been attempts or further attempts at negotiating a settlement after the first appointment but as you are at the second stage of the proceedings, they have not come to anything - yet. The directions given by the court at the first appointment should have been complied with: in particular, some common ground ought to exist on the value of the assets (ok, the values of the bedside lamps and the coal scuttle are agreed) and each side should have answered the questionnaires.

In an effort to beat you down, your opponent's lawyer will have prepared a document called a *skeleton argument* which has nothing to do with what might be found under a Leicester car park. It will summarise the factual background and comment on what remains in dispute and why your opponent maintains that you are a despicable liar, in surreptitious cohabitation, deliberately under employed and with family members who will be bank rolling you in perpetuity. Or the *skeleton argument* may be moderate and balanced. When you read it (and this may not be until the day of the appointment and at court) you might visualise your case collapsing before you. When you read it again, you will probably visualise your case suddenly rejuvenated and realise the document is a balloon of hot air. My advice about taking in a lawyer for the first appointment is even more apposite for this second stage. If you are represented, your lawyer will have produced a skeleton argument on your behalf, perhaps even more aggressive and inflammatory than that from your opponent.

The judge (not necessarily the same judge who conducted the first appointment) will go into crack mode, discovering what offers, counter offers, counter-counter offers and counter-counter-counter offers have been made and what now separates the parties. Having listened to both sides and any lawyers, the judge will do their best to indicate what they consider to be a fair settlement. That won't be easy where there are fundamental factual issues between the parties. You will be allowed time to negotiate at court on the day.

The judge will dip into and out of the negotiations by asking you back to find out how you are getting on and becoming irritable if they are told that neither side has budged an inch. And then as darkness draws in, the public outside make their way home and you and your opponent and any lawyers check your wrist watches (or fobs) and yawn with exhaustion, the judge will want to know whether you have settled.

As before, nobody can force you to settle. Should the best offer from your opponent fall short of the realms of reasonableness, refuse to settle. The judge will then give directions for a contested hearing to take place at a later date. It is unlikely to be for at least three months: it could be considerably later. But negotiations could continue after the appointment and lead to a settlement with both sides having chewed over the arguments which were ventilated at the appointment and the judge's suggestions for how the case should be settled. Many cases which failed to settle at this stage do go on to settle soon afterwards. Bear this in mind, though. The judge at the financial dispute resolution appointment will have directed various things to be done by the parties before the final hearing: statements from the parties and any relevant witnesses of the evidence to be relied on in relation to particular issues, experts' reports (maybe from a pensions expert or a business valuer), property valuations - that sort of thing. These will cost money and that money will be coming out of the parties' assets so you don't want to run up this expense or too much of it if the case is to settle - and you know it.

Incidentally, if the case does proceed to a contested hearing and you thought the judge's settlement proposals at the financial dispute resolution appointment were off the mark, don't worry. You won't be seeing that judge again for the financial proceedings unless you join them in the same ice-cream queue at teatime. They are disqualified from playing any further part in the financial dispute (except to deal with procedural matters).

Interim relief: interim pain

Should you be in financial difficulty (perhaps you have been relying on regular voluntary maintenance or housekeeping from your opponent which has dried up or been reduced), you can apply to the court for temporary maintenance: that *maintenance pending suit* up to decree absolute and *interim periodical payments* from then onwards I have already mentioned. This is particularly useful where you are in the family home and the mortgage repayments are not being made. The object of temporary maintenance is to deal with immediate needs. It will almost invariably be pitched at a figure which is lower than the maintenance you could expect from the court after a final hearing. You can indicate an intention to apply for temporary maintenance on your initial application form: sling it in, just in case and it will not matter if you never follow it up. On the hearing of a temporary maintenance application, each side will be required to produce statements of their financial circumstances where the Forms E are not yet ready. It would be rare for any oral evidence to be allowed on the hearing of the application which is usually decided on consideration of the papers and after representations from both sides. Where you are applying for a legal services order (see above), it will be convenient for that matter and temporary maintenance to be dealt with together.

In an urgent situation, the court may be prepared to make a *Segal Order* (named after the judge who invented it) for global maintenance for the applicant and the children in the applicant's care although in due course the Child Maintenance Service (see chapter 50) may need to be involved.

Don't get bogged down by making a temporary maintenance application unless you are really in trouble because its life will be relatively short and the cost of an application if you are legally represented may make it a disproportionate exercise. On the other hand, it can sometimes give you a tactical advantage, demonstrating to your opponent that even the lower maintenance level is somewhat higher than they may have believed and, if they comply with the temporary order as the application progresses, that's pretty good evidence that they have the financial ability to pay what was ordered. "Blimey, if that's the interim, I'm going to be stung by the final order." Could help in negotiations.

"The Delivery Manager
The Family Court
Family Hearing Centre
Toytown
BE4 9JG

URGENT

Dear Sir or Madam

Troublesore v Troublesore

Case no 2016F2016

I am the applicant/petitioner. In my application for financial remedies, I have asked for an order for maintenance pending suit. I request you to please list the application for maintenance pending suit (I respectfully suggest a time estimate of one hour) as soon as possible and prior to the first appointment (or at the same time as the first appointment if the time estimate for the first appointment can be appropriately increased) (delete as necessary). I am desperately short of money because the respondent is not maintaining me and the matter is extremely urgent.

Yours faithfully

Mavis Troublesore"

Register this

It would be a pity if, before your financial application could be heard, your opponent sold or re-mortgaged some (or all) assets over which they had control and walked off with the money. There are ways in which you can effectively prevent this without procuring an injunction (see above). Take a property which is or was intended to be the family home and it is in the sole name of your opponent. By registering a *notice of home rights* you will frustrate any efforts to sell or mortgage the property without your concurrence. The notice will last until the final decree but the court can extend its life. Unless it is Hampton Court Palace the property will almost certainly be registered at the Land Registry. Use form HR1 (see www.landregistry.gov.uk) and there is no charge. If the property is unregistered - one of those parchment title deeds jobs - there is a different procedure you can follow with the Land Charges Registry. For properties other than the family home which are owned by your opponent but not jointly with you, it is possible to achieve the same frustrating result by registering at the Land Registry a *notice* (but different from a *notice of home rights*) or a restriction (which will probably be more appropriate). There is a mirror entry which can be registered at the Land Charges Registry for parchment title deeds jobs. Be warned. Registering a notice or restriction without reasonable cause could subject you to a claim for damages if your action causes loss to your opponent. So no messing about.

'Aint got it: can't get it

You have asked your opponent to produce certain documents and they say they do not have them and cannot obtain them. Perhaps, they are simply silent. Or in relation to the financial circumstances of a cohabitee or intended cohabitee, your opponent says: "We discuss our love for one another and the storylines of *Emmerdale* but about our finances, we never speak. I don't know where she works. Maybe she doesn't work." The most effective way of dealing with this situation is to apply to the court to order whoever has the relevant documentation to attend with it at court on an appointed occasion so that you can inspect it. Such an order (or just the threat of an application for one) may well lead to your opponent coming up with what is required after all. In the case of the cohabitee, their means may be relevant to what they are or should be contributing towards expenditure which your opponent is incurring and to what with their income being taken into account, your opponent could jointly with them raise on mortgage where your opponent's ability to rehouse is material. Of course, they are under no obligation to maintain *you* or help out your opponent to come up with a financial package for *your* benefit but if the court finds that your opponent and their partner do intend to purchase together that is going to be highly relevant. The cohabitee can be required to produce pay slips and other specified documents which are calculated to establish their financial circumstances. The procedure to be followed is in rule 21.2 of the Family Procedure Rules 2010.

Stay - just a little bit longer

You may need to keep your opponent around so that an order preventing disposal of assets pending the resolution of your application (see above) will not be frustrated or it may be imperative to achieve a just decision on your application that your opponent should attend the final hearing in person to be cross-examined. But he is about to scarper. The court does have the power on a special application by you to forbid them from leaving England and Wales and, as a backup, to order them to surrender their passport. Such an application will be pretty exceptional and will not be lightly granted because an order of this kind restricts liberty. The court will definitely have to be satisfied that, without the beast being present in court, with or without a battery of lawyers, your case will be materially prejudiced.

Any order made is likely to be for a very limited period. However, in the case of the late tycoon Scot Young who was involved in protracted and acrimonious financial proceedings with his wife, his passport had been impounded for nearly three years when the court extended the period by a further nine months. Mr Young died in tragic circumstances in 2014.

Wot a business!

If your opponent's business is a one-man/woman band and simply a vehicle for them to earn a living, its value (if any) as opposed to what they are earning from it, is unlikely to be of relevance. Of course, if the business has substantial assets - especially property - some of which could be realised or used as security for a loan, that is another matter. And it is even more of another matter where say your opponent's business is a sizeable one with goodwill which will one day be sold for a packet or is again sizeable and run through a company in which your opponent has more than a peanut shareholding. In such a situation, you may wish to ask the court to order a business/share valuation. Such a valuation can be expensive and so the court will wish to be satisfied that it would be proportionate to order one. The smaller the business, the more disproportionate the court would reckon the expense of a valuation to be. Any valuation ordered is likely to be by a single valuer who is instructed jointly by both sides and, in all probability, with each party initially paying one-half of the valuer's fee. Asking for a single valuer and not one valuer for each side will make the idea of a valuation more acceptable to the judge.

Conned

The court has made a final order for financial remedies - perhaps with your actual consent - and you have now discovered that your opponent acted fraudulently, misrepresented some matter, failed to disclose some information that should have been disclosed, or accomplished all three! If what you know now but did not know then would have made a material difference, you may be able to upset the order. Your opponent's intention to remarry which would have materially affected what was ordered had it been revealed at the time could be enough. What is essential is that once the truth has come out, you act expeditiously to challenge the order. The most appropriate way of doing so, whether or not you consented to the order, is by an application to the court to rescind or revoke the order under section 31F (3) of the Matrimonial Proceedings Act 1985 and rule 4.1(6) of the Family Procedure Rules 2010. If anyone tells you that you can't take this alternative course, tell them to look at the judgments of the Supreme Court in *Gohil v Gohil* and an associated case.

Sometimes the less than frank party will procure the inclusion in the court order of words to the effect that the other party does not accept that the less than frank party has been....frank. They may do so in the belief that this will preclude the other party from challenging the order when ultimately the truth emerges. "You said you thought I lied so how can you complain about it now? You consented to that order with your eyes wide open." This argument won't wash. Words like these in the order will not achieve what was intended by the less than frank party.

The other situation where you may be able to procure the ripping up of an order you feel is no longer fair is where some supervening event has occurred since the order was made. The supervening event must occur soon after the order was made - probably no more than a few months afterwards with 12 months afterwards almost always being too long - and you must act quickly to challenge, this time probably only by an appeal for which permission would be required. In the leading case on the subject, the husband agreed to transfer the matrimonial home to the wife in consideration of him being relieved of any obligation to pay her maintenance and five weeks later, she killed the two children and committed suicide. The wife's mother resisted the husband's attempt at getting the court order overturned but the husband succeeded.

A remarriage by the other party soon after the order was made which did make a difference and which had not been contemplated might be enough to secure a successful appeal. This is distinct from the other party intending to remarry but keeping quiet about it which may well justify a challenge: a case of misrepresentation or failure to disclose material information to you and the court.

Conned by your own form E

It is possible to complete form E (see above) online. In December 2015 it was discovered that there was an error with the automatic calculator of the assets of the party completing the form at box 2.20. It added the party's liabilities to their assets instead of deducting them so as to give a net asset total figure. This meant that the total was inflated by the amount of the liabilities. Consequence? Both parties may have concluded that the finances of the party completing the form were healthier than was in fact the case. Cue media hysteria. Whether the completing party might have succeeded in fooling themselves is open to doubt although it is possible. It is difficult to see how the other party could have been prejudiced by the error. It may be that the error was picked up subsequently, in particular if the parties agreed an order and submitted to the court a summary of their up to date financial positions which ought to have given correct figures for assets and liabilities. Against that there is the possibility that the error was repeated. It must be emphasised that the error could only have occurred in the first instance with an online completion and with one of three versions of the form - 04.11, 04.14 and 01.15.

HMC&TS (the Courts Service) has been deeply embarrassed and troubled by the error. Court staff have been ploughing through old files and isolating those in which the dodgy form has been completed. They have found 2,235 and written to the parties in these cases. Could anyone have been left out? Definitely, yes. It has also been discovered that there was a similar error with the shorter form E1 (which is used for variation applications and applications for provision for a child under schedule 1 to the Children Act 1989 which was available for completion online between April 2011 and March 2012).

If you fooled yourself, what can you do? Get hold of a copy of your form if necessary. Ask formE@hmcts.gsi.gov.uk to send you a free copy which they will do. Then decide whether you think the error has materially or significantly affected the court's decision where there was a contested financial remedy hearing or your own decision to agree an order where it was made by consent. If you reckon you can prove this then you can seek to appeal against the order but the better course would be to ask the court to review the order. Should you have been notified by the court of the error some time ago you will have to explain to the court the reasons for the delay in making the review application.

A special form has been devised for the occasion: form D650 notice of application to vary or set aside a financial order (form E calculator error) is its sexy title. You will be able to source it on http://hmctsformfinder.justice.gov.uk?HMCTS/FormFinder.do. You won't be charged a fee when you send in the form which should be to the court or family hearing centre which made the original order. If the exercise puts you to expense - whether it be for lawyers' fees or time off work etc - you could make a claim for compensation against HMCTS (see chapter 27).

Oh and a revised version of Form E (01.16) has been uploaded to the form finder site which mercifully no longer has an automatic calculator embedded and improves the layout of box 2.20 to aid completion, with litigants in person especially in mind. Sweet. Calculators at the ready.

Maintenance postscript

I cannot allow you to turn to the next page or chuck this book into the dustbin (whichever your preference) without touching on the court's current approach to applications for one party to pay maintenance to the other party for the benefit of the other party rather than for the benefit of any children. The most common order is for maintenance for the wife who is the sole or main carer of the children (although it could be for the husband or civil partner). The approach is by no means uniform and will vary from judge to judge but the trend is increasingly towards getting the party after maintenance out to work and self-supporting sooner instead of later. In a 2014 case Mr Justice Mostyn, probably advocating the most extreme anti-maintenance approach, explained the relevant principles in play on a maintenance application. He said it was proper for there to be a maintenance order where choices made during the marriage had generated hard future needs on the part of the party wanting maintenance. Here the duration of the marriage and the presence of children were pivotal factors. Apart from the most exceptional cases, the order should only reflect what were the needs of the party wanting maintenance. In every case, the court had to consider a termination of maintenance with transition to independence as soon as it was just and reasonable. Limiting the duration of a maintenance order (for, example, to a specific number of years or to a specific event like the youngest child finishing tertiary education as against an order which ran so long as both parties were alive and the payee had not remarried) should be considered unless the party receiving maintenance would be unable to adjust to no maintenance without undue hardship. A degree of hardship in making the transition to independence was acceptable so long as it was not undue hardship.

And in February 2015 Lord Justice Pitchford in the Court of Appeal refused to give the 51 year old wife permission to appeal against an order which was to scale down over six years the maintenance order originally made in her favour for £33,200 per year. At the time of the original order the judge had made it clear that they had expected the wife to begin working within the following two years but she had made no attempt to find work. The 59 year old husband had complained that he had planned to retire at 60 but as he had been unable to afford to make sufficient pension contributions, he had had to postpone retirement until 65. By virtue of the reduction in the maintenance, the husband will now be completely off the maintenance hook when he comes to retire.

Chapter 50

Money For The Kids

Paying for the trainers

Your relationship has broken down and you have the entire or some care of the child. You will be keen on the other parent paying towards the child's maintenance unless you are daft, very rich or care is fairly evenly shared and your financial circumstances are about equal. Assuming that child maintenance does not flow freely from the other parent's pocket into your purse or won't continue to do so, there are three ways you can go after securing it - from the court, from the Child Maintenance Service (CMS) which now deals with all new maintenance cases in place of the Child Support Agency or (with a bit of nudging, threatening or wrestling) from a formal agreement with the other parent.

Maintenance from the court

Generally, disputes about child maintenance have to be dealt with through the CMS. There are some exceptions which we will look at later where the CMS has to keep out and the court gets a look in. And whether or not the CMS can touch, the court does have jurisdiction to make a child maintenance order if there is an agreement between the parties. Almost always, that agreement and order will specify that maintenance will be paid, how much, on which dates and for how long. This is how a typical order will read:

> *B shall make periodical payments to A during their joint lives for the benefit of C born on 14 July 2014 ("the child") at the rate of £1,000 per calendar month payable calendar monthly as from and including 14 July 2016 until the child attains the age of 17 years or ceases full-time tertiary education to first degree level (whichever is the later) or further order.*

In practice, 18 years is often substituted for 17. The life of such an order can be extended if when it is due to end the child will be continuing in education or training for their career or special circumstances exist, such as the child's disability, which would justify an extension of its duration.

If the parties have been married then the court has the power in matrimonial proceedings such as divorce to make an agreed order for the maintenance of a child against a party to the proceedings who is a non-parent but has treated the child as their own. In proceedings under schedule 1 to the Children Act 1989 the court can only make a maintenance order against a biological parent of a child but whether or not the parents have been married. The court can order a lump sum payment for a child's benefit even where it lacks the power to deal with maintenance though this would usually only occur in a 'big money' case.

How much to go for under court order

There is no set figure. However, maintenance is usually agreed at or around what would be payable under the CMS regime for the obvious reason that in the absence of agreement that is all you could achieve. But in those cases where the court has the power to decide, it will use its discretion on the amount to be paid with the CMS figure probably being the starting point. The court will particularly take into account the child's financial needs; any income or earning capacity of the child and their other financial circumstances; any physical or mental disability of the child; the manner in which the child was being educated or trained and what the parents were expecting about that; and the other considerations which apply where you are applying for maintenance for yourself (see chapter 49). If you are after child maintenance against a spouse or former spouse and it is not their child, the court will additionally look at the extent to which and basis upon which they had assumed responsibility for the child and whether they knew the child was not theirs when they did so. The liability of any other person such as the child's natural father to maintain them will come into the reckoning. The court should be asked to reflect the fact that maintenance has to cover not only the food that goes into the child's mouth and the clothes that go onto the child's back but the outgoings on the child's home which will be greater because of the child's presence there. For example, if in order to accommodate your child you have a two-bedroomed flat instead of a one-bedroomed flat your mortgage instalments, for a start, are going to be higher.

A multi-millionaire has moved into your place and you hope the two of you will live together happily hereafter? The multi-millionaire is not legally responsible for maintaining your child and your relationship does not of itself relieve the other parent of their financial responsibility in relation to the child's maintenance or reduce what they would otherwise have to pay. But if your new partner is ploughing money into your household with the result that you are released from other financial burdens you would have to discharge then the court can reflect that fact in its award.

Keeping out the CMS

Where a court order for child maintenance was made before 3 March 2003 neither parent can go to the CMS. It won't touch. The parent after an increase or decrease in maintenance may go back to court for the order to be varied. But where the court order was made on or after 3 March 2003 the CMS can only be kept out for 12 months: after that either party can go to the CMS. This state of affairs carries its risks for the paying parent who may wish to enter into an arrangement with you which is generous in capital provision but in return for reduced child maintenance or perhaps even no child maintenance at all. Risky as you might make your way to the CMS once the 12 months are up and seek a juicy maintenance assessment from them as any agreement by you which purports to restrict your right to apply to the CMS is legally void!

There are ways around this but they are very, very, very, very tricky yet they are occasionally used though so far have not been the subject of an authoritative court decision as to their effectiveness. You can agree and undertake to the court that you will not go to the CMS and the other parent can pray that you will keep to your word and the court will restrain you from breaking it if you attempt or threaten to do so. You can also agree and undertake to repay to the other parent any maintenance they are compelled to pay over as a result of you getting the CMS involved - and you can back that up with a charge on your property (provided you own it or are going to do so) for a sum equivalent to any CMS maintenance the other parent ends up paying out. This would put the other parent in the position of a mortgage lender from whom you had borrowed that amount of money.

Should you renege on an agreement and undertaking not to go near the CMS and there is still a spousal maintenance order in force for you, the other parent might well apply to the court for that maintenance order to be reduced to reflect their liability under the CMS assessment - and succeed!

When can't the CMS poke its nose in?

The CMS has no jurisdiction when:

- the court made an order for child maintenance before 3 March 2003 in which event either of you would have to go back to the court for any sort of variation;
- the court made an order for child maintenance on or after 3 March 2003 and it has not yet been in force for 12 months;
- the child is a step-child of the other parent (but it does have jurisdiction in respect of an adopted child);
- the child is resident abroad; and
- the other parent is resident abroad unless abroad because they

are serving in the civil service, the armed services, certain local authorities or with a United Kingdom based company paying wages in the United Kingdom.

In these situations, the court will be able to decide maintenance except where a step-child is involved unless the step-child is a child of the family where you and the other party have been married.

"My Jimmy is 32 but prefers not to work as this would clash with Jeremy Kyle"

The CMS can only deal with maintenance for a child who is:

- under 16; or
- under 20 where child benefit would be payable (even if it is not claimed for say tax reasons) and they are receiving full-time education up to A level - provided they weren't fast workers and have been married or in a civil partnership.

How much under the CMS regime?

The present regime has been preceded by two previous schemes with different rules. Cases under the old schemes are being progressively closed down and the parent entitled to maintenance (where the money due from the other parent is not being taken out of their bank or building society account following default) will be required to make their own arrangements or apply under the new regime. Nearly 92% of applications are against men. Let's have a look at how the maintenance will be calculated.

There are nil, flat and reduced rates which will not generate anything or only sufficient for a haircut and a bag of chips. The nil rate is scored by, among others, someone with an income of less than £7 per week and prisoners. Full time students no longer automatically qualify for the nil rate. The flat rate is for those out of the range of the nil rate but with a gross weekly income of £100 or less or on certain benefits. It's £7 per week. The reduced rate applies where the weekly gross income is more than £100 and less than £200 generating, for example, a liability of 17% of that income for one child.

With a bit of luck, the basic and basic plus rates will be effective in most cases. Assuming the other parent is not responsible for other children by another relationship who come into the reckoning, the basic rate maintenance for gross weekly income between £200 and £800 is:

- 12% for one child;
- 16% for two children; and

- 19% for three or more children.

Where the gross weekly income is over £800 - this is the *plus* bit of basic plus - then add on a percentage of the income in excess of £800 BUT UP TO A MAXIMUM OF £3,000 depending on the number of children like this:

- 9% for one child;
- 12% for two children; and
- 15% for three or more children.

Should the other party be caring for other children in a new family their gross weekly income for the purposes of calculating child maintenance to go to you will be reduced by 11% for one child in the new family, 14% for two and 16% for three or more. Your own income will not be taken into account.

And may be a bit more

Provided you have applied to the CMS and it has calculated what the other parent is to pay PLUS that amount is the maximum under the CMS regime you could apply to the court for a *top up*. You would have to show this was “appropriate”. You can also go to the court whether or not the CMS has been involved, for an order for the other parent to pay or contribute towards school fees (including extras and uniform), training for a career or for expenses attributable to your blind or disabled child’s condition.

Shared care

The maintenance payable will be reduced if the other parent has one or more of the children stay overnight with them for at least 52 nights a year although even then the maintenance payable can never fall below £7 per week. The maintenance bill goes down by one-seventh for 52 to 103 nights, two-sevenths for 104 to 155 nights, three-sevenths for 156 to 174 nights and one-half plus £7 per child for 175 or more nights. The stay over must be with the other parent and not say with grandparents while the other parent is elsewhere.

It would be cynical for me to say that a parent who is well-informed will sometimes factor these reductions into the proposals for child contact which they formulate, especially when an extra one or couple of nights would raise them into a higher reduction band. But I will be cynical. 51 nights a year won’t earn them a reduction of one new pence: one more night and their liability is cut by one-seventh. Court contact orders sometimes provide for such reasonable contact as the parents shall agree. This does of course have the merit of encouraging a harmonious relationship between the parties and maximum flexibility but if any argument over child maintenance shared care reduction is anticipated the order might better be more definite.

A shall make C available for contact with B and do all things reasonably necessary to facilitate such contact taking place as from the date of this order on alternate weekends from 4pm on Friday until 4.30pm on Sunday commencing on 15 July 2016 with B being present with C overnight and for such other reasonable contact as the parties shall from time to time agree.

Going to the CMS

Before you can apply to the CMS you have to make contact with Child Maintenance Options (0800 988 0988 - www.cmoptions.org) which runs a live chat service. You will be encouraged to reach a family-based arrangement which is a romantic invention involving parents actually agreeing on a figure and payments being made. If no arrangement is made or if it is made but not adhered to, then you can get on with the application. There is a £20 fee unless you are under 18 or in the eyes of the CMS a victim of domestic violence or abuse.

Week 1: "I don't think I can do better than £20 a week but let me have a look at my bank statements and I'll check how much longer I have to run on the plasma hp."

Week 2: "Daddy is not available to answer your call. Please leave a message."

Week 3: "So sorry I didn't get back to you. I can't find my bank statements anywhere. I'll get a print out this afternoon."

Week 4: "Daddy is at present away on a short break to the USA and offline. He will reply to your email as soon as he returns. Best wishes."

You don't want to hang about for too long in trying to get an agreement because the liability to pay maintenance once the CMS gets to work will not arise until two days after the other parent has been sent notification of the application and they clearly cannot be notified until you have made it! The CMS will calculate the amount of maintenance to be paid and then there's an option - Direct Pay or Collect and Pay. With Direct Pay, payments are made - direct to you! With Collect and Pay (where the other party consents or the CMS reckons they won't otherwise pay), the CMS collects, stings and takes immediate enforcement action where necessary. Stings? Yes. You pay 4% of the maintenance and the other party pays 20%. If that doesn't make the collections service pretty unattractive, what does?

"Dear Father

I may have said a lot of uncomplimentary things about you but never that you lacked intelligence. That is why I cannot understand the reason for you not agreeing to put a standing order in force immediately to pay the maintenance which the Child Maintenance Service has calculated you must pay for Jimmy. Do you realise that if you won't change your mind about this my only option is to use the Collect and Pay system which between us will cost 24% of the maintenance, 20% of it coming from you on top of the maintenance. That's not in your interest. It's not in my interest. It's certainly not in Jimmy's interest. Please confirm now that you will do as reasonably asked.

Best

Mother"

Reaching an agreement

Your contact with Child Maintenance Options could lead to an agreement over maintenance and you and the other parent signing a form (www.cmoptions.org/en/pdfs/Private%20Form.pdf). It contains the parents' promise "to keep to the arrangements, for the sake of the children" and warns that the document is not legal though it is a clear statement of their commitment to the children. Some lawyers suggest that this wording is inaccurate and misleading as the agreement would entitle the court to make an order for maintenance in its terms which in turn would have the effect of keeping out the CMS for 12 months. I am not so sure. It could be strongly argued that the agreement is not binding as the wording shows that the parents did not intend it to be so.

So what do you do if there is arrangement but you want the comfort of being sure you can enforce it should the other party default? It may be safer to steer away from the Child Maintenance Options form and use another agreement form which can be enforced in the same way as any contract. If payments were not made you could sue in the county court for what you were owed under the agreement as a straightforward debt and the usual means of enforcing a civil judgment would be available to you (see chapter 22). True that these means would not be as extensive and robust as available to the CMS when it is collecting and there is default (no disqualification from driving or imprisonment, for example). But against this, an agreement does give you the opportunity to obtain an amount of maintenance which is over and above the amount which would have been required under a CMS calculation (though the other parent could at some stage apply to the court to alter the agreement by reducing the amount or go to the CMS themselves). And you could even seek an agreement against a former partner who is not the parent of the child but treated the child as their own to maintain them in the future and, provided by deed, the agreement would be legally enforceable. It may be that the very safest course if the CSA calculation is to be used and the other party is a parent, is to apply to the CMS and, if appropriate, opt for the direct payment scheme without collection charges. Should the CMS not have jurisdiction (for example, because the other parent is living abroad) then an agreement is a useful alternative to a court order.

That agreement of your own

The agreement - call it a deed, please - may go something like this.

THIS DEED is made on 14 July 2016 BETWEEN MAVIS BULWARK of 149 Magnolia Crescent Twickenham Middlesex KT89 4XZ ("Ms Bulwark") and CLIVE TROUBLESORE of 2b Magnolia Crescent Twickenham Middlesex KT89 4XN ("Mr Troublesore")

BACKGROUND

1. Ms Bulwark and Mr Troublesore formerly cohabited together.

2. Jimmy Troublesore-Bulwark ("the child") was born to Ms Bulwark on 14 July 2015.

3. Mr Troublesore is the biological father of the child.

4. Ms Bulwark and Mr Troublesore ceased cohabiting together on 1 March 2016.

5. Mr Troublesore acknowledges his legal and moral commitment to contribute towards the maintenance of the child and to play a full part in the child's life.

6. Ms Bulwark and Mr Troublesore agree that the child should live with Ms Bulwark and that it is in his best interests to do so.

7. Ms Bulwark acknowledges that it is in the best interests of the child that the child should have extensive contact with Mr Troublesore.

NOW THIS DEED WITNESSES as follows:

1.1 Mr Troublesore covenants to pay or cause to be paid to Ms Bulwark maintenance for the benefit of the child at the rate of £1,500. 00 per month payable calendar monthly by way of standing order to the credit of the current account of Ms Bulwark with Dodgy Bank plc numbered 45799003 at its Twickenham branch sort code 32-19-01 or to the credit of such other account as Ms Bulwark may from time to time direct. The first payment shall be made on 21 July 2016 and subsequent payments on the 21st day of each successive month.

1.2 Subject to sub-paragraphs 1.3. and 1.4 below, the payments shall be made until the child attains the age of 18 years or if later until he ceases full-time tertiary education up to first degree level.

1.3 The payments shall cease upon a maintenance calculation being made by the Child Maintenance Service or such other statutory authority as may perform its functions.

1.4 The payments shall cease upon the death of Ms Bulwark.

1.5 The payments shall not cease by virtue of the death of Mr Troublesore and in the event of his death whilst payments continue to be due they shall be made by the personal representatives of his estate.

1.6 Ms Bulwark shall apply the maintenance hereby covenanted to be paid for the benefit of the child and for no other purpose.

1.7 Ms Bulwark shall make the child available for contact with Mr Troublesore and take all reasonable steps necessary to facilitate such contact each Tuesday, Friday and Sunday for two hours at times to be agreed between them commencing on 15 July 2016 and as from 15 July 2017 for one weekend each fortnight from 2pm on Friday until 2pm on Sunday and for such other reasonable contact as Ms Bulwark and Mr Troublesore shall from time to time agree.

IN WITNESS whereof the parties have executed this instrument as a deed on the day and year first before written

SIGNED AS A DEED BY

CLIVE TROUBLESORE in

the presence of:-

SIGNED AS A DEED BY

MAVIS BULWARK in

the presence of:-

Those old cases

Child support cases under the old schemes are being closed down, as already mentioned. Work begins in August 2016 closing down the final segment of cases which involve those in which enforcement action has been taken because of default and the maintenance due is removed from the bank or building society account of the parent liable to pay. An old scheme case once closed down can be treated like a new scheme case with you making your own arrangements with the other parent or with a Direct Pay or Collect and Pay situation. But there is another option - the compliance opportunity. Assuming there had not been agreement for Direct Pay or Collect and Pay, the other parent will be given an opportunity to demonstrate over six months what a wonderful child cheek-pinching and lovable parent they are by generally making payments of one-half of their liability (which can include an element for arrears) to you direct and the other half being paid over by the employer out of the other parent's earnings. Based on performance over the six months, the CMS will then decide whether for the future Direct Pay or Collect and Pay is to prevail. Collection charges will be waived during the six months.

Index

D

E

F

M

N

O

P